George
MacDonald

George MacDonald during his American tour of 1873.

George MacDonald

A Biography of
Scotland's Beloved Storyteller

BETHANYHOUSE
MINNEAPOLIS, MINNESOTA

Published by Bethany House Publishers
11400 Hampshire Avenue South
Bloomington, Minnesota 55438

Bethany House Publishers is a division of
Baker Publishing Group, Grand Rapids, Michigan.

Printed in the United States of America

Library of Congress Cataloging-in-Publication Data

Phillips, Michael R., 1946-
George MacDonald : Scotland's beloved storyteller / by Michael Phillips.
    p.   cm.
    Originally published: c1987.
    Summary: "A revealing look into the life, spiritual journey, and writings of the popular yet controversial 19th-century novelist George MacDonald. Michael Phillips unveils the life and times of his literary mentor in this portrait of a great writer of faith, set in the Scottish land he loved"—Provided by publisher.
    Includes bibliographical references and index.
    ISBN 0-7642-0034-8 (pbk.)
    1. MacDonald, George, 1824–1905. 2. Fantasy fiction, Scottish—History and criticism. 3. Authors, Scottish—19th century—Biography. 4. Christian fiction—History and criticism. 5. Scotland—In literature. I. Title.
    PR4968.P45   2005
    823'.8—dc22   2004024665

DEDICATION

To
Those of a new generation who are discovering
sustenance, wisdom, and truth in the writings
and person of George MacDonald—a man who
has become, for all of us, a true friend.

Books by Michael Phillips

Is Jesus Coming Back As Soon As We Think?
Make Me Like Jesus
God: A Good Father
Jesus: An Obedient Son
Destiny Junction
Kings Crossroads
Angels Watching Over Me
A Perilous Proposal
Dream of Freedom
A Rift in Time
Hidden in Time
The Eleventh Hour
Legend of the Celtic Stone
An Ancient Strife
Your Life in Christ

CONTENTS

LIST OF PHOTOGRAPHS OF SCOTLAND*

*All the photographs were taken by Michael Phillips (except 1 and 32 and center inserts).

INTRODUCTION TO THE 2005 CENTENARY EDITION

From beginning to end in first writing this biography a number of years ago, I was deeply challenged with the magnitude and complexity of telling this man's life in a way that would unearth its essential themes. Because of the multifaceted depth of a man like George MacDonald and the tremendous variety of his works and literary genres—theologian, spiritual mystic, poet, novelist, preacher, scientist, essayist, highly successful lecturer, teacher, editor, fantasy writer, actor—his ideas defy categorization. His thoughts and words are subject to a wide diversity of interpretation. All this to say that this biography is *my* viewpoint of MacDonald's life. A biographer's role is to speak truthfully but not necessarily to close every door to further inquiry or to definitively answer every question that arises. When there are no major new details to uncover, the biographer must draw his own conclusions from the documentation that is available. In short, this biography is not a mere factual recounting of his life's events, but an "interpretation" of his life.

George MacDonald expressed his personal wish that no biography of him be written, stating that his books contained all he had to say to the world. Realizing MacDonald's tendency to downplay his own importance, and sensing acutely the need for fresh literary inquiry into this man of letters of a century past, I considered this venture worth the risk. In spite of my own inadequacies for the task, I entered into it prayerfully, desiring to be accurate, fair, and truthful.

Though I chose not to heed MacDonald's earthly wish that no biography of him be written, I *did* heed his comment regarding the significance of his books in revealing what he had to say, both about himself and to the world. I have therefore made liberal use of his novels, poetry, and sermons, as well as his letters, to elucidate George MacDonald's life. Some critics disagree with the practice of attributing to an author opinions expressed by voices in his fiction. But it was my hope to convey George MacDonald's thoughts and emotions as he grew and matured, and these are most strongly reflected through his literary works. His son Greville said,

"George MacDonald's books must tell us more of his life than could any biography."

My priority as a biographer, therefore, is not to impart mere facts about George MacDonald's life, but rather to get at his heart. It would be a relatively simple matter to construct a timeline of the data of his earthly existence. But that would hardly reveal his *person* to us. The words he wrote, though not autobiographical in a pure sense, illuminate what he thought about, how he approached his mental quandaries, what kinds of questions he asked, and what answers he found. Thus, his writings *are* autobiographical in an emotional rather than a statistical sense, revealing his view of life. His books are the fullest means we have to get under the surface of his thought-skin to discover what really made him tick.

In the opening lines of the personal essay on his father contained in the collection of essays *From a Northern Window*, Ronald MacDonald makes clear his conviction that in his writings we come best to know the man George MacDonald: "To be known by his fruits . . . was the way . . . by which any man seeking to know him must come again and again into contact with that something greater than George MacDonald. There has probably never been a writer whose work was a better expression of his personal character."

In 1924, Greville MacDonald, then sixty-eight years of age and a successful author in his own right, produced a monumental 575-page dual biography of his parents entitled *George MacDonald and His Wife*. Since that time it has been the standard reference work on the life and work of his father. Without it, our knowledge of MacDonald's life would be vastly incomplete. To say that I "made use of" Greville's work in compiling this present biography would be a gross understatement. Greville's painstaking research is the chief cornerstone, undergirding all other study of George MacDonald, including this one, and it would be impossible to reference every single idea that springs from the pages of his book. Foundational to everything that follows is the *full* credit I, and we all, owe to him. Both Greville's and Ronald's inevitable filial bias colored their portrayals of their father, of course; but this does not diminish the value of their works. They knew the man with an intimacy we can scarcely fathom.

It is impossible to arrive at any deep sense of George MacDonald's person apart from the land of his upbringing. Scotland's unique and colorful history draws us into itself the more one knows of it. A study of MacDonald's life becomes at least partially a study of Scotland's history, lore, and culture, for a foundation must be broadly laid if it is to support the structure that will be built upon it. The growth of the man emerged intrinsically out of the heritage into which he was born, and his life cannot adequately be considered without placing the backdrop of his roots in place.

Beyond the sources and details and attempts to confirm pieces of data and ferret out new facts, the experience of *feeling* the country of MacDonald's birth has been vital to an understanding of his life. Walking the streets and riverbanks of Huntly fostered the emotions that have gone into this work. In his own life, regular visits to the place of his birth proved a great imaginative stimulus to George MacDonald, and something of this same powerful phenomenon of the land quietly stole over me during my time in Scotland. Looking out the very window from which MacDonald as a boy daydreamed, climbing the stairway in his home that he used in his mind's eye for that of the Princess Irene, poking through the ruins of Huntly Castle, imagining a young Scottish lad playing there with his friends, hiking along the River Deveron, climbing the great hill behind the Farm where the young George MacDonald rode his horse Missy, standing overlooking the Cabrach, which became Cosmo Warlock's desolate highland home, walking along Aberdeen's seashore, pondering the same questions that plagued the student George MacDonald during his university days, strolling along Cullen's sandy beach where Malcolm first met Florimel and sensing the love for the sea that grew out of MacDonald's boyhood, meandering quietly through the small English village of Arundel, gathering impressions of his first pastorate, following the River Dee out of Aberdeen toward the highlands while reflecting on Gibbie's poignant flight "up Daurside"—it was the impressions of these places, and of Scotland as a whole, that penetrated most deeply into my spirit in the process of writing this book.

While the essential facts reported in these pages come largely from *George MacDonald and His Wife,* other written sources, contemporary newspaper and other articles I was able to locate, and MacDonald's own letters, the spiritual and emotional conclusions I drew from these facts are often my own. More than providing statistics, I tried to investigate genuine emotional themes that were operating in MacDonald's life on a level deeper than the factual—driving him to become the sort of man he was.

The facts of MacDonald's life, then, have been shaped into a picture of the growth of the man out of a very human childhood and a turbulent youth, set against the background of the land he loved. MacDonald's uniqueness, interacting with the forces around him, made of him a man whom we can now place in his rightful literary, spiritual, and historical context.

I make no apology for the fact that I trust George MacDonald, echoing C. S. Lewis's sentiments when he said that though MacDonald was not error-free, he knew of no writer who was so continually close to the Spirit of Christ. Some biographers and analysts have emphasized all the inconsistencies they can find in his life, thereby attempting to undercut the validity of his message. MacDonald himself stressed that truth can only be arrived at by examining what *is* rather than what is *not.* My motive was to look positively and realistically at the man and his strengths, recognizing his shortcomings and doctrinal incongruities, but viewing them in the larger context of his life's growth.

In 1906, writing in the *North American Review,* Louise Willcox said of MacDonald, "When another generation or two shall have passed . . . a fuller appreciation than he has yet had is awaiting him." Perhaps the time she predicted is now at hand, a hundred years after his initial popularity, for after decades of anonymity a whole new generation of readers is now discovering in him what readers of the last century did by the millions. To that new readership I hope to fairly and truthfully represent MacDonald himself. Then the life of George MacDonald, as he points toward One higher, can exercise its impact on people of our own time.

I cannot begin to recognize all who have contributed to the renewal of interest in George MacDonald with their forerunning work of many diverse kinds: G. K. Chesterton, Joseph Johnson, John Malcolm Bulloch, Elizabeth Yates, C. S. Lewis, Clyde Kilby, Richard Reis, Glenn Edward Sadler, Lyle Dorsett, Rolland Hein, William Raeper, and certainly, foundational to all our work, MacDonald's two sons Ronald and Greville MacDonald.

Moreover, my heartfelt gratitude is due the entire editorial and production staff at Bethany House Publishers. Not only did they work diligently to achieve excellence in their groundbreaking republication of Mac-Donald's classic novels in the early 1980s, they also demonstrated intrepid resolution in their approach to this controversial biography. Their initial decision to publish this book demonstrated a deep trust in God. All his life MacDonald was stretching, reaching, probing, and challenging the theological status quo. He was not a systematic theologian and set forth no summary of his final doctrinal conclusions. His was not a mind that could merely sit back and accept what others told him to believe.

Bethany House has been able to separate this questioning from the high-minded and purehearted aspects of his character that all his life, and for a hundred years beyond, have ministered Christlikeness and holiness to those with whom he came in contact. They view the questions he raised as important from a historical perspective, as illuminating the struggles of the nineteenth-century church to arrive at a deeper understanding of the atonement. We pray that all who read this biography will be able to display this same openness, asking God to illumine their understanding, even through specifics they may disagree with.

Many people had a part in the first edition of this book, either directly or indirectly, by lending emotional support, providing factual information, or aiding in production. Mrs. Morag Black showed me around the MacDonald Farm with typical Scottish hospitality. Mrs. Joss and Mrs. Rough at the Huntly Brander Library were most kind in allowing me full access to the MacDonald collection there, which includes many valuable old original manuscripts, as well as a room in which to work. Mr. G. Moore of the North East of Scotland Library Service gave permission to use several of the photographs and was very helpful in having copies of them made. Mrs. Margaret Troup, also of Huntly, was gracious in sharing many family letters and papers with me. My appreciation goes to Nick Harrison and the others who kept the various facets of our business operating smoothly during my trips to Scotland, and to those individuals who read and critiqued the manuscript in its early stages.

My three sons, Patrick, Robin, and Gregory, were, as always, interested and supportive and, by the project's end, very much involved in its progress. My wife, Judy, occupies far more than a "supportive" role in all my writing, particularly in this project, in which she was genuinely a co-sharer of the vision to bring MacDonald to the world. She was the inspired goad, prodding me toward the fulfillment and completion of the book. She did vastly more than simple proofreading; at every stage she was a thorough collaborator, deserving of my heartiest thanks.

I would like to quote from George MacDonald himself from the opening pages of *Ranald Bannerman's Boyhood* in which he uses an autobiographical format:

"My reason for wishing to tell this first portion of my history is that when I look back upon it, it seems to me not only so pleasant, but so full of meaning, that, if I can only tell it aright, it must prove rather pleasant and not quite unmeaning to those who will read it" (*Ranald Bannerman's Boyhood,* chapter 1).

Throughout the writing it was my constant prayer that I would "tell it aright." I hope you, too, will find it pleasant and "full of meaning."

Now it has been almost twenty years since I went to Scotland to write the first draft of this book. Only a few years before that my wife and I, with our friends at Bethany House Publishers, had tentatively embarked on a joint effort to reacquaint the world with the Victorian writer George MacDonald, most of whose books had for decades been unavailable to the public.

Since that time, the rebirth of interest in MacDonald has exploded beyond what any of us could have envisioned. Now there are newsletters and books and articles and studies and Web sites and symposiums and conferences and entire publishing companies devoted to his work. Given that at the time we began not a single one of MacDonald's realistic novels was in print, unbelievable is the only word for it.

Of course, many throughout the twentieth century had discovered MacDonald. He was highly respected in certain academic circles and was included in the Wade Library at Wheaton College. Others had been trying to increase awareness of his work for years—notably the George MacDonald Society in England, as well as such men as Clyde Kilby, Rolland Hein, Glenn Sadler, and William Raeper. (These four men among them published more than a dozen books of significance.) Before all of us came along, C. S. Lewis had done his best to alert the wider public to MacDonald in the 1940s. But Lewis's efforts were of limited success, as were most subsequent publications. Awareness of MacDonald remained isolated in small pockets of academic, literary, and theologic interest.

As a result of Bethany's publication of his novels in the 1980s, however, interest in George MacDonald exploded. On their coattails, a proliferation of new George MacDonald projects grew unlike anything seen since MacDonald's own lifetime. Their editions sold two million copies and "seeded" the world with fertile and fruit-bearing reminders of a man whose legacy, I am certain, will never be forgotten again. Within a decade the whole Christian world knew the name *George MacDonald.*

We owe a debt to Bethany's courage and vision and for their willingness to undertake what was a risky venture back in 1980, when very few in the general reading public had any inkling who George MacDonald was. Without these efforts, MacDonald might *still* be an unknown.

This year, 2005 marks the one-hundred-year anniversary of George MacDonald's death in 1905. Greville MacDonald's biography of his parents, *George MacDonald and His Wife,* was first released in 1924 to recall the centenary of his father's birth, and now it is with pleasure that Bethany House and I join to commemorate the centenary of MacDonald's death with this re-release of *George MacDonald, Scotland's Beloved Storyteller*.

To place this story in its proper context, and for the sake of Mac-Donald's memory, it is imperative to address a few words to an elitism that has emerged out of the developments of recent years as an unfortunate tarnish on his legacy. These comments are offered as a caution as well as a challenge to discover the *true* MacDonald and what his life meant.

George MacDonald had two primary messages to give the world, which are consistently reflected in his writing: God is a good Father, and obedience to the commands of Jesus is the foundation for a walk of faith.

These messages of MacDonald's life and work have not always been recognized. Indeed, just the opposite has often been the case. There has long been a fascination with George MacDonald for misplaced reasons. Through the years, his poetic, imaginative, allegorical, and visionary uniqueness, and the sweeping range of his corpus, because of their very breadth and vision, have lent themselves to misunderstanding, and thus to mis-focused interpretations. Not "wrong" interpretations, but *mis-focused* ones that cannot, *in themselves*, probe the essence of who Mac-Donald really was and what his life was about. The essence of the man can only be gotten at by understanding the foundation of all the rest: Fatherhood and obedience.

Even during his own life MacDonald was revered for the wrong reasons by many who never grasped the essential and eternal import of his life's work. His close friend John Ruskin, who lived one of the Victorian era's notable examples of a troubled and unbelieving life, was fascinated by MacDonald's writing but confessed himself unable to understand it. He loved MacDonald as a friend, but never personally embraced the full meaning of MacDonald's life. Though Ruskin enjoyed an intimacy with MacDonald the rest of us can but envy from afar, in a sense he remained on the outside, never really experiencing true intimacy with the deepest MacDonald had to offer.

Two of the best book-length studies ever done on MacDonald's work were written by an avowed atheist and an unabashed skeptic. After studying his work in enormous depth, both men entirely missed the *essence* of that work and the underlying foundation which gave rise to it in the first place. Why they were so fascinated by a man they did not understand is a mystery. Yet this misplaced analysis has followed MacDonald for more than a century. And now it has reared its head in our own time. Mac-Donald is the subject of an increasing number of scholarly papers and talks and conferences. Hundreds of graduate theses have been written, numerous studies published, and countless addresses given in workshops and symposiums and various gatherings, which analyze and dissect and laud MacDonald's greatness . . . and all the while the simplicity and eternal power of the foundational *raison d'être* of his own life remains mostly neglected as a mere sidebar to the story.

Certainly MacDonald's diverse range of literary skills and gifts (faerie, myth, symbolic fantasy, poetry, allegory, theological imagery, and even simple "romance") lends itself to review on multiple levels. But can analysis hope to succeed without a correct foundation? Indeed, many have taken this analysis of MacDonald to the extreme, reading the most bizarre manner of Freudian, Kohutian, and Jungian psychoanalysis into MacDonald's writing, and then psychoanalyzing MacDonald himself, quite literally from cradle to grave.

It was to point to his essential message that we first began over thirty years ago to produce redacted editions of MacDonald's novels, and then later to publish those same books in their original formats. Aware of this tendency toward mis-focused analysis, I hoped in our work to concentrate on what was the truest portrait of MacDonald, that to be derived from his books themselves. To do this practically demanded that they be adapted, by redaction and editing, to the contemporary reading public. Better, we felt, that MacDonald get into people's hands, so that he could be *read*, than that he forever remain in the vaults of obscurity.

Within the MacDonald community there were some who had been faithfully working toward a rebirth of MacDonald interest for years. When Bethany's redacted novels ignited MacDonald interest the world over, most rejoiced. Certain scholarly cliques within the MacDonald community, however, condemned Bethany's pioneering work. Since that time, the studies and publications from this quarter have persistently ignored the very redacted editions that have widened MacDonald's influence so dramatically in our time. One finds scant mention of the significance of these groundbreaking editions, all these years later, in the scholarly MacDonald literature. Heeding only such academic sources, one would conclude that the MacDonald revolution, sparked as it was, never took place at all.

The importance of clarifying this point is not to emphasize certain editions over others, for without question the redacted editions have limitations. But their historical place in the MacDonald legacy is important in respect of what they have achieved. The message of Fatherhood and obedience must be kept defined and well-focused as the underlying perspective behind Bethany's innovative new classics. The preservation of this foundation, and the pivotal role occupied in MacDonald's legacy by these particular editions cannot be expunged from the record because critics may wish the MacDonald renaissance had come by some other means.

These facts are also important because what I call the "true MacDonald" has not always been the underlying focus of certain other directions of study that have received much attention of late. Many examples could be cited, but the most glaring is represented by Robert Lee Wolfe's *The Golden Key*, which misrepresents MacDonald in the extreme. Though knowledgeable students of MacDonald give Wolfe little credence, his approach remains a troublesome thorn in the MacDonald literature and steers MacDonald studies toward analysis rather than life.

It was to discover the *true* MacDonald that in 1985 I began this biography. Ever since my own discovery of MacDonald's writings in the early 1970s, I wanted to *know* MacDonald, not merely "study" him as a fantacist or mythopoeic visionary. I determined, therefore, to write a biography that would address the foundation of George MacDonald as a spiritual man and would explore the essence of his message, apart from critical analysis and dissection. Certain peripheral elements of his expansive literary genius would come into it, of course. But I hoped to strike into deeper mines of meaning in George MacDonald's life than mere analysis could ever accurately probe. My own priorities as a biographer reflected my own spiritual debt to MacDonald on a profoundly personal level. Thus, in telling his life, I chose to bring to the surface themes that would properly explain the man as I viewed him, that would give a foundation to a true and right reading of his work, and that would accurately assess his impact as a spiritual giant and theologian whose place in the development of Christian thought has yet to be fully recognized.

As we reintroduce a new generation to the story of George Mac-Donald's life on this centenary of his death, it is our prayer that you will read for foundations. In whatever formats you most enjoy his work . . . whatever are your favorites of his genres and books . . . whatever personal background you bring to your reflections on this remarkable life, I encourage you to discover the true essence of the man George MacDonald.

Michael Phillips
Eureka, California
2005

SCOTLAND

AN APPROXIMATION OF HUNTLY IN THE 19th CENTURY

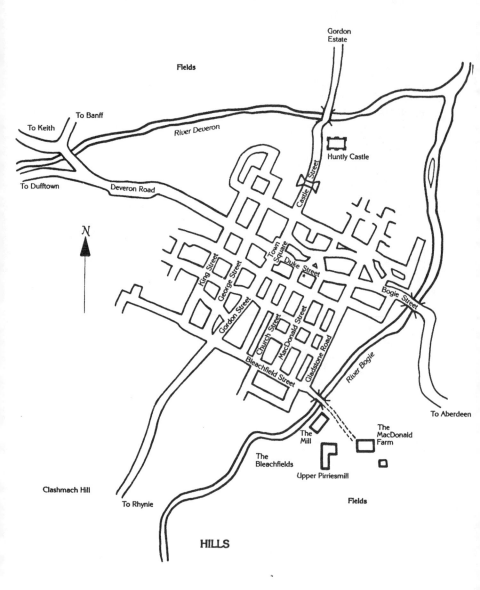

★ George MacDonald's Birthplace

MacDONALD OF CLANRANALD

Crest Badge: *On a castle triple towered, an arm in armor, embowed, holding a sword, proper.*

Motto: *My hope is constant in thee.*

Old Motto: *Dh´aindeoin co´theireadh e (Gainsay who dare).*

Gaelic Name: *MacDhòmhnuill.*

PROLOGUE
(Early Family History)

From the earliest beginnings of the recorded history of Scotland, the clan has played a pivotal role in every aspect of life. In the mountainous north and west, especially, diverse peoples who first occupied the land gradually amalgamated together, yet retained their common Celtic heritage.

This Celtic background made these Highlanders a high-spirited people, as stalwart and vivid as the rugged land they conquered and tamed, devoted to family and soil and principle. If they were sometimes violent in nature, the other side of such emotionalism revealed itself in a love of poetry and music that gave the Highland clans many haunting and lyrical Gaelic melodies, which were passed on from generation to generation. These men and women revered the tribal ballad singer, the bagpipe, the harp, the claymore (two-edged broadsword), and the family tartan as the outward and visible representations of an abiding clan loyalty and faith.

Their life was intrinsically linked to the earth and what it could provide, though the land was usually poor. The clan chiefs usually had no great wealth and could provide little more for those who worked their land than huts fashioned out of a combination of wood and thickly cut sod from the surrounding moors. The clan poet (called a "Bard" or "Sennachie") was as essential to life in the community as the priest himself, and represented the intellectual as well as the imaginative gifts of the Celtic race. His Gaelic songs and chants could be at once tender, wild, historic, and mystical. Similarly, the piper's office, which combined the role of town crier and military trumpeter, paralleled the Bard's. Both were positions of high rank in the clan and sometimes passed from one generation to the next by heredity as did that of the chieftain.

Every clan developed differently through the years, sending out branches of sub-clans in many directions. Their independent and violent spirit kept them constantly feuding with one another, as well as against the English and other threatening foes. Through the centuries, this battle to preserve their heritage contributed to the individuality of the Scots as a people. The Romans, the Anglo-Saxons, the Vikings, the English, the Normans, and the French all attempted incursions into that northern land. But through it all the Scots remained proudly and staunchly independent.

The MacDonalds, the most powerful of all the Highland clans, trace their origin to Somerlad, the 12th-century King of the Isles in western Scotland; from his grandson they take their name. Under Donald (the original name of the clan in Gaelic was *MacDhomhnuill*) the clan attained great eminence, and from him the many branches of the MacDonald tree grew outward, eventually encompassing all of Scotland. Donald's great-grandson John had several sons. His youngest, Ranald, received a grant in 1373 of the North Isles and other lands. From Ranald springs the clan known as *MacDonald of Clanranald*, which eventually held land throughout the western islands and mainland—from North and South Uist down through Rhum, Mull, the Morvern peninsula, the Inner Hebrides, Kintyre, and Argyll.

The recent history of Clanranald came into prominence in the 17th century through their close association with the Jacobite risings. When James Stuart, son of Mary Queen of Scots, became king of both England and Scotland in 1603, loyalty to the native Scottish Stuart monarchy was especially strong in the Highlands. Two generations later, prominent English leaders deposed the Stuart James II in favor of William of Orange of the Netherlands, and this Highland loyalty became all the deeper. When the exiled James began to gather support in an attempt to regain the crown, he found willing followers in Scotland. And though he never did mount a serious threat, a party was formed in the north—called the Jacobites—which opposed the government under William and continued to back the Stuarts.

The king's advisors in London urged him to find a way to teach the troublesome Highlanders a lesson. Thus King William issued an order in 1691 to the Jacobite clan chieftains to take an oath of allegiance before January 1, 1692, or else be treated as rebels in arms against the government.

In the little valley of Glencoe, inland from Loch Linnhe in western Scotland, dwelt the stronghold of a poetical tribe of the Clan Donald—the Maclains. The little narrow glen, with its gloomy barren mountains often shrouded in mist and rain, and swept by fierce winds, was an awe-inspiring setting. But to the MacDonalds who claimed Glencoe for their own, its summer warmth, the richness of the valley soil, the deer-haunted springs, the woods of rowan, and the clear mountain burn that wound through the peaceful glen made it a fit home for the people known as poets for miles around. It used to be said that no man could be a Maclain of the Clanranald unless he could express himself in rhyme. Though all the Highlands were known for their bards and pipers, the Maclains of Glencoe certainly typified such a representation of the 17th-century poetical, loyal, independent Highlander.

Though most of the chieftains had complied with the terms of the

Glencoe, site of 1692 massacre of MacDonald clan by Campbells

king's proclamation by the end of 1691, the MacDonalds were one of the clans most reluctant to accept William of Orange on the throne. Alexander MacIain MacDonald, leader of the Glencoe branch of the clan, postponed making his submission to the very end as a statement of defiance, so as to be known as the last Highlander to submit. When he went to Fort William to take the oath in the last week of the year, he was alarmed to discover there was no magistrate present with power to receive the oath. Quickly he was forced to turn back and travel to Inverary, some forty miles south, the closest point of civil administration. The weather turned against him and a fierce snowstorm held up his journey, delaying his arrival until January 2. To his further dismay, he found that the sheriff's deputy had temporarily left his headquarters, and thus MacDonald's oath of submission did not take place until January 6.

Soon afterward a regiment of soldiers under the command of rival Robert Campbell of Glenlyon (the MacDonalds and Campbells—the Highlands' two most powerful clans—had been feuding rivals for years) was sent to Glencoe with orders signed by King William to execute the Chief of Glencoe. This directive gave the hereditary enemies of the MacDonalds, by virtue of their official position in the area and their connections with the English crown, a chance to wipe out old grievances.

On an ostensible mission merely to collect taxes, made all the more friendly in that Campbell was related to MacDonald's wife, the soldiers were received unsuspectingly by the clansmen, who entertained them hospitably for twelve days, notwithstanding the old feuds between their respective clans. Then at five o'clock on the morning of February 13, 1692, the Campbells turned on their hosts. In obedience to the orders of their officers, the soldiers fell suddenly upon the sleeping MacDonalds. Tradition has it that many Campbells sought to evade the horrible task, warning people up and down the exposed glen to escape before the terrible day came. But when it did finally arrive that cold stormy night before dawn, men, women, and children were slaughtered in cold blood. In the vicious massacre some 40 persons were killed before another 110 managed to escape into the darkness of the early wintry morning—fleeing to the surrounding mountains as the snow fell, some nearly unclothed, saving their lives but carrying nothing away. The majority of these, too, lost their lives from exposure and starvation in the desolate snowbound mountains. The deserted houses were then plundered and burned and the livestock driven away, where it was later divided up among the victorious officers at Fort William.

Alastir MacAonghais,* half brother of the slain chief, was away from Glencoe at Brecklet at the time of the massacre. Receiving warning of the treachery that was falling on his clan, he crossed the River Laroch with his family and livestock to the Ballachulish side of the pass, thus escaping the doom of his ill-fated brother.

---

*Highland families from one clan may have many different names, the prefix *Mac* meaning "son of," thus often confusing the would-be genealogist.

The event outraged other Highland clans and gave renewed impetus to the rebellious Jacobite faction, who vowed to continue their support of the Stuart family, now represented by the son of the old king. In 1715 the Jacobites followed the Earl of Mar in a hapless attempt to restore "the Pretender" to his father's one-time throne. By this time Alastir Mac-Aonghais MacDonald of Clanranald was over 90 years of age. In spite of his advanced years, when his clansmen from Glencoe marched away to fight with Mar at Sheriffmuir, he insisted on accompanying them to battle. His people protested, and to keep him from going, a messenger was sent to inform him that his wife was dying. He returned home at once, only to find her in perfect health; immediately aware of the deception against him, he arose early the next morning, harnessed an old horse, and rode away, never to return. The legends surrounding this old Highland warrior vary: some say the battle was over before he reached the rest of his people, while others claim the Chief of Clanranald was killed on the field of battle. Nevertheless, he was buried at Dunblane. The uprising itself, however, was doomed and the monarchy remained secure.

Alastir's son, who had fled from Glencoe with his father, had migrated northward to the small coastal village of Portsoy, where he became a quarryman. His son William became Portsoy's piper and was destined once again to be swept into the political fray.

The passage of generations did not dim the Jacobite spirit, and many in the Highlands still dreamed of a resurrection of the Stuart monarchy over the Hanoverian Georges who had come to power in London in the mid–18th century. In 1745, Prince Charles Edward Stuart, son of "the Pretender" and grandson of ousted King James II, came to the Highlands from France to rally support for a new claim to the throne. The "Young Pretender," as he was known, found the Jacobite dream thriving. Having

Gravemarker of Clan Donald

Rock formations like this (the Whale's Mouth off the Scaurnose near Cullen) are typical of the coastline of northeast Scotland, where are found many caves like that in which William MacDonald (and the fictional Duncan MacPhail) hid while being chased.

sailed from the mainland with only seven friends, Bonnie Prince Charlie had soon gathered a sizeable army of Highlanders behind him, including many hundreds from the Clanranald.

The Prince, with the Highlanders behind him, marched to Edinburgh and there proclaimed himself King James VII of Scotland. They then blazed their way into England and as far south as Derby. But eventually the northward-marching troops of the King of England forced the Scots to retreat.

Suddenly support for the Prince eroded badly and the morale of his troops began to break down. His retreat continued through Glasgow and north toward Inverness. The King's men, meanwhile, under the Duke of Cumberland, advanced through Aberdeen and along the northern coast through Banff. They finally met the insurrectionary forces at Culloden Moor, east of Inverness on April 16, 1746, and the rebel army of some 5,000 men was crushed and scattered in a final and decisive defeat, signaling the virtual end of the clan system as it had been known for centuries. The Prince escaped and went into hiding, and only a small remnant of his original force survived with him.

William MacDonald, the piper of Portsoy, had fought bravely with the Young Pretender at Culloden and was one of the few to survive the slaughter. He was only able to escape Cumberland's ruthless stalking of every fugitive by the speed of his legs. Tradition tells of his being chased with his eldest son by the people of Nairn, one town's blacksmith brandishing a red-hot iron after them. They hid and were secretly fed for months in the caves along the rugged coast near Portsoy. His home was carefully watched for a time by the authorities and he had to creep into town in the dead of night to visit. How long William had to remain in hiding is unknown. Eventually he lost his eyesight and apparently resumed his duties as the blind piper of Portsoy.

King George II took the events of the 1745 uprising as an opportunity to humble Scotland's obstreperous tribal leaders, and for their insubordination he took away the holdings of the Jacobite clan leaders and outlawed the use of both kilt and bagpipe.

The wife of William MacDonald had given birth just three months before Culloden to a younger son, Charles Edward, named in honor of the Prince for whom her husband was fighting. But the mother died on the very day the news of the terrible disaster reached her. Whether she knew her husband and eldest son had escaped is unknown. After coming out from hiding in the caves, William managed to continue to help raise his large family with assistance from other relatives.

Gaelic was William MacDonald's tongue and Catholicism his religion, but times were gradually changing. After Culloden many in the north of Scotland converted to Presbyterianism (the national religion of Scotland everywhere, except in parts of the Highlands) or other forms of Protestant (or "Dissenting") Calvinism. In addition to religious and social changes brought about by the Highland clearances in the late 18th century, industry was altering the face of Scottish society. Like the rest of Europe, the northern portion of the British Isles gradually became less rural, and the growth of cities and towns had further impact on the dying clan system.

The youngest of the piper's large family, Charles Edward MacDonald, was apprenticed to the weaving business in the growing textile industry, and eventually moved to the small town of Huntly, south of Portsoy. There he married Isabella Robertson and built up a very successful bleaching (dyeing) and spinning business. Their three sons inherited the business, though hard times soon befell the MacDonald family enterprises, whose factories were made obsolete by advancing technology from the south. Their son Charles eventually fled the country because of questionable financial practices. And ultimately their other two sons, George and James, carried the burden of their brother's violations and the sagging family business for another three decades.

Charles Edward and Isabella's son George married Helen MacKay in 1822, and five of their sons survived. Their first was named after George's brother Charles, and the third after his brother James. The two younger were Alexander and John. Their second son they named in honor of his father—George MacDonald, Jr.

Scotland had changed through the years. She had been united with England now for more than a century. Wars and battles had faded into legend. The clan system of the Highlands had waned, and the tales of its poets and warriors could now only be found in stories and ballads and in the histories and poems of contemporary Scotsmen such as Robert Burns and Sir Walter Scott. The tartan and kilt, the bagpipe and dirk had become but ceremonial remembrances of a time long past. The songs of the Sennachie, kindling the vision of a proud people as they sang of nature, romance, peat fires, snow-covered mountain peaks, storm-tossed wintry seas, thatched cottages, legendary battles, and intense love for the homeland, were left behind in the march of 19th-century Scotland into its future. That branch of the Highlands' most formidable clan, MacDonald of Clanranald, had indeed enjoyed a colorful history—from Somerled, who drove the Vikings from the Isles, down through the centuries to Alastir of Glencoe and his grandson the blind piper of Portsoy, to Charles Edward MacDonald, father of George MacDonald, Sr., struggling factory owner and farmer of Huntly. Yet it now seemed all but forgotten as its descendents were absorbed into the mainstream of modern society.

But to the visionary mystic with Celtic blood in his veins, there yet remained a lingering echo of footfalls and voices that had gone before. Out of the union of George MacDonald, Sr., and Helen MacKay of Huntly came a rebirth of the independent Gaelic spirit. Certainly the heritage in which their ancestors had been steeped offered their second son fertile ground for the cultivation of his imagination. On the winds of the past he would bring the voice of the poet and storyteller again to life. By the end of the 19th century, many would look to this latest in the generation of

MacDonalds—clothed in modern garb, yet nevertheless a proper Celt in his imaginative and poetical gifts—as one of the greatest sons of the rugged and historic land of Scotland and one of the most influential bards MacDonald of Clanranald had yet produced.

PART ONE

View from upstairs window of family farmhouse, from which MacDonald must have looked many times and which may have inspired the poem "The Hills."

THE BOY MYSTIC

A ten-year-old boy stood silently gazing out the second-floor window at the small field below. Several black-and-white cows were grazing lazily, and at the far end a small plot of sweet corn waved gently in the breeze.

But neither cattle nor corn caught the boy's eye. His gaze was directed toward nothing in particular on this morning; he merely stood and stared ahead, seeing with his mind rather than his eye. He had climbed the short, winding flight of stairs to his father's room because it brought him a certain sense of repose to be in the inner sanctum where his father's presence lingered. And in the busy household of nearly a dozen people, chances to be alone with his thoughts were rare enough.

As he stared out the window his introspective mind returned to his mother, as it so often did, especially when he was able to sneak past Grannie and spend a few quiet minutes upstairs in the room she had shared with his father. She had been gone two years now, and though his father put up a brave front, the lad could sense the older man's empty heart. He hurt almost as much for his father's loss of his wife as he did for his own loss of his mother. But the two consoled each other in their mutual sorrow and were thus knit together in an inseparable bond of love, which would last throughout both their lifetimes.

As the boy looked out upon his father's fields, gradually the little grassy brae at his feet came into focus. Suddenly into his reminiscences came the face of his younger brother James. He had died only a year ago, but in the miracle of resiliency which is childhood, the tears, as at his mother's death, had been quickly shed and now only returned occasionally at times of particular aloneness. A melancholy smile passed over the boy's lips as he thought of the time he and James had accidentally chased one of those very cows into the patch of corn, later incurring their father's good-natured scolding for the fallen stalks. It had been but six months after the incident that James had been taken, making its memory all the more poignant in the mind of both father and son. Though the tears may have been past, the reminders of the close touch of death were never far from the reflective boy; the focus of his private broodings was often far in advance of his yet tender years.

He lifted his eyes to the expansive golden field of wheat beyond the small, grassy pasture, and then to the distance where, on a clear day, one could just make out the Buck where it stood on the edge of the Highlands. His eyes had left it, and it would be years before his mind would return to the memory of this day to pen the words. But already stored deep in the subconscious mind of this pensive lad were the origins of a poem he would later write—about the little field where he and his brother had so often romped:

> Behind my father's house there lies
> A little grassy brae;
> Whose face my childhood's busy feet
> Ran often up in play.

He stood a few more moments, then turned and left the room. He quietly descended the stairway, the stairs that 38 years later would become the fictional stairway of such significance in the life of his Princess Irene. He reached the main floor of the stone farmhouse his father and uncle had built nine years earlier, known in Huntly as "Bleachfield Cottage."

"Geordie, is that you?" came a voice from the kitchen.

"Ay, Grannie."

Farmland near Huntly

"I thought ye was doon t' the mill."

"No, Grannie."

"Whaur hae ye been, then?"

"In the hoose."

"Doin' what? Up t' nae mischief, I hope."

"Jist thinkin'."

"Whaur i' the hoose?"

"Upstairs, in Papa's room."

"I tell'd ye a hunnert times, Geordie, yer father's room is nae place fer young'uns. Haen't I tell'd ye so?"

"Ay."

"Weel, run alang, noo. Tak this basket o' bread an' butter doon t' yer father an' uncle at the mill. An' dinna be fergettin' that tomorrow's the Sabbath. Jist 'cause it's summer be nae cause fer ye t' be fergettin' the Lord's day."

"I winna ferget."

"Did ye say yer prayers this mornin', laddie?"

"Ay."

"Ye dinna want the Lord angert at ye. He doesn't like it when ye ferget t' say yer prayers."

"I know, Grannie."

"Weel, run alang, laddie. Ye wasted enocht time already wi' yer thinkin' an' sich. Yer papa'll be a hungert an' waitin' on ye."

The boy took the basket and left the house through the front door, while his aging grandmother watched him go with a sigh and a slight shake of the head as if to say, "I dinna ken what's t' come o' him, wi' all his thinkin'. He's sich a strange an' quiet lad."

The stone farmhouse sat some two hundred yards back from the River Bogie, and it was down the grassy incline toward the river that the boy now walked, toward the bleaching mill that his father and uncle operated at the river's edge. Even as he left the house, he could hear the distant sounds of thudding wooden machinery, the swoosh-swoosh of the water that was diverted from the river through the sluice to turn the waterwheel and power various apparatuses inside the mill, and the high-pitched shouts and laughter of his cousins and his two brothers Charles and Alex who spent most of every summer's day playing near the mill and in the river above it. Only his baby brother, John, was left in the house, attended to by his grandmother in the absence of his aunt, who was away from Huntly for a few days.

As he neared the mill, the sounds grew louder and louder. On many days he played with the other children, for the river and the mill never were exhausted in their capacity to provide adventure and enjoyment. And being near his father as he worked was always a special delight. But on this day one of his contemplative moods had unexpectedly come over him and he preferred none but his own companionship—somber though it might be—and that of the fields and trees, the river and the mountains, and the many animals about the place that were his friends. Perhaps after making his delivery he would walk into town or go down to the ruins. This would be a good day for a hike past the castle down the banks of the Deveron through the green pastures to the point where the Bogie spilled into it, and then back along the Bogie to the mill. A long walk by himself suited his quiet frame of mind.

"Ho, Geordie!" came a shout.

"Hello, Uncle James."

"What ye got i' the basket, man?"

"Grannie sent ye some bread."

"Ah, glad I am t' hear't."

Following his uncle inside, the boy saw his father, whose back was turned, engaged in an attempt to repair an aging pulley wheel. The man turned, and at the sight of his son, his face brightened. He dropped the mallet in his hands, took two hobbling strides toward him, and put a strong arm around the lad's young shoulders.

"Ay, George. Hoo's my son this bright day?"

"Well, Papa," returned the boy with a smile.

"Come t' help me keep this mill in good repair, are ye?"

"I jist brocht ye some bread from Grannie, Papa."

"Weel, bless the lady's heart! An' yer's too, my son. We thank ye!"

The boy handed him the basket, his face beaming with pleasure.

"Are ye goin' t' swim wi' the others today, George?" asked his father, taking out a thick slice of the hearty brown bread and devouring a quarter of it in a single bite.

Stone dyke so common in Scotland

"I dinna think so, Papa."

"A bit o' wark on the wee boat Charles an' yersel' are buildin'?"

"Maybe tomorrow."

"What, then? Are ye plannin' t' take Missy an' yer Klopstock's up the hill fer a ride?" said George, Sr.

"Not today. I think I micht walk t' the castle, Papa."

"Weel, whate'er ye like," returned his father. "Be back afore supper an' ye can give me a han' putting this stubborn wheel back in place. I need a strong lad like yersel' t' help me wi' it."

Five minutes later the boy was crossing the small wooden bridge from the mill over the Bogie to Bleachfield Street. He made his way the half mile or so to Gordon Street, where he turned right, passing through the middle of Huntly, and thence to the ruins of Huntly Castle about a mile and a half from his home. He and his brothers and friends often played there during the summer, masquerading as ancient Scottish clan heroes fighting against the Romans or the Vikings or the English, taking turns playing Robert the Bruce. But today he bypassed the castle in favor of the melodic river that wound around its feet. It seemed whenever his mind turned serious, solitude and the sounds of water drew him.

With the pleasant memory of his father still fresh in his mind, the distance progressed quickly. The enjoyment of his walk was not interrupted by any of the troublesome notions that had been plaguing his thoughts lately. Soon he approached the town square, the very hub of business and commerce, not only for the bustling little Scottish village of Huntly, but also for the entire region known as Strathbogie.

Strathbogie valley and the town of Huntly

CHAPTER ONE

HUNTLY

The boy George MacDonald—thoughtful, imaginative, and full of love for his natural surroundings—throughout his childhood made countless walks from his father's farm into the town of Huntly just across the Bogie. He had been born only a block from the town square, and came into town for school, for church, for play, and to visit Grannie. He knew every street of Huntly as intimately as he knew the fields of his father's farm and the now-ruined corridors of Huntly Castle. Not only did he know the streets, he knew the town's surroundings—its fields and farms and the hills, which surrounded the little valley with Huntly at its center. He came to know the Highland regions to Huntly's south and the seashore to its north. But always Huntly and its immediate environs remained most vivid in his imagination.

As George MacDonald grew older and eventually left home for the university, thereafter to migrate to London for the greater part of his professional career, he never forgot the land of his birth and upbringing. Time and again in his memory he found himself walking those same streets, riding those same hills, walking along the banks of those same rivers, and looking out the windows of his childhood upon fields that now seemed so full of meaning with the passage of years. Throughout his life he regularly returned to this small agricultural town from which his roots had sprung. Crisis brought him back, decisive change brought him back, death brought him back. But back he always came—to find rejuvenation for what in life lay ahead, and to find inspiration for the writings he would give to the world.

Historical Backgrounds

The ancient Scottish village of Huntly lies in the northeast of Scotland in Aberdeenshire, some thirty-eight miles northwest of Aberdeen and seventeen miles south of Portsoy on the coast. Situated at a crucial juncture between Aberdeen and Inverness, the area that would come to be known as Strathbogie (the Valley of the River Bogie) first came into prominence in the 12th century when the first castle was built at the critical defensive point near where the river Bogie empties into the river Deveron. The 12th century was a time of momentous change for Scotland as her kings set about solidifying the whole social and political structure of the country from the old loosely knit Celtic tribal kingdom into a well-ordered feudal country under its new Norman rulers. There was determined resistance to the new ways in the strongly Celtic areas, and subjugation could only be achieved by placing loyal noblemen in vital strongholds along all strategic routes that interconnected the north.

Thus, Duncan, Earl of Fife, built a castle known as the "Peel of Strathbogie" on the banks of the Deveron, and occupation of the lands later passed to his son and grandson. In 1307, after falling ill at Inverurie, Robert Bruce was brought to the castle at Strathbogie to recover. But though the king had found shelter in his castle, the lord of Strathbogie turned against Bruce just before his final triumph against the English at Bannockburn. As a punishment, the lands were taken from him and granted in 1318 to Sir Adam Gordon of Huntly, in Berwickshire in the south of Scotland. A border laird, Gordon brought with him to the north the name *Huntly* from his property in Berwick.

A village slowly grew around the castle, and though the Gordons remained the leading noble family of Huntly from the 14th to the 20th century, after two rebuildings and a colorful and turbulent history, Huntly Castle fell into disrepair in the 17th century. Thereafter it became little more than a common quarry, providing building material for houses in the still-growing village. Such plundering did not stop until the 19th century, when at last antiquarian sentiment came to the rescue and declared the ruins a national monument.

Lying in the heart of the Strathbogie valley, with a wide circle of hills standing round it, the village of Huntly eventually expanded to occupy most of the area between the Bogie and the Deveron. The valley was fertile farm and grazing land, standing within sight of the foothills of the Grampian Highlands to the south. Both rivers originated some twelve miles to the southwest, high on the windy storm-swept peat flanks of "the Buck," a 2,400-foot Highland mountain that stood watch over the forests and valleys below. From the Buck a little stream known as the Burn of Craig flowed westward where it emptied into the Bogie, which then flowed toward Huntly, while the Deveron flowed north from the Buck, then west into the village. Gathering size and waters from other contributing burns and springs, the streams took their peat-gold brownish hue from decaying heather, the essence of the Highland mystique. Around the foothold of the ruins of Huntly Castle swirled the Deveron—larger, more open, yet capable of fury when aroused. The Bogie flowed around the town to the east, cascading over rocks and beside ancient but now-quiet mills, topaz-stained, until it poured into the Deveron east of Huntly. Both rivers were easily capable of defying their banks and flooding farms and homesteads

Huntly Castle

in the process, and even once or twice threatening the town between them with their combined ferocity.

The symbolic beauty and fierce nature of these small but rapid waters—like the nature of the ancient Celts who had walked their banks—played a part in inspiring the lads of Strathbogie. The two rivers, along with the ruins of the castle they surrounded, set a mood of adventure, passion, and historic antiquity. Their very color of rich brown suggested a memory of Highland heritage, as the tumbled-down castle stones brought to mind all the vivid heroism of Scotland's tumultuous past.

Huntly in the Nineteenth Century

In the 1820s Huntly was a village of some 3,500 inhabitants, a relatively thriving agricultural town, which also served as a center for the sale of local handicrafts. The life of Huntly, then and now, centered in the town square. In the center of this marketplace stood the thatched little well house, with canopy roof, pulley, chain, and bucket. Around it gathered the country women and bareheaded maids, with baskets on their arms loaded with butter, eggs, cheese, and live fowl. Mingling with them were the town women and domestic servants. Some thirty or forty feet from the well house stood the famous "Stannin' Stanes o' Strathbogie"—a small grouping of several standing stones some four and a half feet tall. This ancient monument dates back to the earliest legends of the area; though, like Stonehenge and other such relics of antiquity, no one knows their original

Huntly—town square and stone enclosure over old well

purpose. In older times it was to the "Stannin' Stanes" that the people were summoned for battle, for court, or for public proclamations. The town square around the well house and the "Stannin' Stanes" was Huntly's center for news, friendship, business, and social life. Surrounding the perimeter of the small square were located gabled merchants' dwellings and stores as well as the toll-booth, or jail. The *Gordon Arms* hotel was one of the square's most imposing buildings, where on market days shepherds and Highland drovers would gather, speaking in Gaelic, or the more Anglicized Doric concerning all matters of interest to do with shepherd and crofter life, just as the ladies would gather at the well.

Though the Industrial Revolution had begun in the cities of England around the 1760s, the use of machinery had not yet even fifty years later found its way into the rural northern regions of Scotland. The primary industry of Huntly, if such it could be called, was an industry of handmade goods. On market days stalls were set up all around the square for all manner of produce, sweets, shoes, haberdashery, leather goods, handmade clothes, smoked or cured meats. Some of the booths sold mossberries (cranberries) or juniper berries, which were used to flavor homemade beer. Around the square stood small, shaggy, long-tailed horses, hitched with ropes to the carts. Behind the carts a group of the town's "nickums" (young mischief-makers) might be seen loitering, keenly on the lookout for an opportunity to pluck hairs from the horses' tails, which they would later use for fishing line. Both the Bogie and Deveron had trout aplenty, free to any who could hook or net them.

From the center of the square, four streets led outward into the maze of little village streets, proceeding in all directions, and thence outward into the countryside beyond. Castle Street led northward through the guard towers, past what would in the late 19th century become the Gordon Schools, into the grounds of Huntly Castle, then across a narrow stone bridge over the Deveron and to the Gordon mansion and estate. Westward from the square the Deveron Road led again across the river and toward Dufftown and Keith. Southward proceeded Gordon Street, and eastward ran Duke Street, which, turning into Bogie Street, crossed the Bogie and became the Aberdeen Road running southeast toward the gray Granite City. Throughout the village were tightly packed one- and two-story gray stone cottages, some thatched, some slated. Many had their ground floors sunk for weaving shops, but by the turn of the 19th century the McVeagh linen factory had mostly displaced the weaver in his cottage. And outside the town, Clashmach Hill, the Bin, and the Hill of Greenfold surrounded the village and looked down on the valley spread out below them.

Twentieth-century minds can hardly comprehend the totality with which British aristocratic noble families maintained their hold over their lands and subjects a hundred and fifty or two hundred years ago. Though the feudal system as such had long disappeared, remnants of its social and class structure remained well into the 19th and in some cases the 20th century, especially in the more remote regions. Prior to the Industrial

Revolution, there was virtually no sizeable middle class as we know it today. There were basically two classifications of people in rural England and Scotland: the landowners, and the peasants who worked their small parcel of land, or croft, on behalf of the landowner, who always managed to claim a significant portion of the profits. The hold these landowners maintained was often unconditional, leaving their tenants little or no negotiating strength. In the late 18th and early 19th century the Highland Clearances began, when the lairds realized it to be more profitable to raise sheep on their lands than to lease it out to tenant farmers; hence the Highlands were "cleared." In massive moves throughout the Highlands, poor crofters were given a 28-day notice to quit, whether they had a place to go or not. To this day, ancient reminders stand throughout the Highlands—vacated, ruined stone shells that once housed Scottish families trying to eke out a meager living from the often unfriendly earth. By the mid-19th century, the chains of this system were breaking down all over England, and though the changes could be felt in Scotland they were slower to prevail. The business classes were expanding, the lot of the crofter and tenant farmer was gradually improving, but it was not until much later that the landowning lairds [lords] fell from their once-mighty positions of almost infinite authority over their local subjects.

In Huntly the Gordon family dictated nearly all aspects of village life, business, and agriculture for centuries. Yet in spite of the personal treacheries, scandals, and historic cruelties of certain of the more well-known

Deserted Highland croft

Gordons, they were in some measure popular in Huntly, even if feared. "Ne'er misca' ["miscall"–berate] a Gordon in the Raws of Strathbogie" was an important local proverb to bear in mind. The Gordons were devoted to the prosperity of their people and the development of their handicrafts and cottage industries. A story told of Alexander, the fourth Duke of Gordon, demonstrates the family's commitment to the welfare of their tenants. In 1821 the Duke's factor, the business manager for the estate, proposed breaking up several small holdings and adding them to the larger farms.

"What are you going to do with the cottars?" asked the Duke.

"They will have to seek a living elsewhere," said the factor.

The Duke thought about this answer for a time, then replied to the factor that he would have all the people taken to the Deveron and drowned.

"Oh, you're joking, your Grace!" said the astonished factor with alarm.

"Not at all," said the Duke finally. "If we are to deprive them of their means for a living, this would be the most humane course. No, they and their forefathers were here before us, and they will be here after I am gone. They will retain their holdings."

However, five years later the Duke died and at last the factor had his way. After that, the frugal and hardy crofters, which had once been scattered abundantly over the glens of Strathbogie, began to disappear one by one. Throughout the 19th century, the life of the crofters who did remain was always a simple one, from those more prosperous tenancies nearer the village to the poorer ones farther into the Highlands, where the land was less fertile, the winds colder, the moors more barren.

It is not possible to think of the Highlands or the people who inhabited them without thinking of the heather that covers its mountains, and the peat that lies several feet thick underneath it—enough peat to provide fuel for the Highlands and surrounding villages for ten thousand harsh northern winters and more. The gray, wiry, scrubby ground-covering bush *Erica Cinerea* is unfriendly and useless, the curse of farmer and sheepherder alike, good for nothing—until the month of August. Then its tiny blossoms break into glorious explosions of pink and purple and white and magenta, blanketing the barren Highland hills and moors in such profusions of radiance that travelers from the world over come to see it, poets and songwriters extol its romantic mystery, and lovers pluck it to exchange their unspoken pledges.

Yet just as surely as the heather blooms and gives rise to Highland gaiety and festivals and haunting ballads, by Christmas those same hills are buried in white, the soil bitter cold, hidden beneath the frozen arctic winds that sweep down over them from the icy North Sea. Winter gives the heather-covered moors opportunity to serve a more practical function than their once-yearly display of royal color. For through the centuries as it grew in these wet regions atop underlying layers of rock, the climate and lack of drainage created unique conditions. As it decomposed under the weight of new growth above, the heather massed together to form "peat."

This partially decayed substance, which burns hot and slow, would, with the passage of sufficient time and pressure, ultimately become coal. Therefore, throughout the Highlands, hardy crofters continue to cut below the heather surface into the rich black matter beneath. Resembling dirt but organic in nature, peat is cut into brick-sized pieces, carried out of the moors, and stored for winter fuel. Just as the heather in August gives a warm and cheerful hue to the hills, in winter the heather of a thousand summers past gives itself to warm the cottages of the Highlands and surrounding valleys.

The mere mention of a peat fire carries one's imagination beyond the town into the little crofting cottages of thatched roof and dirt floor, from which could be seen the friendly curl of smoke rising slowly into the sky, yielding the sweet aroma of the burning peat within. Often the fireplaces and hearths were wide open into the room, the chimney drawing out a scant two-thirds of the smoke, leaving the rest to wander about the two or three rooms of the humble cottage until it gradually found its way through the thatched ceiling. Though the surroundings may have been simple, hospitality was rich and freely given. Storytelling, the singing of ballads, visiting with neighbors or a news-vending beggar, the soothing hum of a spinning wheel, and a reading from the family Bible before prayers and bed were all familiar aspects of the cottar's life.

Thus the Scottish village of Huntly—both within the town and in the hills and farmland surrounding it—was a village of activity, of occasional

Peat cuttings and stacks

Huntly clock tower on Gordon Street

affluence, of frequent poverty on the part of its poorer crofters. Its ancient historical roots, its geographical associations with the Highlands, and commercial links with Aberdeen and the sea made Huntly a village fraught with fertile soil for the roots of a child's imagination.

Much in George MacDonald's writings recalls to mind the simple ways of these unpretentious people and their agrarian lifestyle. To understand the man we must also know the world of George MacDonald's nurture and growth—for the land was always feeding him, influencing him. In his novels, his poetry, and his fairy tales we see themes constantly repeated that hearken back to his own boyhood in Huntly—castles, noble families, cobblestoned village streets, warm summers, icy rivers, golden-brown burns and rivers, fields of ripening grain, heather moors, poverty and wealth, peat fires, and homely meals of boiled potatoes and oatcakes. His boyhood imagination saw beyond the surface appearance of these influences and gave birth to a romantic vision of a time now past.

This, then, is where George MacDonald's life began. And although the whole of his working career was spent outside Scotland, he returned to Huntly time and again throughout his life. A good deal from his writings and much of what he was as a man sprang from this source.

C. Edward Troup, George MacDonald's cousin, wrote:

> "I do not know of any other writer the scenes of whose boyhood were so deeply impressed on him and are so closely associated with his best work. In his English novels he wrote, of course, of English country scenes, but never, I think, with the same love as of Scotland: and when he writes of Scotland, one almost always feels it is Aberdeenshire."[1]

CHAPTER TWO

EARLY DAYS OF JOY
(1770–1835)

George MacDonald's Grandparents

Charles Edward MacDonald, son of the fugitive, the blind piper, from Culloden, arrived in Huntly, probably penniless, sometime around 1770. He went to work as a clerk for Mr. Hugh McVeagh, who some time before, under the auspices of the Duke, had built a linen manufacturing business on the banks of the Bogie that ultimately became highly successful. He was the first to inaugurate this industry in the northeast of Scotland, and his great success brought prosperity to Huntly, employing many weavers in their homes and other workers. MacDonald arrived on the scene at a critical juncture of the growth of the business and was quickly singled out for his grit and acumen. Before long, McVeagh acquired a lease from the Gordons of the farmland of Upper Pirriesmill across the Bogie south of town, and there established bleachworks in conjunction with his linen factory in town. Labor was plentiful, and the soft, brown, naturally acidic waters were perfectly suited to the bleaching process. The fields that sloped down to the river provided a perfect meadow where the sheets of linen could be spread out for the sun to complete the bleaching process. Having already observed MacDonald's energy, McVeagh put his new assistant in charge of this new branch of his industry, and within a few years people from miles around would send their linen to the Bogie to be bleached in its peat-colored waters. When McVeagh died, he left MacDonald in charge of the complete operation of both the linen factory in town and the bleachworks across the river. The young man now had the opportunity of putting his shrewd business sense to work for himself.

As time passed, however, the manufacture of linen ultimately became unprofitable. The factory could not compete with the large mills in the south of Scotland, so the linen factory was closed. But shortly thereafter a new building was constructed, in what would later become MacDonald

Street, for the manufacture of thread—all machinery driven by hand-power. The bleachfields and thread business continued to prosper, and MacDonald became the first man to introduce banking facilities into Huntly. He became the agent for an Aberdeen bank and ran the small operation in conjunction with his other ventures.

Charles Edward MacDonald married Isabella Robertson of Drumblade in 1778. She took to the business as eagerly as her husband, and between their combined efforts the MacDonald name became known as one of the leading merchant families in all of Strathbogie. Though his Highland father had in all probability been a Roman Catholic, Charles Edward identified himself with the Established Presbyterian Church of Scotland, became an elder, and remained in it all his life. His wife, however—a strict evangelical, and fiery Calvinist—was dissatisfied with the Parish minister's ineffectual methods and personality. Arriving at the badly broken-down Parish Church one winter's Sunday morning, the worshipers found snow several inches deep just inside the building. Mrs. MacDonald was so incensed that she turned around immediately with her children and went to the *Missionar' Kirk* (later the Congregational Church). Finding the other church's minister, whose zeal and eloquence were known throughout the area, to her liking, she remained in that denomination, with the entire family except her husband, for the rest of her life.

The banking business in those days was a small operation, and the firm transacted their monetary affairs over the same counter at which orders for goods to be dyed were received. The bank did not even have a safe until Mrs. MacDonald appropriated the family *Chanter Kist,* a treasure chest similar to a footlocker, for that purpose. Such a chest was an impor-

*MacDonald Street in Huntly still runs in front
of what used to be the MacDonald family factories.*

tant item in every Highland household, whether it was the home of the chief or a crofter. This huge, carved-oak chest held the family bagpipes, papers and records, valuables such as a family brooch or jewelry, and, in Catholic regions, perhaps a rosary or other sacred relic.

Isabella's Calvinistic convictions grew stronger and stronger and— whether she had been aware of its contents previously or was appalled at first sight of them—when the well-meaning lady opened the chest for use in the bank, she took it upon herself to destroy all its contents as the snares and wiles of Satan. Thus, any records of her husband's side of the MacDonald family were lost forever.

"The MacDonald Brothers"—George's Father and Uncles

Charles Edward and Isabella MacDonald had four sons and five daughters. As they grew the sons became more and more involved in the family enterprises, which reached their zenith about 1815. After Charles Edward MacDonald died in 1819, his eldest son, William, converted an old and unused bleachworks on the west side of the Bogie into a prosperous brewery. The other three sons—George, Charles, and James—inherited the bleaching and thread-spinning businesses as well as the banking enterprise. Charles got the bulk of the property, managed the banking and finances, and thus assumed the position of senior partner in the firm; George and James operated the bleachworks and threadmill.

In a day when poverty in Scotland was widespread, the MacDonalds were leading merchants and pillars in the community, clearly middle class at a time when "middle class" implied fairly substantial wealth. Yet they were not landowners. Until well into the 20th century the land was owned by whatever aristocratic family controlled the region—the Gordons, in the case of Strathbogie. In the early 1800s the Duke of Gordon owned all the land surrounding Huntly and rented out houses and farmland to his tenants, who would twice yearly pay him his due. In 1821, as he had earlier to McVeagh and probably Charles Edward, the Duke granted a lease of Upper Pirriesmill, known as *The Farm*, to Charles Edward MacDonald's three sons, James, George and Charles. In addition to the bleachworks alongside the river, the Farm encompassed 110 acres of choice farmland that required several full-time hands to operate. Cows were raised on the Farm's meadow near the river as well, their sounds blending peacefully with those of water-driven equipment and the wooden machinery of the factory.

Foreseeing, perhaps, that the threadmill was destined to go the way of the linen mill earlier, the three brothers put most of their energies into the bleachfields. This enterprise was pushed with great activity and developed into an undertaking of remarkable dimensions. George personally supervised the work; Charles kept the books, attended to the correspondence, and maintained the bank; James traveled on horseback throughout the country, collecting accounts and opening up new branches. They were untiring in their efforts to extend their business in the north of Scotland, advertising heavily, an uncommon thing at that time. The following advertisement appeared frequently in the "Aberdeen Journal" throughout the spring of 1827:

HUNTLY BLEACHFIELD

George and Charles MacDonald beg leave respectfully to intimate to their friends and the public that the business of the Huntly Bleachfield will commence for the season in the beginning of April. This establishment being now universally known as one of the first in the line in Scotland, they deem it almost unnecessary to say anything of the nature of the Bleaching system pursued by them, the great increase of business, and the unqualified approbation of the public being the best proofs of its superior excellence. By the mode of Bleaching at Huntly, all the advantages to be gained at Luncarty, Roslin, and other fields in the south of Scotland, of like celebrity, are secured to the public; a beautiful colour being imparted to goods by the most wholesome and harmless ingredients, while the fabric of the cloth remains unimpaired. These advantages are heightened by the natural situation of the Bleaching Grounds, which are finely exposed to the sun, while the supplies of spring and river water are both excellent and abundant; all these under the management of a skilful and experienced Bleacher, combine in securing to the public every advantage that can be desired for such an Establishment.

G. and C. Mc D. beg to return their most cordial thanks for the public patronage of last year, and solicit a continuance of their countenance and support.

The MacDonald Mill (used as a bleachworks, then as a mill) still stands but is in serious decay.

The boom at the bleachfields, however, was only temporary, and a series of events nearly brought doom upon the business. The threadworks, unable to cope with the keen competition of the Glasgow spinning mills of the south, was closed about 1829. Competition became severe for the bleachfields as well. Wages rose, a depression set in, and to crown it all, the devastating flood of August 1829 wrought great havoc at the mill, located on the very banks of the Bogie.

To make matters worse, Charles fell into financial difficulties, became involved in some questionable practices and investments, speculated heavily, and finally fled to America to escape the authorities. He left the bank 6,000 pounds in debt—a huge sum in those days, equivalent to several hundred thousand dollars today. The burden of the debt, as well as the other aspects of the business, fell to his two brothers. They eventually paid the amount off in full, though the payments remained a heavy millstone about their necks throughout the remainder of their lives.

At length, the invention of chloride of lime—ironically, by a cousin of George's wife, a great Glasgow chemist—made the bleaching process of the Huntly mill obsolete, and the MacDonald brothers converted the operation to the manufacture of potato flour and starch. Machinery for that purpose was erected at the bleachfields in Huntly and at other places as well, one of their centers of operation being Lonmay. After many ups and downs, this business became moderately successful, until it was ruined by three successive years of the potato blight in the late 1840s. At that point, the old factory in MacDonald Street was converted into a granary and the bleachfield mills into meal mills, where the old millstones were turned to the grinding of oats. The MacDonald brothers—George and James—established the Huntly Grain Mills, and the mill continued in operation into the mid-20th century. But after the flood of 1829 and Charles' illicit flight, the brothers—despite intermittent success—were constantly hounded by financial difficulties. More often than not, they were only moderately successful tenant farmers relying on the crops from the Farm to sustain them rather than their business enterprises.

In the early 1820s, shortly after the death of his father, George, Sr. had built a two-story stone house in town about a block from the town square. His mother, Mrs. Isabella MacDonald, lived in the adjoining house at the corner of Church and Duke Streets—the house described as Robert Falconer's home in the novel bearing the name. Only the garden at the back of the two houses separated them from the thread-factory on MacDonald Street.*

---

*"There was a building in Rothieden, not old, yet so deserted that its very history seemed to have come to a stand-still, and the dust that filled it to have fallen from the plumes of passing centuries. It was the property of Mrs. Falconer, left her by her husband. Trade had gradually ebbed away from the town till the thread-factory stood unoccupied, with all its machinery rusting and mouldering, just as the work-people had risen and left it one hot, midsummer day, when they were told that their services were no longer required. Some of the thread even remained upon the spools, and in the hollows of some of the sockets the oil had as yet dried only into a paste; although to Robert the desertion of the place appeared immemorial. It stood at a furlong's distance from the house, on the outskirt of the town" (*Robert Falconer*, Ch. 11).

In 1822 George, Sr., married Helen MacKay, a beautiful, sensitive, somewhat mystical woman descended from a distinguished line of military officers, politicians, and scholars. Her elder brother MacIntosh was a friend of Sir Walter Scott, and her other brother George fought at Waterloo as an officer. He later raised his own family in Banff, only seventeen miles north of Huntly, and his influence helped stimulate Helen's second son's love of the sea and his desire to travel.

Thus, on December 10, 1824, George MacDonald, Jr., was born to George and Helen MacDonald in the house on Duke Street in Huntly, Aberdeenshire. The young family lived in that house, next door to little George's grandmother, for another two years. Even at the time of his birth, plans were being made by his father, George, Sr., and his uncle James to build a larger dwelling on the property at Upper Pirriesmill near the bleachworks. The business at that time was booming and they planned to move both their families to the new house at the Farm, there to supervise more closely the activities of the bleaching business and to carry out the farming of their acreage to better advantage.

The three-story farmhouse was built of stone, up the hill about two hundred yards from the mill, which sat on the banks of the Bogie. After

The house where George MacDonald was born (now the Huntly Carpet Centre), adjacent to the house of Grandmother MacDonald (now Reid Flory)—on the corner of Duke and Church Streets in Huntly.

completion the house was sometimes known as "Bleachfield Cottage," but was generally simply called the Farm.

In 1826 the families of the MacDonald brothers, George, Sr., and James, moved into "Bleachfield Cottage" across the river. George and Helen had six sons in all—Charles, George, Jr., James who died at 8, Alexander, John MacKay, who died in infancy, and John Hill. They lived in close quarters with their cousins, with box bunk beds installed in some of the living rooms to provide space for all the children. Though the business would face near-disaster during the years that followed, the two brothers were able to make the close business partnership and the communal living arrangement work.

George MacDonald's First Years

Into this milieu young George MacDonald was born; yet the family and business developments and hardships did not touch him until he became much older. In his earliest years, life was discovery, and Huntly and its environs were full of never-ending delights. This was the world that nurtured his growth and fired his imagination. Though the environment itself was the same to all who viewed it, the world seen through young George's eyes was different than that of his playmates. For the child creates and molds his own world, even as he is fashioned by it. The green bleaching meadows with the great white waves of cloth fluttering in the breeze

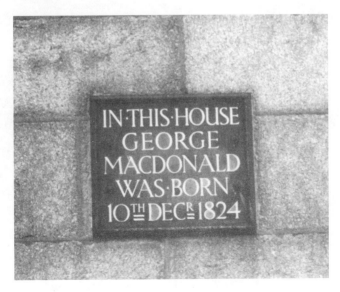

Plaque on the house of George MacDonald's birth.

must have struck resounding chords in his emotions; the brown river Bogie turned the water wheel of his father's mill, and the multicolored fields spread out in the distance. The skies of deep blue filled with billowing white clouds, the cruel snows of winter, the mountains in the distance which broke out into purple every August, and the talk of the country folk who gathered each day in the village square—all may have seemed ordinary enough on the surface, but the keen vision that would later burst forth into poetry was, even from his earliest memory, disclosing to young George MacDonald a magical fairy land, a land of dreams and stories and daring ventures. Whatever occupied the young boy, whether he was mastering his Shorter Catechism for a vicious schoolmaster, playing furious games with his friends, hurling rocks with his classmates at the charging ranks from Huntly's rival school, exploring an old ruin, building a house out of snow, or lying at home sick with pleurisy, he was always surveying and tilling the fertile fields of his experiences and his imagination.

In future years his writings would reflect his early childhood at Huntly. Undoubtedly the later poem entitled "The Old Castle" is a recollection of childhood play at Huntly Castle—either from his own childhood, or recalling to mind a later time when he, as older brother, took his young stepsisters to the castle, only to have them hide from him in the dungeon:

The house called "The Farm" built by George MacDonald's father and uncle and in which he was raised (front of house).

The Old Castle

The brother knew well the castle old,
Every closet, each outlook fair,
Every turret and bartizan bold,
Every chamber, garnished or bare.
The brother was out in the heavenly air;
Little ones lost the starry way,
Wandering down the dungeon stair,
The brother missed them, and on the clay
Of the dungeon-floor he found them all.
Up they jumped when they heard him call!
He led the little ones into the day—
Out and up to the sunshine gay,
Up to the father's own door-sill—
In at the father's own room door,
There to be merry and work and play,
There to come and go at their will,
Good boys and girls to be lost no more!

(The Poetical Works of George MacDonald, vol. 1, p. 308)

Perhaps Huntly was like any other town, but it was also different in several respects. It was, first of all, a thoroughly Scottish town, on the foothills of the Highlands. This in itself gave the place a "history," an aura reminiscent of ancient days, of raids and risings, massacres, clan loyalties, ballads, tartans, and folklore, reminders of Glencoe, the Jacobites, and Bonnie Prince Charlie. What imaginative boy could grow up in the shadow of such memories and not feel himself caught up in the historic flow of Scotland's colorful past? Or who could play with his friends in Huntly Castle—knowing that King Robert the Bruce had once trod those sacred stones, knowing that Mary of Guise, widow of King James V, had visited the castle in 1556—without his imagination rising within him? Such a lad would be carried back over the centuries to envision himself standing beside Wallace or Bruce, defending Mary Queen of Scots against the English foe, fleeing over the countryside with the Bonnie Prince, or fighting valiantly beside him to the death at Culloden Moor—especially a lad such as young George, whose ancestors had been among the few to escape from Glencoe that fateful night in 1692. His great-grandfather had indeed fought with Prince Charles and barely escaped from Culloden in 1746 with his life. Even more, young George's family genealogy could be traced and linked to the Scottish Royal family through the great warrior Somerled, and even loosely perhaps to Robert Bruce himself.

To be a Scottish youngster in the 19th century was to be steeped in such personalities and traditions. Mere legends they could never be, for they were part of *history*. In the very stones and markings—from the "Stannin' Stanes" in the square to the heraldic doorway of the castle—the ghosts of living memories spoke almost audibly to the imaginative son of Bruce. And away to the south stood the Highlands, often shrouded in the vaporous mists, echoing the faint shrill strains of the pipers of old, calling their clan to battle, warning of the coming attack of a rival tribe, or mustering their united forces against the dreaded English foe from the south. To the north, a mere seventeen miles distant, lay the ocean—that terrifying North Sea, never a friend to man. From over its distant horizons a thousand years earlier had come the Norse Viking raiders, brutal and cruel, plundering and conquering. Thus, the wild howl of the bagpipers' pilbroch and the call to arms of Bruce or Wallace mingled with coarse shouts from Viking warships to seize the imagination of the Scottish youngster and take him soaring to heights of romantic danger and adventure of days gone by.

But youthful Scots did not have to rely solely on such reminders from the past and lessons about dead kings from their history books. Indeed, on any day in the market square of Huntly could be heard diverse dialects of peoples and races and clans and nationalities. From the west—rooted in the western isles and spreading to the Highlands—came the Gaelic, rough and yet melodious, ancient, difficult to master without being raised in it. From the south an English visitor was instantly recognizable from his "proper" book-English. From the south of Scotland itself came the "Lalan's" (or "lowlands") dialect, while those natives to the northeast spoke their own rapid and slurred form of the English language known as "Doric." If a visitor from the Shetlands was present with his wares of wool, his mixture of English, Doric, and ancient Norse was enough to confound any well-educated Scotsman. And even travelers from as near as Inverness or Aberdeen could be recognized by their different intonation of the Doric.

The northeast of Aberdeenshire was indeed a cultural, historical, and lingual melting pot for a vast mix of differences. What days of delight such a setting offered! George MacDonald's boyhood can only be fully appreciated with a reading of five of his books that present different aspects of it—*Robert Falconer, Alec Forbes of Howglen, Ranald Bannerman's Boyhood*, and to a lesser degree *Gutta Percha Willie* and *Warlock o' Glenwarlock*. The first three especially are heavily autobiographical and present distinctive perspectives of the same childhood. *Alec Forbes* offers the delight and pleasure of boyhood, *Robert Falconer* fosters appreciation of young George's thoughtfulness, the reminiscences of *Ranald Bannerman's Boyhood* and *Gutta Percha Willie* shed light on the details of childhood and life on a Huntly farm and in a small rural town, and *Warlock o' Glenwarlock* gives us a possible glimpse of George's personality and relationship with his father.

George and his brothers roamed freely during the summer holidays. Their mother was sickly, their father a relaxed disciplinarian who allowed them latitude in their exploits.

"There was plenty for the hungriest boys of all that was necessary . . . but clothes were mostly shabby, and money was always scarce. On the other hand there were cattle in the byre, horses in the stable, wild bees' nests in the stone dykes, whose honeycomb eaten like bread was a priceless joy; there were pools for swimming, and a river for boating. There was fishing with rod and net, the latter especially when the rivers were swollen and muddy and the trout unable to see their way. . . . To these boys the world was a constant invitation to adventure, for they read into its realistic sweetness and terror the trappings of imaginative romance."[1]

Standing in the middle of the upper bridge over the Bogie and looking across the stream to the old MacDonald mill, a visitor inevitably recalls the vast flooding in the northeast of Scotland in 1829. The flood that threatened Glamerton, graphically portrayed in *Alec Forbes*, strengthens the conviction that the events of *Alec Forbes* are indeed true representations of George MacDonald's own youth—from the crudely fashioned "Bonnie Annie," to Alec's snow house, to the misdeeds at school, to the peats thrown on rooftops. From such stories—fact and fancy bound up together—we gain the *feel* of George MacDonald's boyhood in Huntly. Such places, experiences, people, conversations, adventures, boat rides, floods, snowstorms, make-believe battles and victories fueled the already-ignited imaginative fires, which would one day burst into full flame. Today, a century and half later, the streets, fields, riverbanks, and castle ruins of Huntly still retain the mystique and magic that gave rise to the poetic nature of the future bard of Aberdeenshire.

George MacDonald's childhood hinges on two seemingly contradictory points. One is that all his life he was never completely physically well. The family had a long history, both preceding and outliving him, of lung

Near Huntly where the Bogie spills into the Deveron, to which the boy George MacDonald no doubt hiked many times.

disease and tuberculosis. It has been conjectured that the damp climate and the close living quarters at the Farm fostered its spread. In any case, his brother James died at eight. His brothers Alec and John both died of diseased lungs in their twenties. One of his stepsisters died of tuberculosis at fourteen, and four of his own children died prematurely of the same disease later in the century. Even in his youngest days he was constantly battling pleurisy, for which he would be bled from the arm. And later in life, even when free of the recurring symptoms of tuberculosis and hae-moptysis (hemorrhaging from the lungs), which threatened his life on several occasions, he suffered almost continuously from severe asthma, bronchitis, eczema, lumbago, and migraine headaches. There rarely seemed a time from his twenties to his forties when the threat of fatal internal hemorrhage was far from him. On at least a dozen occasions in his adult life he was laid up as a full-fledged invalid for a month or longer, sometimes as long as three or four months. And the times when he was on his back for several days to a week or two are practically too numerous to count.

Yet at the same time he was extremely active physically, and, far from playing the part of the sickly invalid, was rather athletic with a range of physical skills. He grew to be over 5'10" tall, with broad shoulders and muscular build. His son Ronald indicates that in his youth he was an above-average boxer, and he was certainly a skilled horseman, at home in the saddle from his earliest boyhood. Both his sons recall this active and dexterous side of their father. "George MacDonald was a man beyond the ordinary deft with his fingers, and fond of practicing the arts they were master of. A good practical carpenter, a workman-like stitcher of leather, with some practical experience, I fancy, in boyhood, of smith's, or at least farrier's [the shoeing of horses] work, his chief pleasure in this kind during his later years was book-binding; its final phase with him being delicate and loving work in the repair of old books . . . *book-healing*, as he calls it. . . ."[2] "His youngest sisters were then four and two years old [and he twenty-one]. She [his stepmother] saw him upon one occasion whip them up, one under each arm, run around the house with them, and then leap over a hedge which was probably four feet high. Another feat was taking a twenty-eight pound weight in each hand and lifting the two together [with elbows straight] up to the level of his head."[3]

Fictional Insights into Life at Huntly

If we can take *Alec Forbes* as an indicator, summers in the northeast of Scotland must have been glorious for the lad MacDonald with their harvesting, long evenings, inviting rivers, and endless opportunities for play and discovery. Certainly one of MacDonald's greatest outdoor pleasures was to be in the saddle. His passionate love for horses was born out of his extreme tenderness toward all living creatures and a pity for their sorrows. This love he readily displayed to all who knew him, preached from the pulpit, and shared with the world through his writings. The horses in his novels are in some cases almost as memorable as his human characters.

Kelpie of *Malcolm* is perhaps the most graphic, but in rapid succession spring to mind Missy, Lilith, Old Diamond, Lady, Ruber, Niger, and Beelzebub as well. Few, indeed, are his novels where one will not encounter a horse. In *Adela Cathcart*, a vivid description of a mare that he had ridden reveals his love and respect for the animal. The picture he gives tells us as much about the author and his love for and friendship with her as it does the horse. ". . . she was a thoroughgoing hunter; no beauty, certainly, with her ewe-neck, drooping tail, and white face and stocking; but she had an eye at once gentle and wild as that of a savage angel . . . while her hindquarters were power itself. . . . I had never seen such action. Altogether, although not much of a hunting man, the motion of the creature gave me such a sense of power and joy, that I longed to be scouring the fields with her under me" (*Adela Cathcart*, Ch. 7).

This intimacy with animals dated from earliest childhood. One of his earliest favorites was a gray mare called "Missy"—both her real and her fictional name. He tells of half-scrambling, half-leaping upon her bare back to have her rush away like the wind. At other times he would lie peacefully on her back reading a book while "she ground and mashed away at the grass as if nobody were near her." He tells how they first learned to ride the plough horses: "First of all we were allowed to take them at watering-time, watched by one of the men, from the stable to the long trough that stood under the pump. There, going hurriedly and stopping suddenly, they would drop head and neck and shoulders like a certain toy-bird, causing the young riders a vague fear of falling over the height no longer defended by the uplifted crest; and then drink and drink till the riders' legs felt the horses' bodies swelling under them; then up and away with quick, refreshed stride or trot toward the paradise of their stalls. But for us came first the somewhat fearful pass of the stable-door, for they never stopped, like better educated horses, to let their riders dismount, but walked right in, and there was just room, by stooping low, to clear the top of the door. As we improved in equitation, we would go a-field to ride them home from the pasture, where they were fastened by chains to short stakes of iron driven into the earth. There was more of adventure here, for not only was the ride longer, but the horses were more frisky, and would sometimes set off at the gallop" (*Ranald Bannerman's Boyhood*, Ch. 9).

His father would not allow his sons a saddle till they were sure of their seat on the bare back, and after that they needed little teaching. George was apparently quite reckless in his exploits at times. His feat of jumping over the railroad lines was, according to his son Ronald, "local history." A few years after their marriage, his wife wrote to George's father about her husband's love for the saddle. In his reply, George, Sr., recalled his son's younger days: ". . . you express a wish that I had seen him mounted on a noble steed as you had done somewhere in the country. You may just ask himself whether on various occasions I was not most tempted to thrash the rogue's back for his feats at horsemanship. . . ."[4] And whenever as a grown man he would visit the Farm at Huntly, one of his first actions was to saddle a horse and head for the surrounding hills.

Whether he was mounted on Missy, fishing in the river, or romping through the fields, his summers in Huntly were never lacking for activity. In a later letter to his father, MacDonald recalls running with his brother "through the long grass of a certain field on a warm summer night trying to catch the corn scraich till recalled by you and reprimanded for trampling down the grass"; and then of the well, from which "on hot noon days I so often fetched you a jug of cold water when you came into the house hot and thirsty."[5] And we need only recall Robert Falconer and Shargar's positive abandonment when they were set free to romp to Mr. Lammie's farm at Bodyfauld to know such words could only have come from one who was there: "But the delight of the walk of three miles over hill and dale and moor and farm to Mr. Lammie's! The boys, if not as wild as colts—that is, as wild as most boys would have been—were only the more deeply excited. That first summer walk, with a goal before them, in all the freshness of the perfecting year, was something which to remember in after days was to Falconer nothing short of ecstasy. The westering sun threw long shadows before them as they trudged away eastward . . . they crossed a small river, and entered upon a region of little hills, some covered to the top with trees, chiefly larch, other cultivated, and some bearing only heather, now nursing in secret its purple flame for the outburst of the autumn. The road wound between, now swampy and worn into deep ruts, now sandy and broken with large stones. Down to its edge would come the dwarfed oak, or the mountain ash, or the silver birch, single and small, but lovely and fresh; and now green fields, fenced with walls of earth as green as themselves, or of stones overgrown with moss, would stretch away on both sides, sprinkled with busily feeding cattle. Now they would pass through farm-steading, perfumed with the breath of cows, and the odor of burning peat—so fragrant! though not yet so grateful to the inner sense as it would be when encountered in after years and in foreign lands. For the smell of burning and the smell of earth are the deepest underlying sensuous bonds of the earth's unity, and the common brotherhood of them that dwell thereon. Now the scent of the larches would steal from the hill, or the wind would waft the odor of the white clover, beloved of his grandmother, to Robert's nostrils, and he would turn aside to pull her a handful. Then they climbed a high ridge, on the top of which spread a moorland, dreary and desolate. . . . This crossed, they descended between young plantations of firs and rowan-trees and birches, til they reached a warm house on the side of the slope, with farm-offices and ricks of corn and hay all about it, the front overgrown with roses and honeysuckle, and a white-flowering plant unseen of their eyes hitherto, and therefore full of mystery" (*Robert Falconer*, Ch. 16).

In one sense George MacDonald's life ran nearly parallel with the greater part of the Industrial Revolution with all its changes in life, culture, wealth and poverty, social norms, and labor-saving machinery. But in the early part of his life about the farm and mill, everything was done by human and water power, as he later wrote about the water mill: "Its dull wooden sounds made no discord with the sweetness of the hour" (*Donal Grant*). All the activity about his father and uncle's mill provided raw material, which he would later draw upon. Of Robert Falconer he writes: "I have, I think, already indicated that his grandfather had been a linen manufacturer. Although that trade had ceased, his family had still retained the bleachery belonging to it, commonly called the *bleach-fields*, devoting it now to the service of those large calico manufactures. . . . To Robert and Shargar it was a wondrous pleasure when the pile of linen which the week had accumulated at the office under the ga'le-room was on Saturday heaped high upon the base of a broad-wheeled cart, to get up on it and be carried to the said bleach-field, which lay along the bank of the river. Soft-laid and high-borne, gazing into the blue sky, they traversed the streets in a holiday triumph; and although, once arrived, the manager did not fail to get some labor out of them, yet the store of amusement was endless. The great wheel, which drove the whole machinery; the plash-mill, or, more properly, wauk-mill—a word Robert derived from the resemblance of the mallets to two huge feet, and of their motion to walking—with the water plashing and squirting from the blows of their heels; the beetles thundering in arpeggio upon the huge cylinder round which the white cloth was wound—each was haunted in its turn and season. The pleasure of the water itself was inexhaustible. Here sweeping in a mass along the race; there divided into branches and hurrying through the walls of the various houses; here sliding through a wooden channel across the floor to fall into the river in a half-concealed cataract, there bubbling up through the bottom of a huge wooden cave or vat, there resting placid in another; here gurgling along a sprout; there flowing in a narrow canal through the green expanse of the well-mown bleach-field, or lifted from it in narrow, curved wooden scoops, like fairy canoes with long handles, and flung in showers over the outspread yarn—the water was an endless delight.

"It is strange how some individual broidery or figure upon Nature's garment will delight a boy long before he has ever looked Nature in the face, or begun to love herself. But Robert was soon to become dimly conscious of a life within these things—a life not the less real that its operations on his mind had been long unrecognized.

"On the grassy bank of the gently flowing river, at the other edge of whose level the little canal squabbled along, and on the grassy brae which rose immediately from the canal, were stretched, close beside each other, with scarce a strip of green betwixt, the long white webs of linen, fastened down to the soft, mossy ground with wooden pegs whose tops were twisted into their edges. Strangely would they billow in the wind sometimes, like sea-waves, frozen and enchanted flat, seeking to rise and wallow in the wind with conscious depth and whelming mass. But generally they lay supine, saturated with light and its cleansing power" (*Robert Falconer*, Ch. 18).

Harvest time made a great impression on young George MacDonald, and he wrote fondly of it repeatedly in his books, a time loved by all school-bound boys for its months of freedom from books and lessons. "Hugh had watched the green corn grow, and ear, and turn dim; then brighten to yellow, and ripen at last under the declining autumn sun. . . . The long threads, on each of which hung an oat grain—the harvest here was mostly of oats—had got dry and brittle; and the grains began to spread out their chaff-wings, as if ready to fly, and rustled with sweet sounds against each other, as the wind, which used to billow the fields like the waves of the sea, now swept gently and tenderly over it, helping the sun and moon in the drying and ripening of the joy to be laid up for the next dreary winter. Most graceful of all hung those delicate oats; next bowed the bearded barley; and stately and wealthy and strong stood the few fields of wheat, of a rich, ruddy, golden hue. . . .

"At length the day arrived when the sickle must be put into the barley, soon to be followed by the scythe in the oats. And now came the joy of labor. Everything else was abandoned for the harvest-field. Books were thrown utterly aside. . . ." (*David Elginbrod*, Ch. 10).

And from the mouth of Ranald Bannerman, MacDonald further says, "There may be great pleasure in watching machine operations, but surely none to equal the pleasure we had. If there had been a steam-engine to plough my father's fields, how could we have ridden home on its back in the evening? Had there been a threshing machine, could its pleasure have been comparable to that of lying in the straw and watching the grain dance from the sheaves under the skillful flails of the two strong men who belaboured them? There was a winnowing machine, but quite a tame one, for its wheels I could drive myself—the handle now high as my head, now low as my knee—and watch at the same time the storm of chaff driven like drifting snow-flakes from its wide mouth. . . . Let me see: what more machines are there now? More than I can tell. I saw one going in the fields the other day, at the use of which I could only guess. Strange, wild-looking, mad-like machines, as the Scotch would call them, are growling and snapping and clinking and clattering over our fields, so that it seems to an old boy as if all the sweet poetic twilight of things were vanishing from the country . . ." (*Ranald Bannerman's Boyhood*, Ch. 9).

When the summer's labor was done, school would begin with the advancing of the cold weather. And winter provided a whole new range of adventures. Young George, however, was delicate—once in bed for four continuous months—and would thus often be kept from school (though it was but half a mile away) because of the snow or the even more treacherous half-thawed ice. Notwithstanding, the winter always had its own joys, a favorite sport being the excavation of great caves in the snow and battles with snowballs reminiscent of Alec Forbes.

"All the short day the sun, though low, was brilliant, and the whole countryside shone with dazzling whiteness; but after sunset, which took place between three and four o'clock, anything more dreary can hardly be imagined, especially when the keenest of winds rushed in gusts from the northeast, and lifting the snow-powder from untrodden shadows, blew it, like so many stings, in the face of the freezing traveler" (*Ranald Banner-man's Boyhood*, Ch. 31).

George MacDonald's own words, in a letter of 1853 to one of his three stepsisters, recall to his mind these early childhood days of joy. "How much I should like to spend a winter at home again, a snowy winter, with great heaps and wreathes of snow; and sometimes the wild wind howling in the chimney and against the windows and down at the chimney door! And how much I should love to spend one long summer day in June, lying on the grass before the house, and looking up into the deep sky with large white clouds in it. And when I lifted my head I should see the dear old hills all round about; and the shining of the Bogie, whose rush I should hear far off and soft, making a noise hardly louder than a lot of midges. . . . And then the warmer evening, with long grass in the field where the well is, and the corn-craik [noise, talk] crying *craik-craik* [like the faint calling of a bird]—somewhere in it, though nobody knows where. . . ."[6]

CHAPTER THREE

THE YOUNG MYSTIC
(1830–1840)

The Enigma of the Melancholy

Pleasurable though the delights of boyhood were, from a very early age young George MacDonald was different than his peers. His was a typically melancholy temperament—emotional, capable of extremes of both high and low, pensive, analytical, introspective. Amid all the "fun" of childhood, in the second MacDonald son a deeper current was running, a subterranean stream invisible to parents or friends or brothers—a channel of thought and inquiry. He took everything several layers deep, trying to sift and organize and make sense out of what he saw and heard; he questioned what he did not understand, doubted what didn't ring true. His brain was never passive, but ever alert, noticing and responding to everything about him—on both the rational and emotional levels.

This caused another contradiction of his personality—being paradoxically both happy and carefree, yet brooding and withdrawn. In actuality this is no enigma at all, for the melancholy temperament is at once highly emotional and yet deeply analytical. Such persons characteristically rise to heights of ecstasy at one time, and sink to depths of despair at others. Noting his father's "two-sided" nature, Greville MacDonald speaks of the "melancholy which all through his later boyhood dogged his innate gaiety." The melancholic is both outgoing and shy, in love with people and yet craving of time alone. He can be the center of attention, and yet one who walks the solitary hills for hours, alone with his thoughts. Both these attributes came to the fore as George matured. Both are aspects of the same essential make-up, the most complex of human personalities and the richest, fraught with potential for genius and gifted expression, yet most in danger of self-induced failure and emotional bankruptcy.

George MacDonald's "earliest definable memory," as he phrased it, occurred between the ages of two and three at the funeral of the fourth

Duke of Gordon. The Duke had died in London and the body was brought to Elgin via Huntly. As it passed through the town, he remembered seeing countless black carriages drawn by black horses with postillions, all draped in black velvet and nodding plumes. Though happy memories surrounded him, this silent procession of death remained indelibly printed on his young brain, further accentuating the dual viewpoint he held ever after in his mind toward life.

The following poem, the first four lines of which were previously quoted in an earlier handwritten and unpublished form, reveals his interpretive observation of his home's surroundings, and from it one can see even in his early years his mystical depiction of the simplest sights about him.

The Hills

Behind my father's cottage lies
    A gentle grassy height
Up which I often ran—to gaze
    Back with a wondering sight,
For then the chimneys I thought quite high
    Were down below me quite!

All round, where'er I turned mine eyes,
    Huge hills closed up the view;
The town 'mid their converging roots
    Was clasped by rivers two;
From one range to another sprang
    The sky's great vault of blue.

It was a joy to climb their sides,
    And in the heather lie!
A joy to look at vantage down
    On castle grim and high!
Blue streams below, white clouds above,
    In silent earth and sky!

And now, where'er my feet may roam,
    At sight of stranger hill
A new sense of the old delight
    Springs in my bosom still,
And longings for the high unknown
    Their ancient channels fill.

For I am always climbing hills,
    From the known to the unknown—
Surely, at last, on some high peak,
    To find my Father's throne,
Though hitherto I have only found
    His footsteps in the stone!

Clasp my hand close, my child, in thine—
    A long way we have come!

> Clasp my hand closer yet, my child,
> Farther we yet must roam—
> Climbing and climbing till we reach
> Our heavenly father's home.
> (*The Poetical Works of George MacDonald*, vol. 2, p. 3)

One senses in this poem much about MacDonald's perception of the world, threads of which began early in life and were solidified much later—the quest upward, the search, the symbolic interpretation of the places and events of life and nature. Indeed, the next to last stanza capsulizes the essence of George MacDonald's pilgrimage: *"For I am always climbing hills, from the known to the unknown—surely, at last, on some high peak, to find my Father's throne."*

In *The Portent*, the author reflects similarly upon his memory of boyhood: "From my very childhood, I had rejoiced in being alone. The sense of room about me had been one of my greatest delights. Hence, when my thoughts go back to those old years, it is not the house, nor the family room, nor that in which I slept, that first of all rises before my inward vision, but that desolate hill, the top of which was only a wide expanse of moorland, rugged with height and hollow, and dangerous with deep, dark pools, but in many portions purple with large-belled heather, and crowded with cranberry and blaeberry plants. . . . There was one spot upon the hill, half-way between the valley and the moorland, which was my favorite haunt. . . . This was my refuge, my home within a home, my study—and, in the hot noons, often my sleeping chamber, and my house of dreams" (*The Portent*, Ch.1).

If MacDonald's fictional characters and narrative words are not *factually* autobiographical in every case, they are certainly *emotionally* autobiographical. MacDonald shares himself and his feelings in the emotions he evokes through his characters and stories. A person's feelings, emotions, and life-driving motives are, after all, more indicative of that person's truest self than the mere facts of the surface events of his life. Therefore, the boyhoods of Robert Falconer, Alec Forbes, and Ranald Bannerman can be interpreted as autobiographical in that sense—revealing MacDonald's own boyhood emotions. The actual "events" described in these three books, as well as portions of others, blend fact with fiction. But the emotions are without a doubt autobiographical, thus revealing a truer and deeper picture of MacDonald as a person than the facts themselves ever can. Writing in *The Deeside Field* magazine considerably later, C. Edward Troup says, "The essential truth of George MacDonald's boyhood will be found in *Ranald Bannerman* and in *Alec Forbes of Howglen*—not that, save in a few instances, actual incidents are related. But if you will regard Ranald and Alec as George MacDonald in boyhood, you will know what atmosphere he lived in, what were the conditions and outward circumstances of his life, and what were the influences that formed his character."[1]

Alec Forbes and Robert Falconer
—Dual Sides of the Same Childhood

Reflecting the paradoxes of MacDonald's own youth, the characters of Alec Forbes and Robert Falconer are on the surface strikingly distinct. Indeed, the tone of the one book is light, full of joy, boyhood pranks, and fun; the other is somber, thoughtful, and serious. Both, however, shed light on MacDonald's intricate character, and the autobiographical parallels continue beyond the boyhood years: Robert and Alec's love for the medical profession (a love shared by Gutta Percha Willie), their leaving the small towns of their upbringing to attend the university in the city, their searching during youth and early adulthood in settings quite similar to MacDonald's years at King's College (like Alec's) and reminiscent of his travels on the continent (like Robert's).

Two passages from each of these books, in the contrast of their opposite tone, give us a further sense of this dual pull that boyhood exerted on the growing young George MacDonald.

Alec Forbes reflects delight in being alive, fascination with the elements, exhilaration in being part of God's nature—all feelings, judging from his later writings, which George MacDonald shared.

"The winter drew on. . . . Cold and stormy, it is yet full of delight for all beings that can either romp, sleep, or think it through. . . . One morning, all the children awoke, and saw a white world around them. Alec jumped out of bed in delight. It was a sunny, frosty morning. The snow had fallen all night, with its own silence, and no wind had interfered with the gracious alighting of the feathery water. Every branch, every twig, was laden with its sparkling burden of down-flickered flakes, and threw long lovely shadows on the smooth featureless dazzle below. Away, away, stretched the outspread glory, the only darkness in it being the line of the winding river. All the snow that fell on it vanished, as death and hell shall one day vanish in the fire of God. It flowed on, black through its banks of white. Away again stretched the shine to the town, where every roof had the sheet that was let down from heaven spread over it, and the streets lay a foot deep in yet unsullied snow, soon, like the story of the ages, to be trampled, soiled, wrought, and driven with human feet, till, at last, God's strong sun would wipe it all away.

"From the door opening into this fairy-land, Alec sprang into the untrodden space, as into a new America. He had discovered a world, without even the print of human foot upon it. The keen air made him happy; and the face of nature, looking as peaceful as the face of a dead man dreaming of heaven, wrought in him jubilation and leaping. He was at the school door before a human being had appeared in the streets of Glamerton. Its dwellers all lay still under those sheets of snow, which seemed to hold them asleep in its cold enchantment.

"Before any of his fellows made their appearance, he had kneaded and piled a great heap of snowballs, and stood by his pyramid, prepared for the offensive. He attacked the first that came, and soon there was a troop of boys pelting away at him" (*Alec Forbes of Howglen*, Ch. 16).

The boy Alec Forbes does not "represent" George MacDonald in any literal sense, but through Alec's eyes we see his creator's festive spirit.

What a difference we feel, however, in Robert Falconer's emotional response to the same stimulus—perhaps the very same snowstorm—in the same streets of the same Scottish town, a difference that shows us the same creator's other thoughtful, even lonely side.

"It was a very bare little room in which the boy sat, but it was his favourite retreat. . . . There was no carpet on the floor, no windows in the walls. The only light came from the door, and from a small skylight in the sloping roof, which showed that it was a garret-room. . . . But there was less light than usual in the room now. . . . No sky was to be seen. A thick covering of snow lay over the [skylight] glass. A partial thaw, followed by frost, had fixed it there—a mass of imperfect cells and confused crystals. It was a cold place to sit in, but the boy had some faculty for enduring cold when it was the price to be paid for solitude. And besides, when he fell into one of his thinking moods, he forgot, for a season, cold and everything else but what he was thinking about. . . .

"If he had gone down the stair . . . he could have entered another bedroom . . . carpeted and comfortably furnished, and having two windows at right angles, commanding two streets, for it was a corner house, [but] the boy preferred the garret-room—he could not tell why. Possibly, windows to the streets were not congenial to the meditations in which, even now, as I have said, the boy indulged . . .

". . . all at once Robert started to his feet and hurried from the room. At the foot of the garret stair . . . he went down a short broad stair, at the foot of which was a window. He then turned to the left . . . passed the kitchen door on the one hand, and the double-leaved street door on the other; but instead of going into the parlor . . . he stopped at the passage-window on the right, and there stood looking out.

"What might be seen from this window certainly could not be called a very pleasant prospect. A broad street, with low houses of cold gray stone, is perhaps as uninteresting a form of street as any to be found in the world, and such was the street Robert looked out upon. Not a single member of the animal creation was to be seen in it, not a pair of eyes to be discovered looking out at any of the windows opposite. The sole motion was the occasional drift of a vapor-like film of white powder that covered the street, and wafting it along for a few yards, drop again to its repose till another stronger gust, prelusive of the wind about to rise at sundown—a wind cold and bitter as death—would rush over the street, and raise a denser cloud of the white water-dust to sting the face of any improbable person who might meet it in its passage. It was a keen, knife-edge frost, even in the house, and what Robert saw to make him stand at the desolate window I do not know, and I believe he could not himself have told. There he did stand, however, for the space of five minutes or so, with nothing better filling his outer eyes at least than a bald spot on the crown of the street, whence the wind had swept away the snow, leaving it brown and bare, a spot of March in the middle of January" (*Robert Falconer*, Ch. 2).

We observe this same contrast in two of his other novels that tell a great deal of MacDonald's perceptions of childhood: *Wilfrid Cumbermede,* with its underlying heavy and brooding tone, as opposed to the lightness and bliss of *Sir Gibbie.* His own words clarify his lifelong pursuit of the essence of childhood, which he viewed in these two ways. He opens *Ranald Bannerman's Boyhood* with the words, "I do not intend to carry my story one month beyond the hour when I saw that my boyhood was gone and my youth arrived. . . . My reason for wishing to tell this first portion of my history is, that when I look back upon it, it seems to me not only so pleasant, but full of meaning, that, if I can only tell it aright, it must prove rather pleasant and not quite unmeaning to those who will read it" (*Ranald Bannerman's Boyhood*, Ch. 1).

Pleasant and *full of meaning*: the dual sides, not only of childhood, but of all of life as viewed through the eyes of George MacDonald, both the boy and the adult. The sprightly and pleasurable adventures and play contrasted with the pervasion of an eerie melancholy through the narrative. The streets of Huntly were only one level on which he lived his first fifteen years. On a deeper plane, all about him unseen doors were being opened into other worlds—worlds of thought, worlds of dreams, worlds of imagination, worlds of spiritual reality. Whatever he saw or experienced in the physical world immediately became to him a symbol of a deeper reality in the spiritual.

As he lived and played with his friends and attended school and carried out his chores, few observers (except perhaps his father) could have realized to what extent he projected these experiences in his own inner world. All the while his subconscious was taking in the stimuli about him, digesting, weighing, wondering, rejoicing, questioning, and then extrapolating hidden truths about the God who had made it all. The snowflakes falling upon the Bogie as it wound its way through the white snow-covered fields in later years became to him not merely a picture of a river in midwinter, but a symbol of the totality of God's ultimate victory over sin. The gradual melting of the snow from the streets of Huntly under the feet of its busy inhabitants spoke of more than a Scottish village the day after a snowfall; to him it became a representation of the long ages of man's endeavor that would one day vanish in the brilliance of the love of God's Son.

In a passage from *Ranald Bannerman's Boyhood*, so accurately descriptive of the Farm, the mill at the bleachfields, and the surroundings on the banks of the Bogie, MacDonald demonstrates again how he relished life even as he was constantly driven to find its deeper meaning; *pleasant* and *full of meaning* it always would be.

"There was a small river not far from my father's house, which at a certain point was dammed back by a weir of large stones to turn part of it aside into a millrace. The mill stood a little way down, under a steep bank. It was almost surrounded with trees, willows by the water's edge, and birches and larches up the bank. Above the dam was a fine spot for bathing, for you could get any depth you liked. . . . I cannot recall the memory of those summer days without a gush of delight gurgling over my heart just as the water used to gurgle over the stones of the dam. It was a quiet place, particularly on the side to which my father's farm went down, where it was sheltered by the same little wood which further on surrounded the mill. The field which bordered the river was kept in natural grass, thick and short and fine, for here on the bank it grew well, although such grass was not at all common in that part of the country: upon other parts of the same farm the grass was sown every year along with the corn. Oh the summer days, with the hot sun drawing the odors from the feathery larches and the white-stemmed birches, when, getting out of the water, I would lie in the warm, soft grass, where now and then the tenderest little breeze would creep over my skin, until, the sun baking me more than was pleasant, I would rouse myself with an effort, and running down to the fringe of rushes that bordered the full-brimmed river, plunge again headlong into the quiet brown water and dabble and swim till I was once more weary! For innocent animal delights I know of nothing to match those days—so warm, yet so pure-aired—so clean, so glad. I often think how God must love his little children to have invented for them such delights! For of course, if he did not love the children and delight in their pleasure he would not have invented the two and brought them together. Yes, my child, I know what you would say: 'How many there are who have no such pleasures!' I grant it sorrowfully, but you must remember that God has not done with them yet; and besides, that there are more pleasures in the world than you or I know anything about. And if we had it *all* pleasure, I know I should not care so much about what is better, and I would rather be made good than have any other pleasure in the world, and so would you, though perhaps you do not know it yet" (*Ranald Bannerman's Boyhood*, Ch. 15).

CHAPTER FOUR

THE GROWING YOUTH
(1830–1840)

First Awakenings

The growing George MacDonald was a thinker, a juvenile mystic of sorts. As he matured his imaginative instinct sharpened, sending his fertile questioning spirit into more expanded reaches of exploration. In *Ranald Bannerman's Boyhood* he examines, through Ranald's eyes, his own sense of thought and wonder in a most revealing way: "I cannot tell any better than most of my readers how and when I began to come awake, or what it was that wakened me. I mean, I cannot remember when I began to remember, or what first got set down in my memory as worth remembering. Sometimes I fancy it must have been a tremendous flood that first made me wonder, and so made me begin to remember." Considering that MacDonald was but four and a half when the great flood of 1829 hit Strathbogie, the rest of the recollection is amazingly precise. "At all events, I do remember one flood that seems about as far off as anything—the rain pouring so thick that I could put my hand in front of me to try whether I could see it through the veil of the falling water. The river, which in general was to be seen only in glimpses from the house—for it ran at the bottom of a hollow—was outspread like a sea in front, and stretched away far on either hand. It was a little stream, but it fills so much of my memory with its regular recurrence of autumnal floods, that I can have no confidence that one of these is in reality the oldest thing I remember. Indeed, I have a suspicion that my oldest memories are of dreams—where or when dreamed, the good One who made me only knows. They are very vague to me now, but were almost all made up of bright things" (*Ranald Bannerman's Boyhood*, Ch. 1).

Following this passage he then goes on to describe a dream he had repeatedly—very mystical, indeed, for a child of his age to remember. Thereafter come very touching passages about his mother, her death, and his father, all of which we may assume are based, at least roughly, on fact. Certainly, the most complete "impression" of George MacDonald's early years, and indeed of his entire life, comes, not with the reading of this biography or any other, but through the books he has left us as his legacy.

Helen MacKay, George's mother, always somewhat sickly, died in 1832 when George was nearly eight. Christina MacKay, an aunt, came to stay with the family for a time; and since they still lived with his father's brother, James's wife played an active role in helping George the elder with his five sons. Nevertheless, the role of young George's father assumed much larger proportions after this time; he became and remained the primary figure of the boy's childhood.

Helen MacKay MacDonald was a sweet, loving mother and her death no doubt caused great shock and grief, especially in a sensitive child like George at such an impressionable age. Added to this loss of his mother, the death the very next year of his brother James, a year his younger, must also have been a tragic blow. Curiously, the emotions of these losses are not, to my knowledge, explored in depth in any of his books, but the impact must have been profound.

An appreciation for that aloneness—despite wonderful relationships with his father and surviving brothers—comes primarily through the reflective solitude of Robert Falconer (himself with neither father nor mother), and through the life of Cosmo Warlock in *Warlock O' Glenwarlock*, who was also raised by a father and stern grandmother. When George's father remarried seven years later, George was only a year away from leaving home. As much as he loved his stepmother (Margaret McColl, who had been a close friend of his mother) and the sisters she brought him, having had no mother between the crucial ages of eight and fifteen was a severe loss to young George. The only clue of his love for his mother was a letter of hers, saved among his possessions for the remainder of his life—a touching letter to George's maternal grandmother about two-year-old George himself.

The new Mrs. MacDonald no doubt had a great and loving impact on George's younger brothers Alec and John who were with her longer, and all the family loved her Celtic Highland ways dearly. Whenever in later years George wrote to her, she was always "Mother," and a genuine intimacy existed between them all his life, for she died just a month shy of 102 years, outliving him by a year.

George MacDonald, Sr., ruled the home with loving influence, authority, and grace. He was an open-hearted man, and no one in the future poet's life made such a deep and lasting impression. Discipline, manners, and respect pervaded the family relationships, though the father was no stern disciplinarian. Usually a look or single word of rebuke was sufficient punishment. It was not in fashion in those days for men to demonstrate physical affection to their sons, yet the man's love came through clearly in many ways. He would usually only smile at complaints against the wild escapades of his boys, though he might follow it up with a warning or restriction of liberties. Broad, Doric Scotch was never allowed at the table or before the children's elders, indicating again the gentility of the house-hold, though among themselves and with their playfriends they would lapse into the vernacular.

Perhaps because of the loss of mother and brother, and the immediacy of death thus touching him, young George began to frame increasingly larger questions, probing more deeply into the divine purpose. Death and the afterlife came to the fore in his thinking; he himself thought much along the same lines as did Robert Falconer, judging from comments later in adulthood about the wonderings of his childhood. *Why does death strike some early, not others? Is God punishing sin through death?* Such questions began to plague the young mind. Adding fuel to this questioning fire, an incident occurred in July 1835, the memory of which would become the focal point for the book *Robert Falconer.* MacDonald's aging grandmother's heart had nearly been broken over the backslidings of her son Charles after his flight to America. The occasion of his unexpected return that summer's afternoon was witnessed by her impressionable ten-year-old grandson, who had accompanied her home from church. She had earlier been convinced that Charles' prized violin had been a factor in her son's fall from Divine Grace, and to prevent its snaring any other unsuspecting victims, she had burned it while he was away from home—an event later recorded by that same wide-eyed youngster to whom the aging Calvinist woman always remained a most graphic and influential figure. No doubt conversations between young George and his grand-mother, similar to those between Robert and old Mrs. Falconer, contrib-uted much grist for the mill that was already grinding away in the young mind as to the nature and purpose of God's working in the lives of men.

As George's introspection deepened, on the opposite side of the per-sonality spectrum, his wit grew as well, and it, too, manifested itself early. The story is told that when he was strutting about in his first pair of long trousers, his uncle William said that he now needed only a watch and a wife to make a man of him. The little fellow answered quickly, "I can do well enough without the watch, but—but I do wish that I had a wee wifie!"

The Loving Fatherhood of George MacDonald, Sr.

Religion dominated the MacDonald household, as it did most house-holds of that day. Though George's father was a devout man, he kept his faith to himself and did not center his life about the affairs of the church. George's uncle James and his grandmother, however, easily made up the difference, both being very rigorous in their pious adherence to the letter of Calvinistic law. The books that George devoured as an avid reader were *Pilgrim's Progress, Paradise Lost*, and Klopstock's *Messiah*, which he occa-sionally would read lying atop the back of his mare Missy. These same titles were read by Robert Falconer in his cold garret room on the top floor of his grandmother's house. And apparently the thought of being a preacher occurred to George at a very early age, as a humorous story told by his son indicates:

"Once with the young brothers and cousins at his heels, he rushed into the kitchen, jumped upon the clean-scrubbed [basin] table, and [sitting there] began a learned discourse, indicating Bell Mavor, the maid [whose sister Jean corresponded in name and description to the farmer's sister at The Mains in *Sir Gibbie*], as a reprobate past redemption. She flicked at him with her dish-[towel], when he turned upon her in righteous anger, as he set straight the improvised bands about his neck: 'Div ye no ken fan ye're speakin' til a meenister, Bell? Ye's no fleg awa' the Rev. Geordie Mac-Donald as gin he war a buzzin' flee! Losh, woman, neist to Dr. Chaumers, he's the grandest preacher in a' Scotland!'" ["Don't you know when you're speaking to a minister, Bell? You'll not scare away the Rev. George Mac-Donald as if he were a buzzing fly! Losh, woman, next to Dr. Chalmers, he's the greatest preacher in all Scotland!"][1]

This story is substantiated by an even more humorous letter of 1850 from George, Sr., to his son, asking him to stop by in Manchester to preach so that he might see his brothers Charles and Alec (Alexander) who were living there at the time. More than that, it reveals much about the good humor of George MacDonald, Sr., and the sort of relationship he enjoyed with his son.

"I hope you will be able to stop in Manchester," he writes, "on your way South and preach a sermon to your kindred that they may be able to judge of your qualifications and to be otherwise gratified. By the bye, when I think of it, they have repeatedly heard you long ago, when the basin-stand was your pulpit, and when matters purely local and domestic formed the leading subjects of your prayers before your congregation. I believe you had to thank your own slim form that you were not overtaken by the same awkward kind of calamity which befel one of the brother-hood, who, having got by force and the impulse of his own greater gravi-tation into the aforesaid *pulpit* [the small wash-basin in the middle of the counter], found that when he had occasion to slip out again, that to do so was no easy matter; nay, it was an impossibility until he had discharged his audience, and, having more privately peeled off his trousers, made a shift to crawl out of his involuntary imprisonment! Take care, man, and don't ever preach in too small a pulpit for fear of the consequences!"[2]

Surely it is to this man, after whom the character of David Elginbrod was drawn, to whom the world partially owes its gratitude for the man of God his son became. Every instance of the elder MacDonald's character, humor, patience, wisdom, fortitude, and properly Calvinistic austerity which has been recorded causes the reader to wonder, perhaps, which of the two George MacDonalds was in fact closest on earth to the kingdom of heaven. Both, of course, would scorn even the phrasing of such a ques-tion. His description of David Elginbrod certainly reflects MacDonald's remembrance of his own father: "His carriage was full of dignity and a certain rustic refinement; his voice was wonderfully gentle, but deep; and slowest when most impassioned. He seemed to have come of some gigan-tic antediluvian breed: there was something of the Titan slumbering about him. He would have been a stern man, but for an unusual amount of reverence that seemed to overflood the sternness, and change it into strong love. No one had ever seen him thoroughly angry; his simple displeasure . . . would go further than . . . oaths" (*David Elginbrod*, Ch. 13).

In 1823 George, Sr., was treated unsuccessfully for tuberculosis of the knee joint. In 1825, in the days before chloroform, his leg had to be amputated above the knee. The patient refused the customary stupefying dose of strong Scotch whisky, or even to have his face covered during the operation, preferring to watch instead. Only for one moment, when the knife first cut into the flesh, did he look away, uttering at that moment a faint sighing "whiff" of agony.

The first time he left home after the operation he went to Banff for a few days with a friend. A well-known minister was scheduled to preach in the vicinity on Sunday. His friend drove him the couple miles to Macduff for the services. They were both rather startled when the text for the sermon was read, for the Scripture was taken from Psalm 147:10: "The Lord taketh not pleasure in the legs of a man." Notwithstanding, they enjoyed the sermon so much they resolved to hear the man again, and for that purpose drove to Boyndie in the afternoon. Again, to their amusement, the same text was announced and the same sermon preached. As the church in Banff (where he was to complete his day's round of preaching) was near the house of MacDonald's friend, they went to the service there in the evening. They were utterly amazed when again, for a third time, out came the text, "The Lord taketh not pleasure in the legs of a man." The one-legged man had had more than enough on this subject for one day, and for several days to come!

Thereafter George, Sr., rarely lost an opportunity to make fun of his loss. To the village youngsters he took delight in saying, "Div ye ken, laddies, that the mail coach an' four horses rin through atween my legs every day?" And usually no amount of questioning on the part of the boys and girls could extort any sort of explanation. Finally the riddle was made known: though he always had his right leg with him, the other was buried in the graveyard at Drumblade, far away on the other side of the high road to Aberdeen.

There is little doubt that the conversation between Thomas Crann, the dour theological stonemason in *Alec Forbes of Howglen*, and George Macwha originated in George MacDonald, Sr.'s, delight in poking fun at his wooden leg. Macwha baits the Calvinist with questions concerning the resurrection of the body of one with a wooden leg:

"'Wad it be a glorified wooden leg he rase wi', gin he had been buried wi' a wooden leg?' asked he.

"'His ain leg wad be buried somewhere.'

"'Ow ay! nae doubt. An' it wad come hoppin' ower the Paceefic, or the Atlantic, to join its oreeginal stump—wad it no?'" (*Alec Forbes of Howglen*, Ch. 3).

The elder MacDonald's indifference to possessions is illustrated by an incident that occurred when a young friend engaged in business in Aberdeen was visiting at the Farm and happened to remark that "a chap was awkwardly situated in a big city without a watch." Instantly from out of his pocket came the older man's silver watch as a gift to the lad. "The sun's a better time-keeper in Strathbogie than any merchant's watch in Aberdeen," he said. Thereafter, he is said to have never carried or possessed a watch again.

In April of 1846, after his son George had left home, the youngest of the MacDonald daughters was born. His second wife, Margaret McColl MacDonald, gave George MacDonald, Sr., three daughters between 1841 and 1846—Isabella, Louisa, and Jane Duff, after his brother's wife. His wife's state following the last birth was precarious. But no sooner was the crisis past and she lay in her bed just out of danger, at last getting some desperately needed sleep, than a breathless messenger arrived at the house saying that the town was in an uproar and an angry mob was on its way there at that very moment in a dangerously hostile mood.

This was at the height of the worst of the crop failures that devastated Scotland and Ireland; grain was extremely expensive, the local crops had been very poor, and many were going hungry. A portion of Huntly's more contentious element had gotten it into their minds that the MacDonald brothers, as two of the area's leading grain merchants, were storing grain and meal in order to get still higher prices, and were keeping it from those who needed it. The rumor spread, the worst elements of the town were angered, and the hotheads were on their way to the Farm with an effigy of George, Sr., which they intended to burn right in front of his farmhouse.

He had just taken off his wooden leg and set it beside the hearth, as was his custom in the evening when tired. Hearing the news and fearing for his wife's safety if agitated, he quickly replaced it and hurried outside to meet them as they approached. Surprised by his appearance, there was momentary silence, which gave him opportunity to explain that his wife must have absolute silence if she was to make it through the night. He begged them to go down to the market and there tell him what the trouble was about. Without a word of protest, they turned and departed, some-what shamefacedly, carrying the effigy with them.

By the time MacDonald was able to reach them in the marketplace in Huntly's square, however, these had been joined by still others and, their anger revived, a bonfire had been assembled alongside the Stannin' Sta-nes, with the clumsy effigy sprawling on top, its wooden leg obviously and ridiculously placed. When at last they were ready to set the torch to the kindling, MacDonald finally appeared. As he began to address them, their hootings were silenced.

"Bide a wee [Wait a minute], lads!" he shouted, "afore ye set the corpse aflame. Ye've fastened the wooden leg t' the wrang hurdie [hip]."

Then, leaning on his stick, he added seriously, "Noo, ye's gang on we' yer ploys wi' a guid conscience, an' burn yer auld freen' [your old friend]!"

Thus were all the angry and hungry set laughing, and presently they found themselves cheering the man their hearts knew, even if their minds had temporarily misjudged. Then, at his invitation, a few of them followed him back to the Farm where he opened to them his barn and sheds, where they were convinced that his, like their own meal-tubs, were empty. If only they could have seen his letters concerning finances to his son George at the time, they would have known that the crop failures had hit the Mac-Donald brothers as severely as everyone else.

Such was George MacDonald's father, a man whose character profoundly influenced his son. His humor and understanding could not but endear him to all who knew him. When he died in 1858, at the age of 66, the grief was universal.

George, Sr., had grave doubts about his second son's preparation for the future, given the boy's physical weakness, his dreamy and poetic nature, and his propensity to lie on the sofa for hours on end doing nothing but reading. But he did not worry how his son would turn out. Three lines appeared some years later in *A Hidden Life*, which may shed light on the older man's peace about the future of his son.

"The neighbors asked what he would make his son:
'I'll make a man of him,' the old man said;
'And for the rest, just what he likes himself.'"

But already, even at a youthful age, the boy's poetic bent was slowly revealing itself. He would read poetry to his favorite schoolfriends, once repeating a free metrical version of the 14th chapter of Isaiah. But though clearly drawn toward the intellectual and poetical end of life's pursuits, at the same time his imagination longed for romance and adventure.

Among the many delights life offered the MacDonald boys were family holidays in the hills at The Cabrach in the Highlands to the south (the area which later became the setting for *Warlock o' Glenwarlock*), and more often north to the coast. His mother's brother George MacKay lived in Banff, and George's cousin Helen—three years older than he—was a favorite and longtime childhood friend. The MacDonalds would holiday at Banff with their uncle's family, and occasionally in Portsoy or Cullen (one of the most-loved spots) farther west along the coast. Nine-year-old George wrote the following letter to his father, who was not with them. Even though it is the middle of summer, there is a reference to his health.

15 August, 1833
Portsoy

My dear Papa

I return you many thanks for the kind letter I received on Wednesday. I am happy to hear that you are well. I have been unwell for two or three days, my throat was a little sore and my head very painful, but I am quite well now and have been at the sea today and like it very much. . . . We are all quite well. Would you be so good as come down and stay with us till we go home? Aunt makes me drink the [sea]-water, but I am unwilling to do it. I am sorry that my writing is so bad, but my pen is very bad.

I remain, my dear Papa,
Your affectionate son,
George MacDonald[3]

The boy's love of the sea evidently increased year by year, as demonstrated by the following letter—undated, but apparently written when he was about twelve and sent from either Cullen, Portsoy, or Banff. He seems to have at last reached a final decision about his future life, determining that nothing else could possibly be contemplated than the career of a sailor.

My Dear Father
It is now time for me to be thinking of what I should betake myself to, and though I would be sorry to displease you in any way, yet I must tell you that the sea is my delight and that I wish to go to it as soon as possible, and I hope that you will not use your parental authority to prevent me, as you undoubtedly can. I feel I would be continually wishing and longing to be at sea. Though a dangerous, it is undoubtedly an honest and lawful employment, or I would scorn to be engaged in it. Whatever other things I may have intended were in my childhood days, [so] that you can hardly blame me for being flighty in this respect. O let me, dear father, for I could not be happy at anything else. And I am not altogether ignorant of sea affairs, though I have yet a great deal to learn, for I have been studying them for some time back. If it were not for putting you to too much trouble, I would beg an answer from you in writing, but I can hardly expect it, though I much wish it.

Your Affectionate son,
George[4]

*Cullen, looking out over the sea town across the beach toward Scaurnose—
site of the fictional* Malcolm *and family holidays
when MacDonald was young.*

From such words we gather that young George MacDonald's outlook on the future course of his life was still naive and fun-loving. Yet without realizing it, he had reached the age where deeper questions would soon begin to penetrate into his awareness. And it would be these concerns that would occupy his thoughts as he moved into the later years of his youth.

CHAPTER FIVE

THE GREAT CONFLICT BEGINS
(1830–1840)

The initial seeds of doubt as to the validity of the extreme Scottish Calvinistic view of the Christian faith may have begun for young George MacDonald at the Huntly Adventure School which he, along with his brothers, attended. Their first teacher was a certain Rev. Colin Stuart, a Highlander and "a hard man with a severe, not altogether cruel temper, and quite savage sense of duty"—the original of the barbarous Murdoch Malison in *Alec Forbes of Howglen*. Incredible as it seems to our present-day sensitivities, Greville MacDonald ascertains upon good evidence that the fictional schoolmaster is not overdrawn from the reality of Stuart. Mac-Donald, too, may have drawn upon a biography of Burns for the characterization, for the poet's schoolmaster, who also made frequent use of the taws (a hardened leather horsewhip), was coincidentally named Mr. Murdoch.

Life With the Taws

School was a six-days-a-week proposition, Saturday being a half-holiday except for those "kept in" for their failure to properly recite their lessons from the Shorter Catechism—that epitome of Calvinistic dogma that served as the very basis for early 19th-century education in Scotland. The opening phrase of the two hundred-or-so page book reads: "The chief end of man is to glorify God and enjoy Him for ever," about which, in *Alec Forbes*, George MacDonald wrote, "For my part, I wish the spiritual engineers who constructed it had, after laying the grandest foundation-stone that truth could afford them, glorified God by going no further."

They *did* go further, however, covering the whole of their theology with questions ranging from: *What is the chief end of man?*, through creation, the nature of God, the Trinity, and the cornerstone of Calvinism—predestination and the difference between the elect and the cursed. Following the questions came the answers, supportive texts from the Scriptures, and lengthy commentaries and exhortations. Thus following *What doth every sin deserve?* came the necessary reply, "Every sin deserveth God's wrath and curse, both in this life and that which is to come," followed by two pages of fine-print annotations and notes, far too dry, deep, and complex for any but the brightest of fifteen-year-olds to understand, much less seven-year-olds. Pervading the whole was the negative pall of Knox's Calvinism, which viewed the life of Christianity as a lifelong attempt to live out the answer to one of the Catechism's fundamental questions: *What doth God require of us, that we may escape His wrath and curse due to us for sin?* The children were expected not only to recite the answers to the questions verbatim, but also to memorize the accompanying Bible verses. Corporal punishment was meted out for failure by the cruel taws, which the master kept in constant readiness, though even a "lickin'" was sometimes seen as preferable to the hated alternative of being locked in the schoolroom for an entire Saturday afternoon.

Little James MacDonald, the poet's brother, died at the age of eight, and his schoolfellows, if no others, believed his death was in large measure due to Stuart's treatment of him, reminiscent of Malison's crippling of the orphan Truffey.

MacDonald's *Alec Forbes*, though fictional, gives a tolerable notion of what conditions at the Adventure School were like:

"Before the morning was over [Annie] was called up, along with some children considerably younger than herself, to read and spell. The master stood before them, armed with a long, thick strap of horse-hide, prepared by steeping in brine, black and supple with constant use, and cut into fingers at one end, which had been hardened in the fire.

"Now there was a little pale-faced, delicate-looking boy in the class, who blundered a good deal. Every time he did so the cruel serpent of leather went at him, coiling round his legs with a sudden, hissing swash. This made him cry, and his tears blinded him so that he could not even see the words which he had been unable to read before. But he still attempted to go on, and still the instrument of torture went swish-swash round his little thin legs, raising upon them, no doubt, plentiful blue wales, to be revealed, when he was undressed for the night, to the indignant eyes of pitying mother or aunt, who would yet send him back to the school the next morning without fail. . . .

". . . the master had no fixed principle as to the party on whom the punishment should fall. Punishment, in his eyes, was perhaps enough in itself. If he was capable of seeing that *punishment*, as he called it, falling on the wrong person, was not *punishment*, but only *suffering*, certainly he had not seen the value of the distinction . . .

"One Saturday the master made his appearance in black instead of white stockings, which was regarded by the scholars as a bad omen; and fully were their prognostications justified, on this occasion, at least. The joy of the half-holiday for Scotch boys and girls has a terrible weight laid in the opposite scale—I mean the other half of the day. This weight, which brings the day pretty much on a level with all other days, consists in a free use of the Shorter Catechism. This, of course, made them hate the Catechism, though I am not aware that that was of any great consequence, or much to be regretted. For my part, I wish the spiritual engineers who constructed it had, after laying the grandest foundation-stone that truth could afford them, glorified God by going no further. Certainly many a man would have enjoyed Him sooner, if it had not been for their work. But, alas! the Catechism was not enough, even of the kind. The tormentors of youth had gone further, and provided what they called Scripture proofs of the various assertions of the Catechism; a support of which it stood greatly in need. Alas! I say, for the boys and girls who had to learn these proofs, called texts of Scripture, but too frequently only morsels torn bleeding and shapeless from 'the lovely form of the Virgin Truth!' For these tasks, combined with the pains and penalties which accompanied failure, taught them to dislike the Bible as well as the Catechism, and that was a matter of altogether different import.

"Every Saturday, then, Murdoch Malison's pupils had to learn so many questions of the Shorter Catechism, with proofs from Scripture; and whoever failed in this task was condemned to imprisonment for the remainder of the day, or, at least, till the task should be accomplished. . . . Upon certain Saturdays, moreover, one in each month, I think, a repetition was required of all the questions and proofs that had been, or ought to have been learned since the last observance of the same sort . . .

"Now the day in question was one of these of accumulated labour . . . Annie . . . did not know when her turn came, but allowed the master to stand before her in bootless expectation. He did not interrupt her, but with a refinement of cruelty that ought to have done him credit in his own eyes, waited till the universal silence had at length aroused Annie to self-consciousness and a sense of annihilating confusion. Then, with a smile on his thin lips, but a lowering thundercloud on his brow, he repeated the question.

"'What doth every sin deserve?'

"Annie, bewildered, and burning with shame at finding herself the core of the silence—feeling as if her poor little spirit stood there naked to the scoffs and jeers around—could not recall a word of the answer given in the Catechism. So, in her bewilderment, she fell back on her common sense and experience, which, she ought to have known, had nothing to do with the matter in hand.

"'What doth every sin deserve?' again repeated the tyrant.

"'A lickin',' whimpered Annie, and burst into tears. . . .

"A small class of mere children, amongst whom were the orphan Truffeys, had been committed to the care of one of the bigger boys, while the master was engaged with another class. Every boy in the latter had already had his share of *pandies*, when a noise in the children's class attracting the master's attention, he saw one of the Truffeys hit another boy in the face. He strode upon him at once, and putting no question as to provocation, took him by the neck, fixed it between his knees, and began to lash him with hissing blows. In his agony, the little fellow contrived to twist his head about and get a mouthful of the master's leg, inserting his teeth in a most canine and praiseworthy manner. The master caught him up, and dashed him on the floor. There the child lay motionless. Alarmed, and consequently cooled, Malison proceeded to lift him. He was apparently lifeless; but he had only fainted with pain. When he came to himself a little, it was found that his leg was hurt. It appeared afterward that the knee-cap was greatly injured. Moaning with pain, he was sent home on the back of a big parish scholar.

"At all this Annie stared from her pillory with horror. The feeling that God was angry with her grew upon her; and Murdoch Malison became for a time inseparably associated with her idea of God, frightfully bewildering all her aspirations" (*Alec Forbes of Howglen*, Chs. 9, 12, 27).

When George was ten or eleven, Stuart was replaced by the kindly Alexander Millar, and under him he made rapid progress over the next several years, excelling in both reading and composition. Recognizing his ability, Millar gave him much help and encouragement, and in addition George assisted by tutoring the younger students, not an uncommon practice. Morning classes were held before breakfast, and sometimes George would go home with a schoolfellow for breakfast instead of returning all the way to the Farm. There he would share with his friend's family their simple meal of porridge, each person with his wooden beaker of milk: wherever the fare was simple and frugal, hospitality was open and unceremonious. Mr. Millar also invited him to accompany him home occasionally after school for a dinner of potatoes and milk, oatcake and butter, while they read together. Truly as Stuart had stifled the urge to learn in so many, Millar opened the doors of learning to the rapidly expansive mind of the young poet, preparing him in large measure for the university, which was now not far in the distance.

First Questions About the Character of God

What stands out graphically from George's school experience of his early years is the clear dichotomy between the spiritual teachings of the Bible, whose words they were forced to memorize and recite, and the cruel and inhumane methods employed by the pedagogue Stuart. What thoughtful person could not immediately see the bankruptcy of a system wherein scriptural words about God's so-called love were driven into young minds with a whip? These were queries the loyal Calvinistic mind ignored; to wonder about such things was akin to blasphemy. In their view God himself was not unlike the schoolmaster—a wrathful and sovereign tyrant, incensed over mankind's sin, eager to pour out His retribution to the unrepentant. The human heart, and especially the hearts of young children, were deceitful and wicked. Therefore the truth must be forced into them however it could be done—with whip, with lash, with taws, and pain for the most obdurate of young minds.

A dull boy might never question the proceedings, as much as he might hate them. At the other extreme, those like Alec Forbes took it all with a grain of salt, made the best of it, and endured as optimistically as possible. But such options were hardly open to a mind and emotion like George MacDonald's. Something inside compelled him to grapple with it, to make sense of it, to understand it, and to find where truth lay relative to the Shorter Catechism, Mr. Stuart, and the Bible.

Of course such inquiries did not one day simply spring, fully posed, to his mind. On the conscious level, like the others, he memorized his lessons, tried to avoid being kept in, and did what he could to keep from receiving blows from the taws. But his subconscious mind, as he sat in the class, watching the application of the whip and observing the cruelty of the master, noted the emptiness of the spiritual principles which were *said* but not *demonstrated*. And as his subconscious thus ruminated on it all, seeds of doubt were being sown.

Grandmother MacDonald

One other, however, was destined to have an even more thoroughgoing impact upon the young thinker than his cruel schoolmaster. That person was his paternal grandmother, Mrs. Charles Edward (Isabella) MacDonald. A shrewd businesswoman and the most strict and zealous of fire-breathing hyper-Calvinists, her life was bound up in a religious system based on works and predestination, bent primarily, it seemed, on avoiding the impending vengeance and wrath of God.

She lived at the corner of Church and Duke Streets, across a garden and small field from the linen factory she and her husband had operated with the threadmill he had built nearby. Next to her home her son, George, Sr., built the house in which his son the poet was born. The adjoining houses, garden, and factory were nearly exactly as described in the novel *Robert Falconer*; there *was*, in fact, an adjoining door just like that by which Robert entered Mary St. John's house. By the time of George's birth in 1824, Mrs. MacDonald's husband, Charles Edward, was dead, the factories had fallen into disrepair, and the enterprises of her sons had by then been moved to Upper Pirriesmill—the Farm and the bleachmill on the Bogie.

George's own mother was an invalid from tuberculosis even prior to her death. His father approached matters of religion in a quiet and unceremonious way, choosing to live his faith rather than vocalize it. Thus his grandmother came to exert an almost overpowering influence over the family—typifying the image of the aging white-haired matriarch, Bible in hand, trotting off to services with one or two youngsters in tow, making sure they always said their prayers, jealously guarding against any sign of waywardness, pouring out soulful prayers for the salvation of sinners, and constantly reminding whatever young ones came under her charge to flee from the wrath to come. And the degree to which her views worked upon the young mind of her grandson, as experienced by young Robert Falconer, was strong indeed.

About Robert Falconer, MacDonald would later write, recalling to mind his own childhood struggles:

"For now arose within him, not without ultimate good, the evil phantasms of a theology which would explain all God's doings by low conceptions. . . . In such a system, hell is invariably the deepest truth, and the love of God is not so deep as hell. Hence, as foundations must be laid in the deepest, the system is founded in hell, and the first article in the creed that Robert Falconer learned was, 'I believe in hell.' Practically, I mean, it was so; else how should it be that as often as a thought of religious duty arose in his mind, it appeared in the form of escaping hell, of fleeing from the wrath to come? For his very nature was hell, being not born *in* sin and brought forth in iniquity, but born sin and brought forth iniquity. And yet God made him. He must believe that. And he must believe, too, that God was just, awfully just, punishing with fearful pains those who did not go through a certain process of mind which it was utterly impossible they should go through without a help which he would give to some, and withhold from others, the reason of the difference not being such, to say the least of it, as to come within the reach of the persons concerned. And this God they said was love" (*Robert Falconer*, Ch. 12).

Only after many years could George MacDonald follow the childhood confusion thus generated with the next words of the passage: "It was logically absurd, of course. . . ." For the time being, the boy had to try to believe it the best he could, though it was certain to cause conflict in his logical mind.

Mrs. MacDonald, for all the narrowness of her doctrine, was, like Mrs. Falconer, a woman to be loved and a woman who was, if feared, still respected. She was as benevolent as she was a fine businesswoman, adopting a family of four beggar children of questionable parentage, raising three of them to place them out in the world (reminiscent of Shargar). Her antagonism toward Catholics was intense, although she never gave up hope for individuals of her acquaintance who had been misled by the "Scarlet Woman." Her grandson Charles used to tell of a visit he paid her shortly before she died at 92. She was still feisty as ever and able to read the newspapers, which in 1848 were full of revolutions and the toppling of the world's thrones. "Laddie," she said, "the newspapers is tellin' that amang a' the changes takin' place i' the warld, they ha' gotten a guid Pope at Rome; an' I ha' been prayin' t' the Lord a' night t' gie him a new hert an' a guid wife!" She was involved with the London City Mission and was the inspiration of the Huntly temperance movement in the late 1830s, in which young George also played a part.

After the family moved from the center of Huntly to the Farm about a mile away, across the wooden bridge over the Bogie, there continued to be much interplay between the two houses; George and his brothers spent a good deal of time with their grandmother. She helped ease the mothering burdens of young Mrs. MacDonald, and after the mother's death the grandmother's role in the family assumed even larger proportions. While it may be an exaggeration to say that she became a substitute mother for her grandsons during the period between the death of George, Sr.'s, first wife in 1832 and his remarriage in 1839, the woman who was affectionately known as the "real mistress of the Farm" was second only in influence to that of a real mother—especially in the spiritual realm. Robert Falconer's relationship with old Mrs. Falconer gives profound insight into the intensity with which the stern Calvinist attempted to drill the spiritual dogmas of her faith into her grandchildren.

What Is God Like?

Thus in young George were sown the seeds which would ultimately sprout into a tremendous inner conflict. Though he was a mere boy, he could see the inconsistency of belief in these people who portrayed the Christian faith in his life. His schoolmaster, Mr. Stuart, spoke of God, read Scriptures, was addressed as *Reverend*—a word which certainly had the ring of the devout about it—and had studied to be a minister of the Gospel. Yet he was the cruelest man young George had ever known. Did this man epitomize the "elect," the chosen? Was God like Mr. Stuart? Was his horsehide taws a symbol of God's wrath which would punish every sin?

Similarly, George's grandmother spoke in reverent tones about God, prayed intently to Him at all hours, never missed a church service at the kirk, was known throughout the village as one of Huntly's most religious women, and constantly admonished him of his divine duty. Was the Lord like her—cold, dour, uncompromising, and severe, prayerful for sinners, but willing to send them to burn forever in a gigantic lake of fire if they did not repent before they died?

These two remarkable personages—Mr. Stuart and old Grandmother MacDonald—formed young George's first visual picture of God. To him they represented the person of his awesome, terrible, almighty heavenly Father—unsmiling and infinite in His displeasure with man, angry with sinners, and eager to send the jealous vengeance of His curse upon them.

The Bright Face of Nature

At the same time, however, other forces had taken root within the heart and soul of young George MacDonald, contradictory forces which breathed an altogether different spirit. Where the seed initially came from and how it struck root deep in his heart is impossible to say. The divine winds of heaven no doubt are constantly blowing such seeds of refreshment throughout the world, seeking fertile hearts wherein they might plant themselves, there to sprout and grow and bear fruit testifying to God's *true* being and character. George MacDonald's heart-garden was filled with soft, fertile soil, and thus the divine seeds found a home. All about him were signs and miracles that spoke of wondrous things. The trees, the wind, the soft summer fragrances, the two rivers, the blue sky, the white clouds, the barren moors, the breeze in his face, his animal friends, the marvels of the winter landscape, the gold and green fields, the delicate rose, the rough primrose leaves, smiles mirrored back from the faces of those he loved—all these things attested to the joys and wonders and exuberance of life! Say what they would of the curse of God, the world of His making was dazzling in its splendor!

Therefore, as George had already demonstrated something of a two-sided personality, so also to him the world must have seemed as if it had two sides, like the moon—a sunny side and dark side. On the dark side stood his grandmother and Mr. Stuart, fearsome and grim, the one holding his taws, the other her well-thumbed Bible—standing, as it were, on the right and left hand of God, His agents on earth, ready and willing to dispense His terrible, inevitable judgment.

On the sunny side were the natural beauties surrounding him, which he had made his friends, speaking just as loudly (though only to his subconscious at first), saying, "I, Nature, am also the messenger of Almighty God. I too stand at His right hand. I do not dispense His judgment, but rather His joy and His love and His delight with His creation. And His delight with *you* His child. For He has created all this that *you* might be His, and might enjoy it, and Him, forever!"

The Brighter Face of George MacDonald, Sr.

There was one other who stood on the sunny side, whose influence not even his grandmother could match, one whom the boy loved more than any other person on earth—and one who loved him even more—his father, George MacDonald, Sr. If Stuart and Grandmother MacDonald represented "types" of God to the impressionable youngster, so too did his father. But what a different image of God he portrayed—warm, understanding, compassionate, forgiving, always with an arm ready to wrap itself in love about the slender shoulder of his son. From his own father young George received the redemptive love about which he would later write: "Love is the first comforter. . . . Love indeed is the highest in all truth, and the pressure of a hand, a kiss, the caress of a child, will do more to save, sometimes than the wisest argument, even rightly understood. Love alone is wisdom, love alone is power" (*Paul Faber, Surgeon*, Ch. 36).

Here was a man one might, in his wildest dreams, dare to *hope* that God resembled! If only the word *father* had been chosen not by accident, but because our earthly fathers, even more than schoolmasters and grandmothers, were intended in some mystical way to be a "type" and illustration and example of the divine Father who is in heaven and is Father to us all!

Years later, when his ideas of fatherhood were more fully refined, this same boy, grown to manhood, said:

"The truth and faith which the great Father has put in the heart of the child make him the nursing father of the fatherhood in his father; and thus in part it is that the children of men will come at last to know the great Father. The family, with all its powers for the development of society, is a family because it is born and rooted in and grows out of the very bosom of God" (*Paul Faber, Surgeon*, Ch. 49).

"Oh, if only it might be true!" the young lad might have cried out when the revelation struck him. "Maybe, just *maybe*, God is like my own dear father!"

Is it too good to be true?

The answer to his youthful question came in his own words to one of his own children in later years: "It is just so good it *must* be true!"

But for now, as the dichotomy between Stuart and his grandmother on the one hand and Nature and his father on the other widened in Mac-Donald's young mind, the seeds of conflict continued to grow. Throughout his books we sense this tension, a collision of divergent personalities and views. As Glenn Sadler has written, "The phrase 'meadows of childhood' significantly describes MacDonald's lifelong artistic and personal pursuit of the image of the child in his writings. Meticulously he attempts to reconstruct in the poetic language of his novels his recollections of his own moral development as a boy: his encounters with nature and the closely knit life around him in Huntly."[1]

In nearly all his fictional childhood characters we catch glimpses, sometimes full-blown portraits, of himself—wondering, growing, filled with the gladness of life, and at the same time struggling to understand. Wandering little Gibbie has never heard of Jesus, yet his soul soars in one-ness with his Maker as he climbs to the top of Glashgar. When Gibbie comes to know "about" Jesus, the man he meets in the New Testament corresponds with the person he had known all along on the mountain. Little Annie Anderson's confusions over what "faith in God" means, troubles which neither Calvinist Thomas nor simple Mr. Cowie can alleviate, are not settled in her tormented soul until God himself touches her far outside the reaches of the Shorter Catechism. And most poignant and autobiographically telling of all are Robert Falconer's probing and pene-trating youthful questions about God's character, His purpose in the world, His will toward man, and the nature of His love and how it harmonized with His judgment.

Robert's reverent uncertainties after inadvertently hearing his grand-mother's private prayers reflect the same doubts and apprehensions that plagued Falconer's creator in his youth: "Whether it was that the weary woman here fell asleep, or that she was too exhausted for further speech, Robert heard no more, though he remained there frozen with horror for some minutes after his grandmother had ceased. This, then, was the rea-son why she would never speak about his father! She kept all her thoughts about him for the silence of the night, and loneliness with the God who never sleeps, but watches the wicked all through the dark. And his father was one of the wicked! And God was against him! And when he died he would go to hell! . . .

"Robert consequently began to take fits of soul-saving, a most rational exercise, worldly wise and prudent; right, too, on the principles he had received, but not in the least Christian in its nature, or even God-fearing. His imagination began to busy itself in representing the dire consequences of not entering into the one refuge of faith. He made many frantic efforts to believe that he believed; took to keeping the Sabbath very carefully— that is, by going to church three times, and to Sunday school as well; by never walking a step save to or from church; by never saying a word upon any subject unconnected with religion, chiefly theoretical; by never reading any but religious books; by never whistling; by never thinking of his lost fiddle, and so on—all the time feeling that God was ready to pounce upon him if he failed once. . . ." (*Robert Falconer*, Chs. 8, 12).

Such conflicting motives and nagging doubts concerning the religion of his upbringing were an intrinsic part of George's early days, especially beyond the ages of twelve and thirteen as manhood approached. All about him, in the mind's eye of his subconscious, stood the four personalities, which all in their own way seemed to "represent" the Almighty— Mr. Stuart and Mrs. MacDonald on the one side, and the lovely face of Nature and the dear character of his own father on the other.

The driving force of George MacDonald's life over the next several years thus became to integrate these apparently contradictory pictures, and thereby to discover the truth that would answer the foundational question of life: Who is God, and what is He like?

CHAPTER SIX

THE PASSING OF INNOCENCE
(1835–1840)

Nineteenth-Century Scottish Calvinism

The Presbyterian Church of Scotland in which MacDonald was raised had been founded in the 16th century by John Knox (1505–1572). Knox was himself a student of John Calvin (1509–1564) in Geneva, and was almost singlehandedly responsible for bringing the Reformation to Scotland, the country officially converting to Protestantism from Catholicism in 1560. The Confession of Faith drawn up in that year by Knox reflected the Calvinistic leanings of the Reformation far more than it did the Lutheran, and it was elaborated into the even more strongly worded Westminster Confession of the mid-17th century. In the years since that time, and by George MacDonald's day, the church in Scotland had hardened and narrowed, and grown even more exclusive and intolerant through centuries of repetition and lack of change.

The foundational tenets of the brand of Calvinism Knox brought to Scotland were rooted in the absolute power, justice, and holiness of God, and the total sinfulness of man. God's will being forever and irreversibly corrupted by the Fall in the Garden of Eden, man could now do nothing to bring about his own salvation. He deserved only one thing—eternal damnation. The other side of God's holiness was His wrath, His total hatred of sin. The absolute justice of His nature demanded that any who sin—that is, all of humanity—be eternally punished and separated from Him in hell. However, in His mercy, God chooses to give some—the Elect—unconditional salvation from this curse, while, in justice, condemning the rest to their eternal doom. Jesus Christ, God's Son, died on the cross as a substitute for the Elect, taking their punishment upon himself, in order that God's justice be satisfied and the blood offering be made, thus giving God legal justification for sparing them. Their faith and consequently their salvation are bestowed upon them arbitrarily. Neither man's

will, his choices, nor his growth toward personal righteousness and goodness toward his fellows have anything to do with the matter. God has simply "predestined" from the very beginning of time that certain men and
women were *Elect*, while others were *cursed*. Salvation has already been
determined and nothing can be done to sway the divine scales in either
direction. But the leading of an exemplary and spiritual life is an indicator
by which one can determine which side of the eternal fence one happens
to be on.

To Know the Truth

The tendency of youth, especially in modern times, is to rebel against
the dogmas of one's generational predecessors—particularly in matters of
religion and belief. To a lesser degree this has been true for several hundred years as growing intellectual enlightenment, dating back to Renaissance times, has been the standard that youth has raised in all civilized
cultures. No more vivid a portrayal of this tendency exists than in the arts,
where the questioning of old norms at times becomes almost the essence
of the new forms themselves.

To all appearances George MacDonald was a likely candidate to follow
such a path of criticism and negation. There was, however, an additional
ingredient in his innermost self from a very early age; it became the very
foundation stone of his entire life and dictated his response to everything.

Simply put, he had *an intense desire to know the truth*.

Thus, when he began to question the validity of the brand of Calvinism
portrayed by his grandmother, the schoolmaster, and indeed, not only the
Church of Scotland, but also the denominations that had broken away
from it such as the Congregationalist Missionar' Kirk his family attended,
George MacDonald did not set out to prove their teachings wrong. He had
no particular viewpoints of his own. There were no bones to pick, no mis-
sions of destruction against a system he wanted to topple. He simply
wanted to know the *truth*—whatever it was and wherever his quest for it
took him. Once found, his consuming passion was to order his daily life
according to that truth.

Therefore, we find no "rebel" stage in MacDonald's young life, where
he violently threw off the shackles of the past, as did many of his contemporaries. Always respectful of his elders, even of their ways, never condemning or judging, never becoming hostile toward any person, but only
toward what he perceived as erroneous and damaging viewpoints, he simply asked questions at increasingly profound levels. Questioning misapplied Calvinistic notions about God's character, he never questioned the
truthfulness of God himself. Nature and his father were equally at work
molding his thinking, increasing his desire, not to rebel against God at all,
but to find the *true* God. Balance always existed—he never opposed the
totality of Calvin's teaching, only the few points he felt were off target. And
though later in life he was widely known in some circles for his fight
against the Calvinistic doctrines of predestined election and an eternity of

punishment, by others he was considered a ranting fundamentalist. From boyhood to old age, he fit no mold.

Throughout his youth, his desire to find the truth in matters of religion grew stronger and stronger—accompanied all along by the dual personality of joy and melancholy. Yet gradually the innocence of childhood—the warm summers, the snowy winters, the playful "Alec Forbes" side of life—was replaced by the more thoughtful "Robert Falconer" side of his personality; the questions and conflicts of life weighed ever more heavily upon him. We find this same growth progression in Robert Falconer, too, from the frolicking joyful play at Mr. Lammie's farm to the more serious moments when he had to face and wrestle with the great issues of life.

More Serious Questioning

Therefore, as the boy "Geordie" MacDonald became a youth and grew from ten to twelve to fourteen, and by fifteen prepared to leave home for the great city, the university, and his future as a man, it is Robert Falconer who captures the sense of his spirit as he grapples with the questions that haunt him. The roots of change are in place during these years, sending out their probing feelers, as his subconscious mind searches for some way to integrate the two seemingly opposite spiritual personages of his grandmother and his father.

Surely MacDonald is in measure describing himself as he says of Robert: "He took more and more to brooding in the garret; and as more questions presented themselves for solution, he became more anxious to arrive at the solution, and more uneasy as he failed in satisfying himself that he had arrived at it. . . ."

He then goes on to reflect upon Robert's introspective mentality, again recalling his own early years: "I believe that even the new-born infant is, in some of his moods, already grappling with the deepest metaphysical problems, in forms infinitely too rudimental for the understanding of the grown philosopher. . . . If this be the case, it is no wonder that at Robert's age the deepest questions of his coming manhood should be in active operation, although so surrounded with the yoke of common belief and the shell of accredited authority, that the embryo faith, which in minds like his always takes the form of doubt, could not be defined any more than its existence could be disproved. I have given a hint at the tendency of his mind already, in the fact that one of the most definite inquiries to which he had yet turned his thoughts was, whether God would have mercy upon a repentant devil. . . ." (*Robert Falconer*, Ch. 14).

It is scarcely any wonder such thoughts—especially as he could not control them entering his brain—made him feel guilty, as if he might not be one of the chosen elect. "But through the horrible vapors of [his] vain endeavors . . . there broke a little light, a little soothing, soft twilight, from the dim windows of such literature as came in his way . . . and lifted something of the weight of . . . gloom off his spirits. . . . But there was [one book] which deserves particular notice, inasmuch as it . . . rais[ed] a deep question in his mind, and one worthy to be asked. This book was the translations of Klopstocks' 'Messiah' . . . : Amongst the rebel angels who are of the actors in the story, one of the principal is a cherub who repents of making his choice with Satan, mourns over his apostasy, haunts unseen the steps of our Savior . . . and would gladly return to his lost duties in heaven, if only he might—a doubt which I believe is left unsolved in the volume, and naturally enough remained unsolved in Robert's mind:— Would poor Abaddon be forgiven and taken home again? . . . Having no one to talk to, he divided himself and went to buffets on the subject, sid- ing, of course, with the better half of himself, which supported the merci- ful view of the matter; for all his efforts at keeping the Sabbath had, in his own honest judgment, failed so entirely, that he had no ground for believ- ing himself one of the elect" (*Robert Falconer,* Ch. 12).

The frustration was compounded by an environment in which ques- tions about such matters were not raised, knowing that the watchful eye and ear of his grandmother was jealously guarding his budding faith. "'Ow, say awa'. Ye sanna say muckle 'at's wrang afore I cry *haud*,' said Mrs. Fal- coner, curious to know what had been moving in the boy's mind, but watching like a cat, ready to spring upon the first visible hair of the old Adam" (*Robert Falconer,* Ch. 12).

But even this rigid atmosphere could not keep God out of the boy.

"One Saturday in the end of July, when the westering sun was hotter than at midday, he went down to the lower end of the field, where the river was confined by a dam, and plunged from the bank into the deep water. After a swim of half-an-hour, he ascended the higher part of the field, and lay down upon a broad web to bask in the sun. In his ears was the hush rather than rush of the water over the dam, the occasional murmur of a belt of trees that skirted the border of the field. . . .

"He lay gazing up into the depth of the sky, rendered deeper and bluer by the masses of white cloud that hung almost motionless below it, until he felt a kind of bodily fear lest he should fall off the face of the round earth into the abyss. A gentle wind, laden with pine odours from the sun- heated trees behind him, flapped its light wing in his face: the humanity of the world smote his heart; the great sky towered up over him, and its divinity entered his soul; a strange longing after something 'he knew not nor could name' awoke within him, followed by the pang of a sudden fear that there was no such thing as that which he sought, that it was all a fancy of his own spirit . . . But once aroused, the feeling was never stilled; the desire never left him; sometimes growing even to a passion that was relieved only by a flood of tears.

"Strange as it may sound to those who have never thought of such things save in connection with Sundays and Bibles and churches and ser- mons, that which was now working in . . . [his] mind was the first dull and faint movement of the greatest need that the human heart possesses—the need of the God-Man. There must be truth in the scent of that pine-wood: someone must mean it. There must be a glory in those heavens that depends not upon our imagination: some power greater than they must dwell in them. Some spirit must move in that wind that haunts us with a kind of human sorrow; some soul must look up to us from the eye of that starry flower. . . .

"Little did Robert think that such was his need—that his soul was searching after One whose form was constantly presented to him, but as constantly obscured and made unlovely by the words without knowledge spoken in the religious assemblies of the land; that he was longing without knowing it on the Saturday for that from which on the Sunday he would be repelled without knowing it. Years passed before he drew nigh to the knowledge of what he sought.

"For weeks the mood . . . did not return, though the forms of Nature were henceforth full of a pleasure he had never known before. He loved the grass; the water was more gracious to him; he would leave his bed early, that he might gaze on the clouds of the east, with their borders gold-blasted with sunrise; he would linger in the fields that the amber and purple, and green and red, of the sunset, might not escape after the sun unseen. And as long as he felt the mystery, the revelation of the mystery lay before and not behind him" (*Robert Falconer*, Ch. 18).

The Poignant Vanishing of Childhood

If it was slowly vanishing with advancing years and greater concerns, the childhood of young George MacDonald contained yet a few more pleasures to be savored. One was the construction and sailing of a great kite with his brother John, the story of which has been immortalized in *Robert Falconer*—for the histories of the two kites were remarkably similar.

"When they reached the open road . . . the tail was unrolled, and the dragon ascended steady as an angel whose work is done. Shargar took the stock at the end of the string . . . but the creature was hard to lead in such a wind; so they made a loop on the string, and passed it round Shargar's chest, and he tugged the dragon home. . . . On the way they laid their plans for the accomodation of the dragon [and how to get it past Grannie]. . . .

"Before they entered the town they drew in the kite a little way, and cut off a dozen yards of the string, which Robert put in his pocket with a stone tied to the end. When they reached the house, Shargar went into the little garden and tied the string of the kite to the paling. . . . Robert opened the street door, and having turned his head on all sides like a thief, darted . . . up the stairs. . . . From the skylight [he] threw the stone down into the . . . garden, fastening the other end of the string to the bedstead. Escaping as cautiously as he had entered, he passed hurriedly into . . . [the garden], found the stone, and joined Shargar. The ends were soon united, and the kite let go. It sunk for a moment, then, arrested by the bedstead, towered again to its former 'pride of place,' sailing over Rothieden, grand and unconcerned, in the wastes of air.

"But the end of its tether was in Robert's garret. And that was to him a sense of power, a thought of glad mystery. There was henceforth, while the dragon flew, a relation between the desolate little chamber, in that lowly house buried among so many more aspiring abodes, and the unmeasured depths and spaces, the stars, and the unknown heavens. . . .

"All that night, all the next day, all the next night, the dragon flew" (*Robert Falconer,* Ch. 23).

In *George MacDonald and His Wife,* Greville tells how Grandmother MacDonald, heartbroken over the backslidings of her son Charles (George's uncle), burned his prized violin, determined, as he puts it, that "it should lead no other lads beyond reach of the Divine Grace" as she considered it had done him. Greville later used the contrasting symbols of the violin's death throes at the hand of the impassioned Calvinist and the heaven-soaring kite to illustrate Robert's (and his own) "tethered" longings to reach toward the heavens, all the while bound by a restrictive, indeed, a cruel theology which would burn objects of great joy because to her creed, pleasure itself was the antithesis of God's solemn righteousness.

At the moment when Robert could stand and face his grannie, and confront her with words of righteous indignation for what she had done, in that moment manhood was upon him. With the courage to look her boldly in the eye, he cast off the fetters of her theology of cold, negative austerity and began his search for another.

In the same way, though the fictional Robert Falconer, the kite, and the violin are but symbols, they reveal the same crossroads in George Mac-Donald's own life. Grandmother Falconer, too, represents a symbol of narrow Calvinistic thinking. She is not a totally accurate picture of *his* grandmother any more than young Falconer is the *precise* image of George MacDonald, but she is the representation of an abused theology from which he was trying to wrestle free.

Like Robert Falconer, young George was struggling as a youth to soar to the heavens, to know and understand God—whoever He was and whatever He was like. But like Robert's kite, he was tethered to the bedstead, earthbound by the theology of his upbringing. Only when he stood and looked his own symbolic Grandmother Falconer in the face, and in love for the truth spoke against the narrow and restricting confines of her dogma, was he ready, like Robert, to begin his own search for the *true* God—a God who would lead him to distant hills, to the high peak unknown, to the heavens where the kite of his spirit longed to soar.

For George MacDonald that search would soon take him to Aberdeen.

"Robert came home to dinner the next day a few minutes before Shargar. As he entered his grandmother's parlour, a strange odour greeted his sense. A moment more, and he stood rooted with horror, and his hair began to rise on his head. His violin lay on its back on the fire, and a yellow tongue of flame was licking the red lips of a hole in its belly. All its strings were shrivelled up save one, which burst as he gazed. And beside, stern as a Druidess, sat his grandmother in her chair, feeding her eyes with grim satisfaction on the detestable sacrifice. At length the rigidity of Robert's whole being relaxed in an involuntary howl like that of a wild beast, and he turned and rushed from the house in a helpless agony of horror.

Where he was going he knew not, only a blind instinct of modesty drove him to hide his passion from the eyes of men. . . .

"[Later he] walked composedly into his grandmother's parlour, where the neck of the violin yet lay upon the fire only half consumed. The rest had vanished utterly. . .

"'Robert, ye may hae spite in yer hert for what I hae dune this mornin', but I cud do no ither. An' it's an ill thing to tak sic amen's o' me, as gin I hae dun wrang . . . it was only an' auld, useless, ill-mainnert scraich o' a fiddle.'

"'She was the bonniest fiddle i' the country-side, grannie. And she never gae a scraich in her life 'cep' whan she was han'let in a mainner unbecomin'. But we s' say nae mair aboot her, for she's gane, an' no by a fair death on one's own straw either. She had nae blude to cry for vengeance; but the snappin' o' her strings an' the crackin' o' her banes may hae made a cry to gang far eneuch notwithstandin'.'

"The old woman seemed for one moment rebuked under her grandson's eloquence. He had made a great stride towards manhood since the morning.

"'The fiddle's my ain,' she said, in a defensive tone. . . .

"'The fiddle's your nae mair, grannie. . . .'

"Therewith Robert retreated to his garret.

"When he opened the door of it, the first thing he saw was the string of his kite, which, strange to tell, so steady had been the wind, was still up in the air—still tugging at the bedpost. Whether it was from the stinging thought that the true sky-soarer, the violin, having been devoured by the jaws of the fire-devil, there was no longer any significance in the outward and visible sign of the dragon, or from a dim feeling that the time of kites was gone by and manhood on the threshold, I cannot tell; but he drew his knife from his pocket, and with one downstroke cut the string in twain. Away went the dragon, free, like a prodigal, to its ruin. And with the dragon, afar into the past, flew the childhood of Robert Falconer. He made one remorseful dart after the string as it swept out of the skylight, but it was gone. . . . And never more, save in twilight dreams, did he lay hold on his childhood again. But he knew better and better, as the years rolled on, that he approached a deeper and holier childhood, of which that had been but the feeble and necessarily vanishing type" (*Robert Falconer,* Ch. 23).

PART TWO

Beach, sand dunes, with the mouth of the River Don in the distance where student MacDonald went for solitary walks during the days in Aberdeen.

THE SEEKING STUDENT

The night was black, and the fierce winds coming in off the icy North Sea had whipped it up into a cauldron of angry, white-tipped waves.

Along the desolate beach, struggling against the elements trying to halt his forward progress, strode the solitary figure of a youth. Behind him the lights of Aberdeen could barely be seen through the cloudy winter night. He had come to the seashore with two friends—fellow students at King's College—but they had deserted him long ago, retreating to the warmth of their lodgings, while he alone continued the nighttime vigil of welcoming the season's first storm to Scotland's northeast coast.

Perhaps their spirits could be content to let such a moment pass while they sipped their tea in comfortable surroundings. But not his. Perhaps they were less troubled than he by storms of all kinds—external *and* internal.

Whatever the reasons, he now found himself walking alone along the shore bordering the golf links north of Aberdeen proper and east of the College and his lodgings on Spital Brae. It was not the first time he had been here alone. Nor would it be the last.

For a year now, the turmoil in the young man's soul had been steadily growing. Whether he found in the sea some sort of refuge in the midst of his inner confusion, or whether the turbulence of the wind and waves during a storm offered a solace to the raging of his own internal storms, even he did not know. He only knew that the sea drew him, and somehow comforted him. He did not resist its lure. When the questions in his troubled mind grew unbearable, at whatever hour, day or night, he would leave his work, walk across the links east of Kings, a distance of about half a mile, and find himself once more at home on the sandy shore.

He had always loved the sea, since his family's regular visits to Portsoy to visit his uncle and cousins. Back then he had wanted to be a sailor. At twelve the ocean's charm had been focused on the high adventure of a life on board a great sailing ship.

It was different now. In his morose moods he thought the sea drew him because it reminded him of death, with which he had become equally fascinated. In the more optimistic moments, equally a part of his dual nature, he would simply have said he liked the sea because he identified with the ongoing tension it clearly felt—being pulled at once toward the shore and away from it.

That was how he felt tonight, pulled and repelled at the same time. Pulled and attracted toward the notion of a God who could love—truly *love*!—all men; yet repelled by the inconsistencies of the God so many of his friends and relatives seemed content to believe in—an angry God who was able to . . .

He could not even force the notion into his mind!

He was convinced both ideas could not be true! His professor of Natural Philosophy had told him only today that opposites could not coexist.

God could not, he reasoned, be both things at once! He could not, as the Scriptures said, *be* love, and at the same time administer eternal damnation and doom to half the men and women of His own creation.

It could not be so!

Once again the ragings within his mind began afresh.

He stopped and turned toward the sea, the edges of whose waves pounded the shore some forty feet away. Even in the darkness he could see the front of the approaching tempest just a mile or two offshore—its blackness punctuated now and then with a flash of lightning.

He shouted something at the top of his lungs into the wind. But there was no one to hear him. Even as the words were swallowed up by the whistling squall about him, he had forgotten them himself. For he was now running in full stride, off along the sand. Had there been anyone to see, they would scarcely have noticed the tears streaming down his face as he ran, for by now large random drops were falling from the sky as harbingers of the fast-gathering storm, and who could distinguish the tears of anguish from the tears of the sky on a night so dark as this?

On he ran, past the end of the links, until the stretch of dreary beach widened out on his left to make way for the river's exit to the sea. Still he ran, panting heavily now, his large frame sweating freely as his lungs began to ache from the strain.

Gradually he slowed as the mouth of the Don loomed before him. Farther he could not go, for the river had already begun to swell in prelude to the coming of winter.

Exhausted, he stopped, sank to his knees, and was still save for the heaving of his torso replacing the air he had spent.

Suddenly he lifted both hands to the sky and cried, "Oh, God . . . help me!"

Even as the plea left his lips, a white flash of lightning illuminated the sky, followed by a deafening crash of thunder. The torrent was finally unleashed, sweeping over the kneeling youth on the beach. But he hardly felt the drenching rain upon his back.

He only hid his face in his hands, and wept.

CHAPTER SEVEN

ABERDEEN
(1840–1845)

When George MacDonald came to Aberdeen in 1840 a few months prior to his sixteenth birthday, the direction of his life immediately began to change. As he later said of his occasional fictional self, "A life lay behind Robert Falconer, and a life lay before him. He stood on a shoal between. The life behind him was in its grave. . . . The life before him was not yet born" (*Robert Falconer*, Ch. 51). Forces quickly came to bear upon him which, all taken together, contributed to his growth into the man he ultimately became.

George MacDonald came to Aberdeen as a young teenager who, though questioning, still clung in large measure to the values and spiritual viewpoints of his Calvinistic upbringing. He was uncomfortable with them, but he had not yet entirely cut the string. Almost within weeks, however, a wider sphere of social awareness prevailed upon his sensitive mind. Boyhood was behind him and manhood stood waiting on the threshold. And by the time he left the university five years later, the viewpoints he held throughout adulthood—views which were distinctly at odds with what he had been taught in early life, views which formed the foundation of his ministry and writing career, and views which all his life long placed him in the center of controversy—were substantially in place.

Therefore, the years 1840 to 1845 are crucial to an understanding of George MacDonald's life, for they signal the final days of his apprenticeship so to speak, the end of his youth and the beginning of his manhood. His mental and spiritual development during these years, the forces impinging upon him, and the questions he wrestled with as he continued his attempt to integrate the teachings of his past with what he considered to be his own fresh insights and revelations are foundational to a comprehension of his later writings.

Preparation for the University

Fifteen-year-old George MacDonald left Huntly and followed his older brother Charles to the great northern coastal port of Aberdeen, thirty-eight miles to the southeast, to enter King's College, later the University of Aberdeen, which had been founded in 1495 to provide higher education to those living in the north and northeast of Scotland, the Highlands, and the Islands.

Though the quality of education and teaching at Aberdeen was high, the educational system was geared in many ways to the poor scholar; many of Aberdeen's students came from lower on the social ladder than those from the south of Scotland or at the English universities Oxford and Cambridge. They were often from cottar, ploughman, or shepherd background, and the university, seeking to raise educational standards in the north, did what it could to cater to the needs of such students. Frequently, such young men would work at home for the seven months of summer and during harvest earn enough money to support themselves during the five months (November through March) when the university was actually in session, earning after four terms an M.A., or master's degree.

At the beginning of each year's session, a series of tests was administered, forming the basis for the distribution of scholarship ("bursary") funds for the following term. Young lads entering the university for the first time, if they intended to enter the Bursary Competition, would be sent to the city two to six months early for intensive study and coaching in preparation, particularly in Latin. And it was not altogether unheard of to see an occasional bearded man in the midst of these tutored boys, men who had spent their lives on farms, studying in their spare moments while saving every penny in the hope of some day "winnin' t' the college."

Therefore, with Mr. Millar's encouragement, it was decided that George should go to the university, and he arrived in August of 1840, where for three months he studied at the Aulton (Old Town) Grammar School in Old Aberdeen in preparation for the Bursary Competition.

Though his three months at the Grammar School may seem almost negligible in light of the total course of MacDonald's education, it was nevertheless a significant time for his introduction to the life of Aberdeen. For the first time he was away from home and living with other students. At one time George's father had been a prosperous businessman and industrialist, but by now had sunk to the status of a struggling miller, and finances were always a problem throughout the lad's university years. His lodgings were very modest. Coming from rural Huntly with its 3,500 inhabitants to Aberdeen with its 65,000 provided instant exposure to many new people and experiences and social influences. In the coming years this exposure had great impact on his moral development, yet he remained a very private, even a solitary young man. His moods would swing dramatically from peaks of sanguine enthusiasm to opposite periods of quietude and reflection. At one moment the very center of social attention, he could turn quickly into a loner. He took his studies seriously and found himself thinking more and more through the implications of the wider context of the new worlds he was entering.

As his own later writings give the clearest autobiographical glimpses into his childhood, so too, no more vivid portrait of certain of his university experiences and the flowering of his mental and spiritual awareness can be gained than through his own words in *Alec Forbes of Howglen* and *Robert Falconer*, both of whose title characters went from their own Huntlys (Glamerton and Rothieden) to the university in the city.

Describing the studies and play, the varieties of backgrounds represented, and his own erratic involvement through the eyes of one of his favorite fictional characters, he wrote: "If the School work was dry it was thorough. If that Academy had no sweetly shadowing trees . . . beyond still was the sea and the sky; and that court, morning and afternoon, was filled with the shouts of eager boys, kicking the football with mad rushings to and fro. . . . And if the master was stern and hard, he was true; if the pupils feared him, they yet cared to please him; if there might be found not a few more widely read scholars than he, it would be hard to find a better teacher."

Though it is Robert Falconer's experiences thus described, there can be little doubt it was George MacDonald himself who "would rush into the thick of the football game, fight like a maniac for one short burst, and then retire and look on. He oftener regarded than mingled. He seldom joined his fellows after school hours, for his work lay both upon his conscience and his hopes . . . but sometimes, looking up from his 'Virgil' or his Latin version, and seeing the blue expanse in the distance . . . he would fling down his dictionary or his pen, rush from his garret, and fly in a straight line . . . down to the waste shore of the great deep [the North Sea being less than half a mile away]" (*Robert Falconer,* Ch. 30).

In November the tests were held, and again the description of Robert Falconer's experience sheds light on the occasion:

"Slowly the hours went, and yet the dreaded, hoped-for day came quickly. The quadrangle of the stone-crowned college grew more awful in its silence and emptiness every time Robert passed it. . . . October faded softly by, with its keen, fresh mornings, and cold memorial green-horizoned evenings. . . . November came, 'chill and drear,' . . . through whose long shadows anxious young faces gathered in the quadrangle, or under the arcade, each with his 'Ainsworth's Dictionary,' the sole book allowed, under his arm. But when the sacrist appeared and unlocked the public school, and the black-gowned professor walked into the room, and the door was left open for the candidates to follow, then indeed a great awe fell upon the assembly, and the lads crept into their seats as if to a trial for life before the bench of the incorruptible. They took their places; a portion of Robertson's 'History of Scotland' was given them to turn into Latin; and soon there was nothing to be heard in the assembly but the turning of the leaves of dictionaries, and the scratching of pens constructing the first rough copy of the Latinized theme.

"It was done. Four weary hours, nearly five, one or two of which passed like minutes, the others as if each minute had been an hour, went by, and Robert, in a kind of desperation, after a final reading of the Latin, gave in his paper, and left the room. When he got home . . . he returned to the torture—took out his first copy and went over it once more. Horror of horrors! a . . . *maximus error.* Mary, Queen of Scots, had been left so far behind in the beginning of the paper, that she forgot the rights of her sex in the middle of it, and in the accusative of a future participle passive . . . had submitted to be *dum,* and her rightful *dam* was henceforth and forever debarred.

"He rose, rushed out of the house, down through the garden, across two fields and a wide road, across the links, and so to the moaning lip of the sea. . . .

"The next day he had to translate a passage from 'Tacitus'; after executing which somewhat heartlessly, he did not open a Latin book for a whole week. The very sight of one was disgusting to him. He wandered about the new town, along Union Street, up and down the stairs that led to the lower parts, haunted the quay, watched the vessels, learned their forms, their parts and capacities, made friends with a certain Dutch captain . . . and on the whole . . . contrived to spend the week with considerable enjoyment. Nor does an occasional episode of lounging hurt a life with any true claims to the epic form.

"The day of decision at length arrived. Again the black-robed powers assembled, and again the hoping, fearing lads . . . gathered to hear their fate. Name after name was called out—a twenty Pound bursary to the first, one of seventeen to the next, three or four of fifteen and fourteen, and so

The interior of the couryard in the oldest part of King's College where MacDonald (and his fictional Robert Falconer and Alec Forbes) spent many hours.

on, for about twenty, and still no Robert Falconer. At last, lagging wearily in the rear, he heard his name, went up listlessly, and was awarded five Pounds" (*Robert Falconer*, Ch. 30).

In actuality, George MacDonald fared somewhat better, winning what was called the Fullarton Bursary, which amounted to fourteen pounds per year—not a huge sum, but an amount that would generally have been sufficient to cover all of a student's university fees, as well as a good part of his living expenses for the five months of the term. And with the traditional bags of oats and potatoes brought back to the city by the students from the country for winter provisions, he should require only modest additional support from his father. He then entered King's College and began the usual course of curriculum of the four sessions, which were known (instead of freshman, sophomore, etc.) as Bajan, Semi, Tertian, and Magistrand. The first two years concentrated on the standard academic subjects of Greek, Latin, and Mathematics, after which more specialization would generally be sought. A majority of students, planning to become ministers, would study Theology and Moral Philosophy. All students were free to attend classes in any subject whether they intended to pursue it or not. Therefore, in addition to his specialties of Chemistry and Natural Philosophy (Natural Science or Physics), MacDonald more than likely also attended medical and anatomy classes as described in *Alec Forbes;* he remained deeply interested in all the sciences as well as medicine throughout his life.

King's College, Aberdeen

Most students took up lodgings in the Old Town of Aberdeen, and merry pranks and youthful fun became a new ingredient to the university scene once this change was made. George MacDonald appeared to mix well on the social level and to enjoy the company of his fellow students, notwithstanding the distance he occasionally maintained. He lived in a granite house on the top of the hill known as Spital Brae, only about three blocks from King's College in that portion of Aberdeen which separated Old Aberdeen from New. He occupied a garret room overlooking the North Sea, about a half mile away. Of his room and study habits, Glenn Sadler says, "From his attic 'digs' near the top of the Spital Brae in Old Aberdeen . . . he burned midnight oil as he studied chemistry, natural philosophy, history, and dipped into poetry. In his early verses he caught 'the sough [squalor] of the Norlan' Seas' and the northern stars, which became his 'understanding friends.'"[1] Writing to his father in October of 1841, having just arrived in Aberdeen to begin his second term, he appears well integrated into the student life: ". . . I found all our friends well, and our lodgings very comfortable [all his brothers, Charles, John, and Alec, attended the university at more or less overlapping periods, but there is little mention of them in the correspondence], although the lad who lodges along with us is not so much of a gentleman as we could wish; yet I hope he will not be any the worse in that respect for lodging with us. . . ."[2]

The Bajan (freshman) student George MacDonald, to all outside appearances, had "inherited" a substantial portion of the religious faith of his upbringing. Two months into his first term, in January of 1841, his writing clearly reveals the orthodox bent that still held sway in his mind.

> MY DEAR FATHER,
>   I am much obliged to you for the kind letter which you sent me some time ago. I hope I wish to serve God and to be delivered not only from the punishment of sin, but also from its power. . . . Mr. Kennedy was at our Sabbath school soiree in the Old Town. He preaches most excellent sermons, and he never closes without saying something to the unconverted.
>
> I am, your affectionate son,
Geo. MacDonald[3]

Yet even as he wrote these words, forces were at work thrusting ever deeper into the soil of his subconscious the questions that had begun to haunt him years earlier at Huntly. His active young mind was now fully awake, continuing to probe into reasons, meanings, and root causes—searching for the truth in his perspectives. The kite flew ever higher. But unlike Robert Falconer's quick downward stroke, it took George MacDonald four or five years to sever the string that bound him to his past.

Three major factors contributed to a change in young George MacDonald's perception of the world, and at the same time tilled the soil where his active and expanding mind was sending down roots into previously unexplored regions: (1) *Changing social conditions in Britain*; (2) *The religious atmosphere of Aberdeen*; and (3) *The questioning student "mentality."*

Changing Social Conditions in Britain

The 19th century in Great Britain was a period of sweeping, almost cataclysmic, change affecting every level of society. Political reform saw two simultaneous adjustments. In the mid-18th century, during the reigns of Kings George I and II, a severe decline in the power and prestige of the monarchy began, which resulted in a rise in the power of the cabinet form of parliamentary government. At the same time increasing masses of the population began to demand a voice in politics. Whereas previously only the landed classes had controlled British society, now representation began to filter down—first to the wealthy middle classes, then to larger segments of the middle class, and eventually to all men and even women. By the pre-Industrial Revolution standards of 1760, these were astounding, unbelievable changes.

Social change was equally far-reaching. The Industrial Revolution gradually altered England from a rural to an urban society. With the growth of cities came a tremendous increase in the urban working class. This new element began to demand a political voice, and all aspects of society were affected, resulting in educational reform, military reform, and factory reform. Power was shifting. The lower classes were speaking up, demanding their rights, no longer in awe of their aristocratic "betters."

George MacDonald's father, while by no means a wealthy man, was, in the 1820s before the disastrous reversals that hit the family business, nevertheless a member of the middle class by virtue of the quantity of land he farmed and as a result of being a business owner of some means. Class distinctions at that time were considerably more pronounced between the "working" and "middle" classes than they are today. And while the middle classes had risen steadily in wealth since 1760, the working classes and low class tenant farmers remained locked in a much lower social stratum with no way to better themselves.

By the 1820s and 1830s, however, great reform was underway. One of the great political efforts of the mid-19th century was the Chartist Movement, which called for universal male suffrage, annual elections for the House of Commons, reapportionment of electoral districts, and voting by ballot. Along with the call for such political change, there was clamor for a complete overhaul of society, from women's and children's rights to new concern for the poor. The 1830s saw a flurry of reform activity and emerging social awareness. Politically and socially, Britain in the 1840s was a powder keg, waiting to explode. Had circumstances been different she could have found herself in the midst of a civil war or revolution along with many of the countries of continental Europe in 1848.

One of the key points of struggle in Britain concerned the Corn Law of 1815. During the Napoleonic Wars of 1790 to 1815, France and England blockaded each other's coastlines in an attempt to economically starve each other out. Because of the scarcity of new grain coming from the mainland, English landowners were thus able to charge artificially high prices. This went on from 1804 until 1813, until Napoleon was defeated and the blockades were lifted. When grain from the continent began flow-ing into Britain again, inevitably the prices began to drop. Having by this time enjoyed a decade of fat profits, however, the landed classes were reluctant to see prices go down. They pressured Parliament to pass legis-lation to retain high prices by keeping cheap grain out of the country. Since Parliament was still controlled by aristocratic landed interests, the result was the Corn Law of 1815, which preserved the landowners' swollen profits. At the same time it alienated many of the rising lower elements of society. As the years passed, the Corn Law became one of the great rallying cries of the reformers, and though its repeal was regularly demanded, the representation of the working and lower classes in Parliament was never strong enough to bring about its abolition.

Aberdeenshire was predominantly a county of small tenant holdings owned by local land barons or lairds. As a man whose business was on a downhill slide, dependent to an increasing degree on the crops he could grow on the land he leased from the Duke of Gordon, George MacDonald, Sr., found himself suffering the hardships common to small farmers and crofters brought on by the growth of industry. Finally there was sufficient pressure on Parliament to effect the passage of a refinement of the Corn Law, in which a sliding scale was established by which prices were deter-mined. Thus George MacDonald, Sr., along with other grain growers, suf-fered from lower corn prices. Several years of catastrophic potato crop disasters in Ireland and Scotland in the mid-1840s eventually brought about a total repeal of the Corn Law for humanitarian reasons. Combined with the changing economics of the north and the modern developments that made their former bleaching process obsolete, these lower grain prices, along with the potato famine, continued the discouraging trends facing MacDonald's father and his once thriving family business.

In the midst of all these changing social conditions, sixteen-year-old George MacDonald found himself caught in an ideological conflict between the essentially conservative views of his upbringing (and no doubt his sympathetic appreciation for his father's anti-repeal stance on the Corn Law) and the moral necessity of curing the social ills and injus-tices of society. Simply being in Aberdeen, facing the fluctuating social milieu of a reform-hungry country and witnessing the terrible state of the poor in the city, was bound to have its impact on a sensitive nature such as his.

It was little wonder, then, that his involvement in the Blackfriars Con-gregational Church (following his brother Charles' example) under the Rev. John Kennedy, D.D. (pastor from 1836 to 1846) further stimulated his responses to his expanding world. Kennedy was an activist, and, along with progressive politicians, loudly advocated the repeal of the Corn Law. Kennedy's organizational zeal and compassion led to what was called his *School of Industry*, in which were gathered the hordes of beggar children roaming the streets of Aberdeen in order to feed them and provide some means of education. In addition to teaching in the Sunday school, Mac-Donald helped in this work, which further infused him with sympathy for many of the social reforms being called for.

As his second term opened on October 28, 1841, he wrote very sympathetically in a letter to his father concerning the Chartists who were staging a rally in Aberdeen at the time. His reaction was clearly favorable and enthusiastic, even though later in the same letter he makes reference to his father's financial difficulties, which were being made worse by these very reform measures: "I saw a most splendid procession today of the Chartists going out to meet Fergus O'Conner [one of Britain's leading Chartists, then in Aberdeen to speak and drum up support for their cause]. There were about two thousand of them in the procession, and there might have been fifteen thousand on the streets. There were several different bands of music and banners and mottoes innumerable. . . . I was down at the links for a short time while he was addressing the people. The scene was really splendid."[4]

Social change, therefore, was coming to all of Britain, and the young student was swept into it.

The Religious Atmosphere of Aberdeen

Social change was only the beginning. At the same time, great upheaval was occurring throughout Scotland in the religious realm. The church of Scotland was in the midst of fiery internal controversy. For years Aberdeen's churches had tended toward indifferent conservatism. And

Interior of King's College Chapel

indeed, throughout all of Scotland until the early days of the 19th century, people had nothing but the Established Church, or Church of Scotland, to look to. But it had become a "moral waste" to many, driving, for instance, old Mrs. Charles Edward MacDonald, George's grandmother, and others out of the Parish Church altogether. Now suddenly splinter groups were breaking off. Schisms developed. New churches and denominations were begun. Between 1840 and 1844, a veritable storm began to rage throughout all of Scotland in all its denominations. A multitude of theological and doctrinal questions were raised and discussed, especially among students. All the major dissenting denominations were affected—the Presbyterian Church of Scotland, Congregationalists, Baptists, Methodists, Glasites, etc.*

While Calvinistic doctrines still for the most part held sway in all these groups, in the early 1840s there was a great deal of controversy and upheaval within Scotland's churches. Suddenly the granite city's evangelical fervor was awakened, and no better evidence of its vitality could be found than in Dr. Kennedy's ministry, of which young George MacDonald was a part. His own home town of Huntly had been the site for one of the major disputes over church patronage ("the Strathbogie controversy"), and he was right in the thick of it when, in 1843 and centered in Aberdeen itself, the Great Disruption came—a final breaking asunder of the Church of Scotland into two distinct strains.

The Questioning Student Mentality

On many different levels, change was taking place all around young MacDonald in Aberdeen. Everywhere men and women, politicians and clergymen, workers and the poor were seeking reform and asking why things had to remain as they had always been. Immersed in such a mental,

---

*It is difficult for Americans to grasp the British distinction between "Anglican" and "Dissenting" churches, which are both *Protestant* in light of their non-Catholic affiliations. But in most respects the difference between the Anglican *Church of England* and the many "Dissenting" congregations is parallel to the distinction elsewhere between *Catholic* and *Protestant*. *Dissenting* churches took many forms—Presbyterian, Methodist, Baptist, Reformed, etc., all descendants of the great reformers such as Calvin, Knox, the Wesleys, Edwards, etc.—while the Church of England's roots extended back to Henry VIII's break with Catholicism in the early 16th century. In the United States and the rest of Western Europe, the distinction between *Catholic* and *Protestant* is more familiar, while in Great Britain the parallel differentiation is between *Catholic, Anglican,* and *Dissenting.*

These labels are further blurred when studying George MacDonald's life, because of the fact that in Scotland the state church became (in 1560) Presbyterian in a bold break with the Church of England. Thus the "Church of Scotland" was a *dissenting* denomination, as were the many other denominations that sprung up and broke off throughout the years. Despite the common *dissenting* label, the antipathy between the Church of Scotland and other church organizations often ran high, even though most still retained the foundational "Calvinistic" doctrinal mentality. As we have seen, the MacDonald family were "Congregationalists," having been active in Huntly's "Missionar' Kirk." But both the Congregationalists and Church of Scotland Presbyterians were denominations of *dissent* and equally Calvinistic in their outlook.

moral, social, and spiritual climate, it is no wonder that George Mac-
Donald, now a maturing student who was studying to make sense and
order out of his world, would continue to ask questions as he had begun
doing earlier in Huntly.

Students of all ages have been a questioning breed. It is a time of widening horizons, of doubts and theories and quandaries and uncertainties
and moral dilemmas. All these factors were vigorously at work in the student George MacDonald. Many labels have been attached to such times
in life in an attempt to explain the internal reality of what happens—finding oneself, youthful rebellion, overcoming the generation gap, seeking a
new identity, challenging the status quo, shaking off the past, idealistically
trying to better the world. How many of these labels apply to MacDonald
we cannot know with precision. Nor can we ascertain to what degree he
was swept into the fray of student activism in support of the many
"causes" that presented themselves. Undoubtedly the pressures had their
impact on him. He was a typical nonconforming student in a variety of
ways—growing a beard at a time when such a thing was looked upon with
horror as "heathenish," dressing occasionally in outlandish Highland garb
for effect, demonstrating extremes of moods, and so on.

One thing *is* clear. He continued to question. But now he was not only
weighing the tenets of the religion of his upbringing. To this were now
added questions about social injustices, questions concerning how spiritual truths and social problems might be interrelated, and questions about
the relationship among the many factions within Christendom and what
unity among them might mean.

Most importantly, he began to scrutinize the depths and validity of his
own relationship with God. Very early in his days at Aberdeen he became
dissatisfied with a merely "inherited" faith, and began to seek urgently
after something more dynamic. His journey in this search no doubt paralleled that of Robert Falconer, including the despair and misery that came
from his doubts, about whom he later wrote: "I cannot, if I would, follow
him on his travels into the phantasm[s] of his past. I suspect, however, that
much of it left upon his mind no recallable impressions. I suspect that
much of it looked to himself in the retrospect like a painful dream, with
only certain objects and occurrences standing prominent enough to clear
the moonlight mist enwrapping the rest.

"What the precise nature of his misery was I shall not even attempt to
conjecture. That would be to intrude within the holy place of a human
heart" (*Robert Falconer*, Ch. 51).

No longer would the faith of his father, his grandmother, the church, or
whatever doctrines he may have been taught as a child suffice. However
far he had to go (even if the journey was within the depths of his own
mind rather than to Switzerland and beyond as it was for Falconer), whatever personal miseries he had to endure in the process, in coming to Aberdeen George MacDonald had embarked upon a road from which he
could not turn back. He had to discover whether God was real, and if He
was, what was He like? No surviving letters indicate the precise paths this

search took, but by the time he had reached its end he.had been over-whelmed by a desire to be intimately related with his Maker. Yet his conception of the character of God would be vastly different than that of the God he had been taught to fear as a child.

MacDonald the Student

Therefore, in a sense George MacDonald lived in two worlds during his years at King's College in Aberdeen: the outer world of the university, of friends, of classes, of activities; and the inner world of his pilgrimage of faith. For Robert Falconer, too, the journey began in Aberdeen and lasted four years. And there is little doubt that in setting down Falconer's travels on the continent, George MacDonald was offering a rare glimpse into his own soul as it journeyed, perhaps unseen by anyone other than himself, through similar mental, spiritual, and emotional byways.

From surviving statements of others, it is clear that George MacDonald was a mixed and complex personality, alternating between heights of gaiety and depths of anxiety, even depression. He was certainly not anti-social, and was popular in academic circles and debating societies. Games of drawing-room charades had come from France in the early 1820s and had by this time penetrated from England to Aberdeen. He enjoyed these greatly, and it is told that on one occasion he was handed a

*Typical street in Old Aberdeen, mostly unchanged since
MacDonald's student days.*

green coat as part of the act. But it was old and buttonless. So he cut a huge carrot into discs and sewed them on the coat with great effect and laughter for all present. Remembering him years later, one of his fellow students said that George MacDonald was quickly recognized as "a youth of imaginative power, but, like the typical Celt, dreamily careless of fame and classlist positions," and remarked further, "I remember the radiance of a tartan coat he wore—the most dazzling affair in dress I ever saw a student wear, but characteristic of the young Celtic minstrel."[5]

He was well liked and friendly, but deep in thought much of the time. Writing of him in 1898, Robert Troup, who had been introduced to him in 1843 when MacDonald was nineteen (and would later marry his cousin), said, "He was studious, quiet, sensitive, imaginative, frank, open, speaking freely what he thought. His love of truth was intense, only equalled by his scorn of meanness, his purity and his moral courage. So I found him when I became acquainted with him. . . . So I found him ever since.

"I have recollections of him sitting by himself after the meal was over, silent and thoughtful, sometimes apparently musing, and sometimes reading while the others were talking. At other times he took his part heartily in the conversation that was going on. His older friends were anxious about his spiritual state."[6]

Another, William Geddes, afterward Principal of the University, wrote to George MacDonald in 1865, ". . . Though you did not mix much with the students at College, and indeed hardly cared to descend into the ordinary arena of emulation, your fellow-students were not unaware of the talents you possessed. I remember distinctly the universal impression regarding you, that you were master of powers which you had not put to the full measure of proof, but which were touched to fine issues and destined to yield great things. . . ."[7]

Old Aberdeen was situated only about half a mile from the shore of the North Sea, which was bordered by great rolling grassy golf links. MacDonald often walked through the links to the shore, many times leaving his lodgings late at night for a thoughtful stroll on the beach. His moods were variable, he was often depressed, lived in much real loneliness, and felt the need for frequent and long solitary walks. He had always possessed a great love for the sea. Thus when the perplexing doubts of manhood began pressing in upon him, he turned to the lonely solace of the waves upon the shore for comfort. The description of a walk Alec Forbes took with a friend to the very places haunted by young George MacDonald conveys the doleful tone reflective of his spirits at the time:

"The day had been quite calm, but now a sudden gust of wind from the north-east swept across the pier. . . . They were now close to the sea. On the other side of the wall which rose on their left, they could hear the first of the sea-waves. It was a dreary place—no sound even indicating the neighborhood of life. On one side, the river below them went flowing out to the sea in the dark, giving a cold sluggish gleam now and then, as if it were a huge snake heaving up a bend of its wet back, as it hurried away to join its fellows; on the other side rose a great wall of stone, beyond which was the sound of long waves following in troops out of the dark, and falling upon a low moaning coast. Clouds hung above the sea; and above the clouds two or three disconsolate stars . . .

"They climbed the steep rugged steps, and stood on the broad wall, hearing the sea-pulses lazily fall at its foot. The wave crept away after it fell, and returned to fall again like a weary hound. There was hardly any life in the sea. How mournful it was to lie out there, the wintry night, beneath an all but starless heaven, with the wind vexing it when it wanted to sleep! . . . Up the slope the waves rushed, and down the slope they sank again, with that seemingly aimless and resultless rise and fall, which makes the sea so dreary and sad to those men and women who are not satisfied without some goal in view, some outcome of their labours; for it goes on and on, answering ever to the call of sun and moon, and the fierce trumpet of the winds, yet working nothing but the hopeless wear of the bosom in which it lies bound for ever" (*Alec Forbes of Howglen*, Ch. 42).

The quest of his spirit gave rise to a chaos of thoughts and emotions that began to find vent in a great quantity of poetry, much of it bleak and questioning, written during his university years. One of his favorite sayings at the time was, "I wis we war a' deid!" (I wish we were all dead!) And his verses show a lonely preoccupation with death, which reveals not only his poetic fervor, but also the prevailing melancholy and introspective mood that made up his mental condition at the time.

> Bury me, bury me lone
> Where no dirge is sung and no music plays
> In echoes around my sepulchral stone,
>   And the only funeral lays
> Be the hollow moan, in its rocky caves
> Of ocean awaking its thousand waves.
>
> Bury me, bury me deep,
> In some lonely cave on the wild sea's shore
> There are none o'er my grave will seek to weep,
>   And the mad waves' tempest roar
> Will soothe this spirit, when, shrouded in gloom,
> It visits the strange and unrecked of tomb.[8]

CHAPTER EIGHT

THE GREAT LIBRARY
IN THE NORTH
(1842)

The struggle to come to terms with what he believed was a long and difficult one for George MacDonald. He was becoming more and more ill at ease with the Calvinistic doctrine of election, or predestination, which in its less balanced forms seemed to indicate that God had deliberately created some people in order to doom them to eternal torment, while He reserved His special favor for others. Similarly, he was uncomfortable with the stern negativity that characterized the God of his grandmother. The foundational role of the "lake of fire" in extreme Calvinist thought, in which the everlasting punishment of sinners in hell appeared to undergird all else even to a greater degree than God himself, was a particular stumbling block to him. The Christian faith, he thought, *must* be more than a mere adherence to a set of doctrines such as those of the Westminster Confession or the Shorter Catechism. There *must* be more to God than a jealous wrath ready to pour out its vengeance upon unknowing sinners.

At the same time, other Christians were thinking along the same lines. Many such issues were raised and discussed heatedly, especially among students. At that time a bitter controversy was raging within the Congregational Church in Scotland over the doctrine of universal redemption, the antithesis of the very core of Calvinism. In Glasgow some students were expelled from the Congregational Theological Academy for adhering to the belief that Christ's atoning work was available to all men, not just to the "elect," and would in fact ultimately triumph even over hell itself. The notion that a God of love could possibly rest while souls were left tormenting in hell had become an idea such thoughtful students could not scripturally reconcile, and MacDonald took a great interest in the controversy. He along with others in Aberdeen's Blackfriar's congregation found such ideas exciting, offering the possibility of release from the mental chains of past teachings which they could no longer hold in good conscience. Those in authority in the church, however, took a dim view of raising such heretical issues; a number of Congregational churches in Scotland lost their endowments from the denomination for siding with the outspoken rebellious students from Glasgow.

Dr. Kennedy, himself strongly Calvinist in his outlook, and MacDonald's elder brother Charles (then in business in Aberdeen, and who felt it his responsibility to keep watch over his younger brother's doctrinal orthodoxy) both grew quite anxious about his spiritual condition. Too many questions and the raising of too many doubts, they feared, was a sure road to perdition.

A Break in Schooling

The typical student at Aberdeen was often from farming stock and would therefore usually return home from the city after each term to work on the land, thereby earning enough money for the next year's session. Though he was physically strong, George MacDonald was unfit for such work because of the weakness of his lungs. Therefore, he began thinking of other means to earn extra money, especially important in light of his father's declining finances. After two years at King's, his bursary proving insufficient to meet all his expenses and his father having no money with which to help him, he sought and found alternate employment.

MacDonald's new job apparently lasted throughout the summer months of 1842 and long enough into the fall or winter that he was unable to attend the university session of 1842–43. Very little is known of this mysterious time, and there are no letters surviving from the period. But it clearly had a tremendous impact on him. Both his son Greville and Rev. Robert Troup record the fact that this summer was spent "in a certain castle or mansion in the far North . . . in cataloguing a neglected library," and the theme of a young man working in a large library found its way into seven of his novels. Greville adds further, "The library, wherever it was, and whatever its scope, added much to the materials upon which his imagination worked in future years."[1]

For a lover of books such as MacDonald nothing could have been better. The library contained many volumes and authors he had not met before. He sampled the 16th-century poets and the medieval romances. But most of all, his familiarity with the German language led him to tackle many German classics and authors. And these more than anything served to solidify new directions of thought in which he had been moving, propelling him forward into whole new vistas of discovery. In addition to the descriptions of carting dusty books from place to place and building new bookshelves, found in *Wilfred Cumbermede*, the only personal words we can glean about this experience are through the mouth of the narrator of *The Portent* and through the mouth of Mr. Cupples in *Alec Forbes of Howglen*.

"'Efter I had taen my degree,' began Mr. Cupples, '. . . I heard o' a grit leebrary i' the north—I winna say whaur—that wantit the han' o' a man that kenned what he was aboot, to pit in dacent order, sae that a body cud lay his han's upon a buik whan he wantit it. . . . Dinna imaigin' it was a public library. Na, na. It belonged to a grit an' gran' hoose—the Lord hae respec till't, for it's no joke o' a hoose that—as I weel kent afore a' was ower! Weel, I wrought awa', likin' the wark weel, for a buik's the bonniest thing i' the warl'. . . . Weel, ye see, I had a room til mysel', forby the library an' my bedroom—an' a gran' place that was! I didna see onything o' the family, for I had my denner and my wine and a' thing human stammack cud desire served up till me i' my ain room'" (*Alec Forbes of Howglen*, Ch. 30).

Similarly, *The Portent's* narrator goes on:

"Now I was in my element . . . the very outside of a book had a charm to me. It was a kind of sacrament—an outward and visible sign of an inward and spiritual grace; as, indeed, what on God's earth is not? So I set to work amongst the books, and soon became familiar with many titles at least, which had been perfectly unknown to me before. I found a perfect set of our poets . . . although it omitted both Chaucer and George Herbert. I began to nibble at that portion of the collection which belonged to the sixteenth century; but with little success. I found nothing, to my idea, but love poems without any love in them, and so I soon became weary. But I found in the library what I like far better—many romances of a very marvellous sort, and plentiful interruption they gave to the formation of the catalogue. I likewise came upon a whole nest of the German classics, which seemed to have kept their places undisturbed, in virtue of their unintelligibility . . . happening to be a tolerable reader of German, I found in these volumes a mine of wealth inexhaustible" (*The Portent*, Ch. 7).

In his biography, Greville reflects on the possibilities: "It is curious that I can find no record of how the summer months of 1842 were spent. In *Alec Forbes* we find Cupples telling of some 'grit leebrary i' the far North' where he was employed, and some of this I take to be autobiographical. I have been at considerable pains, both in correspondence and in travelling, to ascertain where this library was situated; for its importance in my father's education cannot be questioned. But I have not been successful, though I have a strong suspicion that it was Thurso Castle. . . . It has a fine library, and its owner . . . [was] a collector of German literature, which fact tallies with the account of the library in *The Portent*. The fact that my grandfather [George MacDonald, Sr.] had some sort of intimacy with him is suggested by the use of his name on an advertisement as recommending the potato-flour . . . manufactured by the MacDonald Brothers at Huntly . . .

"The only other possible place is Dunbeath . . . there was formerly a 'wonderful' library there. . . . [The owner] says that friends of hers think it very probable that this was the very library my father catalogued."[2]

Both these castles are located in the extreme north of mainland Scotland in Caithness, and Thurso is today in ruins. This particular interlude is significant in George MacDonald's life, however, not because of the location of the library, but for what the experience represented in his mental and spiritual growth. It seems to have crystallized many of his disordered thoughts and begun the focusing process that would ultimately bring him out of his tunnel of questioning and doubt.

Novalis

In the early 1800s in the theological world of evangelical Protestantism (in the U.S.) and Dissent (in Britain), Germany represented a fearsome monster bent on destroying the faithful. The mere mention of "German theology" was enough to raise the battle cry among any group of staunch Calvinists.[3] How shocking, therefore, for young George MacDonald to begin reading the likes of Schiller, Goethe, Hoffman, and mystics such as Jacob Boehme or Swedenborg—in whose writings can occasionally be seen traces of evolution, pantheism, mysticism, and hints of many Eastern religions whose concepts of God are far removed from the Judeo-Christian ideas indeed.

But instead of weakening his concept of the Christian God, MacDonald's experiences with the German writers and other mystics served instead to strengthen it in a way that conservative Calvinism had never been able to. Rather than adopting the specific doctrines and beliefs of these men, MacDonald took from them support; he could see that he was no longer "alone" in exploring untried regions of faith. Others had been there before. They too had questioned. And too, his reading gave boundaries to his doubts. Instead of accepting the distant and clearly unbiblical tenets of these mystics, their views served to swing young MacDonald back more solidly toward the faith of his past. He took what he could gain from them, left behind what he felt was in error in their theology, and emerged stronger in his own beliefs. In his novels of later years he refers to Jean-Paul, Schiller, Heinrich Heine, and Goethe. Most influential of all the Germans was the more obscure German poet Novalis (Georg Friedrich Philipp von Hardenberg, 1772–1801), in whose debt MacDonald remained all his life.

More than anything, this time away from the university gave George MacDonald a renewed hope. His acquaintance with the poets George Herbert and Henry Vaughan particularly showed him a God who was all goodness and love. He had hardly dared hope that the God portrayed by his grandmother might not be the true God at all! He was finding, instead, a God who was *good*, whose love pervaded all, who was a Father like his own kind father, whose love and kindness and forgiveness overshadowed all else.

These new authors also gave a reverent place to nature, and he took heart in knowing that other men, like himself, saw God's handiwork in every speck of creation. The words of Novalis, whose parents had been Moravians but who himself became a Roman Catholic, appealed to MacDonald's mystical and poetic side and drove him closer to his heavenly Father:

Uplifted is the stone,
And all mankind is risen;
We all remain thine own,
And vanished is our prison.
All troubles flee away
Before thy golden cup;
For Earth nor Life can stay
When with our Lord we sup.

*   *   *   *   *

If I him but have,
     If he be but mine,
If my heart, hence to the grave,
     Ne'er forgets his love divine—
Know I nought of sadness,
Feel I nought but worship, love, and gladness.

Where I have but him
     Is my fatherland;
Every gift a precious gem
     Come to me from his own hand!
Brothers long deplored,
Lo, in his disciples, all restored.

*   *   *   *   *

He lives! he's risen from the dead!
     To every man I shout;
His presence over us is spread,
     Goes with us in and out.

(Twelve of the Spiritual Songs of Novalis)

But though Novalis loved God and put into poetical and prose form his deepest feelings about Jesus, his faith, and the world God had made, he was no *traditional* Christian in the sense that grandmother MacDonald would approve of. He was a mystic in the full sense of the word. And worse—a Catholic! Yet MacDonald was drawn to him and received nourishment in his writings for his hungry soul. He was drawn no doubt also by the tone of melancholy and the themes of death that especially pervade Novalis's *Hymns to the Night* and *Spiritual Songs,* both of which were written under the shadow of his early death at the age of twenty-nine, and which coincided with much of what downhearted student George MacDonald had been feeling. In his reading he was encouraged, sensing in Novalis a man who clearly wrestled with many of the same dilemmas and doubts that he did, who was not a Calvinist, yet who loved God and was not afraid to express his mystical beliefs in imaginative writings. Here was a whole new side of the Christian faith MacDonald had never known existed! All Christians didn't necessarily have to follow the same Calvinistic path!

The months at the library, his reading of the Germans and other authors, and his falling in love with the writings of Novalis did not provide

George MacDonald with a "new theology," so to speak, as if he one day threw out the old and adopted a set of new, modern viewpoints. But with the foundation of the previous two years of reevaluation, his experiences away from Aberdeen in the north seemed to give more focused direction to his search for spiritual truth, opening his eyes to insights he had previously seen only vaguely and incompletely, offering him hope that he might eventually find a faith he could accept and make his own. Greville comments that "this library led him out of doors and beyond the bounds of academic scholarship." His view of everything was henceforth larger and more expansive than before. And from this point on he was able to begin integrating all the factors that would ultimately form the core of his own belief.

Undoubtedly, the library experience marked a major turning point. When it was over, the beginning of the integration process had begun. He returned to Aberdeen stronger within himself, more able to face his doubts and questions in a positive light, realizing perhaps for the first time that God would not judge him for his honesty, and realizing too that his instincts regarding God's character were valid—that God's *goodness* and love were supreme and that His wrath and punishment of sin had to fit into the overriding quality that was the essence of his nature: *love*.

Questions remained. But he came back fortified mentally and emotionally, prepared to continue his quest, and having turned a significant corner. As Greville says, "George MacDonald, his engagement in the great library done, resumed his studies in Aberdeen much strengthened, we may presume, in mind and imaginative outlook. If his life's adventure was no more than opened, to have bravely begun it was a foretaste of victory."[4]

CHAPTER NINE

THE NEW OUTLOOK
(1843-1845)

After returning from his sojourn in the north in the middle of what would have been his third session, George MacDonald acquired a teaching position in the Aberdeen Central Academy (still standing in the middle of Little Belmont Street in Aberdeen), where he taught arithmetic from February to November of 1843 "with great spirit and skill" according to the headmaster, Mr. Thomas Merton. He remained on intimate terms with Dr. Kennedy, his Congregationalist minister, and in addition to his position at the academy, now went to Dr. Kennedy's home three times a week to tutor a student, and was, though a nervous speaker, part of the Debating Society.

Discerning the Meat, Discarding the Bones

The upheaval in Scotland's religious world continued; this was the year of the Great Disruption of the Church of Scotland into the Established Church and the Free Church. Though his footing was sounder, Mac-Donald's struggle to find scriptural solutions to the perplexities of his faith continued. For years he had intuitively sensed that God's goodness must extend to all men, and that His mercy must undergird even His treatment of sinners. After reading many works by Novalis, these convictions were stronger than ever, and the hunger within him grew all the more urgent to discover the nature of God's character.

Many in such a position, discontent with what they have been taught and rebelling against their past, have the tendency to reject the whole system of their upbringing because of the fallacies they observe in it. This is indeed the classic pitfall of youthful revolt in all ages. Carried away with challenging hypocrisy that rightfully should be corrected, young rebels wrongly allow the pendulum of change to swing too far in the opposite direction and succeed only in erecting a new system, just as intolerant (albeit differently) as what they rebelled against in the first place.

Throughout the ages, men and women, fed up with the sham they have witnessed in their superficially religious parents, teachers, priests, and pastors, have made the lethal mistake of discarding Christianity itself rather than the emptiness of a few of its feeble adherents. They raise up an imaginary version of Christianity based on their misconceptions and then proceed to tear it to shreds, never bothering to look at the real thing itself.

Not a trace of this fatal error is to be found in George MacDonald. Never did he throw out the scriptural core of Christianity in his frustration with incomplete forms of it. His desire was always to find the truth, whatever it might be that such truth would require of him. He would later write that to see a truth, to understand it, and to love it are one. His search was not toward dogma, creeds, or theories but always toward the person and character of God, and then his personal responsibility as a man made in the image of God.

MacDonald, therefore, could not content himself, as so many do, with simplistically concluding, "Since there are inconsistencies in my perception of Christianity, I will leave it for a philosophy more to my liking." He was not after a philosophy that suited his tastes; he was after truth. Therefore the queries continued to burn: What is God really like? Are all things in heaven and earth subservient to His wrath or to His love? Is the *peace* the Lord spoke of available, and if so, where? What was the essence of "the gospel"? What was to be his personal response to God, and to his fellow man?

The Search Continues

Thus his internal quest, like Robert Falconer's, continued into his third and fourth years at King's College. Greville says of this time: "In spite of close touch with fellow-men in study and social pleasures, George MacDonald lived in much real loneliness, his poetic longings taking him far afield. The sea particularly called him to share its turmoil and its peace, its mystic solace in rhythmic beat, its kindred protest in evasion of control."[1] He goes on to quote Robert Troup, who says MacDonald and another friend, James Maconochie, would often take walks together. One wild night, about ten o'clock, they went to the golf links and the seashore to watch the storm. Troup recalled: "When Maconochie returned about midnight to his sister's, he looked anxious and disturbed, and said, 'I hope George MacDonald is not going out of his mind. . . . When we got to the shore, he walked backwards and forwards on the sands amid howling winds and the beating spray, with the waves coming up to our feet; and all the time he went on addressing the sea and the waves and the storm.'"[2]

MacDonald continued to write poetry to express the convulsive thoughts swirling within him. His poems of this time reveal a youthful poetic fervor, along with the prevailing introspective tone of pessimism with which his sporadic hope was still fitfully mingled. In verse he explored the concept of the blessing of death, a theme that would find its way into most of his later works. He made translations from the German

The Chapel, King's College, Aberdeen

poets he had discovered. A blank verse narrative called *David* of this period a few years later offered him his first opportunity for publication in January of 1846 when it appeared in the *Congregational Magazine*.

He corresponded regularly with his cousin Helen MacKay from Banff who was now attending school in London. She was highly educated, an accomplished musician, older than himself, and very beautiful; and MacDonald, according to some, imagined himself in love with her. He found great comfort in her sympathy with his moods. Consequently, he wrote her a series of love poems, even writing out an entire album of poems which he sent her. The infatuation was short-lived, however, for she was married in 1844.

Between 1843 and 1845 he completed his Tertian and Magistrand terms at the university, receiving his Master of Arts degree in April of 1845. During these latter years he emphasized the sciences—graduating high in his class in natural philosophy (physics) and with honors in chemistry, though he was still in complete doubt about what he was fit for in life. His mastery of German led him to consider going to Giessen in Germany to continue his studies in chemistry under the renowned Baron von Liebig, one of the discoverers of chloroform, but finances stood in the way. Toward the end of his college career, he became strongly interested in studying medicine (a desire lived out fictionally through Alec Forbes and Robert Falconer), but again money prevented continued education and training. While specializing in the precise sciences of physics and chemistry, he shared with his cousin Helen that he felt that he would one day be a poet, and thus in the end concentrated more and more of his studies on modern languages and literature.

Slowly the light began to dawn upon his long-troubled spirit. His reading and his study of Scripture at last convinced him that God's love was supreme, that everything in the universe, even hell itself, *had* to be subservient to that love, and that a God of love could never predestine the majority of mankind to a life of torment without Him. With such realizations, the person of Jesus Christ came closer and closer to the young man who had been seeking Him so long.

The pilgrimage had been a long one, beginning in early childhood. In 1882 he wrote: "I well remember feeling as a child that I did not care for God to love me if he did not love everybody: the kind of love I needed was love essential to my nature . . . the love therefore that all men needed, the love that belonged to their nature as the children of the Father, a love he could not give me except he gave it to all men" (*Weighed & Wanting*, Ch. 3). And the "revolutionary yeast" was beginning to rise when he came to Aberdeen. Greville speculates "that when he was little more than seventeen he was in some form or other asking himself the general question, What need for the Gospel if the elect and no others are predestined to be saved?" He then goes on to put into perspective this entire period of his father's life. "But probably it was during his sojourn in the far North that his Calvinistic chains became intolerable. Such a view seems to have been general at home, and his Uncle James, who adhered to the old teaching with quiet satisfaction expressed it as his opinion. But my father, conscious that the awakening began long before his eyes were [fully] open, would ascribe no such definite period to his conversion."[3]

The Process of Awakening

Whether or not he could affix a certain moment to the awakening, conversion, or solidification of a confused but real faith, by the time George MacDonald left the university in 1845 he had emerged from the tunnel of his doubts, recognizing the importance of those doubts in the process of formulating his eventual faith—another lifelong truth he stressed in his writings. Though his lengthy poem of 198 stanzas, *The Disciple*, was not written until many years later (it was released in 1868), it largely represented MacDonald's train of thought as he worked his spiritual quandary through to the end. The final words in what Greville calls "that pageant of spiritual moods" in one sense reveal the underlying significance of his entire time at King's:

"The man that feareth, Lord, to doubt,
    In that fear doubteth thee."

Some find it sufficient to accept what they have been taught without question. But often such acceptance is not faith at all but rather a dull, sleepy acquiescence, which finds it easier to submit to a certain precept than to inquire whether it be true. For George MacDonald, however, the validity of a thing was not measured by the number who happened to believe it, nor by what criticism he may have come under by questioning it, but rather by whether or not it rang true to the character of God as revealed in the New Testament.

Thus we find *The Disciple* reflective of his journey "out" of the tradition of his past, and "into" a new and personal faith of his own. Having ridden the swinging pendulum from the rigid confines of Calvinism all the way in the opposite direction toward liberal German theology, he was at last ready for it to swing back and come to rest in the solid biblical middle ground where he could take his stand. The earlier doubts and explorations of his seeking heart had strengthened him and, having been tested to the depths, his new faith was at last ready to send its roots down toward the bedrock from whence it could never again be shaken. The dedication to the poem speaks of the search to find the truth amidst the traditions that surround it: "To all who ... would keep the grain, and cast the husk away—that it may feed the living seed. . . ."

Innocently he opens with regret, almost shame, that he can no longer love the spiritual words proclaimed in pulpit, hymns, and solemn tradition. Though nature speaks to him, the church does not.

I do not care for singing psalms;
    I tire of good men's talk;
To me there is no joy in palms,

Or white-robed, solemn walk.
I love to hear the wild winds meet,
The wild old winds at night;
To watch the cold stars flash and beat,
The feathery snow alight.

But for thy temple in the sky,
Its pillars strong and white—
I cannot love it, though I try,
And long with all my might.

He goes on to reveal his doubts, the lowness of his spirits, and the cry of his heart after God.

I read good books. My heart despairs.
In vain I try to dress
My soul in feelings like to theirs—
These men of holiness.

My thoughts, like doves, abroad I fling
Into a country fair:
Wind-baffled, back, with tired wing,
They to my ark repair.

O hear me, God! O give me joy
Such as thy chosen feel;
Have pity on a wretched boy;
My heart is hard as steel.

*   *   *   *   *

Thou wilt not hear: I come no more;
Thou heedest not my woe.
With sighs and tears my heart is sore.
Thou comest not: I go.

*   *   *   *   *

One hopeless hope there yet may be
A God somewhere to hear;
The God to whom I bend my knee—
A God with open ear.

In vain I cry. The earth is dark,
And darker yet the air;
Of light there trembles now no spark
In my lost soul's despair.

*   *   *   *   *

My books unopened long have lain;
In class I am all astray:
The questions growing in my brain,
Demand and have their way.

Old truths, new facts, they preach aloud—
Their tones like wisdom fall:

> One sunbeam glancing on a cloud
>> Hints things beyond them all.

Recalling the faith of his own father, he then vows to continue his quest in hopes of finding God at last.

> They preach men should not faint, but pray,
>> And seek until they find;
> But God is very far away,
>> Nor is his countenance kind.

> Yet every night my father prayed,
>> Withdrawing from the throng!
> Some answer must have come that made
>> His heart so high and strong!

> Once more I'll seek the God of men,
>> Redeeming childhood's vow.—
> —I failed with bitter weeping then,
>> And fail cold-hearted now!

> The preacher says a Christian must
>> Do all the good he can:—
> I must be noble, true, and just,
>> Because I am a man!

> They say a man must watch, and keep
>> Lamp burning, garments white,
> Else he shall sit without and weep
>> When Christ comes home at night:—

> Yes, I say well—said words are cheap!
>> For action man was born!
> What praise will my one talent reap?
>> What grapes are on my thorn?

> 'Twere well my soul should cease to roam,
>> Should seek and have and hold!
> It may be there is yet a home
>> In that religion old.

> Again I kneel, again I pray:
>> *Wilt thou be God to me?*
> *Wilt thou give ear to what I say,*
>> *And lift me up to thee?*

With his hope kindled, he turns to the Bible, but finds it dry and distant.

> I read the Bible with my eyes,
>> But hardly with my brain;
> Should this the meaning recognize,
>> My heart yet reads in vain.

> *   *   *   *   *

Oh, not like men they move and speak,
     Those pictures in old panes!
They alter not their aspect meek
     For all the winds and rains!

Their thoughts are full of figures strange,
     Of Jewish forms and rites:
A world of air and sea I range,
     Of mornings and of nights!

But then he turns to the story of Jesus, feels His love, and at last recognizes his own sin that he must confess.

I turn me to the gospel-tale:—
     My hope is faint with fear
That hungriest search will not avail
     To find a refuge here.

A misty wind blows bare and rude
     From dead seas of the past;
And through the clouds that halt and brood,
     Dim dawns a shape at last:

A sad worn man who bows his face,
     And treads a frightful path,
To save an abject hopeless race
     From an eternal wrath.

How find the love to pay my debt?—
     He leads me from the sun!—
Yet it is hard men should forget
     A good deed ever done!—

Forget that he, to foil a curse,
     Did, on that altar-hill,
Sun of a sunless universe,
     Hang, dying, patient, still!

A word within says I am to blame,
     And therefore must confess;
Must call my doing by its name,
     And so make evil less.

The struggle comes. Evil or I
     Must gain the victory now.
I am unmoved and yet would try:
     O God, to thee I bow.

The skies are brass; there falls no aid;
     No wind of help will blow.
But I bethink me:—I am made
     A man: I rise and go.

To Christ I needs must come, they say,
     Who went to death for me:

> I turn aside; I come, I pray,
>   My unknown God, to thee.

And as he bows before God, still not even knowing whether his prayer is heard, a silent peace creeps over him, and hope begins to dawn.

> I kneel. But all my soul is dumb
>   With hopeless misery:
> Is *he* a friend who will not come,
>   Whose face I must not see?
>
> I do not think of broken laws,
>   Of judge's damning word;
> My heart is all one ache, because
>   I call and am not heard.
>
> Yet sometimes when the agony
>   Dies of its own excess,
> A dew-like calm descends on me,
>   A shadow of tenderness;
>
> A sense of bounty and of grace,
>   A cool air in my breast,
> As if my soul were yet a place
>   Where peace might one day rest.
>
> And when my heart with soft release
>   Grows calm as summer-sea,
> Shall I not hope the God of peace
>   Hath laid his hand on me?

Then at last, when the longing of his heart after God has begun to be answered, he rises again in protest, as in Robert Falconer's memorable speech to his horrified grandmother, and refuses God's love if he is singled out from the many who are not chosen.

> But if a vision should unfold
>   That I might banish fear;
> That I, the chosen, might be bold,
>   And walk with upright cheer;
>
> My heart would cry: But shares my race
>   In this great love of thine?
> I pray, put me not in good case
>   Where others lack and pine.
>
> Nor claim I thus a place above
>   Thy table's very foot;
> 'Tis only that I love no love
>   That springs not from the root;
>
> That gives me not my being's claim;
>   That says not *child* to me;

> That calls not all men by the name
>   Of children to His knee.

And from this great love of God's, shown to all men, he too realizes how direct and personal is this love to him alone.

> Art thou not each man's God—his own,
>   With secret words between,
> As thou and he lived all alone,
>   Insphered in silence keen?
>
> Ah, God, my heart is not the same
>   As any heart beside;
> My pain is different, and my blame,
>   My pity and my pride!
>
> My story, too, thou knowest, God,
>   Is different from the rest;
> Thou knowest—none but thee—the load
>   With which my heart is pressed.
>
> Love is salvation: life without
>   No moment can endure.
> Those sheep alone go in and out
>   Who know thy love is pure.

Finally recognizing God's life within him, he ascends to the highest question of all: What does God want him to do?

> Thou seest how poor a thing am I,
>   Yet hear, whate'er I be;
> Despairing of my will, I cry,
>   Be God enough to me.

* * * * *

> What is his will?—that I may go
>   And do it, in the hope
> That light will rise and spread and grow,
>   As deed enlarges scope.
>
> I need not search the sacred book
>   To find my duty clear;
> Scarce in my bosom need I look,
>   It lies so very near.
>
> Henceforward I must watch the door
>   Of word and action too;
> There's one thing I must do no more,
>   Another I must do.
>
> But here I am not left to choose
>   My duty is my lot;
> And weighty things will glory lose
>   If small ones are forgot.

I am not worthy high things yet;
    I'll humbly do my own;
Good care of sheep may so beget
    A fitness for the throne.

Ah fool! why dost thou reason thus?
    Ambition's very fool!
Through high and low, each glorious,
    Shines God's all-perfect rule.

'Tis God I need, not rank in good;
    'Tis Life, not honour's need;
With him to fill my every mood,
    I am content indeed.

And if I ponder what they call
    The gospel of God's grace,
Through mists that slowly melt and fall
    May dawn a human face.

What face? Oh, heart-uplifting thought,
    That face may dawn on me
Which Moses on the mountain sought,
    God would not let him see!

Love was his very being's root,
    And healing was its flower;
Love, human love, its stem and fruit,
    Its gladness and its power.

          *   *   *   *   *

I find his heart was all above;
    Obedience his one thought;
Reposing in his father's love,
    His father's will he sought.

          *   *   *   *   *

And where I cannot set my faith,
    Unknowing or unwise,
I say "If this be what *he* saith,
    Here hidden treasure lies."

Lord Jesus Christ, I know not how—
    With this blue air, blue sea,
This yellow sand, that grassy brow,
    All isolating me—

Thy thoughts to mine themselves impart,
    My thoughts to thine draw near;
But thou canst fill who mad'st my heart,
    Who gav'st me words must hear.

Thou mad'st the hand with which I write,
    The eye that watches slow
Through rosy gates that rosy light
    Across thy threshold go;

Those waves that bend in golden spray,
    As if thy foot they bore:
I think I know thee, Lord, today,
    Shall know thee evermore.

Lord, thou hast much to make me yet—
    Thy father's infant still:
Thy mind, Son, in my bosom set,
    That I may grow thy will.

My soul with truth clothe all about,
    And I shall question free:
The man that feareth, Lord, to doubt,
    In that fear doubteth thee.

          (*The Poetical Works of George MacDonald*,
          vol. 1 p. 187; selections from "The Disciple.")

Into the Light

The fixing of "times and seasons" to a moment of rebirth or conversion or awakening is important to many people. However, it is impossible to denote with certainty the precise stages of mind and heart George Mac-Donald went through during this time. He has left us no written personal record. Thus we must look to his later works, like the autobiographical poem *The Disciple* to shed light on his inward journey. And the impression gained from *The Disciple,* from Robert Falconer's four years "in the desert," from Alec Forbes' and Hugh Sutherland's long quests, is a picture of progressive awakening to the Spirit of God within his heart. George Mac-Donald's own awakening corresponded very closely with that of Thomas Wingfold, which began with serious doubt, giving way to a hope that expressed itself tentatively: "No, my hearers, I call not myself a Christian, but I call every one here who obeys the word of Jesus, who restrains anger, who loves his enemies, who prays for his slanderers, to witness my vow, that I too will henceforth try to obey him, in the hope that he whom he called God and his Father will reveal to me him whom you call your Lord Jesus Christ, that into my darkness I may receive the light of the world!" (*Thomas Wingfold, Curate*, Ch. 31).

From such tenuous beginnings it progressed to the prayer: "O Father, thou art All-in-all, perfect beyond the longing of thy children, and we are altogether thine. Thou wilt make us pure and loving and free ... Then shall thy children be of good cheer, infinite in the love of each other, and eternal in thy love. Lord Jesus, let the heart of a child be given to us, that so we may arise from the grave of our dead selves and die no more, but see face to face the God of the Living."

And finally came the confidence that could say to the dying marquis in *Malcolm*:

"'Are you satisfied with yourself, my lord?'

"'No, by God!'

"'You would like to be better?'

"'I would.'

"'Then you are of the same mind with God.'

"'Yes, but I'm not a fool! It won't do to say I should like to be. I must be it, and that's not so easy. It's damned hard to be good. I would have a fight for it, but there's no time. How is a poor devil to get out of such an infernal scrape?'

"'Keep the commandments.'

"'That's it, of course; but there's no time, I tell you—at least so those cursed doctors will keep telling me.'

"'If there were but time to draw another breath, there would be time to begin.'

"'How am I to begin? Which am I to begin with?'

"'There is one commandment which includes all the rest.'

"'Which is that?'

"'To believe on the Lord Jesus Christ.'

"'That's cant.'

"'. . . it is to me the essence of wisdom. It has given me a peace which makes life or death all but indifferent to me, though I would choose the latter.'

"'What am I to believe about him then?'

"'You are to believe *in* him, not about him.'

"'I don't understand.'

"'He is our Lord and Master, Elder Brother, King, Savior, the divine Man, the human God: to believe in him is to give ourselves up to him in obedience, to search out his will and do it'" (*Malcolm*, Ch. 49).

Thus George MacDonald's awakening out of doubt can be seen through his later assertions concerning the faith into which he grew. Like Janet toward Gibbie, he did not worry himself about a fixed moment when "belief" came upon him. "Having long ceased to trouble her own head, [Janet] had now no inclination to trouble Gibbie's heart with what men call the plan of salvation. It was enough to her to find that he followed her Master" (*Sir Gibbie*, Ch. 23). When the time was past, MacDonald could say, with confident authority like his awakened curate Wingfold, "Ye have borne with me in my trials, and I thank you. Those who have not only borne but suffered, and do now rejoice with me I thank tenfold . . .

"But oh what unspeakable bliss of heart and soul and mind and sense remain for him who like St. Paul is crucified with Christ, who lives no more from his own self, but is inspired and informed and possessed with the same faith toward the Father in which Jesus lived and wrought the will of the Father! If the words attributed to Jesus are indeed the words of him whom Jesus declared himself, then truly is the fate of mankind a glorious one—and that, first and last, because men have a God supremely grand, all-perfect in Godhead; for that is, and that alone can be, the absolute bliss of the created" (*Thomas Wingfold, Curate*, Ch. 96).

All MacDonald's later works here quoted point autobiographically back to this period in his life between 1840 and 1845. But *Robert Falconer* always remains the beacon from which the clearest light upon George MacDonald's spiritual pilgrimage is shed.

"He made his way eastward toward the Alps. As he walked one day about noon over a desolate heath-covered height, reminding him not a little of the country of his childhood, the silence seized upon him. In the midst of the silence arose the . . . words . . . 'My peace I give unto you.' They were words he had known from the earliest memorial time. He had heard them in infancy, in childhood, in boyhood, in youth: now first in manhood it flashed upon him that the Lord did really mean that the peace of his soul should be the peace of their souls; that the peace wherewith his own soul was quiet, the peace at the very heart of the universe, was henceforth theirs—open to them, to all the world, to enter and be still. He fell upon his knees, bowed down in the birth of a great hope, held up his hands towards heaven, and cried, 'Lord Christ, give me thy peace.'

"He said no more, but rose, caught up his stick, and strode forward, thinking . . .

"Suddenly he was aware that the earth had begun to live again. The hum of insects arose from the heath around him; the odor of its flowers entered his dulled sense; the wind kissed him on the forehead; the sky domed up over his head; and the clouds veiled the distant mountain-tops. . . . All nature began to minister to one who had begun to lift his head from the baptism of fire . . .

"Walking up the edge of the valley, he came upon a little stream whose talk he had heard for some hundred yards. . . . He sat down on [a] foot of the rock, shut in by the high, grassy banks from the gaze of the awful mountains. The sole unrest was the run of the water beside him, and it sounded so homely that be began to jabber Scotch to it . . . With his country's birch-tree beside him, and the rock crowned with its turf of heather over his head, the quiet as of a Sabbath afternoon fell upon him—that quiet which is the one altogether lovely thing in the Scotch Sabbath—and once more the words arose in his mind, 'My peace I give unto you.'

"Now he fell a thinking what this peace could be. And it came into his mind, as he thought, that Jesus had spoken it another place about giving rest to those that came to him, while here he spoke about '*my* peace.' Could this *my* mean a certain *kind* of peace that the Lord himself possessed? Perhaps it was in virtue of that peace, whatever it was, that he was the Prince of Peace. Whatever peace he had must be the highest and best peace—therefore the one peace for a man to seek. . . . He remembered the New Testament in his box, and resolving to try whether he could not make something more out of it, went back to the inn quieter in heart than since he left his home. In the evening he returned to the brook, and fell to searching the story, seeking after the peace of Jesus.

"He found that the whole passage stood thus: 'Peace I leave with you, my peace I give unto you; not as the world giveth give I unto you. Let not your heart be troubled; neither let it be afraid.'

"He did not leave the place for six weeks. Every day he went to the burn, as he called it, with his New Testament; every day tried yet again to make out something more of what the Savior meant. By the end of the month it had dawned on him, he hardly knew how, that the peace of Jesus . . . must have been a peace that came from the doing of the will of his Father. From the account he gave of the discoveries he then made, I venture to represent them. . . . They were these that Jesus taught:

"First—That a man's business is to do the will of God.

"Second—That God takes upon himself the care of the man;

"Third—Therefore, that a man must never be afraid of anything; and so,

"Fourth—be left free to love God with all his heart, and his neighbor as himself . . .

"All this time he was in the wilderness . . . and he did nothing but read the four gospels and ponder over them. Therefore it is not surprising that he should have already become so familiar with the gospel story, that the moment these questions appeared, the following words should dart to the forefront of his consciousness to meet them:

"'If any man will do his will, he shall know of the doctrine, whether it be of God, or whether I speak of myself.'

"Here was a word of Jesus himself, announcing the one means of arriving at a conviction of the truth or falsehood of all that he said, namely, the doing of the will of God by the man who would arrive at such conviction.

"The next question naturally was: What is this will of God of which Jesus speaks? Here he found himself in difficulty. The theology of his grandmother rushed in upon him, threatening to overwhelm him with demands . . . from which his soul turned with sickness and fainting. That they were repulsive to him, that they appeared unreal, and contradictory to the nature around him, was no *proof* that they were not of God. But, on the other hand, that they demanded what *seemed* to him unjust; that these demands were founded on what *seemed* to him untruth attributed to God, on ways of thinking and feeling which are certainly degrading in a man— these were reasons of the very highest nature for refusing to act upon them. . . . He saw that while they appeared to be such, even though it might turn out that he mistook them, to acknowledge them would be to wrong God. But this conclusion left him in no better position for practice than before.

"When at length he did see what the will of God was, he wondered, so simple did it appear, that he had failed to discover it at once. Yet not less than a fortnight had he been brooding and pondering over the question, as he wandered up and down that burnside, or sat at the foot of the heather-crowned stone and the silver-barked birch, when the light began to dawn upon him. It was thus:

"In trying to understand the words of Jesus by searching back, as it were, for such thoughts and feelings in him as would account for the words he spoke, the perception awoke that at least he could not have meant by the will of God any such theological utterances as those which troubled him. Next it grew plain that what he came to do was just to lead his life. That he should do the work, such as recorded and much besides, that the Father gave him to do—this was the will of God concerning him. With this perception arose the conviction that unto every man whom God had sent into the world he had given a work to do in that world. He had to lead the life God meant him to lead. The will of God was to be found and done in the world. In seeking a true relation to the world, would he find his relation to God?

"The time for action was come.

"He rose up from the stone of his meditation, took his staff in his hand, and went down the mountain, not knowing whither he went" (*Robert Falconer*, Ch. 51).

CHAPTER TEN

ON HIS OWN
(1845–1847)

When George MacDonald received his degree in the spring of 1845, he was in one sense no nearer the choice of a profession than when he had begun. The sea was no longer calling him, and he could not afford the additional years of schooling required to follow medicine or a doctorate in chemistry, which would have allowed him to teach at the university level. He did not inherit the family instincts for business, and following in his father's footsteps never seemed to have been a serious option.

The Young Tutor

In 19th-century Britain the ministry was highly thought of as a "profession," and many middle class young men sought clerical posts for reasons other than spiritual. It is apparent that by this time the idea of the ministry had entered MacDonald's mind as his personal life with God deepened. But he recoiled from the notion of entering the ministry merely as a means to gain a livelihood. And though his faith was now on a sound footing and his desire to serve God growing, there remained uncertainty. His antagonism to the rigid dogmas of his upbringing and his sense that God was more truthfully represented in nature than in many churches kept him in sore doubts about whether he should give his life to the service of the church.

He discussed his indecision with his father, who was sympathetic and supportive. Though there are few surviving letters between the two men from the university period, from 1845 onward there began to be a correspondence that illuminates the son's continued growth. In November of 1845, indicative of his thought about what direction his life should take, he wrote his father, "My greatest difficulty is always, 'How do I know that my faith is of a lasting kind such as will produce fruits?' . . . My error seems to be always searching for faith in place of contemplating the truths of the gospel which produce faith. My spirit is often very confused. My time does not come to much for reading between one thing and another, but I am improving my mind steadily, though it may be slowly. . . ."[1]

Therefore, having taught previously, and having a certain faculty for it, he sought a tutorship. It would provide something profitable to occupy him for the present, while at the same time giving him time to think what should come next.

Dr. John Morison, a close friend of his father's who had taken the liberal side in the universal redemption controversy still raging in Britain, was at the time a popular and fashionable preacher in London, at the Trevor Chapel in Brompton. He had originally come from Aberdeenshire and was influential in London for forty years. So when MacDonald went in search of a tutoring position it was Dr. Morison who found it for him in the home of one of his church members, J. Radermacher, living in the London suburb of Fulham.

Now that he was out of school and on his own, George MacDonald's great hope was to begin earning enough money to pay his own way, eliminate his few Aberdeen debts, and send home what money he could. The potato blights had now begun in earnest and his father's financial straits grew worse with each passing year for the remainder of the decade. Therefore, the younger MacDonald journeyed south to the great metropolis and took up lodgings in the center of the vast and rapidly expanding British Empire, a city that was, in financial, economic, and social matters, the very hub of the civilized world. It was certainly a drastic change for the young man. Yet for most of the remainder of his active life, with brief exceptions and various excursions elsewhere and abroad, he was "based" in and around London.

MacDonald recalled his tutoring experience briefly but accurately in *Warlock o' Glenwarlock*, and in more detail when he portrayed the proud, wealthy Appleditches in *David Elginbrod*. He lived with the family for more than two years, and it was a wearisome assignment. Though the gentleman and his wife were superficially kind to him as far as it went, they took little care for his physical needs, made unreasonable demands upon him, and undermined his discipline with the children. He was paid to teach the three dull and spoiled little boys of the family; but two sisters, whose unruly behavior and screaming were nearly intolerable, and were allowed to come and go, often interfered with the studies. The boys were rude, always boasting about the money their father had given them, and their mother resented their young tutor, who was also expected to take them to the Chapel twice every Sunday. His efforts to conciliate Mrs. Radermacher drained him emotionally and brought mental conflict of a new kind. His letters to his father and his discussions with Dr. Morison during this period reveal that he was not now so much troubled by the implacability of Calvinism, but by whether his own new faith was strong enough to stand the test of time. He usually placed the blame for his difficulties on his own irritability of temper rather than accusing Mrs. Radermacher or indulging in self-pity.

Yet difficult as the position was, it was a period of substantial growth. His letters home reveal a growing assurance in his newfound spiritual walk. Rather than questioning the fundamentals of the faith, he now discussed things like church government and organization, what his role in the church should be, and analyzed Dr. Morison's sermons and pastoral practices. Gradually, MacDonald seemed to develop a growing consideration of himself as "in" the Church (the *Church* at large, not a particular denomination, sect, or faction within it). A confidence was slowly emerging, and less and less he felt the need to apologize for his beliefs. Specifics as to his personal role in the Church still remained to be worked out, but his mental and spiritual footing was more secure. His life gradually became more outward. Letters revealed him involved with destitute friends in London who received most of the extra pennies he could spare from his meager earnings. He even asked his father to send oatmeal for them. At the same time he asked his employer for ten shillings in order that he might send it to the famine-stricken Highlanders. He sent home an accounting of every penny spent, fearing his father would hardly understand the expense of living in London. Still emotionally bound to his father in a healthy way, he began testing the waters of independence and manhood slowly.

Thoughts of the Ministry

The idea of becoming a minister appeared to be growing steadily stronger during this time, and in several letters home he discussed the possibility with his father. From the pulpit, he felt he could convey the new truths he had come to see about God's character. Now that his eyes were opened, it truly was a "gospel" story he felt compelled to share—the great and glorious good news that God's love was over all and in all and covered all. So joyous was the liberation of his own soul that he wanted to share the freeing message of God's true character. With this desire came a blossoming confidence in his authority to speak out what he believed. A bold enthusiasm sprang up within him that he might indeed make a difference in people's lives, that he might minister to others struggling with the same doubts he had overcome.

Despite more serious consideration of the ministry, however, he seemed constantly aware of his unfitness for the task. He continued to be completely frank with his father, surely a result of his father's open acceptance of him. The son had no fear of the father's condemnation, regardless of the severity of the doubts he had traversed recently, which could not have been unknown to the father. The perfectly flowing relationship between father and son continued, as indeed it did in later years between George MacDonald and his own sons and daughters. This example of fatherhood, stemming from the large and accepting heart of George MacDonald, Sr., remained visible throughout the son's entire life—both in his attitude toward God and in his own personal relationships as well, and was characterized fully in *Warlock o' Glenwarlock* in Cosmo's relationship with his father. In *Warlock* he says, "Nobody knows what the relation of father and son may yet come to . . . there must be in it depths infinite, ages off being fathomed yet. For is it not a reproduction in small of the loftiest mystery in human ken—that of the infinite Father and infinite Son? If man be made in the image of God, then is the human fatherhood and sonship the image of the eternal relation between God and Jesus" (*Warlock o' Glenwarlock*, Ch. 24).

A letter to his father during this period (1847) is particularly intriguing—revealing his thoughts of the future, his growing confidence spiritually, his remaining doubts, his devotion to God's Word, his continuing love of nature, his openness with his father—all things which would emerge in his writing in later years. Clearly, the qualities in the character of the George MacDonald the world would later come to love were already settling into place:

"I did not wish you to understand [that I] had finally made up my mind as to the ministry. Tis true this feeling has been gradually gaining ground on me. . . . But on the other hand, I fear myself—I have so much vanity, so much pride . . . I have not prayed much about it, for it has seemed so far in the distance, as if it was scarcely time to think of it yet. . . . I love my Bible more—I am always finding out something new in it. All my teaching in youth seems useless to me. [To validate it] I must get it all from the Bible again [for myself]. . . . If the gospel of Jesus be not true, I can only pray my maker to annihilate me, for nothing else is worth living for; and if [it] *be* true, everything in the universe is glorious, except sin. . . .

"God is the God of the beautiful. Religion the love of the Beautiful, and Heaven the home of the Beautiful. Nature is tenfold brighter in the sun of Righteousness, and my love of Nature is more intense since I became a Christian . . . God has not given me such thoughts and forbidden me to enjoy them.

"I should have much to say to you if I were with you, and many a long conversation I trust we may have before *very* long. May I never cause you a thought of pain, as I have so often done in years that are past. . . . Give my love to Johnny; to grandmama too. . . ."[2]

Our frustration as readers, of course, is that we have no definite evidence of precisely what he meant by "becoming a Christian" or when such an event—if indeed *event* it can properly be called—took place. He subsequently never spoke of an exact time or place of a "spiritual experience" of this magnitude. He did not rigidly try to pin such things down, either in his own life or in the lives of his characters, preferring to think of openness toward God as a gradually unfolding process. Thus we are simply left with this beguiling snatch from a letter of his early twenties, concluding only from it that the crisis of his earlier doubts had passed and that he was thinking of himself as a Christian, yet still wondering about many things and thereby on his way toward a mature walk of faith.

Another letter of the same year to his uncle, James MacDonald in Huntly, is equally interesting. Like that to his father, it reveals a thoughtful, questioning, pondering, discussing mentality. The specific point being considered (the difference in how God orders events for the Christian and the non-Christian) is not nearly so illuminating as is the underlying tone. There is no hint of trying to persuade or convince. He is peddling no viewpoint; he simply wants to get at the truth.

"My very dear uncle," he begins, "I called on Dr. Adams, but had again the misfortune to find that he was out. I do not think I am right to use the word *misfortune*, for the conviction is, I think, growing upon me that the smallest events are ordered for us, while yet in perfect consistency with the ordinary course of cause and effect in the world. I am strongly inclined to think that whatever has a moral effect of any kind on our minds, God manages for us. . . . How far the events of those who do not at all seek to serve Him are controlled by him, in regard to these individuals personally, is a question about which I have no opinion at all—at least not a settled one. Perhaps it would be presumption to form one on such a subject. . . .[3] Your very affectionate nephew, George."

In his later writings MacDonald strongly attacks the mentality that cares more for proving its own position than for discerning the truth. He would prefer to find himself in the wrong, and thereby learn a new facet of truth, than win an argument. The second to last sentence in the letter shows much about the young man: he will not even formulate an opinion until he sees the question more clearly.

Thus, one of the rare qualities that set George MacDonald so far apart from other Christian teachers, preachers, and moralists—namely, the reluctance to put forward an opinion prematurely until the light of truth had been shed upon it—was visibly established in his outlook by age twenty-two.

Additionally, this letter graphically elucidates MacDonald's continuing *growth*. His notions and viewpoints would never be set in concrete. There was a pliability present, illustrating the moving, deepening, forward-looking, still-growing, still-broadening mindset. His was a mind not afraid to doubt and ask questions. It was a mind not hiding behind doors, but knocking on them. His eyes were wide open, alert to any entrance of truth. He read his Bible at the same time as he was writing his father about the scientific account of Darwin's voyage around the world. Young George MacDonald, though a loyal Congregationalist with thoughts of the ministry, was clearly on a different path than many of his religious contemporaries.

CHAPTER ELEVEN

LOUISA
(1845–1846)

From his earliest days George MacDonald was on intimate terms with the family of his mother's brother, Lt. George MacKay, who lived north of Huntly in the coastal town of Banff. The family's frequent vacations at the sea led to his lifelong friendship with his cousin Helen, three years George's senior, who died in 1911 at age 89, the last of the MacKays of her line.

In 1840—the same year that her cousin George won his bursary and began his years at the university—Miss MacKay, as beautiful as she was intelligent and talented, was sent to a finishing school on Abbey Road in London. Even after the period of "love poems" was past, she and George remained in close contact, and throughout the years their friendship was always a special one. Helen would occasionally amuse George by prophesying that somehow he would get his heart's desire, and "as a stout, elderly M.D. would be driving a good horse on his rounds visiting patients." In 1868, just after the honorary degree of LL.D. had been conferred upon him by his alma mater at Aberdeen, she addressed a letter to him as "*Doctor* MacDonald," to which he replied in Scotch dialect, "Quhat the muckle de'il gars ye pit the *Doachter* afore my name? Let it come ahint it gin it likes!" Whereupon his cousin replied: "I thocht ye wad raither hae a Doctor afore ye than a *Lang-Leggit-De'il* [LL.D.=Long-Legged-Devil] rinnin' aifter ye!" His final reply kept the punning and playful ball rolling: "'Deed, lassie, ye hae the best o't aboot the doctor an' the de'il."[1] The two would always, in their many letters, use the broadest tongue of the dialect for a sentence or two, particularly for humor.

When Mr. MacKay sent his daughter to the finishing school in London, he asked his friend James Powell, a leather merchant who lived in the London suburb of Upper Clapton, to befriend her. Apparently Mr. Powell obliged most hospitably, for the young Scots girl soon fell in love with his son Alexander and the two were married in 1844.

When George MacDonald came to London in 1845 to begin his tutoring assignment, he immediately looked up his cousin Helen, now Mrs. Powell. Within a short time Helen must have introduced him to the family of her in-laws, for early in the year 1846 he was already being welcomed regularly into their home, called The Limes. It was an English household of considerable means, and they took in the young recently graduated tutor with as much kindness as they had his cousin five years earlier. And with a similar result.

The family of James Powell* was lavish in its hospitality to their sister-in-law's cousin. And soon George began to have his effect upon the family as well, particularly one Powell daughter by the name of Louisa. He introduced the four younger girls to English literature, reading to them from Sir Walter Scott and Wordsworth, then Tennyson and Browning. Up till then their reading had been strictly devotional and religious. He was interested in the smallest of their doings, and through him the Powell girls came to see how restricted their purely denominational outlook had been. He showed them how much larger one's vision could be without inhibiting faith—indeed, expanding their faith. The younger four girls were especially taken with him. Louisa was away from home on his first visit, but her sister Angela wrote that Helen's cousin would "explain everything" that puzzled her and make life happy. In her later reminiscences she adds, "He showed me new life in everything, understood me as an equal. This was very wonderful to me, as all my life I had been the fool of the family. . . . Great was my astonishment when he wished me to learn mathematics and began himself to teach me."[2]

But if this cousin of Helen's was captivating in his Highland charm, he was at the same time disturbingly nonconformist in some of his ideas. It is difficult today to imagine how large a factor in daily life were matters of religion at that time and how important was conventionality upon doctrinal points. The Powell family was very religious, Congregational, and devoutly Calvinist in their views. Greville illustrates the influence of such orthodoxy by telling of an aunt of his mother's who used to vow that she could never lie comfortable in bed at night if she did not believe in hellfire and everlasting pains for the unrepentant. Another story used to circulate through the family about a dinner party at which one of the family was telling of an infant who had died in the night. "But I hope the poor thing was christened?" asked one of the guests with some alarm.

"Well, ma'am, *no*," came the reply. "The parson couldn't get his pants on fast enough, and the puling [crying, shrieking, wailing] little sinner went to hell."[3]

From such a system George MacDonald was struggling to emancipate himself. But so strong were Louisa's own doctrinal convictions that she deferred accepting MacDonald's love for many months until he could

---

*Of the Powells' thirteen children, eight survived—Charlotte, Alexander, Phoebe, Louisa, George, Angela, Florentia, and Caroline.

satisfactorily formulate his views on the Atonement, which at last he was fortunately able to do.

Yet with all her religious conventionalism, Louisa possessed a spark that was only waiting for the right man to ignite. Her sister Angela said, "The home was always dull when Louisa was away; she was the gay influence. Like the twinkle of her wonderful eyes, she brightened all around her."[4] While doctrinal purity was important in the family, Louisa could never tolerate pat religiosity. Her son later said of her: ". . . Humbug was to her all through her life so absurd and funny that one wonders why it ever made her angry. Either her sense of the ridiculous or her honesty prevented her joining their Church till much older than was customary. When at last she consented to it, along with her young sister Flora, my aunt tells how two grave old deacons came to ask them questions and to pray with them. One was an undertaker, very old and fat. He asked Flora whether she 'wrestled in prayer.' . . . Louisa could [hardly] conceal her naughty delight; for she pictured this sister, who shared her bedroom, so often fast asleep already when [she herself was still] kneeling at her bedside."[5]

It is scarcely any wonder that George MacDonald very soon found himself attracted to this fun-loving twenty-three-year-old who was two years older than himself. Coming out of several years during which dejection of spirit was often his sole companion, she was to him like the breath of fresh air he had recently discovered in the spiritual realm. She was the smallest of the family, slim and beautiful. More than that, here was one so alive, so cheerful, so sparkling; she must have been to her future husband a joyful change from the bleak mental outlook of his college days, and at the same time a great relief from the drudgery of his daily tutoring routine. It is little surprise that he spent more and more time in the Powell home.

Greville quotes his aunt Angela in describing how young George MacDonald seemed to these young ladies the very model of a poet. "He came not a conventional youth, with polite smooth talk, but like a prophet of old. Long before we thought of him as having any religious message to us, gradually we found he knew about everything and could put any difficulty right, [whether it be] to answer 'Is there a God?' or 'What is poetry?' or 'What about ghosts or fairies?'"[6]

By June of 1846 and onward there are letters from George addressed to Miss Louisa Powell, which are always signed (presumably because, through the marriage of George's cousin Helen to Louisa's brother Alexander, they were something like cousins-in-law) "Your affectionate cousin." An indication of his dawning happiness and his invariable industry (both mental and physical) is a letter to his stepmother that describes a pair of slippers he cross-stitched for her. Deft with his fingers and always anxious to learn a new handcraft, the story behind the letter reveals much. In an earlier letter to Louisa he had apologized for having inadvertently carried off her thimble (a reply note which undoubtedly told him to keep it as long as he found it useful). Her delicate fingers, no doubt, taught the young man to use his needle not only for the wool work slippers, but also to patch his trousers now that he was on his own in Fulham—the diminutive mistress, barely five feet in height, while he stood nearly six, showing the large-framed Celt the stitching technique. The laughter and fun of the project must have contributed to the cementing of their budding relationship of love.

"My Dearest Mother," he writes, "will you accept some of my work? You will excuse faults, seeing it is my first attempt. . . . I can sew very well now—always mend my own clothes—use my thimble—a nice silver one—like a lady. I have patched my trousers two or three times—an accomplishment I have attained since I came to England, and a most useful one I find it to be! . . . God is very good to me. Oh! I was so far from him two or three years ago, and I trust I am always coming nearer to him now."[7]

In a rare moment, he outwardly reveals both the depths of his despondency during his college days, but yet the mentality of growth, of wanting to learn new things, of expanding his horizons. The same openness to the previously untried makes him capable of learning a woman's skill with childlike abandonment and joy, while at the same time calling out in his spirit with a desire to grow still further—to be "always coming nearer to him."

There are many, many letters between Louisa and George during this period, from mid-1846 onward. According to their son, "They are very ordinary—like primroses and hedge-roses and shy violets and quiet pools of blue-bells—just ordinary." Therefore he says, in preparation of his biography more than sixty years ago, "So I will, for the most part, leave them where they lie." By July of that year the increasing love between them can be seen. In a letter to Louisa in which he sent her a poem he had written, at the bottom of it, in her own hand she writes:

"My dear, my dearest!" and then her penmanship breaks out into little spasmodic sprays and stars of decorative feminine anguish and she continues, "O, I am an overgrown baby. . . ."

CHAPTER TWELVE

CALLED TO THE MINISTRY
(1848)

By the beginning of 1848, George MacDonald, having just turned 23, had reached the preliminary decision to enter the ministry. The process of thought and prayer to arrive at this point had been long and slow. Questions regarding the tenets of his faith had pressed ever deeper, probing to integrate the Calvinism of his past, the searchings of his youth, and the belief of his manhood into a unity of faith and action. No doubt the first chapter of James was well-thumbed in his New Testament—"If any of you lack wisdom, let him ask of God, that giveth to all men liberally, and upbraideth not; and it shall be given him."

Since his final year at King's College the conviction had grown within him that God's character was founded in His goodness and loving fatherhood over all creation. With that certainty came the next step in the natural progression of growing maturity—the desire to communicate the conviction. So liberating were his discoveries on a personal level, and so slanderous toward God did he consider Calvinism's harsh definition of His character, that the necessity swelled within him that he *must* preach what he now realized God had been revealing to him since his earliest childhood.

Though all his life long he disavowed any sense of "mission" on a lofty spiritual plane, it is certain that in this time period of his mid-twenties an inner intuitive impression of "calling" must have begun to steal in upon him. Whether in later years he chose to call it such or not, the "message" that he had for the world was gathering momentum, and it would become increasingly impossible with every passing year for him to ignore its urgings. And for now, with his still-limited awareness of the scope of options before him, the ministry appeared the only viable avenue through which he could proclaim to people his discoveries concerning his heavenly Father.

Late in the spring of 1848, George MacDonald happily resigned his

tutorship. The following letter to Louisa reveals both his continuing struggle over the decisions facing him about the course of his life, and the
progression in his thinking. He is indeed beginning to sound like the
George MacDonald who would later write with such force and confidence. He never boasted that he had arrived. He still compared himself
with one far from God, desperately in need of drawing closer to the divine
Heart. But how much stronger was his view of God's character! How different, indeed, was the Shorter Catechism from MacDonald's ripening
view that the essence of God's purpose in human history is to bring man
back into what he called our "natural" state of fellowship with Him:

"The difficulties with which I told you I was surrounded are not the
results of my situation. However ill I may bear them at times, I regard my
trials here as helps, not hindrances. But my difficulties are those which a
heart far from God must feel, even when the hand of the Heavenly Father
is leading it back to himself. It seems a wonder that he can bear with me.

"What is it that is the principal cause of everyone's unhappiness who
is not a Christian? It is the [lack] of enough love. We are made for love—
and in vain we strive to pour forth the streams of our affection by the
narrow channels which the world can give—and well is it if, stagnated in
our hearts, they turn not to bitterness. [Faith in] Jesus Christ is intended
to bring us back to our real *natural* condition: for all the world is in an
unnatural state. This will give us that to love which alone can satisfy our
loving—which alone, as we climb each successive height, can show us
another yet higher and farther off—so that, as our powers of loving
expand, the object of loving grows in all those glories which excite our
love and yet make it long for more."[1]

The "difficulties" mentioned in the letter were primarily two: what to
do about theological school and the ministry, and what to do concerning
Louisa.

George MacDonald and his father had always talked about everything.
In conceptualizing God, the model of his own father was ever before
George, Jr., the model demonstrated in the scripture: "What man is there
of you, whom if his son ask for bread, will give him a stone? Or if he ask
for a fish, will he give him a serpent? If ye then, being evil, know how to
give good gifts unto your children, how much more shall your Father
which is in heaven give good things to them that ask him?" (Matt. 7:9–11).
In later life he once said that he had never asked his father for anything,
either as a boy or man, but that it was given to him.

Throughout 1847 MacDonald's hope to visit home had been growing.
Letters between them increasingly discussed specifically the possibility of
his returning to school to prepare for the ministry, and certainly high on
the list of concerns must have been the expenses that would be incurred.
In addition there was another matter of paramount importance: he hoped
to get his father's approval to secure a certain young lady for his wife.

Hence, by 1848 it had become imperative that he should go north to
discuss these things with his father.

Moreover, having lived in London for nearly three years by this time, he was pining for his home, the winds of its hills, the rush of its rivers, the faces of its people, and the simplicity of its pace after three years in the world's busiest city.

So he spent the summer of 1848 at home in Huntly, a time that must have been one of extraordinary joy—not only to himself but to those he loved—except for one shadow. Grandmother MacDonald died that same year at age ninety-two. It is not known whether her death was in the first part of the year and thus preceded her grandson's visit, or if she saw him one last time and died later in the year. Perhaps her failing health precipitated the visit, as was the case in *Robert Falconer*: "The men laid their mother's body with those of the generations that had gone before her, beneath the long grass in their country church-yard—a dreary place, one accustomed to trim cemeteries and sentimental wreaths would call it . . ." (*Robert Falconer*, Ch. 49). The description tallies precisely with that of the Drumblade churchyard near Huntly, where most of the MacDonald family were buried. (Though MacDonald himself was later buried in Italy, a plaque commemorating his life was installed at this same churchyard in the 1990s.)

To 20th-century minds, a grown man asking his father's advice in all matters, large and small, might seem a strange thing. Yet the closeness between George MacDonald, Sr., and all his sons cannot be overemphasized. Even when they had reached independence, they would seek his sanctions and recommendations for their doings. A poem the son wrote some years later is certainly reminiscent of his memory of his father in his advancing years, and recalls the welcome he would receive whenever he returned.

> With simple gladness met him on the road
> His gray-haired father—elder brother now.
> Few words were spoken, little welcome said,
> But, as they walked, the more was understood.
> If with a less delight he brought him home
> Than he who met the prodigal returned,
> It was with more reliance, with more peace;
> For with the leaning pride that old men feel
> In young strong arms that draw their might from them,
> He led him to the house . . .
> Set him beside the fire in the old place,
> And heaped the table with best country-fare.
>
> (*The Poetical Works of George MacDonald*,
> vol. 1, "A Hidden Life")

Few specifics of that summer are known. The play at Huntly Castle, recalled in the poem quoted in Chapter Two, may have occurred then with his stepsisters, who at that time were seven, four, and two. A further reminiscence comes from Robert Troup, who tells of George MacDonald's being requested by some friends to conduct an informal meeting at the home of one Tibbie Christie (who later makes her appearance in *Alec*

Forbes of Howglen), a blind woman of about ninety who was confined to bed and unable to attend church. About ten or twelve friends were present; MacDonald prayed and then spoke briefly words on Mark 6:48, when Jesus came to His disciples on the water in the storm. Equally significant to the text and circumstances is the simple fact that by this time George MacDonald was not only accustomed to the pastoral role, but was recognized in such by his relatives and friends. He was increasingly exercising the pastoral gifts that were beginning to emerge.

In September George MacDonald once again left his homeland of Aberdeenshire, Scotland, as Greville says, "now not launching into the unknown but making sail for a harbour where hard work and romantic joy were awaiting him."[2] Any roadblocks that may have existed in his mind as the summer opened, or lingering doubts about what he felt called to do, had—after several months with his father—been removed. To Louisa and the ministry he was now bound.

A simple line or two written by Louisa during her lover's absence is indicative of their relationship at this point, and of her view of her future husband. "Oh, the air is so sweet, the trees so beautiful, the sky so bright! All Nature looks so glorious, and the silvery clouds soften the heat; and my heart feels so much quieter. . . . I cannot . . . help thanking God for this, and [for] you his instrument. Oh, here I do pray God . . . to give you health, strength and much of his love, that you may glorify him now on earth and for ever in his Heaven."[3]

Still a Congregationalist, MacDonald had five Theological Halls of that denomination in London to choose from. Having several friends there, he chose Highbury College and began the new term in September of 1848. The students lived together under one roof, each with his own study and bedroom. All meals were eaten together and the menu was excellent— accomodations in striking contrast with the Aberdonian student's life. The men met together every morning and evening for Bible reading and prayer.

With a university degree and three years of teaching experience, George MacDonald was both older and more intellectually advanced than most of his fellow students. As a result, before long he had volunteered his help to the slower of them, and on his own had instituted lectures on chemistry and physics. Now that he was pursuing a course he hoped would lead into a fruitful ministry, he was gaining in confidence all the time. Not only was his belief sound, he had at last come to feel confident in his own spiritual standing. Though a healthy suspicion of his own "self" remained an intrinsic part of his nature throughout life, he was now past the haunting doubts about which he had written his father in 1845 and 1846.

Along with this solidarity, the mysticism of his nature was surfacing to a greater extent. A letter to Greville some years later by Charles Green, one of his close student friends along with James Matheson, Hardwicke Smith, and Robert Troup, makes clear that MacDonald stood out conspicuously: "Conscious as he must have been of such manifest superiority, it never generated any . . . grand airs. . . . He had no eccentricities of manner or dress. . . . He was at all times perfectly natural and easy to approach, though so innate was the poetic and mystic element [in him]. . . ."[4]

As soon as George MacDonald settled at the college, he wrote (on October 19, 1848) a formal letter to Mr. Powell, asking to be allowed to visit his daughter in the hope of one day making her his wife. Greville says, "The reply, I cannot but think, must have surprised almost as much as it rejoiced him. He was accepted." He was, after all, only a struggling theology student; his father was but an industrious tenant-farmer in the impoverished north and could offer him no financial help. Nonetheless, he was welcomed as a future son-in-law by this prosperous, stern disciplinarian whose smile was not always close to the surface. Louisa's mother loved the young Scot dearly. And the personality of the young man was perhaps the most persuasive factor of all. To father and mother, as well as to the daughters, here was a different kind of man than any who had been in their house before. Even to this austere merchant who could put his soul into his violin playing, there was a mystical quality in the young Scot's influence, and he must have recognized that he would provide good keeping for the daughter who loved him.

After receiving Mr. Powell's acceptance, he wrote the following letter to Louisa. Again we notice the strengthening of themes, which will later become integral in his writing: his triumphant view of death as man's true birth, his conviction that growth is the essence of life, the overriding necessity of active *doing* to validate faith, and his unceasingly energetic mind, which *must* inquire into the meaning of everything.

"Highbury College, My Study, Oct. 24, 1848," he heads his letter, and then goes on, ". . . I meant to write a much longer letter to my Louisa and many, beautiful and wise things I wanted to say, but now the impulse has left me. May our Father in heaven be with you and bless you. . . .

"Is love a beautiful thing, dearest? You and I love: but who *created* love? Let us ask him to purify our love to make it stronger and more real and more self-denying. I want to love you for ever—so that, though there is not marrying . . . in heaven, we may see each other there as the best beloved. Oh, Louisa, is it not true that our life here is a growing unto life, and our death a being born—our true birth? If there is anything beautiful in this our dreamy life, shall it not shine forth in glory in the bright waking consciousness of heaven? And in our life together, my dear dear Louisa, if it please God that we should pass any part of our life together here, shall it not still shine when the cloud is over my head? I may see the light shining from your face, and when darkness is around you, you may see the light on mine, and thus we shall take courage. But we can only expect to have this light within us and on our faces—we can only expect to be a blessing to each other—by *doing* that which is right. . . ."[5]

CHAPTER THIRTEEN

MANHOOD
(1848–1850)

Already being a Master of Arts, George MacDonald was only required to spend two years at Highbury before being allowed to be ordained and hold a Congregational pulpit. During those two years, in addition, he was given interruptions in order to gain experience in preaching whenever opportunities arose. Because preaching was seen as the minister's chief duty, it was important for students to become expert in pulpit fervor and exposition through practical exposure. Thus they were encouraged to accept invitations from any church temporarily in need of a pastor, for which duties an honorarium was usually given.

A Student Again

At Highbury George MacDonald's ideas continued to be refined. The hard work and close study (New Testament Greek, classical theology, Augustine, Luther, Irenaeus, Calvin, Knox, etc.) contained frequent interludes of minor ailments such as headaches (possibly from the nearsightedness that eventually drove him to the use of glasses), great fatigue, and more than one sharp attack of bronchitis. The physical problems that would plague him throughout manhood began gradually to impose themselves upon him after a relatively healthy ten or twelve years. But there were pleasures and new experiences wherever he turned—concerts and speeches, art exhibits, dramatic performances of Shakespeare of which he was particularly fond, discussions and debates in which he took an active part, and frequent meetings and outings with the Powells.

Of his two years at Highbury, MacDonald's son Greville perceptively notes: "How much he gained from his theological course we do not know. But likely enough, his studies were of other importance than the professors presumed: they were strengthening his suspicions already germinating, that mere scholarship in the interpretation of Christ's words was of small worth, if not often dangerous; though almost up to his last days he was searching his Greek Testament for its innermost meanings."[1]

His friendship with fellow-student James Matheson led to an even greater intimacy with Greville Matheson, James's elder brother. He worked as a bank clerk and lived, along with another brother, William, and their sister, with his widowed mother in Islington, only a few minutes' walk from Highbury Park, where the college was located. Her hospitable home and gentle wisdom, freely open to any of her sons' friends, played a pivotal role in George MacDonald's Highbury days. He became close to the entire family, and years later included his friend's poems in the collection *A Threefold Cord*. About the relationship with Greville, MacDonald's son, who was named after him, called it, "the friendship with a man of his own mental and spiritual degree, one who was destined to do more for him, with wise admiration and keen criticism, than perhaps any man-friend of later years. For both these services were the outcome of that deep un-uttered affection between man and man, potent as it is rare, of which common minds know but little."[2] MacDonald remained the closest of friends with both Greville and William (ten years his younger), and was with them both within days of their deaths.

Then, as now, doctrinal purity was jealously guarded, especially in theological circles. And once the universal redemption controversy quieted down in the Congregational seminaries, anyone whose orthodoxy aroused suspicion was closely watched. One of the professors at Highbury, John Godwin, a man of great intellect who had authored various New Testament commentaries, was liked by the students and possessed great influence with them. He held somewhat independent views by virtue of his leanings toward Arminianism—which opposes Calvin on the concept of predestination, believing instead that man's responsibility and free choice are the determining factors in salvation. He and George MacDonald developed a close relationship (he later became MacDonald's brother-in-law and lifelong friend) despite several intrinsic differences. George was too outspoken even for Professor Godwin, who took him to task for his informality in speaking, for his tendency to be poetical and intellectual, and for what he termed "doctrinal insecurity"—his polite way of saying that his views were too far from what was acceptable and would likely get him into trouble if he persisted in espousing them! Nonetheless, Godwin had a warm affection for his pupil and secured many speaking engagements for him.

At that time the theater was not a particularly respectable institution and was in a rather poor state, both morally and creatively. It was especially taboo in conservative religious circles. Because of his great love for drama and his indifferent attitude toward others' opinions, however, George MacDonald enjoyed attending upon occasion. After one night at the theater with the Mathesons, MacDonald received an anonymous letter the following morning, advising him that he had been closely observed by one who, if such promptings of Satan were ever yielded to again, would secure his expulsion from Highbury. Some trick in the penmanship, however, revealed the perpetrator of the joke to be one of his companions in the iniquity—either Greville or William Matheson.

Despite Professor Godwin's open disapproval, MacDonald went, sometimes with friends, to hear Alexander John Scott lecture at the Marylebone Institute. It was thus that another of MacDonald's permanent and spiritually sustaining relationships was begun. Scott was a liberal thinker who had begun his career as a Calvinist minister in a suburb of Glasgow. But when he was offered a post in London, Scott said he was no longer able to subscribe to the Westminster Confession, and his ministerial license was revoked. By the time MacDonald was studying theology, Scott had become Professor of English Language and Literature at University College, London, and later was to become Principal of Owens College.

Always fond of horses, young George was often given a mount by Mr. Powell and would then accompany one or more of the young ladies for a ride. Indeed, one of the points in the young man's favor with his prospective father-in-law was his excellent horsemanship, a gift that matched his adaptation to the niceties and manners of polite London ways.

Love Letters

Like George, Louisa was not of the healthiest constitution. In the spring of 1849 the doctor ordered sea air for her, and, therefore, with a friend, she traveled to Hastings, on the coast directly south of London. A long series of letters between the two followed, as they were forced to postpone any plans of marriage until George was suitably employed. In one of these letters is the first mention of Mr. A. J. Scott, whose friendship would play a key role in the couple's future.

The many letters between George and Louisa during this period consist largely of the daily details of life. But there are also glimpses of the still expanding reverence for nature as God's magnificent creation, a strengthening of MacDonald's expressions of its beauty, and an increasing clarity of vision. On May 12, 1849, he wrote: ". . . You tell me about the sea and the sky and the shore so beautifully, so lovingly, so truthfully, that I love you more for it. . . . Tell me again about everything round about you; every expression the beautiful face of Nature puts on. Tell me, too, about the world within your own soul—that living world—without which the world without would be but a lifelessness. The beautiful things round about you are the expression of God's face, or, as in Faust, the garment whereby we see the deity. Is God's sun more beautiful than God himself? Has he not left it to us as a symbol of his own life-giving light? But I cannot now explain all that I mean. . . ."[3]

Who could read such words and think the writer of them did not love his God more dearly than anything? And yet hints of potential trouble on the horizon can already be detected. His overpowering veneration for nature; his frequent tendency to quote the Germans; the symbolic and mystical language into which he casts his observations; the underlying assumption that God's love will gloriously triumph over all, even evil; his capacity to see God's glory and His character reflected in everything He has made, from the sun to the tiniest of insects, all reveal that he has already veered from the sort of faith that would have pleased old grandmother Falconer. Such an outlook is too wide, too new, too unfamiliar, and therefore threatening to those who do not share it.

Such change anticipates the next decade in the life of George Mac-Donald. For the present, God was becoming more intimate and personal to him, while his love for Louisa grew and hers for him. And because she loved him, she too, now that questions of his doctrinal orthodoxy for her were past and she *knew* of his love for God, was growing to view God's character in a new light.

A second letter, written just three days later, amplifies on these themes; it is even more figurative and philosophical, poetical, full of imagery, and full of a sense of wonder at God's way. It also discloses his longing for her. "I have just read your letter, dearest . . ." he writes, ". . . I have had a letter from you every day as yet. Only a week today since you went! Well, I would not have you back one hour sooner, if my heart were like to break with its longing. You have beautiful things around you, and beautiful things are creeping into your soul, and making a home for themselves there—and my wife is growing more beautiful for me. Does not He deserve thanksgiving who made male and female? . . .

"Write to me about the sea and sky, and all those never-ceasing beauties, ever changing yet still the same, which are common to all men—like those great truths the *sense* of which makes a man feel great too—those truths ever the same yet ever presenting new aspects of beauty, different to different minds, different to the same mind at different times—yet ever in essence one and the same . . .

"I have been trying to translate a little poem of Goethe's, entitled

NAHE DER GELIEBTEN

I think of thee when of the sun the shimmer
    From the sea streams;
I think of thee when of the Moon the glimmer
    From deep wells beams.

I see thee, when upon the far Way's Ridge
    The Dust-cloud wakes;
In the deep Night, when on the narrow Bridge
    The Wanderer quakes.

I hear thee there, when with a rushing low
    Falleth the Wave,
In the still Thicket loitering oft I go
    Quiet as the grave.

I am with thee, and tho' thou are so far,
    Yet thou art near!
The Sun doth sink, soon lighteth me each Star
    Oh! wert thou here!"[4]

Following these two letters, Greville comments: "If there be such things as milestones on a man's spiritual pilgrimage, then I think these two letters must stand as such. They indicate the long road already traveled and recall something won; but they also suggest the many miles yet to come. My father's words are the poet's who knows what eyes and ears are given for; they are the philosopher's who amplifies and explains every sentiment the senses awaken; they are the prophet's who bids the weary and travel-stained lift their eyes to the hills whence help always comes: and then, on for another milestone. But some of us who have been led by his later imaginative writings to get sense of the fairy realms which not even his poesy can wholly reveal to us, will, in looking back upon their master's earlier journey, see that himself at twenty-five had but reached the little wicket-gate, to which, later he led ourselves—children, lovers, parents— bidding us enter and take each our own way."

He then goes on to illustrate his point with references to his father's fiction: "In his most imaginative stories he is constantly offering help to the divine questionings. In *The Princess and the Goblin* it is a little invisible clue, which when at last we have hold on it, we dare never lose again. And in his novels he teaches the same truth more directly. . . . Compare this passage about nature, from the novel, *What's Mine's Mine*, written almost forty years later than these letters: 'If you would hear her wonderful tales, or see her marvellous treasures, you must not trifle with her; you must not talk as if you could rummage her drawers and cabinets as you pleased. You must believe in her; you must reverence her; else, although she is everywhere about the house, you may not meet her from the beginning of one year to the end of another. . . . I have all the time been leading you toward the door at which you want to go in. It is not likely, however, that it will open to you at once. I doubt if it will open to you except through sorrow. . . . When you have got quite alone, sit down and be lonely . . . fold your hands in your lap, and be still. Do not try to think anything . . . by and by, it may be, you will begin to know something of nature. Nature will soon speak to you, or not until, as Henry Vaughn says, some veil be broken in you.'"[5]

First Pulpit in Ireland

Churches in the Congregational denomination were free to choose their own ministers. When a vacancy occurred, a church would invite various applicants to come and preach, oftentimes young men nearing completion of their theological studies. If an initial sermon proved satisfactory, a trial period might be arranged for the fill-in, or "supply" minister, to see how he suited the congregation over a longer period as he carried out all the pastoral responsibilities. To prepare the young men for preaching, the college often arranged for its students to preach in neighboring churches. Professor Godwin admitted that young George MacDonald usually gave satisfaction upon such occasions. But apparently there was something missing, because none of his first assignments resulted in any further overtures toward him on the part of the churches, and after the second of these he could not help but feel disappointment.

In the late spring of 1849 George MacDonald wrote to his father to discuss the possibility of going to Cork in southern Ireland for three months to take a temporary pastorate. Second only to his longing to do God's work was his craving to no longer be a financial burden upon his father and to pay the modest debts that had accumulated. He left for Ireland in the middle of June.

The Irish welcomed him warmly, and the letters from Cork to his father show that he gained much knowledge of the world. The hospitality of the people surrounded him, and for the most part he had a pleasant time of it. One of the deacons lent him a horse, and his rides were a great release for his spirit. But his emotional and physical ups and downs persisted; he was again laid up with bronchitis and suffered from low spirits—"no new thing with me," he says.

He wrote to his father on July 25: "My conscience has never been more at ease with regard to my studies. I am very glad I came here, to let me try myself a little; and though I have not so much confidence in my capabilities as perhaps you have, yet I get on pretty well, though I am very doubtful how I shall ever be able to write more than one sermon a week. . . . Yesterday morning I went some six miles east from Youghal to see the devotions of the poor Catholics at one of the round towers of Ireland and by two holy wells, and a holy stone, said to be floated from Rome, under which they creep for rheumatism, etc. . . ."[6]

Recalling her destruction of all the ancient Catholic family records as wiles of the devil, his grandmother would no doubt have been horrified to learn of her grandson's having to do with Catholics in Ireland. In a similar vein, after receiving a letter from his fiancée containing unkind words about the man a friend of hers was about to marry, he writes reprovingly for her disparaging remarks about Unitarians. His openness toward others who claimed the faith, no matter how distant their views, was occasionally a bit much even for Louisa.

During the summer Louisa pined terribly for her fiancé. From the very outset theirs was a relationship of deeper friendship than for many husbands and wives. They communicated about everything, shared life completely on all levels, and were not only bethrothed but intimate friends. To be parted was to not be whole. Every little tidbit of life was to be shared, to be lived *together*. This foundation continued, not just through courtship, but throughout the fifty-six years they spent together.

Possibly some of her anguish during his absence in Cork was caused by the beginnings of criticism of her husband-to-be, something she would grow more accustomed to in coming years. In this case it came from George's brother Charles, who came to London for a visit and expressed himself very candidly and critically concerning George's "mistake" in undertaking the work in Cork when his prospects in Manchester would have been so far superior. The discussion in question took place at the Powell home, where her sister-in-law Helen (George's and Charles' cousin) was also present. The first signs of a noticeable tension between the two women flared up, and Louisa wrote indignantly to George at the way Helen spoke "as if she was so much George's superior!"

Such occasions depressed her afterward, making her question whether she should marry at all. Greville writes that she was beginning "to realize the suffering that such consecrated companionship as was theirs must necessarily invite. Her letters written during this period are full of strange variations of mood. . . . Now and again it seems as if she could not bear to read his exalted thoughts. She is oppressed by her inability to share in his joy over God's glories . . . claiming her unfitness, almost begging him to let her go, saying she could bear anything that was for his good. Again she breaks out into simple yet anguished solicitude for his health; his cough is constantly mentioned."[7]

But all was not gloomy. The following letter signals an altogether different mood: ". . . I had such a very beautiful dream last night, dear. I dreamt I had a vision, it was so beautiful! I think it was at sunset. I was looking earnestly at the clouds when one thick volume of pink and white cloud had two faces; the cloud was all the shape and colour to show them. I looked at them for a long time not knowing who it was, but soon discovered your face, only grown into a beautiful old man with the most glorified and perfectly beautiful expression upon it. The other for some time I thought was Mama, but upon looking and thinking, hoped it was I, with long white hair. I held a book out of which you were reading. You had your arm round my neck . . . after looking for some time, the cloud melted away: then someone told me it was a vision sent to me that I might not fear present evil to either of us. Perhaps this is hardly worth telling you about; but I do not know when I have had any so beautiful a dream, or any that has made so strong an impression on my waking thoughts. . . ."[8]

On the contrary, how prophetically worth telling was her dream! For the two did indeed grow old and white-haired together, and never ceased their loving ministrations to each other. Their golden wedding anniversary picture is reminiscent of Louisa's dream of fifty-two years earlier.

Coming back to England, the young preacher risked the supreme disapproval of his future father-in-law. Mr. Powell had always been openly proud of his young friend's breeding—at any rate, until the day when George returned from Ireland. He sported on his face a reminder of man's unregenerate days and savage origin—a dark, black beard! Greville describes the incident: "The delinquent had been three months away, yet when Mr. Powell returned from the city and found him in the drawing-room with his daughters, he hesitated for one moment, gave him a second look, then, without greeting, turned and left the room. My father, so my mother would tell us, immediately went . . . and, with soap and razor, obliterated his offence."[9] It was several years more before he would give up shaving again; the beard was not grown for good until approximately 1854.

After Cork, George MacDonald settled down once again to his studies at Highbury, punctuated occasionally by preaching at various churches in hopes of gaining something permanent. Midway through the school year the possibility of a post opened up at Stebbing. He preached there once and then wrote the following to his father (February 23, 1850): ". . . Yesterday, however, a note came from one of the deacons at Stebbing, telling me that I . . . was not acceptable to many of the people. . . . The more intellectual part, I believe, would have liked me . . . indeed, I think this is the feeling about me generally in other places; [but] many say they can't understand me. I tried to be as simple as possible at Stebbing. They are a nice, kind-hearted country people, but I cannot say I am disappointed . . . God takes care of me—though I don't deserve it. Perhaps my manner is too quiet to please dissenters commonly. However, I must not do violence to the nature God has given me, and [artificially] put anything on. I think, if people will try, I can make them understand me—if they won't, I have no desire to be understood. I can't do their part of the work. . . ."[10]

Notwithstanding this rebuff, Mr. Godwin again found a temporary assignment for his favorite pupil, and in April MacDonald did a month's preaching duty at Whitehaven, Cumberland, far to the north in England, where his father hoped "he would find mountains ready made to please his poetical mind without putting it to the labor of portraying imaginary ones."

Many are the letters of this period between George MacDonald and his betrothed and his father. Though his father's letters occasionally ring with the familiar sound of parental advice and admonishment, George MacDonald, Sr., was nevertheless wholeheartedly supportive of the direction God was leading his son. Late in life as he was, we sense the elder MacDonald's continuing openness as he is still able to discuss his son's uncustomary views with candor. Of this remarkable family bond, Greville says, "it is impossible, let me repeat, to give any whole idea of the son without picturing the father and brothers, the mother and little sisters [born after he left home], who were so literally, though miles might keep their bodies far separate, part and parcel of his welfare."[11]

Toward the end of May 1850, his father wrote of better times at last for the Farm: "My Dear George," he begins, "Almost all the family have gone to meeting save myself, and I am just away from having worship with the farm servants. The children are off to help each other to bed, the voice of the mill has ceased—the falling water alone with its continual buzz is the only thing that falls upon the ear, where I am sitting. The evening is calm, warm, and beautiful. The midges sport in thousands above the water, and nature, long detained from its summer garb, is now getting into lovely verdure. What a change in the course of one short week!—plenty of grass now for the starving cattle, and the corn crops are advancing as if within the tropics. But our seasons are changeable, as you may well remember, and how long such a state of things may remain, it is impossible to say. . . . We have ground for confidence in our God, the author of all blessings, that He who spared not His only son, but delivered him up to the death for us all, will with Him also *freely give us all things*. . . ."[12]

Though he was in the final days of his formal training for the ministry,

George MacDonald continued seeking further illumination. Toward the end of May he wrote his father a lengthy letter discussing the age-old theological conflict between Calvin's predestination and Arminius's "free will" doctrine. His father's open response reveals much, particularly for one who had spent his life in Calvinism. As for the son, settling one issue in his mind only served as impetus to delve into the next thorny dilemma of faith, wherever such inquiry led. His father wrote: ". . . Your long letter yesterday gave me something of variety to think about which pleased me, notwithstanding that part of it was rather too philosophical for the cast of my mind; but in so far as I am able [to] see, the views of both of us are very much alike. . . . Like you, I cannot by any means give in to the extreme points either of *Calvinism* or *Arminianism*, nor can I bear to see that which is evidently *gospel mystery* torn to pieces by those who believe there is no mystery in the scriptures and therefore attempt to explain away what it is evidently for the honor of God to conceal. I see so much of mystery in nature, and so much of it in myself, that it would be a proof to my mind that the scriptures were not from God were there nothing in them beyond the grasp of my own mind. As to the responsibility of man and his power of choice, I think there can be no doubt.

"As to the '*new faith*' folks, I believe they hold many important things in common with ourselves. . . . [But] they have without the least compunction split in pieces many churches. . . . Is it to be endured that for the sake of a few speculative minds a whole community of . . . Christians shall become agitated . . . and the house of God made the place . . . for a sort of *debating society*? I consider the peace of a Christian Church too important a matter to run the risk of the disunions and hatred which have been created in too many quarters around us."

He then closes the letter with words indicating that his son's days at Highbury were nearly done, and with another simple reminder of the ever-troublesome nature of finances: "Let me hear from you before leaving the College, and I shall do my best if need be. . . ."[13]

So in the summer of 1850, at twenty-five and a half years of age, George MacDonald completed his course of study at Highbury Theological College. The long decade of growing, searching, and questioning appeared at last nearly over.

His enthusiasm must have run high, for it had been four years since he had met Louisa, and they had been waiting two years to marry. And he had every reason to confidently anticipate finding a receptive pulpit before many more months from which he could tell people of the Lord's great love, which they had only to open their eyes to see.

Therefore, June of 1850 dawned bright with the hope of the future.

CHAPTER FOURTEEN

THE FAITH OF
GEORGE MACDONALD
IN PERSPECTIVE

The 19th century in Great Britain was one of singular religious and social upheaval. At every point, past norms were being challenged, rewritten, and thrown out. The political and social status quo had never been more uncertain. Scientific advances were accelerating with rapidity. The church was in flux. Splinter and dissenting groups seemed to divide off almost monthly from existing churches—over the smallest doctrinal disputes. Not only was there fierce antipathy between the Church of England and the Catholic Church of Rome, centered around the colorful figure of John Henry Newman and the "Oxford Movement," but there was also great change at the other end of the spectrum. The remarkable success of John Wesley's Methodism gave rise late in the 18th century to a great evangelical revival that led to many social reforms, as well as modification in many growing evangelical denominations.

This fluctuating social and religious environment has given rise to Robert Lee Wolff's perceptive observation: "Innocently we read Victorian fiction for enjoyment," he says, "and fail to realize that often we are not understanding it." He goes on to detail some of these areas where our world of today differs from that of a century ago, limiting our capacity to understand between the lines of what we read.

"We miss not only topical references to news of the day—a parliamentary election, a scandal over the conditions of child-labor in the cotton-mills, a sensational murder, a gold-strike in Australia—but also allusions to whole worlds of opinion, of discourse, and of social relations that have now vanished. The relations between landlord and tenant on a large estate, the attitudes of farmers toward the passage of the local hunt over their ploughed fields, the difference between a prison (gaol) and a penitentiary, the varying social status of undergraduates at the universities, the purchase and sale of commissions in the army: all are foreign to the late 20th century and make readers of Victorian novels cry out for footnotes. However, of all the subjects that interested Victorians, and therefore preoccupied their novelists, none—not love, or crime, or war, or sport, or ancestry, or even money—held their attention as much as religion. And of all the subjects none is more obscure to the modern reader."

We can quickly see how accurate his comments are, especially when we consider the changes in the religious atmosphere between then and now.

"Not since the seventeenth century . . . had religious contention been the stuff of everyday English life . . . families were bitterly divided. The Church of England was rent by party controversy. . . . Quarrels raged over a wide variety of doctrinal issues: what to believe; and of practical issues: how the service should be conducted. Except for a few at the extreme High-Church end of the spectrum, members of the Church of England were united in their opposition to Roman Catholicism. . . . Except for some at the extreme Low-Church end of the spectrum, members of the Church of England were united against the Protestants outside the Church: the many sects of Nonconformists or Dissenters. Before long, the questions broadened in the minds of many, if not most, Victorians. They were troubled not only about what to believe and how to practice their religion, but also about whether to believe at all. . . . Doubts were fostered by the advances of science, which rendered the Bible's account of creation suspect; by the advances of scholarship, which showed that the books of the Bible must have been written down at widely different times; by ethical qualms over certain Christian doctrines; by the impossibility of reconciling the concept of a wholly benevolent and all-powerful God with the doctrine of eternal punishment for sinners. There seems at times to have been as many varieties of doubt as there were human beings in Victorian England.

"Hundreds, perhaps thousands, of novels reflect every aspect of the public religious controversies and the private religious agonies."[1]

Neither Liberal nor Fundamentalist

Through a particularly stern Calvinistic corner of Scottish "Dissention" George MacDonald entered this 19th century milieu, and shortly after the middle of the century, began to try to enlighten and broaden it. As noted by Wolff, there were unbelievable numbers of books written espousing every conceivable doctrine and personal point of view that were eagerly devoured by the public. MacDonald was a man—given his background, his rebellion against the religious views of his upbringing, his cutting intellectual mind, his education, his interest in Darwin, his love for the latest scientific developments, and his poetic and mystical bent—who might have been likely to jump off some deep end or another in search of his own personal obsession and destiny, which he would then foist off on a gullible public.

But George MacDonald's revolutionary spiritual and moral extremism were of an altogether different kind than what might have been expected—certainly different than others of his day who, like him, were rising up against the attitudes they felt needed to be restructured. A revolutionary he certainly was in the closely guarded circles of dissenting Calvinist theology. And his chief influence was exerted at the fundamental Calvinist end of Victorian Britain's religious spectrum, where he had the profoundest impact. Yet at the same time, he would hardly have been viewed as fanatical at the High Church/Catholic end of the spectrum where progressivism reigned, where Unitarianism flourished, and where science and religion were able to meet and even occasionally hold business together. As Louise Willcox said as early as 1906, and is even more true today as the leftward swing of the religious pendulum has continued: "He was to his own age shockingly liberal, and to ours he is amazingly orthodox."[2]

That could be said of him even within his own lifetime. He remained tolerant toward Catholics, unprejudiced toward Calvinists, fiercely denouncing hypocrisy wherever he saw it, clinging to any doctrine he felt was true no matter how ancient and traditional. He based his life and his hope on the person of Jesus Christ as revealed in the gospel; never afraid to probe the previously unexplored, avoiding no taboos, friend of Unitarians and atheists and Calvinists alike, he gave himself and his life's work to that great middle or "common ground," which is always to be found in the center of Christendom and which is defined by how one practically *lives* one's faith. Thus his writings and his person can be viewed either as incendiary in their progressive ecumenicalism, or positively fundamental in their adherence to so many of the traditional reformed Protestant traditions.

But in one thing he was, if not revolutionary, certainly unique: he remained open to all, no matter what their positions. He often said he never met a person he could not learn from. Thus, while others were busy unloading their many viewpoints onto a receptive public, George MacDonald was engaged at an altogether different level. He was busy calling men to what Richard Foster has termed "the authenticity of simplicity, the spirit of prayer, and the life of obedience": obedience to the lifestyle of Jesus Christ. His writings and ideas, therefore, have continued—silently, invisibly, unnoticed—through the years to engender a unity within the sweeping spectrum of the Christian body of believers. Because his primary concern was not to convince the world of *his* particular viewpoints, the seed of his broad, ever-growing, and tolerant faith has taken root and sprouted in the most unlikely places throughout the entire continuum of Christendom, drawing people together in a common unity based on the very principle which was the guiding force of MacDonald's own existence: that life with

God is to be *lived* in relationship with Him and one's fellow man, not doctrinalized.

From a spiritual perspective, George MacDonald's significance lies not in the liberal or the fundamental pigeonhole we may ascribe to him, but rather in the concept of God's character he portrayed in his writings. Perhaps as we read his words today, much does not sound particularly revolutionary. But what made him distinctive in his day was the context from which he emerged. He came out of a misapplied Calvinism, where God's wrath was supreme, to proclaim a God of an altogether different disposition. In doing so he became neither a liberal nor a skeptic. For the God of MacDonald's pen was infinitely more personal and demanding than any vague liberal deity, more human and warm and tolerant than Calvin's harsh heavenly taskmaster.

Therefore, MacDonald was pivotal in the annals of both literature and Christian thought. He was not the first to rebel against the stern legalism that held Scotland in its grip. His more famous countrymen Thomas Carlyle (1795–1881) and Robert Burns (1759–1796) were both raised in the strictest of religious homes, Carlyle's father intending his son for the ministry. Like MacDonald, they too rebelled. But their rebellion was characterized by a complete rejection of fundamental Christian values—Carlyle through the criticism found in his writings, Burns through the self-indulgence of his life. Carlyle, too, read Novalis, but it turned him toward transcendentalism and away from the personal element of faith, while it turned George MacDonald *toward* the personal aspects of God's character. MacDonald's good friend John Ruskin (1819–1900) was another noted English author who was raised for the ministry but then rejected the faith of his childhood, never to return to it despite his intimacy with the Mac-Donalds.

George MacDonald was exceptional in being able to disengage himself so completely from the chains of heavy puritanical legalism that he could go forward *into* genuine Christian truth, which found outlets in many diverse forms—novels, fairy tales, sermons, essays, lectures, and fantasy stories. No Burns or Carlyle or Ruskin, coming out of the Calvinist end, could do so. Neither could any John Henry Newman at the other end of the spectrum. The critics criticized, the skeptics charted their own secular course, the scientists dispensed with religion altogether, the Calvinists entrenched themselves behind the locked doors of their doctrines, and the liberals looked down on the fundamentalists as unenlightened. Though some could perceive issues clearer than others, none of these could see to the end of the spectrum in the opposite direction. George MacDonald, however, embraced viewpoints and individuals from *all* these camps. He had close friends who were Unitarians, befriended unbelievers, wrote admiringly of skeptics, respected his Calvinist father above all living men, was sympathetic with the doctrine of universal redemption while at the same time writing about the tormenting pains of the purifying hellfire, and refused to be boxed in at every point—appearing liberal one moment and conservative and traditional the next. Thus he found that foundational bedrock underlying Christianity—a middle ground based not on doctrine at all but upon obedience, a middle ground so urgently needed and yet so hard to maintain among Christians who are more interested in discussing their disagreements than what they hold in common.

A Truly "Original" Scotsman

MacDonald did not allow his Calvinist background to taint and forever mar his imaginative, mystical, and poetic gifts. Nor did he allow it to turn him into a critic of the church and its people. He found instead, the balanced perspective of the middle. For these reasons his position in the explosive 19th-century's religious world was highly unusual.

A further analysis by G. K. Chesterton (early 20th-century author and theologian) bears consideration. Chesterton wrote a scholarly introduction to the 1924 edition of *George MacDonald and His Wife* by Greville MacDonald. In it, after outlining his own personal debt to MacDonald, Chesterton very perceptively places George MacDonald's historical significance in Scottish Calvinism, with particular reference to others of that country's well-known men of letters and literature: Carlyle and Burns as already noted, and Sir Walter Scott (1771–1832), another Scot raised a Calvinist who later joined the Church of England, but who never developed a personal faith that influenced his writings, a man whose religion remained his own private affair. Chesterton's discussion provides an enlightened context, which gives perspective to George MacDonald's faith:

"The originality of George MacDonald has also a historical significance, which perhaps can best be estimated by comparing him with his great country-man Carlyle. It is a measure of the very real power even popularity of Puritanism [Calvinism] that Carlyle never lost the Puritan mood even when he lost the whole of the Puritan theology. If an escape from the bias of environment be the test of originality, Carlyle never completely escaped, and George MacDonald did. He evolved out of his own mystical meditations a complete alternative theology. . . . And in those mystical meditations he learned secrets far beyond the mere extension of Puritan indignation to ethics and politics. For in the real genius of Carlyle there was a touch of the bully, and wherever there is an element of bullying there is an element of platitude, of reiteration and repeated orders. Carlyle could never have said anything so subtle and simple as MacDonald's saying that God is easy to please and hard to satisfy. Carlyle was too obviously occupied with insisting that God was hard to satisfy; just as some optimists are doubtless too much occupied with insisting that He is easy to please. In other words, MacDonald had made for himself a sort of spiritual environment, a space . . . of mystical light which was quite exceptional in his national and denominational environment. He said things that were like the Cavalier mystics, like the Catholic saints, sometimes perhaps like the Platonists or the Swedenborgians, but not in the least like the Calvinists, even as Calvinism remained in a man like Carlyle. And when he comes to be more carefully studied as a mystic, as I think he will be when people discover the possibility of collecting jewels scattered in a rather irregular setting, it will be found, I fancy, that he stands for a rather important turning-point in the history of Christendom, as representing the particular Christian nation of the Scots. As Protestants speak of the morning stars of the Reformation, we may be allowed to note such names here and there as morning stars of the Reunion."

From this comparison, Chesterton moves on to illuminate MacDonald's position by looking at what he calls the emotional or spiritual "color" of Scotland.

"The spiritual colour of Scotland, like the local colour of so many Scottish moors, is a purple that in some lights can look grey. The national character is in reality intensely romantic and passionate—indeed, excessively and dangerously romantic and passionate. Its emotional torrent has only too often been turned towards revenge, or lust, or cruelty, or witchcraft. There is no drunkenness like Scotch drunkenness; it has in it the ancient shriek and the wild shrillness of the Maenads on the mountains. And of course it is equally true on the good side, as in the great literature of the nation. . . . Nevertheless, by a queer historical accident this vivid and coloured people have been forced to 'wear their blacks' in sort of endless funeral on an eternal Sabbath. . . .

"The passionate and poetical Scots ought obviously, like the passionate and poetical Italians, to have had a religion which competed with the beauty and vividness of the passion, which did not let the devil have all the bright colours, which fought glory with glory and flame with flame. It should have balanced Leonardo with St. Francis; [yet] no young and lively person really thinks he can be balanced with John Knox. The consequence was that this power in Scottish letters, especially in the day (or night) of complete Calvinistic orthodoxy, was weakened and wasted in a hundred ways. In Burns it was driven out of its due course like a madness; in Scott it was only tolerated as a memory. Scott could only be a mediaevalist by becoming what he would call an antiquary, or what we should call an aesthete. He had to pretend his love was dead, that he might be allowed to love her. As Nicodemus came to Jesus by night, the aesthete only comes to church by moonlight.

"Now, among the many men of genius Scotland produced in the 19th century, there was only one so original as to go back to this origin. There was only one who really represented what Scottish religion should have been, if it had continued the colour of the Scottish mediaeval poetry. In his particular type of literary work he did indeed realize the apparent paradox of a St. Francis of Aberdeen, seeing the same sort of halo round every flower or bird. It is not the same thing as any poet's appreciation of the beauty of the flower or bird. A heathen can feel that and remain heathen, or in other words remain sad. It is a certain special sense of significance, which the tradition that most values it calls sacramental. To have got back to it, or forward to it, at one bound of boyhood, out of the black Sabbath of a Calvinist town, was a miracle of imagination."[3]

A Critic From Within the Ranks

Calvinism was a theological perspective, a particular approach to the interpretation of Scripture and the viewing of God, man, and the world. George MacDonald came from no specific denomination as such, but rather out of a theological mindset. The particular brand of Calvinism which had been represented to him in his youth paralleled classic Old Testament legalism, a system based on works in which the least doctrinal incongruity was noted and swiftly dealt with, and in which the faithful had to be constantly on their guard for heretics poisoning the flock. It was such puritanism several generations earlier, both in Britain and in the United States, that so righteously guarded the tenets of faith that heretics were burned at the stake that God's vengeance might be carried out.

Certainly there had been critics before. But as part of their criticism they usually threw out their whole belief in a personal God who had inspired the Scriptures, who desired to relate himself intimately and individually to man, and whose intrinsic essence was love. In stark contrast, MacDonald kept his faith in the Christian God—ever deepening and personalizing it still further—and then repudiated the negative, somber, dark puritanism of his upbringing. To MacDonald, nature was a wondrous display of God's handiwork, equal to the Bible in its manifestation of God's goodness and His love. God himself was a smiling and joyful Father in whom we could find refuge, a Father of infinite love, not displeased with man's every move but delighted in man's feeblest attempt to respond to Him. The Sabbath was God's day to enjoy and delight in. Nothing was too good for God. All the beauty, poetry, music, laughter, imagination, and creative energy in the world originated in His creative heart of love. Indeed, to George MacDonald, God's love was so everlasting that He would continue to love sinners to himself, though it took the excruciating fires of the next life to purge away their sin; for God was so enormous that even hell fell within His dominion. The whole universe was His. The gospel was indeed "good news," not black, not dreary, but joyful and liberating. Such a view of God's character, rather than weakening MacDonald's perspective on the importance of relating oneself to Jesus Christ in salvation and obedience, strengthened it all the more. So good was God in every way, that only in complete obedience to Him could fulfillment in life be attained.

Thus George MacDonald became an extremely controversial figure. He could not so easily be dismissed, because he spoke from *within* the ranks of Christendom. He could not be called an atheist or a skeptic or an unbeliever. He was called a heretic, and yet what heretic was so insistent upon the very premises of orthodoxy which Calvin himself stressed along with everything else—repentance from sin, salvation, death of the old man, and obedience to the Spirit of Christ? What heretic was so insistent upon relating himself to Jesus Christ? What heretic read his New Testament at every opportunity, seeking new and deeper ways of ordering his life by its truths?

In fact, the totality of George MacDonald's theology demonstrates how very orthodox he was, with but a few notable exceptions. His sermons could have come out of many evangelical pulpits. He preached about Jesus, about God's love, about prayer, about salvation, about miracles, about the resurrection, and *always* about living in obedience to the truths of Scripture. But his was no theology to be stuffed into a mold. He developed his beliefs through what he knew of God's nature as revealed in the Bible and in the world, not with respect to any "doctrine of men." Thus he is at once shockingly liberal, and so straightforwardly orthodox one wonders how his name and the word heresy could ever be uttered in the same breath.

He was in no sense out to subvert Calvinist notions, but to call the hearts of men to revival, urging them toward the God who made them. He held far more doctrines in common with Calvin than he opposed. As his son Ronald said, "George MacDonald . . . was in the prime of his great effort to revive personal religion within the fold. He made no war upon the Church as he knew it—whether independent, Presbyterian, or Anglican; his war was upon the faithlessness of the officially faithful, and, incidentally only, upon one or two Calvinist and Augustinian dogmas exaggerated out of all proportion to their service."[4]

His stinging pronouncement stands against this faithlessness of which his son speaks: "I doubt if wickedness does half as much harm as sectarianism, whether it be the sectarianism of the Church [of England] or of dissent [non–Church of England], the sectarianism whose virtue is condescension, or the sectarianism whose vice is pride. Division has done more to hide Christ from the view of men than all the infidelity that has ever been spoken. It is the half-Christian clergy of every denomination that are the main cause of the so-called failure of the Church of Christ" (*Paul Faber, Surgeon*, Ch. 28).

He was seen, however, by those on the extreme right as "dangerous," and opposition followed him throughout his life. Chesterton's warm words are tempered by many who thought MacDonald's writings evil. Even his own devout uncle James at one point convinced a local paper not to review his nephew's book because of the offense sure to be generated by the characters he had portrayed. Of this negative side of the reaction, Wolff notes:

"In MacDonald's own day, there were many who were outraged at his brisk refutation of Calvinism: . . . His revulsion against Calvinism, they felt, had broken all bounds. His idea that it was possible to repent in hell, and so to qualify for redemption, created—the critics declared—a sort of 'Protestant purgatory.' . . . Sentimental overemphasis on love alone led to the neglect of the meaning and implications of sin. MacDonald's 'benign determinism,' his over-optimism, his use of 'domestic emotions'—the love of sons for fathers—as the scale by which to measure God and the principles of God's rule, was to derive theological conclusions from 'facile surface emotion for the offspring,' and to reduce ethical mysteries to 'a sweet and effeminate type of domestic love.' . . . In the MacDonald theology, they scornfully declared, 'we are each of us blessed with a nature good enough from the beginning, and, once we cleanse away a trifle of rubbish that overlays or obscures it, we 'find ourselves,' and very soon find our God.' Such reasoning was 'sentimental vaporing.' These strictures serve to show the continued power of Calvinism down to the turn of the twentieth century. The vehemence of both MacDonald's supporters and his opponents reflects his key importance as a sympathetic portrayer of individual Scotch Calvinists (both Church-of-Scotland and 'Missionar') and as a powerful critic of their doctrines. When one remembers in addition his own career in the Congregational ministry in England and his first-hand knowledge of the small-town English nonconformist congregation, one unhesitatingly puts him into the front rank of the novelists of Dissent."[5]

Thus George MacDonald emerged, in 1850, with his career and all that accompanied it still ahead of him, into the spiritually and socially charged world that was 19th-century Victorian Britain. Of what lay ahead for him and his wife-to-be he had not a glimmer. He knew only that his faith in God, and in God's life within his own heart, was stronger than it had been at any time in all his twenty-five years. With that confidence and optimism, he moved forward, and into the mainstream of history.

PART THREE

Arundel on England's South Downs, site of George MacDonald's first pastorate—Arundel Castle on the far right.

THE POET PREACHER

A young man of about twenty-seven sat at a small desk in the corner of an upstairs bedroom. The lodgings were small, even though they must house himself and his wife and their newborn daughter. This was the only spot he could find that might legitimately pass for an office. In any case, it was all he had.

And he was ecstatically happy for it! He had at length completed school. He and his beloved wife were at long last together and married, on their own, and blessed with a beautiful baby girl. His health was on the mend, and his dream of the last few years—a pulpit of his own from which to preach—had at last been realized. God had indeed blessed him richly!

He sat at the tiny desk and stared out the window. He could just see the top of his church, across the rooftops, where it stood on the other end of Tarrant Street at the lower end of the village. The houses of his parish were scattered up the hill in front of the church, and spread out on either side toward the river in one direction and toward the flat pastureland in the other. Directly behind the church, at a distance of some five miles over the south downs, lay the English Channel.

He sat still, gazing out the window. Tomorrow he would stand in the pulpit of that very church.

And say what?

He had been sitting there for an hour now, and so far the only thing he had written down were a few lines of verse.

But poetry did not make particularly good sermons. Not that he hadn't tried it a time or two. But he was gradually discovering that his parishioners were not, by any stretch of the word, intellectuals. As much as he loved them, they were of a different sort than he had been accustomed to speaking with at Highbury, and he realized he had to modify his words to suit their needs.

But it was not always easy. The poetry and imaginative illustrations seemed bent on coming out, even when he didn't plan it. Just two

Sundays ago there had been that conversation after church about Mrs. Hemway's dog. Thinking to help ease the sorrow of the poor widow's losing her four-legged friend, he had inadvertently let slip a comment about getting to see old Guffy again in the next life! How could he have known what an uproar his innocent statement would have caused?

And that poem he had read two months ago had received such a somber reaction among his listeners. It had positively thrilled him when he first read the words. It was a good thing he hadn't mentioned the name Novalis to anyone, or that he was a German!

Perhaps a walk along the river would help formulate his thoughts.

He rose, picked up his hat and walking stick, kissed his wife, and went out. The air was pleasantly crisp, with just enough of a hint of the coming autumn to invigorate the senses.

He walked briskly through the narrow streets of the village, stopping to chat for a few moments with the carpenter. The door to his shop was wide open, and a thick trail of shavings poured out from the floor under his workbench and toward the walk outside.

As he continued on he waved to the baker's wife, poked his head inside the butcher's shop to say hello to his husky friend Stephens. Farther along he exchanged a few words with the muscular blacksmith, whose forge would be one of the chief attractions of the village children when winter came on in earnest. At length he reached the edge of the village, and the bridge over the river where he had met Old Rogers his second afternoon in town. Crossing it, he turned left and made his way along the riverbank. The green pasture on his right was filled with grazing cattle in the distance. Across the river to his left rose the impressive walls of Arundel Castle, a sight which always moved him.

"I shall have to write a story about that place some day," he said to himself.

On he walked thinking of nothing in particular, having for the moment forgotten all about tomorrow's sermon. The sound of the slowly meandering river drew him and he walked down the bank to its edge. There he sat upon a large stone, staring into the water as it passed, knocking a pebble here and there into the water with the end of his stick.

All about him Mother Nature was busy with her housework. He drew in a deep breath. How he loved the out-of-doors! Since before he could remember, he had loved all the things that made nature what it was. And now, as he looked around, the most ordinary scenes were delightfully alive with God's life! The cattle grazed, but knew not why. The water ran, but could do no other. The sun shone, yet knew nothing about it. The ferns waved in the breeze. The clouds went drifting overhead. But none of them knew what they did, nor was even capable of knowing at all.

The glories of all these sights were for God and man alone to share. They alone were capable of perceiving and enjoying their glory. And man alone was capable of allowing his love for nature to demonstrate to him the character of God and cause him to worship his heavenly Father. Man alone!

How sad it was that some men partook of nature's goodness, and the truths to be found in nature, as the cows partook of the grass—seeing but perceiving not, partaking but comprehending not.

"Oh, God," he prayed, "help me to draw near to these of your people that you have given me. In your world it is spring. Everything is coming to life, yet that life is not yet born in so many of your children. Bring it yet more to life in me, Lord. Let my love for you and your people blossom as do your flowers and your trees and your ferns. Let my love for you and your people bubble up out of your life inside me as do the streams that feed this river. Take my life, Lord, where you will. Let my life flow according to your purpose as this great river flows to the sea. Let me not make plans where my life should or should not go, Lord, but be guiding and directing my steps though I may feel it not."

He fell silent.

At length he rose and slowly walked home, thinking once more how happy he was to be a servant to God's people.

"Perhaps I shall speak to them about seeing God in nature," he mused. "I will talk to them of primroses and buttercups, of cows and spider webs, of icicles and rivers, of clouds and caves. I will tell them how God is all around them every moment of every day, if only they open their eyes to see Him in the things He has made."

When he reached home, to his unmatched delight he found that his wife had built him a fire to take the late afternoon's chill out of his study, as they called it. He thanked her, then sat down in his favorite chair and continued to think about what he might say on the morrow.

But when at last he rose and again approached his desk, it was not to write down thoughts for his sermon. What he wrote instead were the following words:

> I love the skies, thy sunny mists,
> Thy fields, thy mountains hoar,
> Thy wind that bloweth where it lists—
> Thy will, I love it more.
>
> I love thy hidden truth to seek
> All round, in sea, on shore;
> The arts whereby like gods we speak—
> Thy will to me is more.
>
> I love thy men and women, Lord,
> The children round thy door;
> Calm thoughts that inward strength afford—
> Thy will than these is more.
>
> But when thy will my life doth hold
> Thine to the very core,
> The world, which that same will doth mould,
> I love, then, ten times more!
>
> (*Poetical Works of George MacDonald*,
> vol. 1, "Noontide Hymn")

Trinity Congregational Church in Arundel, now in disuse.

CHAPTER FIFTEEN

THE CALL TO ARUNDEL
(1850-1851)

The latter half of the year 1850 was full of change. In mid-June Louisa's mother, Mrs. Powell, died and two months later Mr. Powell temporarily rented a furnished house for his family directly below London on the Channel seacoast at Brighton, he himself traveling up and down every day to London, though he was now seventy. In August MacDonald had an invitation to take up temporary ministerial duties at the Trinity Congregational Chapel in Arundel, a sleepy little town twenty miles west of Brighton about two miles from the coast. The church was a very small one, with less than 100 members, and had been in existence only some fifty or sixty years.

Two factors about the offer were attractive: one, though the position offered was only as "supply" minister, the congregation at Arundel was in search of a full-time pastor, and it soon appeared highly probable that he would be asked to remain permanently. Second, being only a third the distance that London was from Brighton, trips to the Powells' would not be so difficult. He accepted the offer without hesitation.

Preparations for the Ministry

On August 27, Charlotte, Louisa and cousin Helen visited Arundel, and the following day, after her return to Brighton, Louisa wrote George about her impressions of the place and the thought of living there, as the minister's wife, after they were married: ". . . I did not go to bed before we had unpacked our treasures [from Arundel], looked at the figs and butter, put the sweet flowers into water, and gave the bits of wild roots and flowers a little too; I felt so happy . . . I cannot imagine my ever living in so lovely a place; so near to such beauties. There would be one disadvantage . . . that in such a secluded place I should not be enough for you, dearest. My heart sinks sometimes, oftentimes, when I think of my unsuitableness in so many ways. And oh, if you found it out too late! . . . How kind Mrs. New was to think of taking us to see your rooms. . . . Believe, my dearest George, in the love of your most unworthy child, LOUISA."[1]

Though touching, to contemporary ears Louisa's frequent reference to herself as her lover's "loving child" perhaps sounds a bit quaint. Nevertheless, it reveals the regard she had for the man she was about to marry; he was not only the man she loved, but a spiritual pioneer as well. Also between the lines of this letter are glimpses of what will cause ongoing problems between Louisa and Helen. For years Louisa struggled with feelings of inferiority as she compared herself with the beautiful and talented Helen who had once so charmed her own George. Some time later she would write, ". . . this is my happiness—to know that you love me so truly in spite of my plainness and ignorance. . . ."[2] They were eventually able to work their problems through into a solid familial relationship, although later Louisa would nevertheless refer to Helen's "pin pricks" through the years.

The new minister's own description of Arundel's surroundings was given some time later in a letter to his twelve-year-old half sister: ". . . Behind the town there are very low hills, with sweet short grass, on which numbers of fallow deer are feeding. Here and there are plantations of very fine trees, and down in one of the hollows rises and runs a stream of water, clearer than the Bogie, and so nice to drink in the hot days. . . . We have a river that runs through the town, up which vessels come of a good size, bringing things and taking away things; but it is a very quiet little town—not so much bustle as Huntly. . . . The fields grow much richer crops than with you, and there are many more trees growing about the fields; but it is not such a beautiful country to my mind, nearly, as the one I left. . . ."[3]

The following Sunday Mr. Powell himself traveled to Arundel with his daughter to hear George preach, and early the next morning, before breakfast, he wrote his future son-in-law a lengthy letter concerning his methods.

"MY DEAR SIR," opens Mr. Powell, ". . . Perhaps I ought to apologize for assuming the critic. I only, however, do it on the plea of age, and I then only make these remarks to be received by you if you on consideration think they have any reason in them. I ought perhaps to have commenced with saying how very much I was pleased with your professional services. . . ."[4]

And though what follows is openly modest and respectful, it is yet very definite in advice to the aspiring young preacher, saying at one point that, though he avoided monotony, he did not speak like a divine oracle as he should. George MacDonald, like all young men working their way into manhood in a chosen field, was subject to the universal blessing and curse of advice from his elders. His father, too, had written him in an "old-fashioned tone of parental advice, criticism, and admonishment," in which he had said: ". . . I hope you will by and by be in circumstances to pay off your small debts, and make conscience of never venturing on taking a wife before then. If you begin by thinking lightly of such a case, depend upon it the carelessness will increase until none but yourself . . . can paint the agony it will entail."[5]

For the remainder of September he was at Arundel, and in October, pleased with what they saw in the young man, the congregation extended an official "call" to him to become their permanent minister. In two letters to his father, we learn about his new position, the people, and himself.

"In great haste and half-dressed I am writing, my dear father, to tell you that the Church at the meeting last night [determined] that I should be their minister. . . . They [will] give me 150 Pounds [a year]. . . . I expect to find the work of preaching grow easier and easier, but will be oppressed at first, I fear. That will teach me more faith. Mr. Godwin told me that the accounts he had heard lately of my acceptableness were very gratifying to him. This is something from him, as my sermons have seldom been other than censured by him as unsuitable for the people. I will send you some of my poetry and a sermon or two soon; for I have not time to spend on the composition of sermons, which I preach in a very different style from that in which I write them. . . ." (Oct. 4, 1850).[6]

". . . The invitation was signed by all the Church except five, who had not heard me. . . . I preach for the first time as their Pastor next Sunday. . . . In all things I hope God will teach me. To be without him is to be like a little child, just learning to walk, left alone by its mother. . . .

"We hope to be married in the spring—to which Mr. Powell is quite favourable—and if you would receive us, we should like, if we could, to visit you then—perhaps in April. I should, of course, have much pleasure in letting you and Louisa know and speak to each other, and should like her to see the sky and the hills which first began to mould my spirit.

"You ask whether the Church is of long standing. I cannot say how long—but there is a very old lady still alive, though in her dotage, who was principally the means of forming the Church. There are fifty-seven signatures to the *Call*. . . . They seem a people that would make much of their minister. . . . The people are a simple people—not particularly well informed—mostly tradespeople—and in middling circumstances. They chiefly reside in the town, which has between two and three thousand inhabitants. There are none I could call society for me—but with my books now and the beautiful earth, and added to these soon, I hope, my wife—and above all that, God to care for me—in whom I and all things are—I do not much fear the want of congenial society . . ." (Oct. 16, 1850).[7]

During September, while expecting the offer of this call, the young preacher had been approached by a church in Brighton to see whether he would accept an invitation from them. Not only was he attracted to the simpler ways and affection of the folk at Arundel, but he felt under an obligation to them. He definitely believed, therefore, that he had been led to their pulpit rather than to Brighton with its more well-to-do and better-educated society.

George MacDonald's completion of his studies at Highbury did not include a formal "ordination." This was usually done at the time when a minister took up his first post, and in most Congregational churches the offer of pastorate, or "call," was considered as constituting ordination enough. However, some of the Arundel congregation had questioned the legitimacy of a minister's administration of the sacrament of Communion until some rite of ordination had been performed. Therefore, plans for a formal service were made. MacDonald himself had no strong feeling as to its necessity, while his father was strongly in its favor on the grounds that without it "a suspicion might arise of something wrong in doctrine or character." And now that George could support a wife, definite plans for the wedding were at last made with hopes of a trip to Huntly following.

About this same time George wrote to Louisa and asked her a rather delicate, as it turned out, and embarrassing favor: would she go to Helen and ask his cousin to give her the notebooks of poetry he had sent her years ago? Most of their contents were simply well-known poems by renowned authors copied out for Helen; for it seems Helen had destroyed those of a more personal nature. It is clear George had nothing to hide from Louisa, and in fact wanted her to have the things he had written in his early years. She resisted at first, but eventually did go see Helen, with the interesting result described in her next letter to George.

". . . I went to Helen's last night . . . I felt very much inclined to beg you to write to her, instead of my asking about the books; but when I thought how seldom I can show my love to you by doing anything I do not quite like, I determined not to miss the opportunity, and found it much easier than I expected. She pretended not to know what I meant at first. She thought I meant some of her note-books that you had of hers, and which, as I understood her, you had returned to her. However, she soon understood me, and when I asked for them, saying Papa would perhaps take them, she said, 'Very well, Louisa, I will make up a little packet for *him*.' . . . She was very pleasant and more natural than sometimes, I think, and so we were more cordial friends. I should not like her to go away with the uncomfortable feeling that I am sure has existed on both sides. . . . I hope your pocket-books have not shared the fate of the poetry she told me was for no eyes but her own and was therefore put on the fire. . . ."[8]

A letter to his father in the last week of October 1850 provides interesting details: ". . . My congregation I think increases, and the week meetings on the whole are better. We have a prayer-meeting every Monday, and a lecture on Thursday, for which I do not make much preparation—but gather up the gleanings of the Sunday. I mean on those same evenings to have Bible classes, one for young men and the other for young women. I shall have plenty to do. . . . I hope to be able to visit a good deal amongst the poor and unwell.

"I expect the ordination will take place towards the end of November. I don't like it. . . .

"It will depend on Mr. Powell whether I take a house at once—there happening to be a desirable one vacant now, and houses being very scarce in Arundel. He is coming down to [visit] me Saturday to stay till Monday. . . ."[9] Mr. Powell had agreed, if a suitable house for the young couple could be found, to furnish it for them.

The First of Many Setbacks

But a catastrophe was awaiting all these plans. In the first week of November, Louisa boarded a train bound for what had been intended as a rather lengthy visit to her aunts'. As she sat down in the coach and settled on her way, leaving the dreary London November fog behind, she opened a pencil-addressed letter from George that had arrived just as she left home, but which she had not had a chance to open in the hurry of departure. It contained only six lines, telling that a blood vessel had broken and that he was bleeding seriously from the lungs.

The next stop was not until Bletchley, fifty miles north of London. But the moment the train had pulled into the station, she was off and back to London on the next. Arriving home, she told her father of the letter. In his distress he took her in his arms and said he feared it might be a sign that she was not to marry George MacDonald. "No, Papa!" she exclaimed; "it is a sign that I *must* marry him at once and nurse him!"

Realizing the impropriety of going down to Arundel to take care of him herself, Louisa contented herself to stay where she was. A second letter soon followed with reassuring news that her fiancé's life was not in danger, and Mrs. New, his landlady, cared for him, though he was condemned to lie motionless on his back, with leeches on his chest. Her brother Alexander went down to Arundel for the weekend and brought back news of continued improvement, along with penciled notes from George to Louisa.

The night of Alexander's return Louisa wrote, ". . . How dear of you to write; but you must not do it if it is at all likely to hurt you one bit. . . . God keep you and both of us in willingness for his goodwill. . . . Papa has been so very kind to me. I know he loves you. He says he will find a corner somewhere when you are quite better enough to come. [Back in London for the winter, the Powell house was then full of guests.] Good night, my best and dearest . . . I should like to be an angel or fairy just to see how you are sleeping. But He is keeping you and I will praise Him. . . ."[10]

Mr. Powell urged his coming to them as soon as the doctor would permit. After about three weeks he was well enough to make the trip to London, where he consulted the eminent specialist Dr. C. J .B. Williams, who diagnosed pulmonary tuberculosis. The next day MacDonald wrote to his father, but did not appear to realize the gravity of his condition—though he knew the hemorrhage was liable to strike again.

"Louisa has told you of my visit to Dr. Williams and of his orders not to preach for six weeks or two months. He has ordered me cod-liver oil. I have very little fear that my complaint is slight and will soon leave me with proper care. But I believe the lungs are in some measure affected. It is somewhat discouraging to be thus laid aside at the beginning—but the design of God in doing so will perhaps appear soon—or if not now we shall know afterwards; and if never, it is well notwithstanding. There is a reason, and I at least shall be the better for it. [He would later write, "I do not myself believe in misfortune; anything to which men give the name is merely the shadow-side of a good" (*Warlock o' Glenwarlock*).]

"Now the question is, what am I to do with myself. . . . All my spare money I laid out on books—very necessary to do when going to a country place like Arundel where I can have no society, and no books of any kind except what I have of my own. . . . I expect the people will wait for me, though two Pounds a week [to pay substitutes] out of 150 Pounds a year won't leave much. . . ."[11]

He never did go to the Powells, but instead spent his days convalescing with an aunt, his father's sister, on the Isle of Wight. Though full of encouragement, the elder MacDonald's letters are nevertheless anxious. The family curse of weak lungs seemed universal, and when later his brothers (at about the same age) suffered similar hemorrhaging, rapid destruction of the lungs followed quickly.

A week before Christmas he wrote his father: "It is very kind of you to write to me so often. . . . I feel very doubtful whether I shall preach much longer. I feel if I were to begin again now, it would bring back the attack . . . lately I was sure something was wrong. It was in the very midst of forcing myself to do what I did not feel as if I were able for, that my attack came. However, it may partly be fancy. All that I know is that when I have work to do, I will try to do it with God's help, and then if I fail, it is not my fault. But I am not unhappy about it. . . . Perhaps such attacks might come and go . . . for some years. But I have no *idol of chance*, as many Christians seem to have. All will be well with me. I know you would give me my heart's desire if you could. And I know God is better than you—and it was Christ himself that taught us to call him *Father*. If I were to die tomorrow, I would thank God for what I have had, for he has blessed me very abundantly: I could say 'I have lived.'"[12]

Recovery

Without realizing it, this illness and time of recovery proved to be a turning point in George MacDonald's life. He had undoubtedly been writing poems since he could write at all. But more and more he was considering it a serious part of his life; in writing to Louisa he refers to poetry as his "work," and he must have thought of the possibility of publication at some future time. He had been working on translations of some of his favorite Germans (notably Novalis). But most important, his long dramatic poem *Within and Without* was written entirely during these two months of recuperation.

His letters to Louisa and his father are full of continued meditation concerning his spiritual saga and news of his writing, always reflective of Nature's voice speaking to his heart.

To Louisa he wrote: "I had your sweet letter today, when I posted my one to you. . . . Most people are always peeping through pin-holes in bits of paper; and often very ready to tell the man on the hill top with his eyes wide open what wonderful things they see. . . . I wish the Church [of Scotland] were better. I think I should almost go into it. Don't fancy I am changing. Indeed I am not saying more than I have always said, that my great objection to it was the kind of ministers the system admitted. . . .

"*Saturday night.* I had your letter to-day and the poor flattened rose—crossing your violets on the way. I was out nearly an hour and a half and enjoyed it, this bright beautiful day. I walked down nearer the sea, but yet a long way above it. I could see the blowing of the irregular tiny waves over the level sand, of which a little was bare, and a man or boy, I don't know which, was walking on it, with such a clear black shadow. The sun flashed on the sea, and a sloop-rigged boat left a snail track behind it. The horizon was a luminous mist, I enjoyed it more than yesterday.

"*Sunday morning.* I lay simmering in bed, till half-past ten this morning, without mental energy enough to look at my watch. I have been out before the door and it is very mild, and the sea sounds on—the first time I have noticed its low monotonous tune. I have had your dear little letter this morning. Thank you for all your dear love. . . . I shall write a little of my poem this evening. I fear it will disappoint me as usual. . . . It is little more than a week now till I see you once more. I am sure I shall never be well until I have you with me always. . . ."[13]

And to his father: "I have just come from consulting Dr. Williams. He seems so far satisfied with me—but not pleased that I did not take the oil constantly—which now I will do, sick or not—but he says that [nausea] will go off. He allows me to preach if I begin gently. . . . Many thanks to you, my dear father, for writing so often and so kindly. I hope to be married in March. . . . I fear we shall not be able to come to Scotland. Dr. Williams does not approve of it. But we will hope to see you in the South."[14]

He resumed his duties in mid-January and his congregation received him with a quiet joy that was very gratifying. But he was clearly still weak and had to spare his energies as much as possible. Writing to his father again, he said, "Most preaching seems to me greatly beside the mark. That only can I prize which tends to make men better—and most of it 'does na play bouf upo' me' [does not even bark at me]. . . . I finished my poem . . . but it must wait for your perusal when you come to see us, for I cannot copy [it] out. . . . Will you come and see us in the summer?"[15]

George MacDonald and Louisa Powell were married on March 8, 1851, in northeast London. The wedding took place on a Saturday. They immediately left for Leamington, where Louisa's two aunts had lent their house for the honeymoon. En route he was scheduled to preach the next day at Rugby. Humorously Greville recounts their wedding night: "But if George MacDonald looked to no 'idol of chance' to set things right, some demon of mischance awaited the happy pair on unpacking their luggage at Rugby: the bottle of cod-liver oil was broken, its contents reaching even the Sunday trousers of the morrow's preacher!"[16]

George's wedding present to Louisa, beautifully handwritten to her, was a poem entitled "Love Me, Beloved," which ultimately later found its way into the poetic drama on which he had been working so assiduously. In haunting, tender, and prophetic mood, after tracing the progression of their love through life, he arrives at the end, with each of them having to face the thought of losing the other in death:

> Love me, beloved; for thou mayest lie
> Dead in my sight, 'neath the same blue sky;
> Love me, O love me, and let me know
> The love that within thee moves to and fro; . . .
>
> Love me, beloved; for I may lie
> Dead in thy sight, 'neath the same blue sky;
> The more thou hast loved me, the less thy pain,
> The stronger thy hope till we meet again; . . .
>
> Love me, beloved; for one must lie
> Motionless, lifeless, beneath the sky; . . .
>
> Love me, beloved; for both must lie
> Under the earth and beneath the sky; . . .

And then on to the triumphant conclusion, the words ringing with the tone of victory which would mark George MacDonald's later writings and, indeed, the course of the rest of his life:

> Love me, beloved; Hades and Death
> Shall vanish away like a frosty breath;
> These hands, that now are at home in thine,
> Shall clasp thee again, if thou still art mine;
> And thou shalt be mine, my spirit's bride,
> In the ceaseless flow of eternity's tide,
> If the truest love that thy heart can know
> Meet the truest love that from mine can flow.
> Pray God, beloved, for thee and me,
> That our souls may be wedded eternally.

> (*Poetical Works of George MacDonald*,
> vol. 1, "Within and Without")

CHAPTER SIXTEEN

HAPPY DAYS
(1851–1852)

George MacDonald's health was on the mend, he and Louisa were at last able to settle down to the married life for which they had waited so long, and it seemed the little village of Arundel would agree with them. Perhaps after a decade in Aberdeen and London a certain contentedness accompanied MacDonald's return to a setting more like—though warmer than—his beloved Scotland in the north.

His son reflects: "Those were happy days indeed, with plenty to do among a people, simple, eager to learn, and very grateful. The majority were tradesmen, though a sprinkling of pure country-folk gave the minister easier touch with the elemental virtues, which among people belonging to the soil are less likely to be hid under a bushel of worldliness."[1]

Arundel provided the setting for the novel *Annals of a Quiet Neighborhood*, published many years later. Greville says: "It was at Arundel that he stored, without, I think, any definite intent, material for ... *Annals of a Quiet Neighborhood*. Its descriptions tally closely with Arundel; while one at least of the characters, Old Rogers, is the portrait and name of a member of his congregation who would come regularly to chapel in his round frock, red cotton handkerchief, and tall beaver hat. His conversation in the book is based upon the old man's shrewd observations, his imaginative outlook accounted for by his having been a man-of-war's man. So that when he likened the pulpit to a mast-head, one is not surprised. 'I love a parson, Sir! ... He's got a good telescope, and he gits to the mast-head, and he looks out. And he sings out, "Land ahead!" or "Breakers ahead!" and gives directions accordin'.' It was on Arundel's beautiful bridge that my father first met Old Rogers. 'All sorts of bridges have been from very infancy a delight to me [he said in the book in connection with this one in particular]. For I am one of those who never get rid of their infantile predilections, and to have once enjoyed making a mud bridge, was to enjoy all bridges for ever'—a remark that holds one clue to my father's thoughts and imagery: the child was father of the man."[2]

Greville goes on to say, "The serenity of the place is nowhere better suggested than in the words of my mother . . . to my father [when he was away from home]. . . : 'What a sweet, sunny, breezy Sunday afternoon this is! The street is so still, [they lived in a little house on Tarrant Street, which Mr. Powell furnished as a wedding gift] and our one tree is whispering most sweetly to me all about you, and Him who cares about both of us. The river is full and the lights and shadows in the meadows beyond are very beautiful.' "[3]

Much of MacDonald's intense questioning regarding the legitimacy of the Christian faith was behind him. Yet taken in the wider context of his life as a whole, we must remember that he was only twenty-seven, was newly married, had rather serious health problems, and could not help but be aware that he was "different" in some ways—his ideas and methods of expression could catch the more traditionally minded off guard, causing them to wonder about his faith. Had not his own Louisa hesitated getting involved with him at first because of his unorthodoxy? Was not his father always worrying about someone misinterpreting him? Wasn't Professor Godwin, with all his encouragement, constantly badgering him to make his sermons more "suitable" for the common people?

All this must have puzzled the young minister. Knowing his own heart toward God, why were people so prone to mistrust and doubt? Why were certain exalted doctrines seemingly more important to many than relationships with fellow members of God's family, and even more important than the highest doctrine of all—love?

Questions were still being posed at Arundel. No longer was there doubt as to his own personal standing with God. His search for faith had yielded a rock-solid faith that would not and could not be shaken. But now what was he to do with it? At this point the focus of his prayers was the church and his role in it. How was he to carry himself to these people? How was he to communicate the message that burned inside him? What if they didn't want to hear what he had to say?

In light of such questions, portions of the opening chapter of *Annals of a Quiet Neighborhood* are illuminating, revealing the directions of certain thoughts which may have been going through his mind—even at a subconscious level. On the surface he enjoyed the work; the first months of being a pastor and a husband were delightful. But below, things were brewing that would take years and many additional experiences to identify. "When I was thirty," his fictional self says in the book, "I was made a vicar, an age at which a man might be expected to be beginning to grow wise; but even then I had much yet to learn.

"I well remember the first evening on which I wandered out from the vicarage to take a look about me. . . . It was depressing weather. Grave doubts as to whether I was in my place in the church would keep rising and floating about, like rainclouds within me. Not that I doubted about the church; I only doubted about myself. . . . 'Were my motives pure?' . . . Perhaps seeing we are in this world in order to become pure, it would be expecting too much of any young man that he should be absolutely certain that he was pure in anything. But the question followed very naturally: 'Had I then any right to be in the Church ... without knowing whether I was fit to do her work?'" (*Annals of a Quiet Neighborhood*, Ch. 1).

At the same time, a reading of *Annals of a Quiet Neighborhood* yields a rich harvest of another sort in its illumination of the mind and heart of the young pastor. The subtle, peaceful, "quiet" tone of the book (before the plot takes it rather far afield from the autobiographical) certainly reveals the young man's sensitivity, his love for the town and its people, and his love for the *church*, the fellowship of God's people. Though he may have questioned his fitness for the task, young pastor Walton as depicted in the book is "at home" in the ministry. And how he reflects his literary creator! Everything about him provides food for thought and growth, especially the gentle voices of nature and the spirits of the people he encounters. It is a time for observation and reflection—as Arundel certainly was for the young MacDonald; a time to put into practice ten years of growth and learning—at first tentative in his steps, yet with growing confidence.

As a deeper appreciation of MacDonald's childhood comes with a reading of books already mentioned, and of his college and tutoring days with portions of *David Elginbrod* and *Donal Grant*, so too the first half of *Annals of a Quiet Neighborhood* adds color and depth to a sense of the new pastor's heart:

"As I went again through the village, I observed a narrow lane striking off to the left, and resolved to explore in that direction. It led up to one side of [a] large house.... As I came near, I smelt what has been to me always a delightful smell—that of fresh [wood] under the hand of the carpenter. In the scent of those boards of pine is enclosed all the idea the tree could gather of the world of forest where it was reared. It speaks of many wild and bright but chiefly clean rather cold things.... Turning a corner, I heard the sound of a saw. And this sound drew me yet more. For a carpenter's shop was the delight of my boyhood; and after I began to read the history of our Lord with something of that sense of reality with which we read other histories, and which, I am sorry to think, so much of the well-meant instruction we receive in our youth tends to destroy, my feeling about such a workshop grew stronger and stronger, till at last I never could go near enough to see the shavings lying on the floor of one, without a spiritual sensation such as I have in entering an old church.... So I drew near the shop, feeling as if the Lord might be at work there at one of the benches" (*Annals of a Quiet Neighborhood*, Ch. 4).

Then he muses about his love for books:

"When I reached my own study, I sat down by a blazing fire ... and soon fell into a dreamy state called *reverie*, which I fear not a few mistake for *thinking*, because it is the nearest approach they ever make to it. And in this reverie I kept staring about my bookshelves.... I am very fond of books. Do not mistake me. I do not mean that I love reading. I hope I do. But ... I am foolishly fond of the bodies of books as distinguished from their souls.... I delight in seeing books about me.... Nay, more: I confess that if they are nicely bound, so as to glow and shine in such a firelight as that by which I was then sitting, I like them ever so much the better. . . . [But lest they become as mammon to me as my love for them went] through a process more than analogous to that which the miser's mind goes through—namely, that of passing from the respect of money because of what it can do, to the love of money because it is money . . .—I would rather burn them all. Meantime, I think one safeguard is to encourage one's friends to borrow one's books. . . . That will probably take some of the shine off them, and put a few thumb-marks in them, which are very wholesome. . . ." (*Annals of a Quiet Neighborhood*, Ch. 11).

Finally he thinks aloud about God's work in the world:

"I walked home, as usual on Sunday mornings, by the road. It was a lovely day. The sun shone so warm that you could not help thinking of what he would be able to do before long—draw primroses and buttercups out of the earth by force of sweet persuasive influences. But in the shadows lay fine webs of laces of ice, so delicately lovely that one could not but be glad of the cold that made the water able to please itself by taking such graceful forms. And I wondered over again for the hundredth time what could be the principle which, in the wildest, most lawless, fantastically chaotic, apparently capricious work of nature, always kept it beautiful. The beauty of holiness must be at the heart of it somehow, I thought. Because our God is so free from stain, so loving, so unselfish, so good, so altogether what He wants us to be, so holy, therefore all His works declare Him in beauty; His fingers can touch nothing but to mould it into loveliness; and even the play of His elements is in grace and tenderness of form.

"And then I thought how the sun, at the farthest point from us, had begun to come back towards us; looked upon us with a hopeful smile; was like the Lord when He visited His people as a little one of themselves, to grow upon the earth till it should blossom as the rose in the light of His presence. 'Ah, Lord,' I said in my heart, 'draw near unto Thy people. It is spring-time with Thy world, but yet we have cold winds and bitter hail, and pinched voices forbidding them that follow Thee and follow not with us. Draw nearer, Sun of Righteousness, and make the trees bourgeon, and the flowers blossom, and the voices grow mellow and glad, so that all shall join in praising Thee, and find thereby that harmony is better than unison. Let it be summer, O Lord, if it ever may be summer in this court of the Gentiles. But Thou hast told us that Thy kingdom cometh within us, and so Thy joy must come within us too. Draw nigh then, Lord, to those to whom Thou wilt draw nigh; and others beholding their welfare will seek to share therein too, and seeing their good works will glorify their Father in heaven.'

"So I walked home, hoping in my Savior, and wondering to think how pleasant I had found it to be His poor servant to this people. Already the doubts which had filled my mind on that first evening . . . as to whether I had any right to the priest's office, had utterly vanished, slain by the effort to perform the priest's duty.—And how can doubt ever be fully met but by action? . . . And I hoped that if ever a cloud should come over me again, however dark and dismal it might be, I might be able . . . to rejoice . . . and say with all my heart to my Father in heaven, 'Thy will be done'" (*Annals of a Quiet Neighborhood*, Ch. 11).

Solidifying Priorities

Writing to his father in April of 1851, MacDonald revealed the minister at work with reviving physical energy and growing self-assurance, pitting himself against the "Shorter Catechism system" in which he had been schooled. Not only was his stand becoming firmer, he had the boldness to preach his views—a combination which before long was used against him. He wrote: "Will you excuse my writing to you on these scraps of paper, as I am not willing to call Louisa from the garden where she is sowing some flower seeds. . . . She has been very well, I am happy to say. I am far happier, much more at peace, and I hope learning more rapidly the best knowledge. . . . As I expect to be on very good terms with the church people here, I hope for better congregations in the evening when there is no service in the [Church of Scotland] parish church. Amongst our visitors the week before last was the vicar—I mean at our house, not the chapel. . . .

"I firmly believe people have hitherto been a great deal too much taken up about doctrine and far too little about practice. The word *doctrine*, as used in the Bible, means teaching of duty, not theory. I preached a sermon about this. We are far too anxious to be definite and to have finished, well-polished, sharp-edged *systems*—forgetting that the more perfect a theory about the infinite, the surer it is to be wrong, the more impossible it is to be right. I am neither Arminian nor Calvinist. To no system would I subscribe. . . ."[4]

How daring are his words, given the spiritual climate of the time! With authority he affirmed—*To no system would I subscribe*. Firmly he turned his back on dogma—whether Calvinist or Arminian. The priority of his life, which pervades every book he later wrote, is fixed—the *doing* of God's word, not the forming of finished, well-polished theories about it.

He later wrote: "Theology is not my origin, but God. Nor do I acknowledge any theology but what Christ has taught, and has to teach me . . . What he requires of his friends is pure, open-eyed truth" (*Paul Faber, Surgeon*, Ch. 20).

Equally revealing is the overriding foundational priority of his heart—to *grow* in his knowledge of and obedience to God. Spoken here to his father, and later echoed frequently through the words of his memorable character Thomas Wingfold in *Thomas Wingfold, Curate* and its sequel *Paul Faber, Surgeon*, is MacDonald's unpretentious attitude, which never said, "I *have* faith," but was always open to say, "I need more faith." In everything he wrote—every letter, every poem, every book, every sermon—this theme is repeated, the theme of growth: the openhearted and open-minded quest always for *more* truth, *more* wisdom, *more* understanding, *more* humility, *more* brokenness, *more* love, *more* knowledge, *more* compassion. This was the essence of George MacDonald's character and his message—humble, open growth which is rooted in *carrying out* the Word of God.

Doing God's Word was critical in the economy of a truth-loving man such as George MacDonald because of his overriding conviction that only in *obeying* God's principles in the small moments of every day can the truth become known. Growth comes about only through obedience to God, by living the kind of life that God instructs. He wrote: "To him that obeys well, the truth comes easy; to him who does not obey, it comes not. . . . The true, that is the obedient man, cannot help seeing the truth, for it is the very business of his being—the natural concern, the correlate of his soul" (*Warlock o' Glenwarlock*, Ch. 43).

To George MacDonald, growth, learning more of the truth, and obeying God so as to know Him better was the great delight of life. "That is the joy of existence!" his character Ian says in *What's Mine's Mine*. "We are not bound to *know*; we are only bound to *learn*."

In *Paul Faber* he wrote: "There is in the man who does the truth the radiance of life essential. . . . To know God is to be in the secret place of all knowledge . . . not to be intellectually certain of a truth does not prevent the heart that loves and obeys that truth from getting its truth-good, from drawing life from its holy factness, present in the love of it. . . ." (*Paul Faber, Surgeon*, Ch. 49).

There were no barriers for MacDonald. While Christians throughout Britain were defining their doctrines and drawing dividing lines according to their differences, George MacDonald was demolishing the lines, attending the devotions of the Catholics in Ireland while serving as a Protestant pastor, inviting the parish vicar to his home, throwing out theories altogether in favor of the doctrine of obedience—exactly as did Wingfold.

Throughout his life, great speaker that he was, MacDonald was an even greater listener—he was always patiently waiting for the truths that another could teach him. He shrank from debate, always afraid that the justifying of one's opinions in argument might outrun the desire to find the truth at the bottom of whatever question was under consideration. He wrote: "The man who is anxious to hold every point, will speedily bring a question to a mere dispute about trifles, leaving the real matter . . . out in the cold. Such a man, having gained his paltry point, will crow like the bantam he is. . . . Few men do more harm than those who, taking the right side, dispute for personal victory. . . . But even genuine argument for the truth is not preaching the gospel, neither is he whose unbelief is thus assailed, likely to be brought thereby into any mood but one unfit for receiving it. Argument should be kept to books. . . . God alone can convince . . ." (*Paul Faber, Surgeon*, Ch. 24).

It was not only from people and issues that he was eager to learn and grow. Every flower, every seascape, every insect, every change in the weather had truth to reveal to him of the universe and its Maker. This wide-eyed attitude is prevalent in his characters: Malcolm Colonsay, Robert Falconer, Donal Grant, Harry Walton, Janet Grant, David Elginbrod, Alister

Macruadh, Barbara Wilder, Joseph Polwarth, and Alexander Graham. Through each of these characters, in each of his books, different facets of MacDonald's vision of God's character emerge. Through no single one do we obtain the complete scope of his perception of God, yet each contributes to the total picture. Surely the man Thomas Wingfold stands out strongly, however, as a forceful and radiant example of the image of Christ that MacDonald sought to present to the world. For here was a shallow man with no personal faith, a man who plagiarized his sermons, a man with little personality, unequipped to occupy the pulpit and still less to lead even the humblest of his parishioners.

And yet Thomas Wingfold quickly endears himself to us, for Wingfold possessed the one quality which MacDonald revered above nearly all others—*openness*. His ears were not plugged with self-satisfaction and tradition, but were ready to listen, ready to look for truth outside the usual boundaries, ready to learn from any quarter.

With this openness came an honest heart, one willing to take a thorough look at whatever new presented itself. In the character of Wingfold appear a host of qualities that accompany openness and were high personal priorities with MacDonald himself—humility, a willingness to admit oneself ignorant, a lack of airs, an absence of defenses. Thomas had no walls standing between his true self and the outside world. Therefore, while *Thomas Wingfold, Curate* is not autobiographical, it certainly provides a window into the priorities of character and heart which were MacDonald's own.

Thomas Wingfold, along with the characters in MacDonald's other books, represents another facet of that "ideal" character after which MacDonald himself was trying to model his own life. In his characters MacDonald was painting a portrait of Christ—a portion of the Ideal Man here, another quality there. Gibbie portrays the eyes of love; Malcolm Colonsay, the authority which comes from simplicity; Robert Falconer, the hands of service; Annie Anderson, the radiance of humility. In Hugh Sutherland and Alec Forbes, MacDonald demonstrates the prodigal's search and return; in Hester Raymount, the ministry of God-given talents; in Joseph Polwarth, thankfulness in spite of afflictions; in Alister Macruadh, the humility of true authority. And all taken together they illumine MacDonald's lifetime masterpiece: the portrait of the Christ he loved and served. The story of Thomas Wingfold adds one of the most vital ingredients of all—the picture of the Christlike heart. In Wingfold we are shown the response of the open heart when confronted with truth, a response of openness and humility, which leads to growth and spiritual maturity.

Challenging Words

This attitude is so clearly revealed in his words to his father, "I am . . . I hope learning more rapidly the best knowledge." The ungrowing, unsearching, unquestioning heart is one becoming hardened to the immediacy of God's voice. MacDonald remained in touch with that Voice because he never closed himself to anything, remaining ever hungry for *more*.

Yet between the lines, even of this same letter, lie many questions: how are the people going to respond to their new pastor's bold proclamations and his refusal to embrace doctrines? And how are they going to respond to his insistence upon duty, upon obedience as the focal point of faith, not *what* is believed? The people's reaction to the unusual sermons of Wingfold in *Thomas Wingfold, Curate* raises the possibility that MacDonald was drawing somewhat upon his own experience at Arundel in describing the mixed reactions of the congregation. "When he read his text, it was to a congregation . . . listless and indifferent. . . . He had not gone far, however, before that change of mental condition was visible on the faces before him . . . they were actually listening. But . . . it was no wonder, for seldom . . . in that church, had there been heard such . . . a sermon. . . . A few of the congregation were disappointed. . . . A few others were scandalized at such an innovation on the part of a young man who was only a curate. Many, however, declared that it was the most interesting sermon they had ever heard in their lives—which was perhaps not saying much . . .

"[By the next week] news of that strange first sermon had of course spread through the town, and the people came to church the next Sunday in crowds—twice as many as the usual assembly— . . . mostly bent on witnessing whatever eccentricity the very peculiar young man might be guilty of next, but having a few among them who were sympathetically interested in seeing how far his call, if call it was, would lead him" (*Thomas Wingfold, Curate*, Chs. 20, 36).

There is no evidence that there was such strong reaction to the sermons of George MacDonald in Arundel. But silently, over the course of two years, the leaven of his preaching worked slowly in the minds of certain of his congregation, fermenting gradually—rising, warming, waiting. In addition to *Annals of a Quiet Neighborhood* and *Thomas Wingfold, Curate*, the Arundel years are rounded out and given depth and breadth by *Paul Faber, Surgeon*, in which a sermon that was undoubtedly typical of its author is given:

"God hides nothing. His very work from the beginning is *revelation*—a casting aside of veil after veil, a showing unto men of truth after truth. On and on, from fact to fact divine He advances, until at length in His Son Jesus, He unveils His very face. Then begins a fresh unveiling, for the very work of the Father is the work the Son Himself has to do—to reveal. . . .

"He loves light and not darkness, therefore shines, therefore reveals. True, there are infinite gulfs in Him into which our small vision cannot pierce, but they are gulfs of light, and the truths there are invisible only through excess of their own clarity. . . .

"But see how different *we* are. . . . See the tendency of man to conceal his treasures, to claim even truth as his own by discovery, to hide it and be proud of it, gloating over that which he thinks he had in himself, instead of groaning after the infinite of God! We would be forever heaping

George MacDonald at thirty-seven in 1862, at the time he was just beginning his career as a novelist

George MacDonald, Sr.

Mrs. Charles Edward MacDonald,
George MacDonald's grandmother

George MacDonald's brother
Alexander in 1852

George MacDonald's brother
John in 1853

George MacDonald at thirty in 1855

*Mrs. George (Louisa) MacDonald in
her early thirties—approximately 1855*

Louisa MacDonald and the four eldest children, Lilia, Mary, Carolyn, and Greville, with their friend Lewis Carroll in 1862

GROUP OF CONTEMPORARY WRITERS. Top row: George MacDonald, J. A. Froude, Wilkie Collins, Anthony Trollope. Bottom row: W. M. Thackeray, Lord Macaulay, Bulwer Lytton, Thos. Carlyle, Charles Dickens

George MacDonald at about forty-five, approximately 1870

Chromolith of MacDonald of the kind used for literary men of the time on pomade boxes—approximately 1872

*George MacDonald in 1873 about
the time of the American tour*

George MacDonald at about fifty-five near the height of his popularity (NESLS)

MacDonald family with E. R. Hughes (who had proposed to daughter Mary) in 1876

George MacDonald in 1880

Louisa MacDonald in 1885

George MacDonald in 1884 dressed for the role of Mr. Greatheart in the family's dramatic presentation of Pilgrim's Progress

George MacDonald in his early to mid-sixties

George MacDonald at sixty-seven in 1892

George MacDonald at about seventy-five, shortly before or after the time of his stroke (NESLS)

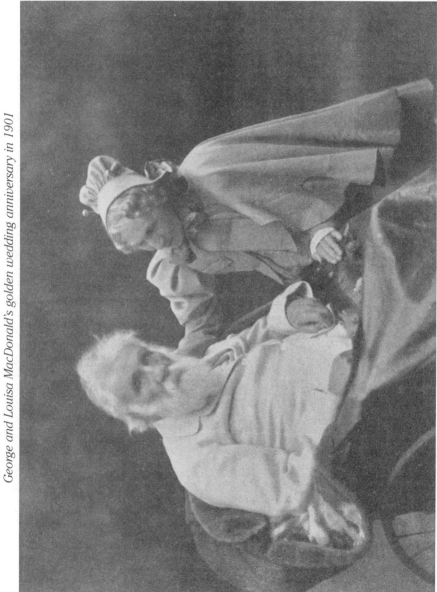

George and Louisa MacDonald's golden wedding anniversary in 1901

together possessions, dragging things into the cave of our finitude, our individual self, not perceiving that the things which pass that dreariest of doors, whatever they may have been are thenceforth but 'straws, small sticks, and dust of the floor.' When a man would have a truth in thither as if it were of private interpretation, he drags in only the bag which the truth, remaining outside, has burst and left . . .

"Let us make haste to open the doors of our lips and the window of our humility, to let out the demon of darkness, and in the angels of light— so abjuring the evil. . . . If we do not thus open our house, the day will come when a roaring blast of His wind, or the flame of His keen lightening, will destroy every defense of darkness, and set us shivering before the universe in our naked vileness, for there is nothing covered that shall not be revealed, neither hid that shall not be known . . .

"Brothers, sisters, let us be clean. The light and the air around us are God's vast purifying furnace; out into it let us cast all hypocrisy. Let us be open-hearted, and speak every man the truth to his neighbor. Amen" (*Paul Faber, Surgeon*, Ch. 31).

In the meantime, with the majority of his people, a bonding took place with the new preacher and his wife, who took an active part in visitation. The sensitivity of the man, his stories of pathos and humor and wit, his respect for the common man, and his attitude that God draws near to the poor and simple of heart undoubtedly endeared him to the plain folk of his congregation; they loved their new minister. He had God's heart toward the people and they loved him in return.

The ordination (long postponed because of illness and then the marriage) finally took place in June of 1851, and MacDonald's former professor at Highbury, by now his good friend, Mr. John Godwin, came down from London to officiate. Louisa's sister Charlotte had been invited to help entertain the childless widower. It was there they met for the first time, and they were married two years later by the former student of the one, the brother-in-law of the other. George's two brothers Alec and John were also present at the ordination. In July his father wrote from Huntly, "John and Alec are greatly delighted with Arundel and with the minister's *wife* thereof. I am happy to think you have been so fortunate, and I pray God you may appreciate at all times the blessing. . . ."[5]

George and Louisa had frequent visits from their London friends, notably Louisa's sisters and Greville Matheson, among others, although George was for a while, according to his son, "still much of an invalid." George, Sr., was not altogether happy about his son's physical condition, attributing some of its cause to the overwork of trying to mix writing with preaching. He wrote urging him to "give [up] the fruitless game of poetry, and apply yourself to the preaching of the Gospel and the instruction of your people. A nervous [i.e.—emotional] temperament and a poetical imagination are too much for a frail clay tabernacle. . . ."[6]

But he grew accustomed to the idea of his son's compulsion to express himself not only from the pulpit and through his deeds, but also through his pen. Writing some time later to Louisa he says, ". . . Is not . . .

[emotionalism] the *tap-root* of all genuine poetry? The nervous system acts, and is reacted upon until it becomes a shaken, wasted, and tattered thing. Don't get alarmed: for I say what I have done jocularly. . . . It is now no longer wonderful [i.e. hard to realize and accept] to me that the independent minister of Arundel *is a poet*. . . ."[7]

An occasional visit to London for a day or two kept the writer's mind stirred with people and places beyond the relaxing and sleepy climate of Arundel. His friend Greville Matheson provided him literary help, and at the end of 1851 he had his translations of *Twelve of the Spiritual Songs of Novalis* printed. Though it was but twenty-seven pages in length and the private printing was intended solely for the purpose of giving to his friends as a Christmas gift, this inauspicious beginning nevertheless launched MacDonald's literary career. The mystical pietism of these songs of anguish over Novalis's bereavement after the death of his betrothed had gripped MacDonald's imagination ever since his student days in Aberdeen. Though they did not rank among the German's greatest achievements, and though MacDonald was equally influenced by his other writings as well as by the other German romanticists, the tragic figure of Novalis (who had died young of tuberculosis) and his *Spiritual Songs* continued to exercise a powerful attraction on the young Scotsman, who reworked his translations at least three times over the next forty-five years and always intended a more complete edition of Novalis's works in English. In 1851, with his deep poetic instinct, he was at least able to fulfill a portion of his own appreciation for the songs by giving of their riches to his friends.

MacDonald's poetic tendencies endeared some people to him and alienated others. Brief portions from a few of these translations represent MacDonald's first published words:

> Then came a savior to deliver—
> A Son of Man, in love and might!
> A holy fire, of life all-giver.
> He in our hearts has fanned alight.
> Then first heaven opened—and, no fable,
> Our own old fatherland we trod!
> To hope and trust we straight were able,
> And knew ourselves akin to God.

*   *   *   *   *

> My faith to thee I break not,
>   If all should faithless be,
> That gratitude forsake not
>   The world eternally.
> For my sake Death did sting thee
>   With anguish keen and sore;
> Therefore with joy I bring thee
>   This heart for evermore.

*   *   *   *   *

Thou with thy love hast found me!
    O do not let me go!
Keep me where thou hast bound me
    Till one with thee I grow.
My brothers yet will waken,
    One look to heaven will dart—
Then sink down, love-o'ertaken,
    And fall upon thy heart.

        (Twelve of the Spiritual Songs of Novalis)

CHAPTER SEVENTEEN

THE HERESY HUNT
(1852-1853)

After opening on a bright note of great joy (in the first week of the year George and Louisa's first child, Lilia Scott, was born), the year 1852 soon brought the faint sounds of criticism within the congregation; rumors and talk began to circulate, which expressed doubt in the minister's orthodoxy.

Bold Preaching

Both George MacDonald's volumes of sermons and his novels containing sermons reveal one factor that consistently runs through such discourses: George MacDonald cared nothing about potential negative reactions. He said what he had to say, irrespective of persons who might take exception. Never a man-pleaser, he was driven toward one thing—to speak what he considered the truth, in love but boldly. He declared what he had to say and let the chips fall where they might. The three volumes of *Unspoken Sermons* reveal this tendency, as do *Thomas Wingfold, Curate* and its sequel *Paul Faber, Surgeon*, in which the young curate Wingfold speaks challenging words of discomfort to the complacent flock. As he does, his finger always points toward himself as well, as did MacDonald's. He must be the first to take his own counsel:

"The Lord says, *Love your enemies.* Sayest thou, *It is impossible?* Then dost thou mock the word of him who said, *I am the Truth,* and hast no part in him. Sayest thou, *Alas! I can not?* Thou sayest true, I doubt not. But hast thou tried whether he who made [thee] will not increase the strength put forth to obey him?

"The Lord says, *Be ye perfect.* Dost thou then aim after perfection, or dost thou excuse thy willful shortcomings, and say *To err is human*—nor hopest that it may also be found human to grow divine? Then ask thyself, for thou hast good cause, whether thou hast any part in him.

"The Lord said, *Lay not up for yourselves treasures on earth.* My part is not now to preach against the love of money, but to ask you, *Are* you laying up for yourselves treasures on earth? As to what the command means, the honest heart and the dishonest must each settle it in his own way; but if your heart condemn you, what I have to say is, call not yourselves Christians, but consider whether you ought not to become disciples indeed. No doubt you can instance this, that, and the other man who does as you do, and of whom yet no man dreams of questioning the Christianity: it matters not a hair; all that goes but to say that you are pagans together. Do not mistake me: I judge you not. But I ask you, as mouthpiece most unworthy of that Christianity in the name of which this building stands and we are met therein, to judge your own selves by the words of its founder.

"The Lord says, *Take no thought for your life. Take no thought for the morrow.* Explain it as you may or can; but ask yourselves, Do I take no thought for my life? Do I take no thought for the morrow? and answer to yourselves whether or not ye are Christians.

"The Lord says, *Judge not.* Didst thou judge thy neighbor yesterday? Wilt thou judge him again tomorrow? Art thou judging him now in the very heart that . . . sits hearing the words. . . ?

"The Lord said, *All things whatsoever ye would that men should do to you, do ye even so to them*. . . . do you obey this law? Examine yourselves and see. Ye would that men should deal fairly by you: do you deal fairly by them. . . ? If conscience makes you hang the head inwardly, however you sit with it erect in the pew, dare you add to your crime against the law and the prophets the insult to Christ of calling yourselves his disciples?

"Not every one that saith unto me Lord, Lord, shall enter into the kingdom of heaven, but he that doeth the will of my Father which is in heaven" (*Thomas Wingfold, Curate,* Ch. 36).

Both in his actual preaching and through the lips of his fictional preachers, MacDonald's words of honesty against false priorities, mammon, and self-righteous pride drove straight to the heart of the open-minded. But to the more comfortable and well-to-do who did not want their minister challenging them discomfortingly, his words were not always welcome. Men and women like Mr. Drew (of *Thomas Wingfold, Curate*) welcomed him into their hearts and were changed forever as a result. The Robert Bruces (*Alec Forbes of Howglen*) and Mrs. Ramshorns (*Thomas Wingfold, Curate*) went away seething, his words hitting too close to home.

At the beginning, describing what must have been MacDonald's initial reaction to the people, Greville calls them "a people, simple, eager to learn, and very grateful." But after a year and a half in Arundel, the tone with which the congregation is described is measurably altered, as seen through the eyes of the curate in *Paul Faber, Surgeon,* which novel provides an echo of MacDonald's Arundel experiences. Commenting on that book, Wolff reflects MacDonald in calling them "petty-minded, sanctimonious lower-middle-class tradesmen, many of whom cheat despite their piety . . . They care not 'to grow in grace, but in social influence' . . . The minister in *Paul Faber* at times gives vent to mystical speculation in the pulpit, and the quotations that MacDonald supplies from his sermons almost surely reproduce what he himself had said to outrage the Arundel congregation more than a quarter-century earlier. And as with himself, so with his fictional minister: the congregation accuses him of Germanism."[1]

If Wolff is correct, what must the people of Arundel have thought when MacDonald preached to them after the fashion of Wingfold?

"*Ye cannot serve God and mammon.*

"Who said this? The Lord by whose name ye are called. . . . And yet how many of you are, and have been for years, trying your very hardest to do the thing your Master tells you is impossible! Thou man! Thou woman! I appeal to thine own conscience whether thou are not striving to serve God and mammon. . . .

"Let us consider for a moment the God you do not serve, and then for a moment the mammon you do serve. The God you do not serve is the Father of Lights, the Source of love, the Maker of man and woman, the Head of the great family . . . the God who can neither think nor do nor endure any thing mean or unfair; the God of poetry and music and every marvel; the God of the mountain tops, and the rivers that run from the snows of death, to make the earth joyous with life; the God of the valley and the wheat-field . . . the God and Father of our Lord Jesus Christ, the perfect. . . . The mammon you do serve is . . . Death. His temple is a darkness, a black hollow, ever hungry. . . . His wages are death, but he calls them life. . . . I will tell you some of the marks of his service—a few of the badges of his household. . . . If, when thou makest a bargain, thou thinkest *only* of thyself and thy gain, thou art a servant of mammon. The eager looks of those that would get money, the troubled looks of those who have lost it, worst of all the gloating looks of them that have it—these are sure signs of the service of mammon. . . . If thou favor the company of those whom men call well-to-do . . . and declinest that of the simple and the meek, then in thy deepest consciousness know that thou servest mammon, not God. If thy hope of well being in time to come, rests upon thy houses, or lands, or business, or money in store, and not upon the living God, be thou friendly and kind . . . or a churl whom no man loves, thou art equally a server of mammon. If the loss of thy goods would take from thee the joy of thy life . . . thou servest mammon. If with thy word . . . thou confessest that God is the only good, yet livest as if He had sent thee into the world to make thyself rich before thou die; if it will add one feeblest pang to the pains of thy death, to think that thou must leave thy fair house, thy ancestral trees, thy horses, thy shop, thy books, behind thee, then art thou a servant of mammon. . . .

"Friend, be not a slave. Be wary. Look not on the gold when it is . . . in thy purse. Hoard not. In God's name, spend—spend on. Take heed how thou spendest . . . let thy good be thy rays, thy angels of love and life and deliverance. Be thou a candle of the Lord to spread His light through the world. . . .

"But if thou art poor, then look not on thy purse when it is empty. He who desires more than God wills him to have is also a servant of mammon, for he trusts in what God has made, and not in God Himself. He who laments what God has taken from him, he is a servant of mammon. There are men in this town who love and trust their horses more than the God that made them and their horses too. . . . Friends, cast your idol into the furnace; melt your mammon down, coin him up, make God's money of him. . . . Make of him cups to carry the gift of God, the water of life, through the world. . . . To hold fast upon God with one hand, and open wide the other to your neighbor—that is religion; that is the law and the prophets, and the true way to all better things that are yet to come.—Lord, defend us from Mammon. Hold Thy temple against his foul invasion. Purify our money with Thy air, and Thy sun, that it may be our slave, and Thou our Master. Amen" (*Paul Faber, Surgeon,* Ch. 7).

It is no wonder that some in his congregation reacted like the aunt of Wingfold's wife! "'Extraordinary young man!' exclaimed Mrs. Ramshorn as they left the church. . . . 'Is he an infidel or a fanatic? a Jesuit or a Unitarian. . . . Such buffoonery! such coarseness! such vulgarity! such indelicacy! . . . My poor Helen. She has thrown herself away upon a charlatan! And what will become of her money in the hands of a man with such leveling notions, I dread to think.'"

Of course, not everything that came from the pulpit was "flaming words" of rebuke. Equal with his prophetic denunciations of hypocrisy could be MacDonald's tender words of compassion—both revealing contrasting scriptural sides of Jesus. "'Come, then, sore heart, and see whether his heart can not heal thine. He knows what sighs and tears are, and if he knew no sin in himself, the more pitiful must it have been to him to behold the sighs and tears that guilt wrung from the tortured hearts of his brethren and sisters. Brothers, sisters, we *must* get rid of this misery of ours. It is slaying us. It is turning the fair earth into a hell, and our hearts into its fuel. There stands the man who says in the might of his eternal tenderness and his human pity, *Come unto me, all ye that labor and are heavy-laden, and I will give you rest. Take my yoke upon you, and learn of me; for I am meek and lowly in heart: and ye shall find rest unto your souls. For my yoke is easy, and my burden is light*'" (*Thomas Wingfold, Curate,* Ch. 46).

Greville says, "My mother took wise and tender share in the pastoral work, her quick and sound sympathy making her loved by all. My father's flaming words against mammon worship and cruelty and self-seeking were as thoroughgoing as the giving of himself to all who needed him." The young preacher wrote to his father, "Some of all classes *do* understand me and I am happy not to be understood by those that do not understand. Some say I talk foolishness, others go away with their hearts burning within them."[2]

Storm Clouds Approach

Whatever the initial cause—whether the discomfort of certain influential persons such as the dishonest butcher of *Paul Faber, Surgeon,* doctrinal disputes with stern legalists such as Mrs. Falconer, personality conflicts with persons like the Appleditches of *David Elginbrod*, or the preacher's convicting words about the nature of their faith and obedience—talk gradually began to circulate against the minister.

His teaching and lifestyle with regard to Sabbath-keeping was one of the first things to be noticed. His lifestyle stood in stark contrast to extreme Calvinistic custom, which was the widely accepted reformed Protestant tradition of the day. Whereas the 18th-century Puritan Jonathan Edwards had once resolved "never to utter anything that is sportive, or matter of laughter, on a Lord's day," MacDonald viewed the Sabbath as truly a day of joy. His relaxed attitudes—"The Sabbath was made for man and not man for the Sabbath"—directly opposed the Old Testament legalism that still bound much of fundamental Christianity in the 19th century; in *Alec Forbes of Howglen*, for example, Mr. Cupples was accosted by Robert Bruce for having picked a handful of flowers on the Sabbath. Though there was nothing heretical in MacDonald's stance, his leniency was suspect.

Another point even less important raised furious indignation among certain elderly ladies of the congregation. Gossip had it—for it was not heard from the pulpit—that the pastor had expressed a hope that animals would share in the life to come, even though the scriptural warrant for any such hope ("The creation itself will be set free from its bondage to decay . . ." Rom. 8:21) was thin. And whether he ever preached such a view at Arundel or not, it is certain MacDonald did come to believe in an afterlife for animals, for definite arguments in favor of such a notion were later found in many of his books, including an entire sermon in *Paul Faber, Surgeon*: "I more than suspect a rudimentary conscience in every animal. . . . My hope is, that in some way, concerning which I do not now choose to speculate, there may be progress, growth, for them also. While I believe for myself, I *must* hope for them. This much at least seems clear—and I could press the argument further: if not one of them is forgotten before God—and one of them yet passes out of being—then is God the God of the dead and not of the living! But we praise Thee, we bless Thee, we worship Thee, we glorify Thee, we give thanks to Thee for Thy great glory, O Lord God, heavenly King, God the Father almighty! Thy universe is life, life and not death" *(Paul Faber, Surgeon*, Ch. 27).

Wrestling With Difficult Scriptures

There were, however, even more serious problems than these. The worst had originated during the course of a sermon during which he had expressed his belief that some provision was made for the heathen after death. This of course struck root at the very base of traditional reformed Protestantism, and such a statement could never be taken lightly.

Anyone who has read his novels and sermons with care knows the extent to which George MacDonald struggled with the whole scriptural dilemma of how to reconcile eternal punishment with God's redemptive plan for the universe. Like so many other perplexing issues, the Bible appears inconclusive when its seemingly contradictory words are taken at mere face value; for example, when, *"Depart from me, ye cursed, into ever-lasting fire, prepared for the devil and his angels"* (Matt. 25:41) is compared with, *"And I, if I be lifted up from the earth, will draw all men unto me"* (John 12:32). Enough evidence exists on both sides of the question to provide ample fuel for a heated theological debate.

Through the years as he studied the issue in depth in the original languages of the Scriptures, George MacDonald found he could not rationalize away such scriptures as 1 Timothy 2:3–4: "For this is good and acceptable in the sight of God our Saviour; who will have *all* men to be saved, and to come unto the knowledge of the truth"; or Philippians 2:10–11: "At the name of Jesus *every* knee should bow, of things in heaven and things in the earth, and things under the earth, and *every* tongue should confess that Jesus Christ is Lord"; or Colossians 1:20: "and having made peace through the blood of his cross, by him to reconcile *all* things unto himself"; or Revelation 5:13: *"Every* creature which is in heaven, and on the earth, and under the earth . . . and *all* that are in them, heard I saying, Blessing, and honor, and glory, and power, be unto the Lamb for ever and ever."

He had questioned the creed of a predestined elect and an eternal separation from God almost since he was able to think. Assured from his studies of early Greek that the words *life eternal* bore no relation to time but rather spoke of the quality of life (an interpretation held by many renowned scholars of the time), as he grew into adulthood he could not lightly dismiss such scriptures merely because they seemed to go against the traditionally held doctrine.

As he grew older his questions grew increasingly more profound. Never satisfied with pat answers, MacDonald's quest for truth forced him into many corners of theological thought that more comfortable Christians never dared even consider. He feared no inquiry, no matter what the objections might be from his onlooking critics. Robert Falconer poses the incredible question that the boy George MacDonald must himself have considered: "What would God do if a devil [one of Satan's fallen angels] were to repent?"

It's a staggering notion—one for which we have no answer. And perhaps MacDonald himself never postulated a firm response either. But the guardians of the ecclesiastical gates of his day were aghast at his audacity even to inquire in that direction.

George MacDonald feared no query, even of such weighty theological magnitude. He was so confident of a great-hearted, loving, tenderly compassionate God that to him nothing was too large or too small to bring before Him. MacDonald's straight-hewn mind always remained focused on the core of God's loving character.

The questions about this troublesome issue continued into MacDonald's adulthood. In the end he found he simply could not accept Calvin's argument, logical as it seemed on the surface, that God's justice and holiness demanded the condemnation of some souls to eternal punishment.

Though Calvin, a great Biblical scholar, concluded from his reading of the Bible that God's goodness was not compromised by such eternal suffering, that His omnipotence was not compromised by His inability in the end to work His will in the universe (1 Tim. 2:4), MacDonald could not accept Calvin's conclusions. Turning to the same Bible, MacDonald—himself well versed in the Greek language—found much which to him supported the idea of punishment for sin and suffering as a purifying necessity of life, but he found little that convinced him of eternal condemnation as part of God's plan. He had no choice, as he interpreted the Scriptures, but to conclude that Calvin's interpretation was limited and incomplete and did not look far enough into the inexhaustible depths of God's loving plan. It was there, MacDonald felt, that the true nature of punishment, suffering, and godly wrath is to be understood—in the distance where many did not look. Those who focused on the short range and incomplete picture saw only the outpouring of God's vengeance against sin. But he was certain they did not see toward what that punishment was leading, that even God's righteous anger falls under the dominion of His love, that even hell lies within the scope of God's infinite plan of reconciling the world to himself, and that the essence of hell is redemptive rather than retributive. They did not look far enough into the future, according to MacDonald's nonconforming view, to see that hell is finite: ". . . and death and hell delivered up the dead that were in them . . . and death and hell were cast into the lake of fire. . . . And God shall wipe away all tears from their eyes; and there shall be no more death, neither sorrow, nor crying, neither shall there be any more pain: for the former things are passed away . . . And he said unto me, It is done. I am Alpha and Omega, the beginning and the end. I will give unto him that is athirst of the fountain of the water of life" (Rev. 20:13—21:6). Hell, rather than representing an everlasting punishment for earthly sins, was to MacDonald the final and most inescapable means of God's drawing all men to repentance and thus to himself, as He promised to do—an extension into the next life of God's loving redemptive plan (John 12:32). The psalmist confidently proclaims that God's presence exists even in hell, verifying to him that hell was an intrinsic part of the redemptive process, for where God is, there is love—"If I make my bed in hell, behold, thou are there" (Psalm 139:8).

These scriptures, combined with a lifetime of thought and study, at length enabled the dilemma to come into focus for George MacDonald— that *all* things are ordered by God and fall under His sovereignty, that His will for the universe *will* be done and will not be thwarted. He concluded that the word "all" in the Scriptures genuinely means what it says. He interpreted the scripture, "For as in Adam all die, even so in Christ shall *all* be made alive" (1 Cor. 15:22) to mean simply what it says—*all* things, *all* men—without his childhood indoctrination rationalizing away the sheer simplicity and force of the words. This original and unorthodox interpretation at length enabled him to suggest that the very thing the Calvinists had always accused those at the liberal end of Christianity of doing—that is, not taking the words of Scripture literally—they had themselves been doing with these scriptures. MacDonald became convinced that, far from robbing the cross of its power, such a purposeful view of hell as fitting into God's master plan of love was the only way to see the atonement in the fullness of the glorious power for which it was intended—for Christ did indeed die for *all* men. Many critics maintained that if what MacDonald and others said was true, there would have been no need for Christ's death. On the contrary, however, MacDonald replied, it is only through His death that salvation can come, and through His death, according to Jesus' own words, that salvation will come to all men—"I will draw *all* men unto me." Thus MacDonald viewed the death of Christ on the cross as an even more wonderful act of redemption and the only full interpretation of the atonement. For what victory would the cross be, MacDonald reasoned, if in the end, only a tenth, or a fifth, or even half of the people of God's creation were able to spend eternity with their Maker, while the rest spent eternity being punished for their sins? Such questions MacDonald now became bold to pose. That could be no victory for a God of love, he said. To believe that, MacDonald concluded, would be to disgrace the character of God. Far from demanding vengeance as the Calvinists maintained, God's holiness in fact demanded that the cross *not* fail, that Satan *not* be allowed to win over the souls of the majority of mankind, and that hell *be* an instrument for God's redemptive use rather than Satan's final victory. And in the final analysis it was this belief in God's ultimate *total* rather than partial victory over Satan that George MacDonald became convinced was the "hope" of which Paul spoke, and the "mystery" of the kingdom of heaven.

Love, Justice, and the Fire of God

In *David Elginbrod, Unspoken Sermons,* and *What's Mine's Mine*, MacDonald elaborated upon these controversial viewpoints, which he ultimately came to hold with sufficient confidence to put them on paper. MacDonald's own words shed light on his view of this issue that was so divisive in his own day, and remains controversial in our own:

"Nothing is inexorable but love. . . . Love is one, and love is changeless. For love loves into purity. Love has ever in view the absolute loveliness of that which it beholds. . . . There is nothing eternal but that which loves and can be loved, and love is ever climbing towards the consummation when such shall be the universe, imperishable, divine. Therefore all that is not beautiful in the beloved, all that comes between and is not of love's kind, must be destroyed."

For MacDonald the fire of God is not an illustration of His wrath, but rather is the deepest symbol of His love, for it burns until nothing but love remains, "And our God is a consuming fire."

"For this vision of truth God has been working for ages of ages . . . and for this will the patience of God labour while there is yet a human soul whose eyes have not been opened, whose child-heart has not yet been born in him . . . let us have grace to serve the Consuming Fire, our God, with divine fear. . . . It is the nature of God, so terribly pure that it destroys all that is not pure as fire, which demands like purity in our worship. He will have purity. It is not that the fire will burn us if we do not worship thus; but that the fire will burn us until we worship thus; yea, will go on burning within us after all that is foreign to it has yielded to its force, no longer with pain and consuming, but as the highest consciousness of life, the presence of God. When evil, which alone is consumable, shall have passed away in his fire from the dwellers in the immovable kingdom, the nature of man shall look the nature of God in the face, and his fear shall then be pure. . . .

"May it not then hurt to say that God is Love, all love, and nothing other than love? It is not enough to answer that such is the truth, even granted that it is. . . . For when we say that God is Love, do we teach men that their fear of him is groundless? No. As much as they fear will come upon them, possibly far more. But there is something beyond their fear—a divine fate which they cannot withstand. . . . The wrath will consume what they *call* themselves; so that the selves God made shall appear, coming out with tenfold consciousness of being. . . . They will know that now first are they fully themselves. . . . The destructible must be burned out of it, or begin to be burned out of it, before it can *partake* of eternal life. When that is all burnt away and gone, then it has eternal life. Or rather, when the fire of eternal life has possessed a man, then the destructible is gone utterly, and he is pure. Many a man's work must be burned, that by that very burning he may be saved—'so as by fire.' . . . If still he cling to that which can be burned, the burning goes on deeper and deeper into his bosom. . . .

"The man whose deeds are evil fears the burning. But the burning will not come the less that he fears it or denies it. Escape is hopeless. For Love is inexorable. Our God is a consuming fire. He shall not come out till he has paid the uttermost farthing."

MacDonald makes it clear that he believes in a painful hell which is waiting for those who continually resist the truth of God. Occasionally this "hell" is internal and comes prior to death, as the final full-length book of his life makes clear. But when an individual does not repent in this lifetime, God's energetic quest after his heart does not stop. As MacDonald said of young Blatherwick in that last of his novels, "there was no way round the purifying fire; he could not escape it; he *must* pass through it!" (*Salted with Fire*, Ch. 16). "If the man resists the burning of God, the consuming fire of Love, a terrible doom awaits him, and its day will come. He shall be cast into the outer darkness who hates the fire of God. What sick dismay shall then seize upon him! For let a man think and care ever so little about God, he does not therefore exist without God. . . . But when God withdraws from a man . . . then will he listen in agony for the faintest sound of life from the closed door; then . . . he will be ready to rush into the very heart of the Consuming Fire to know life. . . . Imagination cannot mislead us into too much horror of being without God—that one living death. . . . The outer darkness is but the most dreadful form of the consuming fire—the fire without light—the darkness visible, the black flame. God hath withdrawn himself, but not lost his hold. His face is turned away, but his hand is laid upon him still. His heart has ceased to beat into the man's heart, but he keeps him alive by his fire. And that fire will go searching and burning on in him, as in the highest saint who is not yet pure as he is pure."

But even more strongly he believes in the final victory of God: "But at length, O God, wilt thou not cast Death and Hell into the lake of Fire— even into thine own consuming self? Death shall then die everlastingly, 'And Hell itself will pass away, and leave her dolorous mansions to the peering day.' Then indeed wilt thou be all in all. For then our poor brothers and sisters, every one—O God, we trust in thee, the Consuming Fire—shall have been burnt clean and brought home. For if their moans, myriads of ages away, would turn heaven for us into hell—shall a man be more merciful than God? Shall, of all his glories, his mercy alone not be infinite? Shall a brother love a brother more than The Father loves a son?—more than The Brother Christ loves his brother. Would he not die yet again to save one brother more?

"As for us, now will we come to thee, our Consuming Fire. And thou will not burn us more than we can bear. But thou wilt burn us. And although thou seem to slay us, yet will we trust in thee even for that which thou has not spoken, if by any means at length we may attain unto the blessedness of those who have not seen and yet have believed" (*Unspoken Sermons*, vol. 1, "The Consuming Fire").

The third series of *Unspoken Sermons* was not published until 1889, and in the intervening years MacDonald's views continued to be refined. When at last he was bold enough to put his highly debatable interpretation of God's justice and his view of the atonement on paper, it was with a strong sense of conviction. First he poses the question of what God's "justice" means to most people:

"If you ask any ordinary congregation in England what is meant by the justice of God, would not nineteen out of twenty answer, that it means his punishing of sin? Think for a moment what degree of justice it would indicate in a man—that he punished every wrong. A Roman emperor, a Turkish cadi, might do that, and be the most unjust both of men and judges. . . . Oh the folly of any mind that would explain God before obeying him! that would map out the character of God, instead of crying, Lord, what wouldst thou have me to do? . . . The justice of God is this, that . . . he gives every man, woman, child, and beast, everything that has being, *fair play;* he renders to every man according to his work; and therein lies his perfect mercy; for nothing else could be merciful to the man, and nothing but mercy could be fair to him. . . . When we speak of the justice of God, let us see that we do mean justice! Punishment of the guilty may be involved, but . . . I will accept no explanation of any way of God which . . . involves what I should scorn as false and unfair in a man. . . . More and higher justice and righteousness is required of him by himself, the Truth— greater nobleness, more penetrating sympathy. . . . To uphold a lie for God's sake is to be against God, not for him. . . ."

He goes on to inquire what lasting good is to be accomplished by the punishment of sin, if the sin itself remains. "The common idea, then, is, that the justice of God consists in punishing sin: it is in the hope of giving a larger idea of the justice of God in punishing sin that I ask, *'Why is God bound to punish sin?'* . . .

"Punishment is *nowise* an *offset* to sin . . . What merit is there in it? . . . The notion is a false one altogether. Punishment, deserved suffering, is no equipoise [counterbalance] to sin. . . . If it were an offset to wrong, then God would be bound to punish for the sake of the punishment; but he cannot be, for he forgives. Then it is not for the sake of punishment, as a thing that in itself ought to be done, but for the sake of something else, as a means to an end, that God punishes. . . .

"Primarily, God is not bound to *punish* sin; he is bound to *destroy* sin. If he were not the Maker, he might not be bound to destroy sin—I do not know; but seeing he has created creatures who have sinned, and therefore sin has, by the creating act of God, come into the world, God is, in his own righteousness, bound to destroy sin. . . ."

Instead of its being punished, says MacDonald, God wants sin utterly destroyed and made up for. "But vengeance on the sinner, the law of a tooth for a tooth, is not in the heart of God, neither in his hand. If the sinner and the sin in him are the concrete object of the divine wrath, then indeed there can be no mercy. Then indeed there will be an end put to sin by the destruction of the sin and the sinner together. But thus would no atonement be wrought. . . . There must be an atonement, a making-up, a bringing together. . . .

"Punishment, I repeat, is not the thing required of God, but the absolute destruction of sin. What better is the world, what better is the sinner, what better is God, what better is the truth, that the sinner should suffer—continue suffering to all eternity? Would there be any less sin in the universe? Would there be any making-up for the sin? Would it show God justified in doing what he knew would bring sin into the world, justified in making creatures who he knew would sin? What setting-right would come of the sinner's suffering? If justice demand it, if suffering be the equivalent for sin, then . . . the making of man was a tyrannical deed, a creative cruelty. . . ."

MacDonald concludes that there is no more lasting way to destroy sin than by making the sinner unwilling to sin again. "The only vengeance worth having on sin is to make the sinner himself its executioner. . . . Sin and suffering are not natural opposites. . . . The opposite of sin is not suffering, but righteousness. The path across the gulf that divides right from wrong is not fire, but repentance. If my friend has wronged me, will it console me to see him punished? . . . I am not saying it is not right to punish. . . . I am saying that justice is not, never can be, satisfied by suffering. . . . God is triumphantly defeated, I say, throughout the hell of his vengeance. Although against evil, it is but the vain and wasted cruelty of a tyrant. There is no destruction of evil thereby, but an enhancing of its horrible power. . . . The notion that a creature born imperfect . . . with impulses to evil . . . which he could not help having, a creature to whom the true face of God was never presented . . . should be thus condemned, is as loathsome a lie against God as could find place in heart too undeveloped to understand what justice is, and too low to look up into the face of Jesus. It never in truth found place in any heart, though in many a pettifogging brain. There is but one thing lower than deliberately to believe such a lie, and that is to worship the God of whom it is believed. . . ."

That, says MacDonald, is truly what "being saved" is, and the end of God's punishment, to take a man to the point of loathing sin and loving God. That is God's justice seen in its fullness. "When a man loaths himself, he has begun to be saved. Punishment tends to this result. Not for its own sake, not as a make-up for sin, not for divine revenge. . . . Punishment is for the sake of amendment and atonement. God is bound by his love to punish sin in order to deliver his creature; he is bound by his justice to destroy sin in his creation. Love is justice. . . . This is the reason of punishment; this is why justice requires that the wicked shall not go unpunished—that they, through the eye-opening power of pain, may come to see and do justice, may be brought to desire and make all possible amends, and so become just. Such punishment concerns justice in the deepest degree. . . . Repentance, restitution, confession, prayer for forgiveness, righteous dealing thereafter, is the sole possible, the only true make-up for sin. . . .

"Justice then requires that sin should be put an end to . . . and where punishment can do anything to this end, where it can help the sinner to know what he has been guilty of, where it can soften his heart to see his pride and wrong and cruelty, justice requires that punishment shall not be spared. And the more we believe in God, the surer we shall be that he will spare nothing that suffering can do to deliver his child from death. . . .

"The notion of suffering as an offset for sin . . . comes first of all, I think, from the satisfaction we feel when wrong comes to grief. Why do we feel this satisfaction? Because we hate wrong, but, not being righteous ourselves, more or less hate the wronger as well as his wrong. . . . In this way the inborn justice of our nature passes over to evil. It is no pleasure to God, as it so often is to us, to see the wicked suffer. His nature is always to forgive, and just because he forgives, he punishes. Because God is so altogether alien to wrong . . . there is, I believe, no extreme of suffering to which, for the sake of destroying the evil thing in them, he would not subject them. . . . God, being the God of justice, that is of fair-play . . . is in himself bound to punish in order to deliver us. . . .

"The notion that the salvation of Jesus is a salvation from the consequences of our sins, is a false . . . notion. Jesus did not die to save us from punishment; he was called Jesus because he should save his people from their sins. . . ."

MacDonald then goes on to question the logic of an innocent being punished for the sins of others. Such punishment, he insists, is not only contrary to God's character, but cannot ever truly atone for sin.

"If there be no satisfaction to justice in the mere punishment of the wrong-doer, what shall we say of the notion of satisfying justice by causing one to suffer who is not the wrong-doer? And what, moreover, shall we say to the notion that, just because he is not the person who deserves to be punished, but is absolutely innocent, his suffering gives perfect satisfaction to the perfect justice? . . . The thing gets worse and worse. . . . What! God, the father of Jesus Christ like that! His justice contented with direct injustice! The anger of him who will nowise clear the guilty, appeased by the suffering of the innocent! Very God forbid! . . . How did it come ever to be imagined? It sprang from the trustless dread that cannot believe in the forgiveness of the Father. . . . You ought not to be able to believe it. It is the merest, poorest, most shameless fiction, invented . . . to satisfy the intellect. . . . It has seemed to satisfy also many a humble soul, content to take what was given, and not think; content that another should think for him, and tell him what was the mind of his Father in heaven. Again I say, let the person who can be so satisfied be so satisfied. . . . That he can be content with it argues him unready to receive better. . . . Opinion, right or wrong, will do nothing to save him. I would that he thought no more about this or any other opinion, but set himself to do the work of the Master. . . .

"Truth is indeed too good for men to believe; they must dilute it before they can take it. . . . Unable to believe in the love of the Lord Jesus Christ, they invented . . . a satisfaction for sin which was an insult to God. . . . They thought him bound to punish for the sake of punishing. . . . They could not believe in clear forgiveness; that did not seem divine; it needed itself to be justified. . . . He sought no satisfaction, but an obedient return to the Father. . . . The thing was too simple for complicated unbelief and the arguing spirit. Gladly would I help their followers to loathe such thoughts of God; but for that, they themselves must grow better men and women. While they are capable of being satisfied with them, there would be no advantage in their becoming intellectually convinced that such thoughts were wrong. I would not speak a word to persuade them of it. Success would be worthless. They would but remain what they were—children capable of thinking meanly of their father. When the heart recoils, discovering how horrible it would be to have such an unreality for God, it will begin to search about and see whether it must indeed accept such statements concerning God; it will search after a real God by whom to hold fast, a real God to deliver them from the terrible idol. It is for those thus moved that I write, not at all for the sake of disputing with those who love the lie they may not be to blame for holding; who, like the Jews of old, would cast out of their synagogue the man who doubts the genuineness of their moral caricature of God, who doubts their travesty of the grandest truth in the universe, the atonement of Jesus Christ. Of such a man they will unhesitatingly report that he does not believe in the atonement. But a lie for God is against God, and carries the sentence of death in itself.

"Instead of giving their energy to do the will of God, men of power have given it to the construction of a system by which to explain why Christ must die . . . and . . . have clung to the morally and spiritually vulgar idea of justice and satisfaction held by pagan Rome, buttressed by the Jewish notion of sacrifice. . . . To represent the living God as a party to such style of action, is to veil with a mask of cruelty and hypocrisy the face whose glory can be seen only in the face of Jesus; to put a tirade of vulgar Roman legality into the mouth of the Lord God merciful and gracious. . . . Rather than believe such ugly folly of him . . . I would say, 'There is no God; let us neither eat nor drink, that we may die! For lo, this is not our God!' "

To those who insist that he formulate a new theory to replace what he has just thrown out, MacDonald says he is uninterested in raising any new theories or doctrines.

" 'Well, then,' will many say, 'if you thus unceremoniously cast to the winds the doctrine of vicarious sacrifice, what theory do you propose to substitute in its stead?'

" 'In the name of the truth,' I answer, *None*. I will send out no theory of mine to rouse afresh little whirlwinds of dialogistic dust mixed with dirt and straws and holy words, hiding the Master in talk about him. . . . Only eyes opened by the sun of righteousness, and made single by obedience, can judge even the poor moony pearl of formulated thought. Say if you will that I fear to show my opinion. . . . What faith in this kind I have, I will have to myself before God, till I see better reason for uttering it than I do now. . . . Trust in God. Obey the word—every word of the Master. That is faith; and so believing, your opinion will grow out of your true life, and be worthy of it. Peter says the Lord gives the spirit to them that obey him: the spirit of the Master, and that alone, can guide you to any theory that it will be of use to you to hold. . . . Jesus is the creating and saving lord of our intellects as well as of our more precious hearts. . . . No man can think as he thinks, except he be pure like him; no man can be pure like him, except he go with him, and learn from him. To put off obeying him till we find a credible theory concerning him, is to set aside the potion we know it our duty to drink, for the study of the various schools of therapy. . . . Obey the truth, I say, and let theory wait. Theory may spring from life, but never life from theory."

He then proceeds with a grand and clear statement of his belief, apart from doctrine.

"I will not then tell you what I think, but I will tell any man who cares to hear it what I believe. . . .

"I believe in Jesus Christ, the eternal Son of God. . . . I believe that he has a right to my absolute obedience . . . that to obey him is to ascend the pinnacle of my being. . . . I believe that he died that I might die like him— die to any ruling power in me but the will of God. . . . I believe that he is my Saviour from myself. . . . I believe and pray that he will give me what punishment I need to set me right, or keep me from going wrong. I believe that he died to deliver me from all meanness, all pretence, all falseness, all unfairness, all poverty of spirit, all cowardice, all fear, all anxiety, all forms of self-love, all trust or hope in possession. . . . I believe that God is just like Jesus, only greater yet, for Jesus said so. . . . I believe that God has always done, is always doing his best for every man. . . .

"I believe that there is nothing good for me or for any man but God, and more and more of God, and that alone through knowing Christ can we come nigh to him. . . .

"I believe that justice and mercy are simply one and the same thing; without justice to the full there can be no mercy, and without mercy to the full there can be no justice; that such is the mercy of God that he will hold his children in the consuming fire of his distance until they pay the uttermost farthing, until they drop the purse of selfishness with all the dross that is in it, and rush home to the Father and the Son, and the many brethren—rush inside the centre of the life-giving fire whose outer circles burn. I believe that no hell will be lacking which would help the just mercy of God to redeem his children.

"I believe that to him who obeys, and thus opens the doors of his heart to receive the eternal gift, God gives the spirit of his son, the spirit of himself, to be in him, and lead him to the understanding of all truth; that the true disciple shall thus always know what he ought to do, though not necessarily what another ought to do; that the spirit of the father and the son enlightens by teaching righteousness. . . . I believe that the inspiration of the Almighty alone gives understanding. I believe that to be the disciple of Christ is the end of teaching."

And answering the final objection, which had been raised against him all his life, he categorically says, "I believe in the atonement of Jesus Christ!"

"'The sum of all this is that you do not believe in the atonement?'

"I believe in Jesus Christ. Nowhere am I requested to believe *in* any thing, or *in* any statement, but everywhere to believe in God and in Jesus Christ. In what you call *the atonement*, in what you mean by the word, what I have already written must make it plain enough I do not believe. God forbid I should, for it would be to believe a lie. . . . But, as the word was used by the best English writers at the time when the translation of the Bible was made—with all my heart, and soul, and strength, and mind, I believe in the atonement. . . . I believe that Jesus Christ *is* our atonement; that through him we are reconciled to, made one with God. . . . I am not writing, neither desire to write, a treatise on the atonement, my business being to persuade men to be atoned to God; but I will go so far . . . as to say . . . that, even in the sense of the atonement being a making-up for the evil done by men toward God, I believe in the atonement. Did not the Lord cast himself into the eternal gulf of evil yawning between the children and the Father? . . . Did he not thus lay down his life persuading us to lay down ours at the feet of the Father? Has not his very life by which he died passed into those who have received him, and re-created theirs, so that now they live with the life which alone is life? Did he not foil and slay evil by letting all the waves and billows of its horrid sea break upon

him, go over him, and die without rebound—spend their rage, fall
defeated, and cease? Verily, he made atonement! . . . It is God who has
sacrificed his own son to us; there was no way else of getting the gift of
himself into our hearts. Jesus sacrificed himself to his father and the children to bring them together. . . . If the joy that alone makes life worth living, the joy that God is such as Christ, be a true thing in my heart, how
can I but believe in the atonement of Jesus Christ? I believe it heartily, as
God means it. . . .

"Who is the mover, the causer, the persuader, the creator of . . . repentance. . . ?—Jesus, our propitiation, our atonement. . . . Shall I not now love
him with an infinitely better love than was possible to me before? That I
will and can make atonement, thanks be to him who is my atonement,
making me at one with God and my fellows! He is my life, my joy, my lord,
my owner, the perfecter of my being by the perfection of his own. I dare
not say with Paul that I am the slave of Christ; but my highest aspiration
and desire is to be the slave of Christ" (*Unspoken Sermons,* vol. 3, "Justice").

Inevitable Controversy

Clearly, one reared on the traditional viewpoints, such as Louisa, would
have a difficult time accepting twenty-one-year-old George MacDonald,
fresh out of the university, until he had "satisfactorily" formulated "his
views on the Atonement." We must remember that these words from his
printed sermons were penned fifteen, twenty, and in some cases thirty
years after his pastorate at Arundel. The "formulation" process took a long
time and years of prayerful thought. And though he was coming into some
measure of conviction concerning these truths in the early 1850s, he still
did not dogmatically say such things to his congregation openly. He recognized the controversial nature of his ideas and thus reserved them for
later years as "unspoken" sermons. He fully recognized the danger of
erecting his *own* doctrinal system. Therefore, though he himself held
strong personal viewpoints on many issues, beyond urging obedience and
living the example of Jesus, he did not forcibly attempt to catechize his
views. He recognized all too clearly his own human fallibility. He knew
many of his own earthly viewpoints would in the end, in heaven's light,
turn out to be wrong. He knew all too well the equally scriptural arguments that could be mustered against everything he said. Therefore, he
urged people to think, to question, to pray, to read their New Testaments,
to ask God what he would have them do; above all he urged people to *act*
upon the Lord's instructions.

Thus it is unlikely that words such as these were heard quite so forcefully from the pulpit of Arundel. He was aware of the contentious nature
of the question, and did not want to be a stumbling block to his

congregation. When pinned down on a certain doctrinal issue, his reply might have been, "I am still seeking further light on the matter." Or, as he said through the mouth of Polwarth: "'I know so little,' he answered, 'that I dare hardly say I *think* anything. . . . His will *is*, and that is everything. But there can be no harm, where I do not know His Will, in venturing a *may be*. I am sure He likes His little ones to tell their fancies in the dimness about the nursery fire. Our souls yearning after light of any sort must be a pleasure to him to watch'" (*Paul Faber, Surgeon*, Ch. 51).

But for the conservative people at Arundel, already nettled by the pointed barbs of his sermons, the least hint of doubt concerning the truth of fundamental Calvinist doctrine was enough. At the mere suggestion that possibly, as the Bible says, God does in fact purpose to save *all* men, tongues began to wag. He had already offended a small but wealthy and powerful group within the church, and this was just the sort of excuse they needed to get back at him.

There was still one further charge against the young minister, this one having no doubt originated with his book on the Songs of Novalis. The new liberal theology, an outgrowth of what is philosophically referred to as the "Enlightenment," had in the 19th century come to Britain from Germany. Conservative churchmen were up in arms over the new ways of approaching biblical interpretation (the so-called "higher criticism"), which, in their view, undermined the literal accuracy and truthfulness of the Scriptures by explaining away everything of a miraculous nature. Therefore, when it began to be said of George MacDonald that he was "tainted with German theology," the charge was a serious one indeed.

Although George MacDonald was a firm believer in the miraculous, and later devoted an entire book to the miracles of Jesus, loved the Scriptures, loved the Lord, and loved the church with all his heart, such criticisms brought him into a dilemma, which no degree of Christlike character could resolve. In his day "German theology" was symbolic of all that was modern, mystical, unscriptural, fearsome, and evil. Unknown, it was feared; therefore it had to be rooted out. It is doubtful any of the leaders in the Arundel church carefully studied the cries of Novalis's heart toward his God; to them it was an indictment against their minister that he had anything to do with Novalis at all. The content of the "Spiritual Songs" mattered little. That MacDonald had translated and then published them placed him in the same camp as the dreaded Germans.

More Practical Matters

Coincident with this undercurrent of gossip came George and Louisa's conclusion that their house was not large enough for their expanding family. It soon became known that they were looking for another. Their present home, however, was being rented from one of the church's richest and most influential deacons. Whether the respectable man could not bear the thought of harboring a heretic, or was offended that the minister no longer found his lodgings "good enough for him," the situation provided even more fuel on the part of this man against the young pastor. The mere suspicion of heresy, coupled with the offense of one influential local merchant, more than outweighed the love of any twenty lesser church members.

Characters of the deacon and his wife were later drawn in *David Elginbrod* as Mr. and Mrs. Appleditch. Though the circumstances between Arundel and the London of the novel are totally dissimilar, the personalities are so parallel that they shed a great deal of light on the nature of MacDonald's frustration. Appleditch is a rich grocer. Almost starving, Hugh Sutherland is browbeaten by Mrs. Appleditch into agreeing to teach their sons at a paltry eighteen pence a lesson. One of the boys, on his first introduction to the tutor, boasts that he has five bags of gold in the Bank of England. Such a remark was actually made to MacDonald in Arundel by this very deacon's son. When the penny-pinching Mrs. Appleditch can no longer tolerate Sutherland's straightforward ways, his honesty, and his beard, she—like the deacons at Arundel—resorts to backhanded subterfuge in order to attempt to force Hugh to give up his post gracefully:

"As it would involve some awkwardness to state reasons, Mrs. Appleditch resolved to quarrel with him, as the easiest way of prefacing his discharge. It was the way she took with her maids-of-all-work; for it was grand in itself, and always left her with a comfortable feeling of injured dignity.

"As a preliminary course, she began to treat him with still less politeness than before" (*David Elginbrod,* Ch. 63).

The Charges

In June of 1852, the deacons formally called upon their minister. They came, having themselves conspired to base their deception upon his salary. Convincing themselves that since he was contemplating a larger house he must have excess money, their conclusion was that his yearly stipend must therefore be unnecessarily generous. They came, therefore, not to confront the issues at hand nor to ask about his views, but with the "unpleasant" duty of informing him that it was no longer possible to pay him as much as 150 pounds a year—the MacDonalds' growing infant and the deacon's son's bag of gold notwithstanding.*

Greville MacDonald colorfully picks up the essence of the dialogue after his father had heard of their decision:

"It was hard enough to make both ends meet, but for him such a matter was in the hands of God.

"'I am sorry enough to hear it,' he replied, 'but if it must be, why, I suppose we must contrive to live on less.'

"The answer surprised them: 'O, but—er—we thought—' stammered out the minister's landlord, 'er—we thought you would take it—er—as a kindly hint, so to speak—'

*Though 150 pounds went considerably further than it would today, in 1850 the poverty level was probably around 100 pounds; 150 pounds was barely a working class wage. A "middle class" income would have been 400 to 1000 pounds per year.

"'Of what?' asked George MacDonald.

"'That your preaching is not acceptable, and that you should resign,' was the reply."[3]

The MacDonalds accepted the deacons' reduction of their pay (which, according to the chapel books, was reduced to approximately 115 pounds per year), but as to the question of resignation, that he would not do without submitting the matter to a meeting of the whole congregation. The resolution calling him to Arundel had been signed by nearly sixty members. He would willingly resign if need be, but only if the congregation as a whole was no longer satisfied with him.

How many actually attended the meeting the following month is not known. The number agreeing to the resolution that was passed is so small (between one-fourth and one-third of the membership that had grown slowly since MacDonald's coming) that it is unclear whether the meeting was poorly attended, whether the actual objectors were few, or whether the majority had not the pluck to stand up to the deacons and speak out against the resolution.

The minister read a brief handwritten address:

"It having been represented to me that a small party in the church has for some time been exceedingly dissatisfied with my preaching, it has become my duty to bring the matter before the assembled church. My first impulse was at once to resign, as the most agreeable mode for me to be delivered from the annoyance. On mentioning this to some of my friends in the church, the proposal was met with no opposition, although it drew forth expressions of sorrow, and the declaration of benefit derived from my labours. But from the advice of two of my friends engaged in the same work, and from the awakened perception in my own mind that, as I came at the invitation of the whole church, it would be unfair to the other members of the church to resign unconditionally on account of the dissatisfaction of a few, I resolved to put it in the following form: Will you, the Church, let me know whether you sympathize or not with the dissatisfaction of the few? Such a communication from you will let me know how to act: I put it thus from the feeling that this is my duty. With my own personal feelings I have nothing to do in this assembly. I retire and await your decision."[4]

He then left the meeting, and the official record of the ensuing proceedings, concluded in admittedly gracious language, runs as follows:

"At a Meeting of the Church of Christ assembling in Trinity Chapel, Arundel, held July 5th 1852 to consider a request from the Revd. G. MacDonald.

"Mr. New in the Chair.

"1st. It was proposed and resolved unanimously to express their respect and esteem towards him as their Pastor.

"2nd. In reference to the dissatisfaction expressed by some members of the Church.

"We do not by any means sympathize with the statement which has been made that there is 'nothing in his preaching.' But we do sympathize with those who were dissatisfied with the statement from the pulpit 'that with the Heathen the time of trial does not (in his, the Rev. G. MacDonald's opinion) cease at their death,' which certainly implies a future state of probation. And this Church considers such a view is not in accordance with the Scriptures and quite differs with the sentiments held by the Ministers of the Independent Denomination.

"It is by no means our wish that the Revd. G. MacDonald should relinquish the office of Pastor of this Church; such a course would cause much regret. But if on reflection he continues to hold and express such an opinion it is evident that it will cause serious difficulties in the Church.

"These propositions were agreed to by about 20 members."[5]

As a result of the inconclusiveness of the meeting and this resolution, George MacDonald did not resign, feeling that he could not in good conscience take his dismissal at the hands of such a small minority.

The Lines of Truth

No doubt, people such as these Arundel deacons and this situation in his first church gave rise to the following passage from *David Elginbrod*, written not many years later, which reveals the very foundation of Mac-Donald's thought in this area. Robert Falconer and Hugh Sutherland are speaking about a certain minister—drawn from the real-life F. D. Maurice, who became MacDonald's close friend—whose preaching and ideas many found uncomfortable and heretical:

"'He looks upon the formulae of the church as utterances of *living* truth. . . . He trusts in God so absolutely, that he leaves his salvation to him. . . . Let God's will be done, and all is well. If God's will be done, he cannot fare ill. To him, God is all in all. If it be possible to separate such things, it is the glory of God, even more than the salvation of men, that he seeks. He will not have it that his Father in heaven is not perfect. He believes entirely that God loves, yea, *is* love; and, therefore, that hell itself must be subservient to that love, and but an embodiment of it; that the grand work of Justice is to make way for a Love which will give to every man that which is right and ten times more, even if it should be by means of awful suffering—a suffering which the Love of the Father will not shun, either for himself or his children, but will eagerly meet for their sakes, that he may give them all that is in his heart. . . .'

"'How is it that so many good people call him heterodox?'

"'I do not mind that. . . . To these, theology must be like a map—with plenty of lines in it. They cannot trust their house on the high table-land of his theology, because they cannot see the outlines bounding the said table-land. It is not small enough for them. They cannot take it in. Such can hardly be satisfied with the creation, one would think, seeing there is no line of division anywhere in it. . . .'

"'Does God draw no lines, then?'

"'When he does, they are pure lines, without breadth, and consequently invisible to mortal eyes; not . . . walls of separation, such as these definers would construct. . . .'

"'But can those theories in religion be correct which are so hard to see?'

"'They are only hard to certain natures.'

"'But those natures are above the average.'

"'Yes, in intellect and its cultivation—nothing more.'

"'You have granted them heart. . . . Is it not hard, then, to say that such cannot understand him?'

"'Why? They will get to heaven, which is all they want. And they will understand him one day, which is more than they pray for. Till they have done being anxious about their own salvation, we must forgive them that they can contemplate with calmness the damnation of a universe, and believe that God is yet more indifferent than they.'

"'But do they not bring the charge likewise against you, of being unable to understand them?'

"'Yes. And so it must remain, till the Spirit of God decide the matter, which I presume must take place by slow degrees. For this . . . can only consist in the enlightenment of souls to see the truth. . . . Till then, the Right must be content to be called the Wrong, and—which is far harder— to seem the Wrong. There is no spiritual victory gained by a verbal conquest. . . .'" (*David Elginbrod*, Ch. 59).

Writing to his father later in the same month as the meeting, Mac-Donald reveals thoughts moving beyond the ministry; he wonders what else he might do—wanting to help people without being in bondage to the whims of a few. This is one of the first hints we have of his dissatisfaction with the clerical life. ". . . I have been very much occupied with some annoyance given me by some members of the church who are very unteachable. I thought it not unlikely at the time that I should have to leave. . . . If God put the means at any time in my power, I mean to take another mode of helping men; and no longer stand in this position towards them [the deacons], in which they regard you more as *their* servant than as Christ's. . . ."[6]

Nevertheless, the preaching went on. And with his income now reduced, simple gifts such as fruit, cauliflower, and potatoes were offered the MacDonalds by poorer friends. "The few young," he wrote to his father, "who are here and not [adversely] influenced by their parents, [and] the simple, honest poor are much attached to me."[7] Louisa demonstrated her determination to help with the financial burden by printing an advertisement offering to take girls into the home for a thorough English education. However, no pupils came.

In the fall George went to Manchester to see his brother Charles. While George was in the cotton capital, Louisa's letters were full of tidbits of pastoral news. Old Rogers visited in his smock with a gift of golden gooseberries from his garden. Louisa gave him the remains of a cold mutton, which, having cleaned what remained to the bone, he pocketed, saying, "The missus will get summat out of it yet."

A little girl, Mary Ann, brought a present of home-brewed beer, "very strong and good for nursing." Louisa went on, "She was looking out of my bedroom window and exclaimed, 'O, what a beautiful garden!' Whereupon I gave her plenty of carnations and went into the garden to get her some jasmine, roses, etc. which delighted her immensely. She kept saying, 'I shan't know what to do with myself if I have such a lot of flowers! Oh what will my mother say to such a beautiful nosegay!'"[8]

Another friend, Mr. Smith, was always considerate—especially when the minister was sick. At such times he would send them all sorts of delicacies they could never have afforded on their own—jellies, cream-custards, cold chicken.

Then came Mr. Bull, calling to tell how sorry he was not to get his way at the meeting. Louisa tells her husband, "He proposed a 'resolution of attachment and affection' which was most warmly responded to, until someone referred to your sermon."

Thus things continued after his return to Arundel, for the remainder of that year and on into the next. Louisa was pregnant again, expecting in the summer. But though the support and love of many of the folk never wavered, the dissension at work could not but do further damage. And for George MacDonald, chief among Christian duties was peace, chief of all terrors was schism. For all his efforts, the breach between the factions within the church grew wider and wider.

Greville MacDonald implies that the deacons continued to try to find subtle means to "ease" the young pastor out. "By what steps," says Greville, "by what annoyances, by what spiritual wickedness in high places, the resignation became at last inevitable is not on record."[9]

No doubt during this time in the north with his brother, George MacDonald had been prayerfully searching his soul in consideration of the best course of action for him to take. No greater contrast of environment—physical, social, intellectual, or spiritual—could be imagined than between Arundel, the beautiful, sleepy town of the South Downs with its ill-educated society and old-fashioned theology, and Manchester, that great northern metropolis at the center of the cotton industry, with its ugly factories, political radicals, and spiritual progressives.

On the one hand, certainly, Arundel was attractive as a setting. But for a spirit such as MacDonald's, air and room and freedom were required—space to think and grow and discuss the deep concerns of soul and spirit with like minds. Although its physical surroundings were not nearly so alluring, after almost three years in Arundel, Manchester must have seemed to the frustrated young preacher as the more attractive place of the two. New friends awaited him, as well as the presence of his brother, and the attraction of the highly revered Alexander John Scott, who had moved from London to Manchester in 1851 to become Principal of Owen College (later Manchester University), in whom MacDonald had discovered similar yearnings toward God.

In May of 1853, therefore, in order to keep the church from dividing any further, George MacDonald resigned his pastorate in Arundel, planning to try his fortunes in the cotton capital of north-central England.

His former teacher and future brother-in-law, the Rev. J. H. Godwin, whom he was scheduled to marry that same summer to Louisa's sister, wrote chastising his former pupil for not working harder to gain "success in the ministry." He counseled him to be more sympathetic to those he would influence and to try to imitate other preachers who had been a success. Then he criticized MacDonald's library: "In looking over your books I could see very few that appeared to me likely to be of much service to you, in respect of your chief work. . . ."[10]

Perhaps Mr. Godwin's eyes would have been opened wider to see what the "chief work" of this growing young man of God actually was had he seen some of MacDonald's letters to his father in these days of trial.

On April 29, 1853, he wrote: ". . . But indeed my way of thinking and feeling would not help to make you more sad. I grow younger and happier. . . . O I know a little now, and only a little, what Christ's deep sayings mean, about becoming like a child, about leaving all for him, about service, and truth and love. God is our loving, true, self-forgetting friend. All delight, all hope and beauty are in God. My dear and honoured father—if I might say so to you—will you think me presumptuous if I say . . . ponder The Gospel—the story about Christ. Infinitely are the Epistles mistaken because the Gospels are not understood and felt in the heart: because the readers of the Epistles too often possess nothing of that sympathy with Christ's thoughts and feelings and desires which moved and glorified the writers of the Epistles. The Epistles are very different from the Apostles' preaching; they are mostly written for a peculiar end and aim, and are not intended as expositions of the central truth. . . .

"God has provided for us very lovingly. Our salary is reduced—but not so much as we feared, and our sister's boarding with us had helped much to take us through. . . ."[11]

On May 20, immediately after the resignation: ". . . I am always finding out meaning which I did not see before, and which I now cannot see perfectly—for, of course, till my heart is like Christ's great heart, I cannot fully know what he meant. The great thing for understanding what he said is to have a living sense of the reality that a young man of poor birth appeared unexpectedly in the country of Judea and uttered most unwelcome truths, setting at nought all the respectabilities of the time, and calling bad, bad, and good, good, in the face of all religious perversions and false honourings. The first thing to know is to know Jesus as a man, and any theory about him that makes less of him as a man—with the . . . notion of exalting his divinity—I refuse at once. . . . The life, thoughts, deeds, aims, beliefs of Jesus have to be fresh expounded every age, for all the depth of Eternity lies in them, and they have to be seen into more profoundly every new era of the world's spiritual history. . . .

"You must not be surprised if you hear that I am not what is called *getting on*. Time will show what use the Father will make of me. I desire to be His—entirely—so sure am I that therein lies all things. If less than this were my hope, I should die.

"I expect to find a few whom I can help in Manchester. . . . If I were in a large town I do not think I should yield . . . and leave—but it is better for me to be driven away than to break up such ties as may be supposed to exist between a true pastor and true people for the sake of getting a larger salary. . . ."[12]

His letter of June 3 reveals his future plans: ". . . Mr. Godwin says I want a place with a number of young men. He says they can't understand me in Arundel; but I know that *some* of all classes *do* understand me, and I am happy not to be understood by those that do not understand. . . . Some say I talk foolishness, others go away with their hearts burning within them. May God fashion me after *His* liking. . . .

"Whether I shall go at once to Manchester and preach wherever I have an opportunity, remains not yet decided. I should be glad to rest, and preach nowhere for a month. . . .

"I can hardly say I have any fear, and but very little anxiety about the future. Does not Jesus say, Consider the lilies? We have only to do our work. If we could be forgotten, all Nature would go to wrack. . . . Jesus lived a grand, simple life in poverty and love. . . . His spirit is working in the earth—and in my heart too, I trust. But no man can speak the truth in a time of insincerity—like this and like most times—and tell people to their face that they cannot serve God and Mammon, without making foes. . . .

"How strange the dear old fields will look to me with the iron nerves run through it, which makes the dear, rugged North one body with the warm, rich, more indolent South! [The railway line had just been laid down in Huntly, cutting straight across the MacDonalds' property, dividing the house from the mill.]"[13]

And finally, a letter in July reveals again his childlikeness and the simple pleasures that give him joy. ". . . I have been very idle with the girls all the morning. . . . We romped a good deal at the Forest. I laughed very much, and was merry, and seemed to have clearer brains for it. I am sure it is good. I understand the Bible better for it, I think. . . . Carrie and I found a dead bird yesterday and we went out this morning and got a spade and went and buried it under a tree, and Carrie put roses over it before the earth. And when we had buried it, we found another lying close to the grave, which we buried too. . . . [The marriage of Mr. Godwin and Charlotte Powell had just taken place.] Mr. Godwin and I were very good friends. I wish he would say nothing more—we should get on so nicely—for I cannot help and do not wish to help loving him. . . ."[14]

CHAPTER EIGHTEEN

MANCHESTER
(1853–1854)

George MacDonald traveled to Manchester alone, staying with his brother Charles while looking for work, and Louisa remained at the house in Arundel until after the expected summer arrival. A second daughter, Mary Josephine, was born in the third week of July, while Louisa's sisters attended her.

The Loss of a Friend

In the midst of all these upheavals and changes, MacDonald faced in the preceding spring of the year an additional trial, the loss of his brother Alec. In order to convey the depth of camaraderie that existed between the MacDonald men, and thereby to appreciate the emptiness of loss, Greville devotes considerable space to the relationship between George Mac-Donald, Sr., and his sons, and among the sons themselves.

Greville's account of their relationship tends to lionize the family of his father with flowery words. But as "one who was there" he gives a true sense of the relationship among these people.

"The love which is mutually instinctive, which is centered in parents and children, brothers and sisters, to radiate from the home in diminishing intensity over clan and nation, is purely religious. It is firmer-rooted than the love of lovers; though if these become husband and wife it thrusts roots into the heavenly ground, and remains, among simple and virtuous folk, as ineradicable as the love of mother and child. And when the natural bonds of family and home are strengthened by sympathy in spiritual outlook and intellectual culture, then we have love of the very highest order. Thus my father and mother had found this greatest love. George, Alec, [Charles,] and John MacDonald, bound together in the first instance by the most tender family-love—with a father of exceptional wisdom always thinking of them, the memory of a beautiful and idolized mother, and a mother of adoption than whom no actual mother could have more wholly endeared herself—discovered a common spiritual taste in literature and philosophy. George and John, fearless in poetic imagination, and Alec, with less genius, simpler in mind, though not less honest, were equally beloved by one another. My mother took them both into her heart and keeping."[1]

Briefly characterizing the MacDonald boys—his father and three living uncles—Greville goes on to say: "The inherited instinct for enterprise and adventure showed itself in all four brothers. In Charles the ambition to get rich without labour seemed most easily indulged by . . . other men's money. In George it inspired the need of a wider spiritual knowledge than could be found in the mother-country of Calvinistic doctrine and literary convention. Alec's enterprise took form in an eager throwing of himself into reform movements, his quick sympathy with his more gifted brothers' different lives, his keen poetic intelligence rather than creative gift. But in John the inherited strain produced a restlessness that made of him a wanderer, and accounted for his lack of persistency in everything he undertook."[2]

With John especially, a mystic like himself, George was very close; a definite portrait of him is given as Ian (the Gaelic form of John) in *What's Mine's Mine*. John spent Christmas of the year 1852 with George and Louisa at Arundel before his trip to Russia in 1853, a trip that lasted three years.

"Little signs of this brother-love constantly scintillate from . . . faded letters. All of them poor, Alec with his 100 Pounds a year, John with his 50 Pounds and board, are rich compared with their older brother, the minister. Little sums pass between them—and indeed from them to their father—and all happily, as though money when in hand was so light a thing, though heavy enough when not to be got at. Clearly it was lack of money more than anything else that kept my grandfather from coming south to see Louisa and little Lily, as he was so constantly hopeful of doing 'next summer.' Such perfect understanding as these men's is perhaps found only on the rich soil of mutual poverty. Both younger men crave for every scrap of George's verses; and John in his turn sends his own poetry—sonnets, odes and what not—to his big brother for advice and criticism."[3]

Alec had been living in Manchester but had recently strained himself by picking someone up on his shoulders. This indiscretion caused hemorrhaging much like his older brother George had experienced two years earlier. In late 1852 he was moved from Manchester back home to Huntly to be nursed. He narrowly missed George's visit to Manchester, and over the course of the next several months lost ground. The deterioration of his condition shows how close his elder brother George had been to death two years before. For in April of the following year, just a month before George's resignation at Arundel, Alec died in his father's arms in Huntly. George had not seen him in almost a year, but his brother Charles arrived just before the end and could not suppress his emotion. To him the dying young man said, with his old smile, "Never mind, Charles, man! This is nae the end o' it!"

The letter of April 5, 1853, which followed the death of the brother who was three years his younger, revealed ever more clearly how George Mac-Donald's love for God was making him a mystic and poet who saw God's love at the heart of every living thing and every event of life.

"MY VERY DEAR FATHER," he begins. "I thank you gratefully for your last precious letter, which I shall not lose sight of as long as I live. It was very kind of you to write so much and so freely about my beloved brother, who is dearer to us all now than ever before. Of him we need never say he *was;* for what he was he is now—only expanded, enlarged, and glorified. He needed no change, only development. Memory and anticipation are very closely allied. Around him they will both gather without very clear separation perhaps. He died in his earthly home and went to his heavenly. . . . He is more to be envied maybe. . . . But for them that love God, no one is to be envied more than another; for all are clasped to the bosom of love and fed daily from the heart of the Father, whether here or in the other world—all one.

". . . Let the body go beautiful to the grave—entire as the seed of a new body, which keeps the beauty of the old, and only parts with the weakness and imperfection. Surely God that clothes the fields now with the wild flowers risen fresh from their winter-graves, will keep Alec's beauty in His remembrance and not let a manifestation of Himself, as every human form is, so full of the true, simple, noble, and pure, be forgotten."[4]

North to the Cotton Capital

At twenty-eight, then, George MacDonald moved north to Manchester, leaving his first pastorate behind him—apparently a failure—one of his brothers gone to the next world, his wife expecting their second child, and with no money and no prospects for the future. No offers from other churches had been made, for in the eyes of the denomination his brief career had been far from creditable. He was not alone, however; there was much free thinking going on at this time. A general awakening seems to have been occurring among many of the clergy. Heresy hunts were being conducted throughout the country, and many ministers were being removed from their pulpits.

In the eyes of those closest to him, however, George's move to Manchester with no employment seemed as foolhardy as his failure at Arundel. He hoped in time to find either a church or at least a small circle to whom he might minister. Meanwhile, his concerns about finances appear to have been minimal.

One of the drawing forces about Manchester, of course, was the presence of Alexander John Scott, the renowned teacher and lecturer with a great gift of wisdom, revered by many men—Carlyle, Ruskin, and others—more famous than he. George MacDonald always considered him the greatest intellect he had known, and in his dedication to *Robert Falconer* in 1868 he wrote: "To the memory of the man who stands highest in the oratory of my memory, Alexander John Scott, I, daring, presume to dedicate this book." Though he had not personally met the man before, George MacDonald gravitated to Manchester primarily in response to the compelling force of this bold preacher and teacher, hoping he might be able to recommend him to some position there. To Scott (twenty years his senior), therefore, he went introducing himself and telling him that his heterodoxy had driven him out of the church, that he had no work, and would employ himself in whatever he could until the right work of a more lasting nature was found. "Mr. Scott came close to me," he wrote to Louisa, "to help and encourage me."

Of the time in the cotton capital of Britain, Greville MacDonald wrote: "The story of the two and a half years' life in Manchester is one of unfailing hope and recurrent disappointment. But they held, too, some happy consolations—intimacy with men and women of rare excellence, a home once more, his own place of preaching, and, most notably, the instant success of his first book. *Within and Without* (1855) brought a succession of new friends, amongst them Lady Byron (the poet's widow), Thomas Erskine of Linlathen . . . the Russell Gurneys, Frederick Denison Maurice, John Ruskin, and so, indirectly, a host of others."[5]

But however Greville's words attempt to romanticize this time, life in Manchester was, nevertheless, difficult. Louisa was not able to join her husband with the two little girls until the following year. She spent several of those intervening months with her father in London (who did not approve of his son-in-law's decision to go north), and then in Liverpool where Alexander and Helen Powell were then living. George joined them there in December. Life had been frugal in Arundel, but now genuine poverty met them and would continue to be their companion for quite some time.

Louisa wrote, "I would rather be with you on a starvation diet than anywhere without you but with all the luxuries of creation." And just after Christmas of 1853, as they contemplated finding a home and getting settled in the big city, George wrote: ". . . It is rather a sad time for us to begin housekeeping, for everything is very [expensive]—coals themselves 20s. a ton, and war threatening [the Crimean War involving Russia and Turkey and most of Europe]. But it is all the same to God whether we begin with 10 Pounds or a thousand. . . . I am very rich in my wife and children, but wish I could support them. . . ."[6] (About this same time he also wrote his father asking if he could send them some grain meal.) In addition to financial struggles, Manchester represented a grim time for MacDonald physically. Frequent hemorrhages interrupted his work and made long periods of convalescence necessary. Five children were born between 1852 and 1857, multiplying not only financial needs, but complicating living requirements, travel, and the daily demands of life.

New Quandaries

Manchester brought spiritual changes as well. Though the resignation from Arundel cannot wholly be viewed as the "tragic turning point" in

MacDonald's life that some have made it, certainly life after Arundel would never be the same. In the years following this experience, years descriptive of which Greville entitles a chapter in his biography "In The Wilderness," another period of reflective refinement of MacDonald's faith occurred, centered now about the question of what his "ministry" in the church was to entail, and how to integrate the narrow orthodoxy he more and more disliked into a unity with the greater *church* he felt called to serve.

George MacDonald was still a young man. In Manchester he turned thirty. He felt he was to give his life to preaching, though he was writing more and was hopeful that it would become profitable enough so as to provide another means to help support his increasing family. Other factors gnawed at him, too. In Scotland the tradition of the "stickit" minister [shut or kept out of the pulpit, silenced, ostracized, removed] was a strong one. Failure in the pulpit was a keen social stigma. To be a "stickit" minister was to forever walk with head low, a mockery to other townsmen. Mac-Donald could not escape this mark of disgrace that now clung to him. He was torn, still wanting to preach, yet drifting farther from the organized "fold." He wanted no division, but after attending chapel services when he first arrived in the city, he became more disgusted than ever with them. He found he no longer even cared to be associated with the established church, and questioned whether he would ever serve as a Congregation-alist again.

The thought of forming a small fellowship of his own grew stronger. But even after he did, the "fellowship" went nowhere. As Muriel Hutton says, in Manchester George MacDonald heard "few voices but his own."[7] Perhaps between Hutton's and Greville's interpretation of MacDonald's Manchester days lies the balance of truth. It was a time of struggle, hard-ship, renewed doubting, of listening to voices that perhaps weren't always valid, of ill-advised decisions, of convincing himself that people would flock to hear him, when in reality it proved far different. And yet through it all, as Greville points out, the hand of God can be seen, furthering the shaping of this young man, testing him through hardship, preparing him for the work He had for him to do.

Meanwhile the frustration continued. George did not even have the money to bring his family to be with him. And though he sensed himself digressing further from the "norm" of conservative Christianity (which process gradually opened him toward the Church of England), he wanted to come still closer and closer to God himself. Attempting to work "within the system," he found only discouragement and rejection. Opening him-self honestly to the people at Arundel, in all good faith and enthusiasm, he now faced the stark realization that his heart's hunger for God was *not* universal. The people did not want the kinds of personal challenges he laid before them. Had he been wrong in his attempt? Should he have kept his viewpoints to himself? And what should he do now, after giving so many years of his life in preparation for and in hopes of the ministry? Had it all been for naught?

The Beginnings of Literary Work

Little things kept starvation away—occasional substitute preaching, a few lectures, literary work (articles and stories) for "The Christian Spectator" magazine, tutoring—in short, anything he could find, sometimes including, no doubt, the generosity of friends. He left no stone unturned for work, but there were many disappointments. He applied for the post of librarian to Owens College at the salary of 100 pounds a year and sent in testimonials on his behalf from various notables. But even his intimacy with the principal did not help him secure the position. Several months later he applied for the post of *sub*librarian at the college, though in this he was also unsuccessful.

On the basis of strong recommendations from friends, a certain publisher by the name of Freeman had agreed to publish his narrative poem. MacDonald was very excited, but upon reading it himself, Freeman changed his mind. MacDonald wrote to his father saying that Freeman "wishes to be clear of the engagement; which he certainly shall be. I am thankful to God for the pleasure the expected publication gave me, and so helped to keep my spirits up. Now I am able to let it go.

"We are with Alex and Helen now [he was writing from Liverpool at Christmas], but we long much for a home of our own. Much rather will we live in poverty than be longer dependent. . . . It is a blessed thing for me that my wife does not pull one way and I another. Our children are well and consequently happy. We are going through the hard time now, without which never man was worth much in the world—I mean for its salvation. May He keep me from being a time-server. . . ."[8]

Later he again wrote his father: "My book, *Within and Without,* is in the hands of an Edinburgh publisher, and I think he will publish it. He is strongly urged to do so by a sister of Sydney Smith into whose hands he put it for her opinion. . . ."[9]

But the book was again refused. In addition, notice came from the deacons in Arundel that he still owed a quarter's rent on his home there. The disappointments seemed to pile one on top of the other.

A trip to Huntly had been planned, but in early 1854, not long after Louisa's arrival in Manchester and in the midst of their search for a better and more permanent home, MacDonald was laid up for three weeks by a severe attack of "congestion of the lungs" and a warning of hemorrhage. Recalling Alec's death only a year earlier, the doctor forbade the trip to Huntly, and MacDonald was forbidden to preach for several weeks.

This period of uncertainty and apparent floundering was made all the more difficult by the knowledge that, if he would only modify his ways, keep certain of his beliefs quiet, and make greater efforts to "fit in" to the system, he could without much difficulty secure a promising pulpit with a stipend of perhaps 200 pounds or more, which would support his family with ease. Even his own father could not help but "wonder" about this son from whom he had expected so much. There were a number of pastorless chapels about Manchester, and he could have filled any of them at once if, following Professor Godwin's counsels, he had given just such attention to success in the pulpit as other walks of life demand of ambitious men. Many were the arguments, by others than his brother-in-law, in favor of giving people no more than they could accept, urging that by offering only what is within their present understanding, they may be brought to higher and wider visions of truth. But toning down his viewpoints, whether practically advisable or not, was never George MacDonald's style. To Louisa, therefore, he wrote, "There will be many vacant chapels in Manchester soon, but I have no chance of any of them." Going on, he refers to his hope of gathering together those who might benefit from his teaching: "But if I could get begun, I should probably have a large congregation soon. . . ."⁹ In reality, however, this hope proved groundless. His desire to preach was a personal dream rather than a leading of God. The Lord's anointing on his words lay elsewhere.

The remainder of this same letter, written within only a few months of his arrival, is touching in its hints of his discouragement; yet through it all as always, he clings to God, desiring to grow through his doubts. The poet ever bursts forth within him.

". . . Here is a little hymn I made for you last night, to keep away other thoughts, and because I could not sleep. . . .

"Thank you for your much precious love—the most precious thing I have: for I will not divide between the love of God directly to me and that which flows through you. Your love makes me strong. . . .

A MOTHER'S HYMN
My child is lying on my knees;
    The signs of Heaven she reads:
My face is all the Heaven she sees,
    Is all the Heaven she needs.

And she is well, yea bathed in bliss,
    If Heaven lies in my face;
Behind it all is tenderness
    And truthfulness and grace.

*   *   *   *   *

I also am a child, and I
    Am ignorant and weak;
I gaze upon the starry sky
    And then I must not speak.

For all behind the starry sky,
    Behind the world so broad,
Behind men's hearts and soul doth lie
    The Infinite of God.

If I, so often full of doubt,
    So true to her can be,
Thou who dost see all round about,
    Art very true to me.

*   *   *   *   *

And so I sit in thy wide space
My child upon my knee:
She looketh up into my face,
And I look up to Thee.[10]

Three weeks later he wrote her: ". . . I have spent a rather sad morning in my own company. Purely physical sadness—if such a thing could be: as if all our ailments were not mental! But I mean it was the sadness, which, if I had been a woman, would have been relieved by tears, and, as I am a man, was bettered by a long walk through wind and sunshine, and green fields and cows. I came home better. I could know that all around me was peace, that it was well with all the world and with me; that God was at the heart of things; and yet I was one Unrest in the midst of the Rest. Well, it is God's business, and he will mend it. Oh, the great Fact of God shooting up into great heights of space, grand indisputable Reality! God and I—I a creek into which ebbs and flows the infinite Sea! . . . It is worth all suffering to be at length one with God; when my being shall be completed by having all the veils between it and the full consciousness of the Divine rent asunder—when it will be flooded with the central brightness. . . ."[11]

Father and Son

Surely one of the most trying aspects of this period for MacDonald was the feeling that he was not understood even by those closest to him. His brothers had had some difficulty with certain of his decisions. His uncle James did not approve. Mr. Powell seemed for a while to have been "a little less cordial." Perhaps he was being influenced by his new son-in-law, the professionally successful Professor Godwin; or perhaps he was simply concerned at finding his brave Louisa and her two babies without a home. But certainly, in his eyes, George MacDonald was not "getting on" as one would have hoped to expect of a proper clergyman by this time in his career.

And even George's own father had some nebulous questions, thinking he might be presumptuous in the stand he was taking, refusing to compromise in order to gain somewhat in "respectability." Greville comments: "—his own father seems to have doubts and fears. With the debts of his long deceased brother Charles still weighing upon him, it is small wonder if at times he wished his sons were more like other men. Alec, so full of promise, was dead; John, the youngest, only just twenty-three, and the most brilliant [whom George called the greatest in all the family], was constantly flying off at unreasonable tangents, and now proposed going to Moscow. Charles had made a humble marriage, and before long was to plunge his father in new money troubles. Finally, George, his favourite, whom he had not seen for four years, was utterly unsuccessful, beyond getting an incomparable wife and two bairns: and yet he was refusing the manna offered from above!"[12]

But even though "concerned"—in vague agreement, perhaps, with the notion that success in the world is a sign of God's hand of blessing—George's father knew his son too well to harbor any lasting mistrust. And the open and free discussion between them was a continuing testimony to this remarkable relationship. Greville says that the elder MacDonald "fears that his son, in refusing those means of respectable livelihood that ordinarily seem right, may be 'presumptuous.' . . . But I think the elder's admonishing is impelled rather by a sense of duty than real anxiety. Sometimes his lectures break down in a little laugh at himself or in a ridiculously funny illustration of his wordy advice, or in a reminder that he is 'never given to laudation of his sons.' . . . Now and again his tenderness breaks out in a word: in thanks for a poem, he says, 'I like your little poem very much and so does your mother. I thank you, laddie!'"[13]

George's responsive letters of these early days in Manchester reveal the state of his mind and the processes of growth he was experiencing. He was still struggling to learn to trust in God, not in the provision of men. To his father he wrote:

"I am sorry that you should feel any uneasiness about me and my position. It is unavoidable that the friends of any public man who cannot go with the tide, should be more or less anxious about him. . . . But your faith in God, and the faith of individual good men in me, should quiet your fears. As to the congregational meetings and my absence from them, perhaps if you saw a little behind the scenes, you would care less for both. I will not go where I have not the slightest interest in going, and where my contempt would be excited to a degree very injurious to myself. Of course, when I disclaim all favour for their public assemblies, I do not deny individual goodness. I have no love for *any* sect of Christians as such. . . . There is a numerous, daily increasing party to whom the charge of heterodoxy is as great a recommendation, in the hope of finding something genuine, as orthodoxy is to the other, in the hope of finding the traditions of the elders sustained and enforced. . . . For my part I do not at all expect to become minister of any existing Church, but I hope to gather a few around me soon—and the love I have from the few richly repays me for the abuse of some and the neglect of the many."

He continued with a critical question about how change comes about: "But does not all history teach us that the forms in which truth has been taught, after being held heartily for a time, have by degrees come to be held merely traditionally and have died out and other forms arisen? which new forms have always been abused at first. There never was Reformation but it came in a way people did not expect and was cried down and refused by the greater part of the generation amongst whom it began. There are some in every age who can see the essential truth through the form, and hold by that, and who are not alarmed at a change; but others, and they the most by far, cannot see this, and think all is rejected by one who rejects the *form* of a truth which they count essential, while he sees that it teaches error as well as truth, and is less fitted for men now than it was at another period of history and stage of mental development. . . .

"But why be troubled because your son is not like other people? Perhaps it is *impossible* for him to be. Does not the spirit of God lead men and generations continually on to new truths? And to be even actually more correct in creed with less love to God and less desire for truth, surely is INFINITELY less worthy! But if you believe in the spirit of God—why fear? Paul, I think, could trust God in these things and cared very little about orthodoxy, as it is now understood. 'If in anything ye be otherwise minded, God shall reveal even this unto you' are words of his about the highest Christian condition. And Jesus said 'If any man is willing to do the will of the Father he shall know of the doctrine.' Now real earnestness is scarcely to be attained in a high degree without doubts and inward questionings and certainly divine teachings; and if you add to this the presumption that God must have more to reveal to every age, you will not be sorry that your son cannot go with the many. . . . If there is to be advance, it must begin with a few, and it is *possible* (I cannot say more, nor does modesty forbid my saying this) I may be one of the few." And then MacDonald affirms further that to be held in error is no more nor less than to follow in the footsteps of Jesus.

"Increase of Truth will always in greater or less degree look like error at first. But to suffer in this cause is only to be like the Master; and even to be a martyr to a newer development of truth (which certainly I do not expect to be required of me) is infinitely nobler than success in the common use of the word. . . . I believe there is much more religion in the world than ever, but it is not so much in the churches, or religious communities in proportion, as it was at one time. Your Huntly young men would not refuse me, however the . . . pompous doctors of the law would set me down . . . with the terms of 'German' and 'new view.' . . . For if it be alleged against me that some condemn me, what have I to say but that others, and they to my mind far more estimable, justify and receive me? Your own Troup [Robert Troup, his friend and classmate at Highbury, now pastor in Huntly, whom George would shortly marry to his cousin Margaret] would be cast out by many. But I will not write more about it, sure that one day, either in this world or the next, my father and I will hold sweet sympathetic communion with each other about God and Jesus and Truth.

"A few young men in Manchester are wishing to meet together in some room, and have me for their minister. That is what I have wished from the first; and if they give what they can to support me, I will be content and try to make it up in other ways . . . But may God keep me from trying to attract people. . . ."[14]

CHAPTER NINETEEN

EXPANDING OPPORTUNITIES
(1854–1855)

The year 1854 gradually ushered in new opportunities for work, an expanding circle of friends and acquaintances, and periodic easing of the financial strains. Once again the little family was united, although the near-hemorrhage canceled the proposed trip to Scotland. They remained hopeful about *Within and Without* even though toward the end of the year still another publisher (Macmillan) had seen it and rejected it. Nevertheless, with Louisa's arrival in Manchester the sun seemed to come out. She quickly made friends, for she was gifted in a social sense. They rented a nice home for 35 pounds a year. The large house gave the poet-preacher a study, had an extra room they were able to rent out to a friend and former Highbury student, and provided ample space to give the intended lectures on English literature.

Preaching Again

In addition, George was now writing fairly regularly for *The Christian Spectator* magazine, preaching somewhat consistently on a Sunday-by-Sunday basis in churches in need of a fill-in, and had a few earnest disciples gathered around him. Thus at length he consummated the plan that he had held in his mind for some time, and rented a room in Renshaw Street where he would be able to preach freely. Following his brother Charles's example, he regrew his beard—in defiance of the fashion, and encouraged to do so by his doctor, who thought that it might offer some protection for his condition.

He wrote to his father: "You send us good news, too, of John. I wish he were near us now. Alec and he would be such comfort to us. Charles is a true friend—but how strong we should be if we were all together! But we are all together in God; and that is enough. . . .

"You seem amused and somewhat indignant at my wearing my beard.

Don't fancy it a foot long though. . . . I feel nearer to nature by doing so. Having been an advocate for it from my boyhood, I hope ere I die, when my hair is as grey or white as this paper, and when no one for whose opinion I care a rush will dare to call me affected, to wear it all just as God meant it to be. . . ."[1]

His next letter finds him almost exultant in happiness over the prospects of starting to preach again. Writing to his father toward the end of June 1854, he comes closer than at any other time to actually claiming for himself a humble sense of mission. A sense of purpose was growing within him. It was no longer merely a question of finding work; that he could do. It was finding the *right* work—that which God put him on this earth to accomplish. He wrote to his father:

". . . Louisa and I send our best thanks for your very kind gift. Indeed it goes into my heart to think you should be sending us this when I fear you are ill able to do without it. It is a precious gift to me, as coming from you especially, whom, but that I think God has chosen me for other work, I ought to be [there at the Farm] helping now. The only reward I wish you to have for it, is to know certainly at some time that in thus helping your son and his family, you have been helping one whom the Father has been teaching through suffering to help the rest of his children.

"Meantime I was never so happy all my life. . . . Next Sunday evening I begin the realization of a long cherished wish—to have a place of my own to preach in where I should be unshackled in my teaching. . . . May God be with me. No one can turn me out. . . . If anyone does not like what I say, he can go away and welcome; but not all can turn me away. I call them together—not they me. A few friends contribute the rent of the place, and a box will be at the door for contributions of free will for me. . . ."[2]

The numbers attending the Sunday services in Renshaw Street were small and did not increase much. They were mostly intellectual personal friends. The working people did not seem much attracted, and there were others who did not attend for their reputations; but for those attending, these small services were undoubtedly rich. Nevertheless, at the time there seemed something missing. It didn't "take." Whether this work was motivated by his own desires rather than God's leading, or whether God was using it to direct him from the organized pulpit toward a whole new type of pulpit He would create for him, the "anointing" of God did not seem to be on George MacDonald's preaching efforts as it would later rest upon his writing.

Following the last letter was this intensely personal word to his father. "Thank you for your kind letter containing the good news about John's safety. I suppose he could not now leave Russia if he would except by stealth.* . . . I have preached three Sundays now, and am quite satisfied as

---

*John was in Russia during the very tense period of the Crimean War. The wolf-hunting expedition reproduced in *What's Mine's Mine* was fact, and through the British Embassy, John became intimate with a beautiful Russian lady of rank. Fearing for his

far as I have gone. I want no hasty success. I want to do God's work and be God's servant. Who ever did this fully without more or less failing?—according to the world's idea of failure and success. The world's judgments are simply those of Peter when he opposed Jesus, and said, 'This be far from thee, Lord.' No man ever failed, according to this judgment, as Jesus himself failed.

"My principal temptation to desire success is that you should one day have the pleasure of seeing your son honoured before you die. In a small (and I may without ostentation, and quietly to you, say) select circle, you would find this the case already. Popularity I can hardly expect, for reasons which my friends could tell you better than I.

"I am so pleased you like my writings [in 'The Christian Spectator']. Much of my taste for literature has come from you. . . .

"I don't know if I told you I am making 9s. a week—that is by three lessons a week—during the College vacation [tutoring]. . . .

"Now, could you not come and see us this summer or autumn?—for I do not see how I can go Northwards—for lack of money and time too. We could receive you very well now—for we are quite settled. We expect another little child in September. . . ."[3]

The Lecturer

George MacDonald's time was now fully occupied, not only with the Sunday preaching and the writing and tutoring, but with lectures as well. And Louisa was kept busier by the arrival in September of a third girl, Carolyn Grace.

The lectures that fall and winter in the drawing room of their new home were more well attended than his Sunday services, and ultimately proved to be instrumental in the founding of the Ladies' College in Manchester. He was one of the original lecturers, teaching on English literature, physical science, chemistry, and physics.

The latter half of the 19th century was a period of explosive discovery in the sciences. In geology, mathematics, chemistry, biology, and physics, new developments were progressing by leaps and bounds. Darwin's evolutionary theories, new mathematical equations, and exploration of the atom by chemists and physicists all had the tendency to make the religious person run and hide, threatened by the apparent dichotomy (as many of the scientists would have it) between rational inquiry and faith. "The Church," as MacDonald's British biographer Kathy Triggs says, "began to suffer a sort of schizophrenia: Christians, thinking that Reason and Faith

safety, some of his friends hastened John's departure. A misunderstanding at the last moment with his passport caused the police to refuse to let John go. The train was later held up by robbers and every person on it killed, except the conductor, who pretended to be dead. Whether the crime was connected to the lady's relatives is not known, but John's narrow escape from death by assassins was fact. He did manage to get away from Moscow, traveled to Leipzig, and then appeared unexpectedly in Manchester in August of 1855.

were at odds, felt obliged to side with one or the other."[4]

George MacDonald, however, knew that reason and intellectual inquiry were among God's highest gifts to man. For him no dichotomy could exist; science simply provided one more area in which man was able to live out his praise for God's magnificence. He remained a scientist all his life, interested in technical advances, new discoveries, and the latest theories in philosophical and scientific knowledge. He read widely, from the English poets and ancient mystics to Darwin and modern scientific journals. He mastered Milton, Shakespeare, and Dante. He read the German, French, and Italian classics in their original languages. He knew his New Testament best in Greek, but had also read it—in addition to the above languages—in Dutch, modern Greek, and Spanish. He knew Latin as well. Reflecting on this great diversity, Greville says, "I would give much to have some record of my father's lectures on Natural Philosophy and Chemistry. His delight in turning yet again into the paths of his Aberdeen days must have been great, for we remember the assurance to his father, amid theological doubts, that he could at least make a good chemist. His talks about the rigid Law of the atoms, their unascertainable minuteness yet indivisibility and unalterable ratios; the contrast of their fixed dimensions with the plastic dimensions of Life, which are always making for increase and freedom, and yet penalize any aberration from type; such thoughts coursing through his brain would have found choice words for their utterance. He . . . would find innumerable instances of physical law tallying with metaphysical, of chemical affinities with spiritual affections; of crystallization with the formulation of purpose; of solution with patient waiting till the time for action was come. . . . my father's master mind had its integral subordinates: the philosopher sitting in the observatory of the brain; the priest in its oratory, the musician at its organ, the poet before its open window, the student in its library, the experimenter in its museum and laboratory, would all join mind to mind so that their learning would find single-souled utterance to claim God as the life, and Christ the type, of all incarnation, of all obedience, of all salvation. . . ."[5]

In *What's Mine's Mine*, after a lengthy conversation with the girls, Ian and Alister departed to be alone with one another and with God on the hills. Talking of spiritual things, then of the two sisters, this high moment of relationship between the two brothers ends with a "spiritual" discussion of a mathematical formula. For MacDonald *all* the universe was alive with the life of God—from the equations of triangles to deep relationships to the beauty of a desolate hillside. "The brothers did speak of them [the girls], and readily agreed in some notion of their characters; but they soon turned to other things—and there passed a good deal that Mercy could not have followed. What would she, for instance, have made of Alister's challenge to his brother to explain the metaphysical necessity for the sine, tangent, and secant of an angle belonging to its supplement as well?" (*What's Mine's Mine*, Ch. 13). This simple last sentence illustrates the total unity of MacDonald's thought.

After a slow beginning, Manchester now seemed to blossom with friendships and opportunities, while an occasional visit to London kept him in touch with the Powells and other old friends. The Ladies' College became fairly well established, and besides his other lectures he added classes in mathematics, for all of which he received 30 pounds a year. He was preaching in one place or another (if not in Renshaw Street, then as a guest elsewhere) almost every Sunday, and many brought in at least some small honorarium. He was writing too, in every spare moment— more lectures and essays, poems, short stories, and though it had already been to two or three publishers, he was still polishing *Within and Without.**

Christmas of 1854 was spent with the Powells in London, after which George returned north to resume his teaching while leaving his family for a few weeks for the grandfather's pleasure. While Louisa was in London, certain devoted women friends of theirs looked after her husband, helping him with his lecture research at the library, copying passages for his literature talks, making him dinner or tea, and "even invading No. 3 Camp Terrace and carrying off socks in need of darning." In her heart—as revealed in their exchange of letters—Louisa's thanks to these women was genuine: they were deeply appreciated friends. Yet another side of her finds it hard to accept their ministrations, and she is "a little naughtily satirical about their worship!" So loyal is her husband that all such little services, even at the hands of other women, have to be told, just as he tells her of his headaches, his better or worse success with this or that lecture, the terrible coal bill that must be paid, or the dirty and asthmabreeding fog. On the other side, she tells of the children's doings, and that Mr. Powell is reading *Within and Without*, and how she found him with the volume in his hand and the tears streaming down his stern old face. Nothing was ever kept secret from husband or wife by the other; such was the free-flowing communication between them.

First Publication

Around the first of February (1855) an offer was made for *Within and Without* by Longmans, at the time one of the foremost of all publishing houses. An agreement was signed on February 7, and as can be expected, the author's spirits ran high. Writing to Louisa he calls it a "very advantageous agreement for an unknown author" (though another letter hinted of a possible dispute relative to payment), but we do not know what it actually entailed. Most contracts in those days offered a flat fee for the copyright, the author receiving no share of future sales or profits; this was the case with most, if not all, of George MacDonald's books. Presumably he received between 25 and 40 pounds for this, his first major publication.

It was not—so Louisa confided to Greville in later years—without some

---

*His son tells of an incident that occurred in his own boyhood as illustrative of his father's near-religious devotion to getting his work just right. "'Be sure,' he said to me as a boy, when, tired over a little carpentering job, I had exclaimed, 'O, that will *have* to do!' 'Be sure if you say that, it will *not* do; it mustn't be allowed to *do!*'"[6]

genuine heartbreak and soul-searching that she consented to the publication of this dramatic poem, which was so personal a story of her courtship with George. For years she struggled with feeling unworthy of her husband, who she could see loved God so greatly. She could not help feel that his love for her fell short of what it might have been had she been more gifted as she thought some other women were. And yet on his part, the poem expressed George's love for Louisa, and, as Greville says, ". . . it suggests very plainly that my father had long since discovered this truth—that in bringing the firstfruits to his wife he was still rendering to God the things that were God's."[7]

Within and Without appeared in May of 1855, a "decided literary success," and the reception of the new writer was remarkable. The reviews quickly became very enthusiastic. *The Scotsman*, then perhaps the most literary of the newspapers, said of it: "This strange and original drama is full of the most exquisite poetry sustained at the pitch of sublimity with immense yet apparently effortless power. . . . A very remarkable production of intellect and heart united as perhaps they seldom have been before. . . ." The personal dedication of the book recalls to mind the circumstances of its writing in late 1850, his solitary convalescence, his separation from Louisa, and the delay of his ordination and their wedding.

TO L. P. M. D. [Louisa Powell MacDonald]

Receive thine own; for I and it are thine.
Thou know'st its story; how for forty days—
Weary with sickness and with social haze,
(After thy hands and lips with love divine
Had somewhat soothed me, made the glory shine,
Though with a watery lustre,) more delays
Of blessedness forbid—I took my ways
Into a solitude, Invention's mine;
There thought and wrote, afar, and yet with thee.
Those days gone past, I came, and brought a book;
My child, developed since in limb and look.
It came in shining vapours from the sea,
And in thy stead sung low sweet songs to me,
When the red life-blood labour would not brook.

May, 1855 (*Within and Without*)

Return to Huntly

Plans were made for a much-needed holiday to Huntly, but money was still scarce and no arrangements could be made to leave the children. In June serious news came from the Farm: George's fourteen-year-old sister Bella had been stricken with the lung disease. Louisa insisted that George should go on without her. After hearing the news he wrote to his father: "Thank you for letting me know about dear Bella. . . . How does dear mother bear it? It must be a dreadful trial to her, but no trial is too sad which makes us look more to the eternal love—the great sea on which all other loves are but the surface waves. None of us will live very long here, and then we shall go into the great unknown wondrous world, which so many of our dear friends know already, and where they are quietly waiting our arrival. . . ."[8]

On July 1 he left Manchester for Huntly, the first time he had visited his birthplace since his marriage. Though the return was full of sadness because his sister was dying, the reunion with those he loved was no less joyful.

His letters to Louisa tell of the journey and the joy of his arrival:

From Edinburgh: "It has been a long day since I saw the last of your eyes at the station. The rain cleared off when half our journey was over. I lay down and slept. I hardly remember anything, but I wish you had seen a sweet-looking Scotch woman with whom I fell in love—a country woman between 40 and 50—oh, so sweet and simple! . . ."

On the train from Aberdeen to Huntly: "I am seated alone, a few miles on my way to Huntly. I have passed in the distance the stone crown which tops the square tower of my old college, and the pagoda-looking towers of the old cathedral—and beyond lies the sea. . . . When I get nearer home I shall want to be looking out, and not to write. It would be pleasant to point out to you the old places where your husband wandered and grew, and partly became the man you love now, notwithstanding his faults— which I hope will always be growing less. . . . I shall feel something like the Ancient Mariner. 'Is this the kirk? Is this the mill! Is this my own coun-tree?'"

From Huntly: "Dearest, I am sitting on grass with water bubbling on both sides of me. We have all met and I am loved to my heart's content. My father is not much changed, only stouter, and fuller in the face. My mother is very dear. . . . My sisters met me at the station, and now as I sit here they are ministering to me with wild roses and wild peppermint beloved, like two fairies. They are sweet dear things. Bella and I both cried. She is so thin. I should not have known her. . . . Uncle and Aunt and cousins are all so loving. . . ."[9]

George MacDonald's visit to Huntly in the summer of 1855 lasted five weeks. It was an extremely difficult time for Louisa. The three little girls, normally tiring enough, were ailing and teething. She had hired a nurse-maid to help her who turned out to be both insolent and irresponsible— she ruined the stroller, which then had to be replaced, an expense Louisa could hardly afford. On top of everything else, Louisa was three months pregnant at the time and physically tired. Invited to her sister Flora's in Liverpool for a couple of weeks, an unenthusiastic and depressed Louisa finally consented. But then she found herself frustrated to the point of despair over their financial position and embarrassed by what she imagined the patronizing of her by others of her family. All she had left to get her and the girls home was 15 shillings, and she wanted to dismiss her nursemaid but hadn't the money to pay the wages she owed her. Her son writes of her reaction: "Contrasting her younger sister's luxurious home with the poorer furniture her husband had to put up with—he who worked so much harder and had so few comforts, who was always fragile and was now acknowledged to be a great poet—she finds a little hard to bear. . . . In truth the mother is having a very hard time . . . the fear of outstaying her welcome, the provokingly comfortable and roomy wardrobe, the drawers of which absolutely refuse to stick and squeak and run askew like the cheap things at Camp Terrace [their own home]!"[10]

Greville says, "To understand my mother's determination that my father should have perfect rest and recreation now that it was vacation, one must remember how his irrepressible intellectual energy was always in conflict with his frail health. She knew how much to him was opportunity for dreaming, and that it could seldom come to him through the rain and fog of a great city, however dear its fireside and friendships. Huntly, his home and cradle, must ever be to him the land of dreams; and she was Celt enough to realize that his genius must hunger and thirst for its inspirations. One who remembered him on that visit to his home spoke of 'the tall, delicate, kindly-eyed Glengarry-bonneted man taking his walks by the castle, or his rides among the heather and dark topaz streams of his native hills.' The man was offspring of that boy who would lie on the sofa or on the horse's back for hours reading when others were at play, or who none the less would be first and most furious in their 'ploys'. . . ."[11]

Thus Louisa tried to make him feel at ease about staying, and tried to sound cheerful. She wrote: ". . . Do not come back for me a day sooner than you need, if you are well and enjoying yourself, which I know you are intensely."[12]

George's peaceful and touching letters of this summer stand in marked contrast with the stressful time his wife is having.

July 5, 1855

"Dear love, I can hardly bear your not being here. . . . It comes so often when I see beautiful things. There is not much beauty here, but much to my heart: and there would be to yours, and you would love my home, with its rough stones nearly covered with ivy. . . . I must write a story here. I am looking for one somewhere in my brain. . . ."[13]

July 8

"I wish you were here. My father and mother are so kind. . . . My beard is safe, I think! I talk Scotch to all the people, and one old school-fellow tells me that will get me over the effect of my beard and moustache! . . . O, I want you so much. It is so often on my lips, dear wife. . . . What money have you? I am going to write something for *The Spectator*, and ask him to advance something on it. . . . Oh that fine old man, my father! He *is* the man to tell anything to. So open and wise and humble and kind—God bless him! . . . It has been so hot to-day, and Bella has been sitting out in the shade, but there is very little hope. . . . She is very patient, the dear child. . . ."[14]

July 9

"My uncle offered me a guinea for my moustache today, seriously though funnily. If he knew how bitterly hurt his own son was at his compelling him to shave, he would not have risked it. If fathers knew how liberality makes their sons love them, they would exercise it oftener. But my noble old father told me that for his part I might let it grow till I stuffed it in my trousers!"[15]

July 10

"My days pass so quietly—I hardly go anywhere but saunter about. . . . If you had been here after I wrote you last night, you might have seen me in less than an hour on the far horizon—the top of a hill [Clashmach] nearly 1000 feet high 2½ miles off. You would have seen my white mare and myself clear against the sky. . . . She is a dear old mare. I love her, and

Scottish Highlands

cannot believe that she returns to the elements when she dies. She will perhaps be *our* mare in a new world—though this thought is too covetous to enter the new heavens and the new earth perhaps. However, if only she lives I don't care so much about having her. . . ."[16]

July 11

". . . I had such a nice ride last night, and met a countryman who had heard me preach (and who had been at school with me, I am since reminded). His face was radiant through a profusion of dirt caused by a hot day's work in the peatmoss. He went back with me and accompanied me through a great part of my ride, talked about the different birds and flowers, and showed me a nest of the rose-linnet. . . ."[17]

July 14

". . . Surely our hard time will wear over by degrees. It will, if it please God: that is, if we are ready to stand the harder trial of comfort—not to say prosperity. . . . I am glad you have enjoyed your papa's visit. Never mind that he makes more of Flora. *I* know something of what my wife is worth. You have a harder trial than the others, dear, both from your husband being what he is, and poor besides—but perhaps that may be made up to you some day. . . . May the wonderful Father draw out the end as He pleases. Oh, God is so true and good and strong and beautiful! The God of mountain lands, and snowdrops, of woman's beauty and man's strength—the God and Father of our Lord Jesus Christ. I wish you saw the sky away to the North. It is so lovely—orange on the horizon, fading up through yellow and pale green into blue. This is at 11 o'clock at night. There is a slight frost. . . ."[18]

July 20

"I have been out since twelve o'clock, have had 18 miles on horseback, and some delightful feelings floating into me from the face of the blue hills, and the profusion of wild roses on some parts of the road. The heather is just beginning to break out in purple on the hillsides. Another week of warm sunshine will empurple some from base to summit. How much more I understand nature than I did! . . ."[19]

He was not asked to preach upon his arrival in Huntly, later saying, "I hear some unfavorable notice had reached Huntly before, in what paper I don't know, and probably made the first impression." He said many were afraid of him from what they heard. But in this connection he adds, ". . . I think there is scarcely one other manly, straightforward man to equal my father. But he takes very little hand in outside things. I have more and more cause to rejoice that I am not connected with any so-called church under the sun. . . ."[20]

Though the elder MacDonald was a deacon, he took little part in church or public affairs. But his more orthodox brother James had a great influence among the Congregationalists, and did not look with favor at his nephew's "emancipation" from the old ways. He now actually opposed the wish of many that Huntly should hear the young preacher who had returned, his avowed objection being the beard.* But he gave way at last, and Huntly did in fact hear from the man who would become the town's most famous, favorite son.

July 25

". . . I cannot bear to force my departure. They are very sad sometimes, and I am sure I am a comfort to them. . . . That dear child Bella has been saving up her money for some time, as she always does to give presents— she had nearly a pound—and today she gave me two sets of flannels for the winter, which I should think took all she had. Her little body will be cold before I wear them. I am going to preach next Sunday evening. I cannot write more just now. . . ."[21]

July 28

"I preached yesterday about the little child. After, one old woman said she thought I went rather too far on *that side* of God's character. Another said to my father: 'When I saw him wi' the moustaches I thocht he looked gey and rouch-like; but, or he had been speakin' lang, I jist thocht it was like Christ himsel' speakin' to me.'"[22]

But then came a distressing letter from Louisa: the grocer had asked for his money by the end of the week—over four pounds!—reminiscent of poor Mr. Drake's difficulties paying his butcher's bill in *Paul Faber, Surgeon.* She had just arrived back in Manchester with 12 shillings to her name. George wrote to her saying he had 2 shillings and 6 pence. "My father is so often talking about the book and me," he said to his wife. "He at least receives his son with honour. I am afraid I have troubled him very much to-night by telling him how ill-off we are. . . ."[23]

A week later, however, George's uncle gave him a pound for his having married his daughter Margaret (George's cousin) to Robert Troup. Then a few days later, he wrote to Louisa, ". . . My father has just come in (I am writing in my bedroom) and offered me 3 pounds to send to you. I have not taken it yet, for I daresay you will not want any before you can answer this and tell me how much you will need till I see you again. . . ."[24]

Louisa wrote back, ". . . So dear, after thinking over everyone, right and left, and all the pros and cons and some tears . . . I have determined to write to Mr. Bateman [an old Powell family friend] to-night. I shall ask him to lend me 5 Pounds. I am sure it is the best way. . . ."[25]

The next letter shows her distressful and in need of rest. ". . . I am so glad you are not coming home tonight, for I got no sleep till 4 o'clock this

---

*Twelve years later, when *Robert Falconer* first appeared in serial form, James sternly wrote to his nephew about the offense it was sure to give because so many of its characters were portraits drawn from the real life of Strathbogie. He even drove in his carriage to Banff to warn the editor of that town's paper against reviewing it.

morning, the children screaming in turns, and sometimes all together, and alternatively playing till then. I am so tired. The new carriage is very heavy, and I have been pushing them out to-day. It has done them good. I do think they will sleep to-night.

"I was almost mad with weariness, children and jam-making all day long, when Charles and Ellen Coleman began talking about honesty and truth in friendship and real friends and true people, and I talked such stuff about not believing in anyone, and the last six months' experience having taught me a great deal! I said a great deal I didn't mean but thought I did then—but she and I were in very different physical conditions. She looks so very well and plump and pretty and cheerful and full of hope . . . it is all drained out of me, everything looks so impossible—so unlike the beauty and life there is in flowers. Ellen looks like a flower, I like a potato rind. . . . Everyone wants you back. . . ."[26]

But George had to write about sadder, though more peaceful surroundings: ". . . Since dinner I have had a saunter up towards the hilly regions, and have looked down on all the Huntly valley beneath me. What a multitude of harebells there are this season! I brought home two or three white ones this afternoon to Bella. . . . Poor Bella had a bad night again, and seems to me looking worse than I have seen her before. . . . I think I shall leave in the beginning of next week—and I hope to be a better husband to you and father to my children. . . . I shall be altogether yours some day. You know what I mean. I am not all Christ's yet."[27]

Drumblade country church and cemetery near Huntly where most of the MacDonald family is buried.

"Just a few words, dearest, for the last time from here. I have been with my father to see Alec's grave, five miles away. He lies beside my mother and my two brothers. I thought—oh, there is room for me between him and the wall. But I must be where you are, my own—only I should like if we could both be in that quiet country churchyard. My father was a good deal overcome, for it is not only the dead, but the dying he has to think of." Little could he guess, as he wrote these words, that each of his three eldest girls and one of his sons would die, later in life, just as their aunt Bella died. ". . . Thank you for your two letters received yesterday. I have been troubled about your talking so before those who cannot understand you as I can. Do not let your horns out of your shell, darling, except to your own friends—for you have two or three yet, though you may not believe it! You are true except in trust. But . . . I know the darkness and trouble you are in, and you are safe with me."[28]

Back Home in Manchester

"And so the visit ended," says Greville, "and my father brought back with him armfuls of imaginative grain waiting for future germination and life—to be increased, there can be little doubt, when, less than a year later, the whole family went to Huntly on a three months visit. The stimulus he got from the literary praise of his dramatic poem coincides well with this return to the land whence was to come the rich milk and honey, the sturdy oats and roses and wild peppermint of his finest novels. Those long and loving talks with his father had been full of family lore and racial traditions—full also of the wisdom, austerity and deep, if hidden, tenderness of his grandmother."[29]

The parting was overflowing in its sadness because of little Bella. In a letter dated from Edinburgh, on his way back to Manchester by train, George wrote: ". . . Give my love to them all—especially Bella. I fear I shall have no better news of her. But, dear father and mother, death is only the outward form of birth. Surely it is no terrible thing that she should go to Alec. And we can't be very long behind her. There is room for us all between Alec and the wall in the churchyard. I hope it will not hurt you more to write thus. Surely if we are sure of God, we are sure of everything. He never gave a good gift like a child to take it back again. . . ."[30]

As soon as he had returned to Manchester he heard that Lady Byron, the poet's widow, had been greatly moved by *Within and Without*. He also received a visit from his dear friend, possibly who had heard of their poverty-stricken straits in spite of the success of the book. He wrote of it to his father:

". . . Mr. Scott called on Friday, and before he left, told Louisa that, not thinking either of us very worldly wise, he must enquire into our circumstances, etc., for though he was not rich himself he knew many who were, and who at a word from him, would be glad to render us assistance. He is indeed a true friend. Is it not a great thing to me to have the man whose intellect and wisdom I most respect in the world for my friend, he not being ashamed to acknowledge the relation? He said he heard of my book from many quarters while in London, and that it has got into the best literary circle. . . ."[31]

His brother John, who stayed with them for a while upon his return from Russia, came for a visit soon after George's return from Huntly. But another major development of a different kind also occurred within a month: George MacDonald at last was offered a pulpit where he could preach freely, at a salary which would greatly ease the family's financial pressures. To his father he wrote, "I am glad to tell you that I was unanimously invited last Sunday by a company of 70 seat-holders to preach to them. I agreed to do so for a year to see how it will do. I was never treated with so much respect. They say: 'Speak out; tell us what you think; no one will interfere with you; that desk is yours.' And all that the chapel raises, which will not probably exceed 100 Pounds and may be less, will be mine. . . . Indeed they give me all the liberty I could wish. . . . I am gradually becoming known in Manchester, but I have not much to do that brings in money. Only when one thing is taken away, another comes—from God I think and hope. . . ."[32]

On August 24 Bella died. George wrote to his stepmother:

". . . Bella has only gone nearer to One who loves her more dearly and tenderly than you do. Or if you even think that she has gone to Alec, who has been waiting for her, it seems no such dreadful thing. God will let him take care of her till you go. I feel that if I had been in the spirit world before she came, I should have taken her to my heart so warmly that my little sister would soon have felt at home in the new place. We must weep often in this world, but there are very different kind of tears. Bella will be kept quite safe for you there, and you will never be separated from her in heart. Schiller says—'Death cannot be an evil because it is universal.' God would not let it be the law of His Universe if it were what it looks to us. And dear Mother, who could wish an easier, quieter, simpler death than my dear sister's? I should like to wither away out of the world like the flowers that they may come again. . . ."[33]

This letter reminds those who read it of David Elginbrod's prayer after Hugh Sutherland's loss of his father:

"O Thou in whase sicht oor deith is precious, an' no licht maitter; wha through darkness leads to licht, an' through deith to the greater life!—we canna believe that thou wouldst gie us ony guid thing, to tak' the same again; for that would be but bairns' play. We believe that thou taks, that thou may gie again the same thing better nor afore—mair o't and better nor we could ha' received it itherwise. . . ." (*David Elginbrod*, Ch. 11).

Thus in his triumphant views of death, George MacDonald has not categorically dismissed Calvin's viewpoints, for in this most foundational area the two men were in wholehearted agreement. Calvin wrote: "Strange to say, many who boast of being Christians . . . are so afraid of [death] that they tremble at the very mention of it. . . . However . . . no man has made much progress in the school of Christ who does not look forward with joy to the day of death and final resurrection."[34]

MacDonald's father wrote and warned his son against the dangers of so much praise as was coming his way as a result of his writing, telling him that the only protection against conceit was to stretch forward to higher and ever higher attainment. The reply can only have relieved his father's mind.

"I thank you for your anxiety about the so far success of my book. True love *must* be uneasy. I hope I know enough of my own failings and ignorance to keep me from becoming conceited, and perhaps I don't think the success as great as you do. Certainly there is always danger, and perhaps a usually modest man may at moments be over favourable in his judgments of himself. I think I have more consciousness of weakness than of strength. But our safety is in God's keeping, not in our own. May He take care of me, and do what He will with me. . . ."[35]

Agreement was made with the Bolton church people, and the hopeful young preacher's dream of having a church with freedom to preach and write at last seemed about to be realized.

Laid Low Again

As if his words to his father a few weeks earlier had been prophetic, even this dream was to be taken away. Barely two months after his beginning, in November (1855) he was suddenly struck down with the worst hemorrhage from the lungs he had yet suffered. For many days he lay near death, and the doctors were unable to stop the flow of blood. Nothing but absolute immobility—not the slightest cough, no speech—with ice bags on his chest would offer him the greatest chance of survival. Louisa, seven months pregnant, was unfit to care for him, so her sister Angela came from Liverpool, and other friends came flocking to help.

The blood flow did not lessen, and at last the doctor bled him at the arm, hoping to give the breach in the vein opportunity to close. The blood-spitting at once ceased. By the end of the year, though weak, MacDonald was much better and was able to write letters. The church kindly paid him further in advance, and he received several other gifts from unexpected sources—in some cases, from people he scarcely knew.

On January 20, George and Louisa's first son, Greville, their future biographer, was born.

As soon as he began to feel his strength returning, George naturally began talking about resuming his many duties. He was, however, still critically weak; this attack had been far more severe than any to date. As soon as was practical, Mrs. Scott fetched him away to their home where he could be nursed, leaving the mother and new baby to the care of her friends and sister. Though separated from Louisa and having to resort again to letters, though the distance was not great, George was in high spirits. He was attended by the Scotts whom he so dearly loved, and well enough to begin reading. "I need hardly tell you I enjoy myself," he wrote his wife. "They are all so kind."

With his high hopes seemingly dashed, his despair returned at the thought of providing for his family and of holding his two sets of disciples together—at Renshaw Street, the intellectual; and at Bolton, the working folk. Everything seemed to be falling into chaos.

> "My harvest withers. Health, my means to live—
> All things seem rushing straight into the dark.
> But the dark still is God. . . .
> . . . Am I not a spark
> Of him who is the light?"
>
> (*Diary of an Old Soul*, January 15th)

It became clear to those around him that he needed more sun, especially now in the dead of winter. As promising as the prospects for George MacDonald's future had begun to look in Manchester, it now appeared doubtful that its climate was conducive to his lasting health. A change appeared inevitable.

CHAPTER TWENTY

MIGRATIONS
(1856–1858)

The dawning of the year 1856—with the 32-year-old poet-preacher lying flat on his back, having narrowly escaped the death that had already claimed his mother, two brothers, and a stepsister—began a time of uncertainty for the young family. Had George MacDonald known at the time that his days of ministry in Manchester were over, just when they seemed on the verge of truly blossoming, his heart would likely have broken. However, at the time the main concern centered around the necessity of getting the invalid south to a warmer climate for the remainder of the winter.

To the South

Therefore, with the help of Mr. Powell, whose fondness for his grandchildren had served to reinstate his compassion and understanding toward his son-in-law, the family—with the father still weak and the mother only a month past childbirth—made the strenuous journey south in early March to Kingswear, on the mouth of the river Dart in Devonshire, in extreme southwest England. They had hardly set up in their rented house when George was seized with another hemorrhage, though less severe than that of two months earlier. Louisa nearly killed herself racing down some thirty steps in the dark to the vicar's house next door for help.

Though the atmosphere of the place was very relaxing, the strong, cold east wind off the sea kept the patient's bronchial tubes from healing, and his recovery was slow. To his father he wrote, "My spirits are not very bad now. Nor can I pity myself very much when they are, for I have hope that no dejection can touch. At the same time I shall never be in good spirits till I can employ myself in something that seems worth doing. I cannot even write verses for any length of time."[1] Having always disliked the title his father insisted on using with him, he wrote him at length, ". . . Will you please give up *the Rev.* to me. I never liked it."

The weather turned warmer in the spring, and he used his leisure moments to copy out the collection of poems he had written into a pretty notebook for Louisa. Once again the inevitable summer plans were made for a visit to Huntly. However, on this occasion—at long last and despite his health problems—the plans came to fruition and the whole family journeyed north by train.

Since there were no letters between wife and husband, or father and son to relate news of the visit, imagination must suffice to describe the three months spent at Huntly: of Louisa's delight in at last meeting the father whom she already loved, but had never seen face to face; of the young couple's pride in showing their four children; of George's happiness at being home again. Greville speculates further, ". . . we can picture the old father's and somewhat younger stepmother's quiet joy in realizing at last how tender a wife God had given their son—a joy that could hardly have been greater had they known that a few years thence it would be said, 'George MacDonald had done for Scotland what St. Paul did for Asia Minor: he opened the windows.' . . . My mother could rest, my sisters could grow fat upon porridge, white scones, eggs and cream without stint, the baby having no need of better food than he had always got. . . . But my father, we must infer, did not gain much strength; and the need of his wintering in the South was urged by all his friends."[2]

In the discussions regarding the poet's health, a new personality entered the scene at this point, a woman who perhaps was more responsible than anyone else for the preservation of his health and for contributing to his peace of mind with her financial assistance. It is quite possible that without this remarkable woman—portrayed as Lady Bernard in *The Vicar's Daughter*—the world may never have enjoyed anything but fragmentary pieces rather than the great body of his life's writing. Lady Noel Byron, the widow of the poet Lord Byron (1788–1824), began to exert a lasting influence upon the course of George MacDonald's life and work.

Lady Byron had been deeply affected by *Within and Without* and, as a result, began corresponding with the new young poet. She was on close terms with A. J. Scott as well, and through him, no doubt, she first began to learn of MacDonald's poor health, empty purse, poor yet growing family, and stymied literary gifts. She wrote initially acknowledging her debt to his book. This initiated a correspondence that ripened quickly into a lasting and intimate friendship. By the time of the Huntly visit, she was already familiar enough with the family's affairs—though the two had not yet met—to strongly advocate Algiers in north Africa for the winter, feeling that a change of scene and society might be as beneficial to his poetic gifts as the dry air would be to his lungs. In addition she offered to pay the necessary traveling expenses and give him introductions to new friends there.

Thus began a pattern of wintering in the warm and sunny south, which, as often as it could be managed, was to last through most of the remainder of his life. Difficult as the traveling was, there is little doubt that these southern winters saved his life and contributed significantly to his long years. All the others in his generation and the next of his family who died of tuberculosis had died before reaching 35. MacDonald himself, now 32, had already suffered two life-threatening attacks.

Financial Hard Times

Though the MacDonald side of the family was accustomed to hard times, those on the Powell side did not understand George and Louisa's plight and had little compassion for them, judging that their difficulties were caused primarily by their own foolishness. Sister Flora could hardly help but notice the little socks darned and then darned again, the mended trousers, the much-wrinkled ribbons that were too old to be smoothed back into "youthful smiles." And the similarly well-off Alex and Helen Powell, considering it wrong to interfere too much with the dealings of Providence lest Louisa never learn prudence and economy, handed her a sovereign upon one occasion as if to humble her, then scolded her for her lack of diligence in completing the refinishing of a table top she was doing for them.

Though in many respects George and Louisa MacDonald were penniless in a very literal sense (having more than once less than a pound between them), theirs was not the sort of poverty that kept them entrenched in the city slums. Though they had no "ready cash," they were nevertheless able to live a more or less middle-class existence. The Lord always made provision for them to live, in a sense, above their means. Food was sometimes scarce, clothes simple, furniture the plainest. Yet they were able to travel, to mix in higher circles of society, and to move about when necessity demanded it. Family and friends were always available to help, and there was never a shortage of nurses and ministers when sickness or children proved more than George and Louisa could handle, and they were not ashamed to accept either help or money.

Theirs was a classic life of faith, provision for which was often made through the charity, generosity, and compassion of friends like the Scotts, of gifts from the simple folk of Arundel, and particularly through loving and generous fathers who both, though sometimes with a bit of difficulty, seemed to recognize that something "more than ordinary" was bound up in the well-being of Louisa's husband. To be on the receiving end of such wealth, while finding himself physically unable to carry out the work he now knew could earn the bread his family needed, must have been a sore trial for the young writer and preacher. Yet he, too, was beginning to grasp something of the "unusual" nature of his life and situation, and was therefore not too proud to act the part of gracious recipient of his father's and Lady Byron's endless generosity, in the same way that he could, when circumstances allowed it, be as giving and open-hearted as they.

From Algiers to his father he wrote: ". . . I feel with you in the fact that your sons have needed so much to be done for them.* For me, if it please God, I shall do better by and by. If not, I hope He will let me go very soon—for if I cannot provide for my family, I would rather not add to the burden. At the same time, some of what is given to me must be regarded in a very different light from charity in the ordinary sense of the word. True, it would not be offered to me if I did not require it; but if I contribute to make life endurable or pleasurable or profitable, I do not see why I should be ashamed of having that acknowledged in the way I need, any more than if I were paid for keeping a merchant's books. . . . You may hope that I shall not refuse to do anything that I can honestly undertake to provide for my family as soon as I return. I would far rather take a situation in a shop than be idle.

"A new edition of *Within and Without* will be published in the spring; and I expect it will be accompanied by a new volume. . . ."[3]

Many of those about him—his own father, to an extent his father-in-law, the Scotts, and certainly Lady Byron—grasped, as his own son says, that George MacDonald's "work had to be apprized rather by some law of spiritual economics than condemned by the world on the score of his not 'getting on.' His work was the scattering of seed wide flung and free for whomsoever . . . might need them."[4]

So even in earthly want, the MacDonalds were provided for, and grew always richer in the circle of friends and associations that came to them. Algiers presented to them many cosmopolitan people; there they were thrown into contact with many from Britain for whom the area was a wintering locale. Wherever he went George MacDonald gravitated toward the intellectual and progressive-thinking element, moving ever more deeply into English literary circles as his contacts and friendships widened.

But even in this southern climate George MacDonald could not overcome his bronchitis, and he had more than one severe attack in the spring. At the end of April 1857, they returned to London to seek a home that offered some hope of permanency. Though he was still officially minister to the Bolton congregation, medical advice was against a return to Manchester, and most of their friends recommended living in or near London. As the center of literary and educational activity, it would provide him the most opportunities and contacts, giving his poetry and lectures a wider audience. The idea of continuing in the pastorate was receding from his mind, and at the same time, he felt strongly he should take definite steps to support his family more actively, despite his recurring illnesses. With the success of *Within and Without*, the thought was growing on him that this could potentially be accomplished through writing, supplemented with lectures and tutoring. Therefore, after still another bronchial attack, the southern coast of England was settled upon as the best place

---

*George, Sr., had apparently just written in a rather despondent mood. At the time, George, Jr.'s, brother Charles was leaving for Australia after his father had bailed him out of heavy debt. And the elder MacDonald, along with his brother James, was even at this late stage of his life paying the bank the final installments of the crushing debts of his own brother, incurred more than 30 years earlier.

to locate, from which he could begin in more earnest to seek a career in the literary world.

A Publication of Poems

In May George traveled (via Warrington where his brother was teaching) north to Manchester to settle his affairs and to bid farewell to the people at Bolton and his many dear friends. On his return to London, he at last met Lady Byron for the first time, and his family spent the summer months at the Powell residence in London while they sought a house of their own. During his convalescence he had been working on the compilation of a collection of poems, which the publisher Longmans wanted as a follow-up to *Within and Without*. He completed it and delivered it to them in April, and it was published in June, nearly the same time he arrived back in London to stay. Approximately 400 pages, it contained 72 poems; the lead one being "A Hidden Life." The volume was dedicated to his father.

The dedication opens with the words, "Take of the first fruits, Father, of thy care . . ."; later come the very personal lines:

> Thou has been faithful to my highest need;
> And I, thy debtor, ever, evermore,
> Shall never feel the grateful burden sore.
>> Yet most I thank thee, not for any deed,
>> But for the sense thy living self did breed
>> That fatherhood is at the great world's core. (*Poems*)

How could any father read such words from a son, written for all the world to see, and not weep for gladness?

The Scotsman's critique in August read: "This second volume from the pen of Mr. MacDonald is marked with the striking characteristics which distinguished his former work; the earnestness of thought, the deep religiousness, and the mingled simplicity and power of utterance are the same. . . . His poetry is not for the few who have erected a particular standard of taste, but for the many who are scattered, for the sheep having no shepherd. The dogmatist, if he lingers there, will find the tightly-wound coil of his prejudices unwinding he knows not how, and the child-heart, somewhere hidden in the breast of every living man, awaken and yearn towards the truth. . . ."[5]

Even though the volume (simply entitled *Poems* and later released as *A Hidden Life*) was entirely in verse, it reflected the same qualities that would later set his adventure and romantic novels apart from the norm— the imaginative and poetic "eyes" with which MacDonald viewed everything about him—eyes which perceived the eternal in the midst of the ordinary, as in:

LESSONS FOR A CHILD

> There breathes not a breath of the morning air,
> But the spirit of Love is moving there;

Not a trembling leaf on the shadowy tree
Mingles with thousands in harmony;
But the Spirit of God doth make the sound,
And the thoughts of the insect that creepeth around.
And the sunshiny butterflies come and go,
Like beautiful thoughts moving to and fro;
And not a wave of their busy wings
Is unknown to the Spirit that moveth all things.
And the long-mantled moths, that sleep at noon,
And dance in the light of the mystic moon—
All have one being that loves them all;
Not a fly in the spider's web can fall,
But He cares for the spider, and cares for the fly;
And He cares for each little child's smile or sigh.
How it can be, I cannot know;
He is wiser than I; and it must be so. (*Poems*)

Similarly, in another poem MacDonald extols the life of simplicity and
focuses the reader's attention upon God's priorities for humanity:

BETTER THINGS

Better to smell the violet
Than sip the glowing wine;
Better to hearken to a brook
Than watch a diamond shine.

Better to have a loving friend
Than ten admiring foes;
Better a daisy's earthy root
Than a gorgeous, dying rose.

Better to love in loneliness
Than bask in love all day;
Better the fountain in the heart
Than the fountain by the way.

Better be fed by mother's hand
Than eat alone at will;
Better to trust in God, than say,
My goods my storehouse fill.

Better to be a little wise
Than in knowledge to abound;
Better to teach a child than toil
To fill perfection's round.

Better to sit at some man's feet
Than thrill a listening state;
Better suspect that thou art proud
Than be sure that thou art great.

Better to walk the realm unseen
Than watch the hour's event;

> Better the *Well done, faithful slave!*
> Than the air with shouting rent.
>
> Better to have a quiet grief
> Than many turbulent joys;
> Better to miss thy manhood's aim
> Than sacrifice the boy's.
>
> Better a death when work is done
> Than earth's most favoured birth;
> Better a child in God's great house
> Than the king of all the earth. (*Poems*)

George made a short visit to Huntly in August, almost certainly the last time on earth he would see his father alive. Returning to England, the anxiety to find a suitable house of their own mounted. And on the last day of that month another baby girl, Irene, was born.

A day or two earlier George MacDonald had dined alone with Lady Byron. She had spoken very candidly, asking him to tell her everything about his financial affairs. "I hope it is no disgrace to me to be rich," she said, "as it is none to you to be poor." In the course of the conversation, she added in her simple and matter-of-fact manner, "If I can do anything for you, you must understand, Mr. MacDonald, it is rather for the public I do it than yourself."

Apparently the candor flowed equally in both directions, for a few days later she wrote him a letter, enclosing a check for 25 pounds and promising another 50 at Christmas. Thereafter, such gifts came on a somewhat regular basis from the generous lady.

At length a large old house was found on the Tackleway in Hastings on the south coast, just fifty miles east of Arundel. It had thirteen good-sized rooms, but the rent was low because of the unfashionable neighborhood. It was immediately named "Huntly Cottage."

At some point during this period, the germination for *Phantastes* must have originated, for he began to make references to a "fairy tale" he was working on, and he conveyed his high hopes for the prospects to his father once they were in the new house: ". . . I hope to keep well enough to be very busy, and deliver lectures as I did in Manchester. . . ." But hardly were they settled before he was laid up again, this time for a couple of months, during which time he was hardly able to write. When the furniture arrived out of storage several months later, its unpacking—thanks to the cayenne pepper used to keep moths away—gave the master of the house a severe attack of asthma and bronchitis, so that, until the sorting and cleaning was over, he fled to friends in Brighton for a week.

On December 2, 1857, he wrote his father:

". . . I had hoped to have a fairy tale or something of the sort ready by Christmas, but that has been quite prevented by my illness. . . . You must not lose heart, my dear Father, for your family. You have got through so far with great difficulty, and so shall we, but as long as God thinks it worth while to let us suffer, it is worth while. If success in this life were an end, we might say all our family has failed, on all sides; but this life is but a portion and will blend very beautifully into the whole story. May the one Father make us all clean at last, and when the right time comes, wake us out of this sleep into the new world, which is the old one, when we shall say as one that wakes from a dream, *Is it then over, and I live?* I for my part would not go without one of my troubles. The only one I fret at is being dependent. . . ."[6]

Inside the MacDonald Family

In his biography, Greville MacDonald devotes an entire chapter to Louisa's energetic efforts to make the Christmas holiday of 1857 a special one for her father, celebrating his seven-fifth birthday, and for the rest of her family at their new home in Hastings. It is a light, touching chapter, full of fun and little children—the old-fashioned joy of Christmas with plum pudding and a Christmas tree and surprises and gifts and cakes and treats and the story of the baby Jesus and even a trip to the beach:

"At five o'clock we lighted the tree in the middle of the tea table, at the top of which was the day's luxury, the Plum Pudding . . . How happy everyone looked! . . .

". . . A teetotum, Sarah's present for Greville, which had been hanging and twirling on the tree all tea-time, was now brought down, and reels of cotton, candlesticks, nuts, figs, oranges. . . . Then followed the mysterious bran-cake which had been the cause of much wondering anticipation all day.

". . . A history of Punch and Judy was one of the presents the tree afforded Papa, and great glee was there over the display of his elocutionary talents in giving it to our party. . . .

"A beautiful holyday! Husband and I and all the children down on the beach. . . . the exclamations, 'Oh, there is my darling baby, how sweet she looks! Papa! Mama!' scampering to our sides. We were as glad and light-hearted as she. . . ."[7]

After Christmas the household settled down to its regular life. George had a study and a measure of his health back, and was again able to write with consistency and regularity every day. To his father on January 2, 1858, he wrote:

". . . I am wonderfully better. The weather is fine. Christmas Day and New Year's Day were both fit for Algiers. . . . The house is pretty comfortable now, but the floors are very open between the boards. Through these the wind blows like knives. But I shall put the demon out by degrees. I have pasted brown paper over the cracks in the floor in two rooms, and we have two more that want it very much.* . . . I am writing a kind of fairy tale in the hope it will pay me better than the more evidently serious work. This is in prose. I had hoped that I should have it ready by Christmas, but I was too ill to do it. . . ."[8]

---

*This experience may have provided the germinal idea for *At the Back of the North Wind*.

The children were growing, to all appearances healthily, and spreading out in age—there were five in all, ages 6, 5, 4, 2, and 1, with another on the way! Love and obedience, firmness and understanding, tenderness and affection (unlike many parents of the Victorian era) were all intrinsic in family life; the succinct principles of child rearing, outlined several years later in *The Vicar's Daughter*, represent principles which originated in MacDonald's own family with the raising of his brood, which eventually numbered eleven.

"The marvel to me is that so many children turn out so well.

"After all, I think there can be no harm in mentioning a few general principles. . . . They are such as to commend themselves most to the most practical.

"And first for a few negative ones.

"1. Never give in to disobedience; and never threaten what you are not prepared to carry out.

"2. Never lose your temper. I do not say never be angry. Anger is sometimes indispensable, especially where there has been any thing mean, dishonest, or cruel. But anger is very different from loss of temper.

"3. Of all things, never sneer at them; and be careful, even, how you rally them.

"4. Do not try to work on their feelings. Feelings are far too delicate things to be used for tools. It is like taking the mainspring out of your watch, and notching it for a saw. It may be a wonderful saw, but how fares your watch? Especially avoid doing so in connection with religious things, for so you will assuredly deaden them to all that is finest. Let your feelings, not your efforts on theirs, affect them with a sympathy the more powerful that it is not forced upon them. . . .

"5. Never show that you doubt, except you are able to convict. To doubt an honest child is to do what you can to make a liar of him; and to believe a liar, if he is not altogether shameless, is to shame him. . . .

"6. Instill no religious doctrine apart from its duty. If it have no duty as its necessary embodiment, the doctrine may well be regarded as doubtful.

"7. Do not be hard on mere quarrelling, which, like a storm in nature, is often helpful in clearing the moral atmosphere. Stop it by a judgment between the parties. But be severe as to the *kind* of quarrelling, and the temper shown in it. Especially give no quarter to any unfairness arising from greed or spite. Use your strongest language with regard to that.

"Now for a few . . . positive rules.

"1. Always let them come to you, and always hear what they have to say. If they bring a complaint, always examine . . . it, and dispense pure justice, and nothing but justice.

"2. Cultivate a love of *giving* fair-play. Every one, of course, likes to *receive* fair-play; but no one ought to be left to imagine, therefore, that he *loves fair-play*.

"3. Teach from the very first, from the infancy capable of sucking a sugarplum, to share with neighbors. Never refuse the offering a child brings you, except you have a good reason—and *give* it. And never *pre-*

tend to partake: that involves hideous possibilities in its effects on the child.

"4. Allow a great deal of noise—as much as is fairly endurable; but, the moment they seem getting beyond their own control, stop the noise at once. Also put a stop at once to all fretting and grumbling.

"5. Favor the development of each in the direction of his own bent. Help him to develop himself, but do not *push* development. To do so is most dangerous.

"6. Mind the moral nature, and it will take care of the intellectual. In other words, the best thing for the intellect is the cultivation of the conscience, not in casuistry, but in conduct. It may take longer to arrive; but the end will be the highest possible health, vigor, and ratio of progress.

"7. Discourage emulation, and insist on duty [obedience]—not often, but strongly" (*The Vicar's Daughter*, Ch. 40).

Never in any hurry with formal education for his children, considering that morals, discipline, and obedience founded in the home were the foundation for all the best in learning, George MacDonald kept his oldest children at home longer than usual. Their education of an informal sort was given by both the father and mother until they deemed it appropriate to begin either class attendance or tutoring. Greville, for example, did not go to school until the age of 11, and then found himself, though older than everyone else in his class, far behind in specific knowledge. He spent two years at the school, hated it, and thereafter did his best learning at the hand of tutors. The MacDonalds seemed to have based educational decisions upon their location at any particular time and a given child's needs. Some of their friends thought them neglectful of learning as it "should be done." If Greville is at all typical, however, although "school" may have been minimal, "education" was not lacking, for he later attended the university, became a highly successful surgeon,* and authored more than a dozen books on diverse topics.

An insight into life "within the MacDonald home" comes from a letter written by a visitor who was struck with the home's order, peacefulness, and routine:

"I was delightfully received by a strikingly handsome young man and a most kind lady, who made me feel at once at home. There were five children at that time, all beautifully behaved and going about the house without troubling anyone. On getting better acquainted with the family, I was much struck by the way in which they carried on their lives with one another. At a certain time in the afternoon you would, on going upstairs to the drawing-room, see on the floor several bundles—each one containing a child! On being spoken to, they said, so happily and peacefully, 'We are resting,' that the intruder felt she must immediately disappear. No nurse was with them. One word from the father or mother was sufficient to bring instant attention. . . . In the evenings, when the children were all in bed,

---

*Perhaps Greville formed something of a model for Gutta Percha Willie, whose history was remarkably similar.

Mr. MacDonald would still be writing in his study—*Phantastes*, it was—and Mrs. MacDonald would go down and sit with her husband, when he would read to her what he had been writing; and I would hear them discussing it on their return to the drawing-room. To hear him read Browning's *Saul* with his gracious and wonderful power was a thing I shall never forget. Mrs. MacDonald's energy and courage were untiring and her capabilities very unusual."[9]

The Passing of Two Friends

A letter to his father in the early months of 1858 reveals a new acquaintance, F. D. Maurice, who came to occupy a key place in the poet's life. MacDonald and his friend Greville Matheson had gone to hear Maurice speak in 1854 at the Working Men's College in London, where the liberal preacher was involved with the Christian Socialist Movement, helping the poor and educating the working classes. MacDonald had been impressed, as he had been with Scott, and the attraction inevitably led in later years to an intimate relationship. Maurice introduced the author to Smith, Elder, and Co. as possible publishers for *Phantastes*. Their immediate acceptance of it and handsome payment clearly showed MacDonald that writing could indeed be the key to supporting his family, as well as the door of the future, through which he might find the audience that had eluded him from the pulpit.

"I had a most successful visit [to London]—got some books I much wanted at a moderate cost—visited Mr. Maurice and Lady Byron—put a little MSS. that took me two months to write without any close work—a sort of fairy tale for grown people, into a new publisher's hands and two days after had 50 Pounds in my hands for it. I likewise have plenty of work on my hands for printing in one way and another. Indeed I shall now be *fully* occupied for some time. I am going to give some lectures, too, here, as I did in Manchester. . . ."[10]

February 1858, however, brought news of another kind: John MacDonald was ill, his lungs gravely affected with tuberculosis. As his home between Liverpool and Manchester was closer to them, in early April he came to Huntly Cottage in Hastings to be nursed. George and Louisa did all they could for him, but the doctors gave him very little hope. To his father George wrote:

". . . Our Doctor says it is out of the question for John to go to Scotland in May. He must not think of doing anything for eight or ten months. . . . We are most happy to have this charge given to us. Louisa is only most pleased that *we* should have it to do . . . we both know something of the sick-room. So you may be comfortable about him. The Doctor attends him as my friend, and charges nothing. . . . I am very glad to have him with us; for we understand each other so well. And as to expense—never think of that. Thank God He takes all anxiety off us. The more we want the more we have and shall have. Things are looking well for us—but God is the giver—and He has plenty. It is very sad for those who cannot trust in him; it is miserable slavery."[11]

George was now giving lectures on English Literature in the drawing room of their home, which, though not as widely attended as those in Manchester, were bringing in a modest income. He continued to meet influential people gradually, and was hopeful of taking John back to Huntly, where the invalid wanted to be above all else. George's relationship with his father was apparently not unique: it was shared by his brothers as well, who, like him, turned to the old man in times of crisis. But his condition remained highly uncertain. In his last letter to his father, written in June of 1858, George tells of John's condition and then reflects on the will of God:

". . . We both read to him when we can, but he is only able for a bit of a story at a time and is soon tired even of that. He is certainly in a very doubtful condition—but God's will is best. As to what you say in your last letter about giving up to the will of God, and then taking it again—I would just say that it is only by having wishes of our own that we are able to give up to the will of God. It is live things, not dead carcases that must be brought to his altar. And when we do not know what his will is—it may be the same as our wish, for all that we know.

"God is good to me. I have prospects of lectures in London that will bring me in the necessary money for another few weeks. . . . John bids me to say that if he is able he will accompany me to London, and sail from there for Aberdeen. . . ."[12]

George's brother Charles had recently returned from Australia, and Greville says that "either my father or my Uncle Charles" took John north to Huntly, where he arrived safely and died on July 7 at the age of 28. The next month his father followed him: it was indeed a summer of great loss for George MacDonald! Greville's poignant words tell of the final days of George MacDonald, Sr., after the death of his youngest son, John.

"A few days after the burial, my grandfather was at dusk going out at a little gate that opened from the farm precincts to a back road running up on to the moor, and saw a figure coming towards this gate. He stepped back within the gate. The figure passed on, but then turned, and my grandfather saw it was John, with plaid over his shoulder in his customary manner. The old man hastened after, but, because of his lameness, failed to overtake the wayfarer before he disappeared at a bend of the ascending road. When my grandfather reached the turn, the figure could not be seen anywhere, though the road and country were so open that no one could have found cover. A man not readily conceding supernatural manifestations, my grandfather hurried home, quite awed and disturbed—so my grandmother told me; for he did not doubt that his beloved son had come back to him and was conducting him somewhither. [This is the sole recorded instance of Celtic second sight in my father's family.]

"It was but a few weeks later, August 24th, that himself, apparently in perfect health, was seized by a fatal heart-attack. The previous night he had as usual walked round the farm to see that everything was in order.

On his return he was stricken with violent pain in the left side of his chest. His brother was summoned and the doctor sent for. They poulticed him all night, and with some apparent relief. At eleven o'clock in the morning little Jeanie, then twelve years old, came to the room to ask her mother something. He was then lying in bed, the child's mother sitting by his side. He turned his head to see who was at the door, looked straight at his little daughter and smiled to her. But her mother then saw a deathlike change pass over his face and called out to the child to run for the doctor; but he died immediately.

"My Uncle Charles was at home. My father, who hurried northwards instant upon the telegram, did not see him alive.

"My grandfather left his property, amounting in all to 1,100 Pounds, to his wife, who at the end of the year left the old home."[13]

Whether or not one believes in such other-worldly manifestations, to this day—almost a hundred and thirty years later—stories still circulate in Huntly of the elder George MacDonald's "presence" at the house on the Farm, which still stands much like it was built in 1826. The current resident of the property has never heard him, but attests to many who have, and has herself had a certain housekeeper quit her job in dread, finding it too unnerving trying to work with the constant *thump, thump, thump* of the old man's wooden leg walking up and down the stairs and all about the place. She never returned to the house again. Indeed, tales of "second sight" are in Scotland far from a phenomenon of the past!

Greville goes on to say of his grandfather's death, "... the grief was universal. Writing to my mother the day after the funeral, my father, having arrived too late to bid him good-bye, says: 'Charles and I went to see some poor people this afternoon. It is very pleasant to hear how they all talk about my father. You would almost fancy he had been a kind of chief of the clan. . . . I am glad my father has got through. I love him more than ever. . . .'[14]

"No such sorrow as this loss of father and brother had yet ever touched George MacDonald ... though tears would readily come over any tale of suffering, or when sharing another's joy or hearing fine music, he seldom wept even when his children were taken. Yet those who have found touch with him in his writings, particularly in the *Diary of An Old Soul*, need not be told how the death, almost as if together, of these two men—the one his tower of strength, the other so much leaning upon him—wrung his very soul. The two dearest brothers and the strong father from whom their 'earthly history began' were now gone, and himself stood in the front rank of those who wait."[15]

After the body was laid in the family plot in the Drumblade church-yard, George MacDonald remained in Huntly long enough to be assured that his mother would survive her time of suffering. For days she paced the meadows, with bowed head, clenching her hands to her chest in silent appeal. Few wives have had such husbands. But she could not live on at the Farm without him. She knew she had to take her two children away. George offered them their home, saying they could now well afford it, but she declined and moved back among her own relatives, who lived not far away.* To Louisa, George wrote, ". . . My mother seems a little more cheerful today. . . . I have had your sad, sad letter. I do love you, and am so grateful for the love you give me. I think God will show himself very kind somehow or other to us both—not that I deserve it, but you do. . . . Do not think I am unhappy. . . . I am cheerful and hopeful. My love to Lily. Tell her I will pull her tooth out for her if she likes. My love to them all and to you, good, kind, beautiful wife. . . ."[16]

From this time on George wrote as regularly to his stepmother as he had his father, though the letters are more often relating to family matters. At thirty-four, George MacDonald, Jr., became, with his brother Charles, one of the heads of his family. In October he wrote her: ". . . My new book is just out, and I am asking the publisher to send you a copy. I am very well, and have the prospect of a tolerable amount of employment. I dreamed last night I saw my father. I felt I loved him so much and was clinging to him, when to my surprise I found he was so much taller than I, that I did not reach his shoulder. There is a meaning in that, is there not? His great soul has already learned so much more than we know. But we

"The Farm" where MacDonald was raised (rear view of house).

shall all find him again, and that will be a blessed day. . . . Louisa joins me in warmest love to you. . . .

"May God help you, dearest Mother, to go nearer to Him—that is the only thing that can comfort you for the loss of my father. There is no gift so good, but its chief goodness is that God gives it, and what he gives is not to be taken away again. Whatever good things we can fancy for ourselves, God has better than that in store for us. Even your sorrow is turned into joy, if you can say to God, 'I am willing to be sorrowful, since it is thy will.'"[17]

PART FOUR

George MacDonald in 1872 (NESLS)

THE VISIONARY NOVELIST

Though the sun had been up less than an hour, already the day was warm. By noon it would be too hot to remain out of doors for any stretch of time.

A man was walking along the placid shores of the sea, his face bent downward; but whether because he was deep in thought or that he was merely watching his footing among the uneven, rocky surface was not clearly evident.

He was watching the path, to be sure, for the coastline near his small but secluded Italian villa was notably rough, steep in parts, and portions of the trails none too dependable. But this was a man who, whatever else he might be doing, was *always* deep in thought. For his mind not to be vigorously at work would have been as unlikely as for the sun not to shine on this place that he and his English family had made their home only a year earlier.

Behind him the soft, clear blue waters of the Mediterranean wound in and out of the northwesternmost portions of the Italian coast, revealing here and there small bays and inlets and islands stretching toward Genoa in the distance. As he walked, none could have known simply by observing him what a tumult of rousing and excited brainwork was going on inside the man's head. The idea had come to him in the early hours of that very morning. At first there had just been the image of a face, out of which two eyes of the deepest blue he had ever seen were gazing. He had wondered if thoughts of the deep blue of the Mediterranean had prompted the vision of the child.

But whatever had prompted it, the image of that face and those eyes had startled him awake an hour before dawn. He had been out, walking up and down the shore and all about the small wood that surrounded their home, ever since. Whenever his mind was busy, he sought whatever water was to be found, whether stream or river or ocean. Today the gentle lapping of the sea upon the rocky shoreline settled his agitated energies, and now that he had been out for a couple of hours, his experienced mind had already formulated well over half of the story which was sure to follow the morning's revelation.

A stranger might have taken the man for sixty. No doubt such an estimate of the solitary walker's age would have been founded on the full, untrimmed beard that was beginning to fill in with considerable amounts of gray, especially about the edges and up through the sideburns. And despite the enthusiastic fire in the man's eyes, there was yet a melancholic droop to the eyebrows, accompanied by creases in the forehead and around the eyes, all of which lent a subtle air of sadness to his look, which even the excited vision of a new novel could not quite erase.

These signs of age were, in fact, the remaining symptoms of a constitution that had in recent years been far from well. Only a few months before he had been flat on his back for six weeks, troubled as he had been so many times throughout his life by his weak lungs. And in the midst of this most recent convalescence, the consumption of his daughter had reached its end. Her death added emotional pain to his physical pain, made all the more unbearable by the depths of agony to which he saw it had taken his wife.

He had himself been at death's very door at twenty-five just after taking his first pastorate, at thirty-five, at forty-four aboard the Blue Bell to Norway, and so now—at fifty-three—if he looked slightly beyond his years, he was actually on the road toward the healthiest period of his life. The dry warm heat proved to be a rejuvinating tonic to his body.

But as he walked he was thinking neither of the heat nor of his lungs, nor even about the daughter he had so recently lost, nor about his beloved wife, whose faith had been so shaken by the events of recent months. His brain had taken flight two hours earlier and had not yet come back to rest. His mind was over a thousand miles away, mostly north and slightly west. This fifty-three-year-old man was a child again in the eye of his imagination, walking out of Aberdeen, the city he so loved, up the banks of the River Dee into the regions known as the "Deeside," following the winding river in his mind's eye up and up, still farther to the point where it emerges, as little more than a stream, from the central Highlands. Though he had not seen the land of his birth for years, in his memory it remained as real and vivid as if it had been the peat-brown waters of the Dee at his feet at that moment rather than the crystal blue waters of the warm southern sea. And throughout the wanderings of his imagination over heather-covered fields and up barren Highland mountains, ever and always the image of the face, with its eyes of blue, remained.

Suddenly from behind him the shouts of children could be heard.

"Papa! Papa! We've been looking for you!"

He turned, then laughed as he saw his three youngest sons racing toward him.

"Can we take the boat out today, Papa?" cried eleven-year-old George and thirteen-year-old Bernard in unison.

Their father laughed again. "You like that boat, do you?"

"Please, Papa!" chimed in fourteen-year-old Maurice, himself unwell like his sister and bringing up the rear.

"Before breakfast?"

"Oh yes! Just a short ride out in the bay!"

"Well, I think a short adventure might be arranged."

The shouts of delight breaking from the lips of the three boys sounded more like the squeals of young children than teenagers. But they had not been hurried as they grew, and their father found pleasure in the innocence of their capacity to relish in the enjoyment of life.

"But first," he added, "I must go in and see your mother for a moment. I have something to tell her. In the meantime, you prepare the boat for launch!"

Before the words had left his mouth, the three boys were off down the hill to where the small rowing boat was tied, while their father made his way back toward the villa.

"Louisa," he called quietly as he entered, "Louisa . . . are you up yet?"

"Yes, dear," came a soft voice from the kitchen. "In here."

He walked in, kissed his wife gently, then said, "You are looking well this morning."

"I feel better today. I'll get over it soon. Thank you for being so patient with me."

"Of course, my dear. It has been a hard time for us all. Did you see our Maurice this morning?"

Louisa nodded, trying to smile, but the shadow of a cloud passed over her face.

"You noticed too, I see," he said. "He's so pale, God bless him!"

He paused. "But," he went on in an upbeat tone, as if to steer the conversation away from the state of their family's poor health, "guess what?"

"I can always tell that look in your eye," Louisa replied. "It's a new book, isn't it?"

"It was so strong it woke me this morning."

"What's the plot about?"

"I don't have much of a plot, so to speak, in mind yet. It's just a person . . . a face . . . a boy."

"Just a boy, nothing else?"

"None of that matters. Not yet at least. The events of the book will write themselves once we get to know him. That's the kind of person he is. He will carry the book, with or without a plot. You'll know what I mean. Even the simplicity of his name tells so much."

"What is it?"

"Gibbie."

CHAPTER TWENTY-ONE

THE DOOR IS OPENED
(1858–1863)

Phantastes

With the publication of *Phantastes: A Faerie Romance for Men and Women* in October of 1858, George MacDonald's literary career took an immediate new direction. Up until that point he had conceived of himself, and was considered in the eyes of the literary public, a poet. He had written stories for magazines, which would later show up in collected volumes, but *Phantastes* gave credence (both its payment and the positive reviews) to the fact that he had skills as an author in genres other than poetry. Before long not only Lady Byron would appreciate his talents, but many in London's intellectual circles would be taking notice that the northern land of Burns, Scott, and Carlyle seemed about to produce another Celtic muse of distinctive gifts and national importance.

To many who read it now, having been exposed previously to Mac-Donald's Victorian novels, *Phantastes* is bewildering, difficult to grasp, mysterious, even a bit weird. But at the time of its writing, literary tastes were vastly different, and it was greeted with enthusiasm for its heavy imagery and what some termed its "prophetic," illuminating, and mythical fantasy. MacDonald borrowed heavily from the German romanticists he had always been fond of, but infused his symbolic dream-romance with sufficient originality that the allegory of the spiritual pilgrimage out of this temporal world into the Kingdom of Heaven was a fresh adventure for its readers. The reviewers certainly appreciated it, and very quickly Mac-Donald became a "known" literary personality in London.

Phantastes was not for everybody. One reviewer called it "nothing but a secondhand symbol shop." However, those to whom it did appeal were always strangely gripped by it. And something of its hidden, even mystical power can be seen from its life-changing impact—some sixty years later—on a certain atheist who picked it up in a train station because he needed something to read. Within hours, young Oxford student C. S. Lewis, destined to become one of the 20th century's most influential expositors of the faith, was on the road out of his atheism toward conversion to Christianity, largely because of what he terms the *goodness* he discovered in *Phantastes*. Lewis writes: "Now *Phantastes* was romantic enough ... but there was a difference. Nothing was at that time further from my thoughts than Christianity and I therefore had no notion what this difference really was. I was only aware that if this new world was strange, it was also homely and humble; that if this was a dream, it was a dream in which one at least felt strangely vigilant; that the whole book had about it a sort of cool morning innocence, and also, quite unmistakably, a certain quality of Death, *good* death. What it actually did to me was to convert, even to baptise ... my imagination. It did nothing to my intellect nor ... to my conscience. Their turn came far later.... But when the process was complete ... I found that I was still with MacDonald and that he had accompanied me all the way and that I was now at last ready to hear from him much that he could not have told me at that first meeting.... The quality which had enchanted me in his imaginative works turned out to be the quality of the real universe, the divine, magical, terrifying and ecstatic reality in which we all live. I should have been shocked in my 'teens' if anyone had told me that what I learned to love in *Phantastes* was goodness ... the sweet air blowing from the 'land of righteousness'...."[1]

Although MacDonald had the beginnings of a "reputation" after *Phantastes*, it was not immediately accompanied by any significant financial benefit. He continued to tutor privately for the next several years, and his popularity as a lecturer was rising steadily, thus increasing the demands on his time. Gradually thoughts of the ministry, which for so many years he had considered his true calling, diminished; it seemed increasingly clear that he could, if not yet actually "make a living" by his writing, certainly profit modestly by it and, in combination with the lectures and tutoring, manage to keep starvation away. Furthermore, the deepening intimacy with Lady Byron helped all the more to alleviate his financial burdens, so eager was she to promote his career.

Into London Society

Lady Byron had introduced him to the Recorder of London, Russell Gurney and his wife, and they to Frederick Denison Maurice. Through the Gurneys a warm friendship was struck with Mrs. La Touche; through her MacDonald met John Ruskin, and theirs proved to be a deep and lasting friendship. Hindered by scanty finances, ill health, and the demands of family, the MacDonalds were scarcely able to move rapidly in the so-called social world—a world they cared little enough for anyway. But many new associations were nevertheless formed during this time with London's leading citizenry. As Robert Wolfe says: "At the height of his career, in the sixties and seventies, MacDonald knew everybody.... John Ruskin made MacDonald his closest confidant.... Frederick Denison Maurice ... invited him to collaborate in writing a book he was planning on the unity of the church.... Ruskin and Maurice joined with Lord Houghton, Charles

Kingsley, Dean Stanley of Westminster, and others in supporting Mac-
Donald in 1865 . . . for the chair of Rhetoric and Belles Lettres at Edin-
burgh. . . . Tennyson came [to MacDonald's house] and borrowed a Gaelic
edition of Ossian. . . . With Thackeray and Leslie Stephen, Leigh Hunt,
G. H. Lewes, and others, MacDonald . . . used to dine with Thackeray's
publishers and one of his own, George Smith, of Smith and Elder. . . .
Matthew Arnold became a friend. So did the aged Crabb Robinson. . . .
Dickens is said to have praised *Phantastes*, and a photograph survives
showing MacDonald with Dickens, Thackeray, Wilkie Collins, Trollope,
Bulwer-Lytton, Carlyle, Froude, and Macaulay."[2] Other friends and acquain-
tances included Miss Mulock (the Scottish novelist), Mrs. Margaret
Oliphant, Mrs. Reid (founder of Bedford College), Dr. Elizabeth Garrett,
Mrs. Josephine Butler, John Stuart Blackie, Arthur Hughes, the Rosettis,
Maddox Browne, Alexander Smith, and Norman McLeod. The Rev. C. L.
Dodgson, better known as Lewis Carroll, was an especially close family
friend. Alexander Munro, the sculptor, used MacDonald's son Greville as a
model for his boy and dolphin statue in Hyde Park, and once when visiting Hastings, upon seeing his friend coming indoors on a windy day with
his thick curling hair blowing all about, the sculptor's eye was arrested by
the sight. He modeled a medallion of MacDonald, two replicas of which
were later cast in bronze and hung in the Scottish National Portrait Gallery
in Edinburgh and in King's College, Aberdeen. Later in life MacDonald
grew close to an array of national and international personalities—Lord
Mount-Temple, Mark Twain, General Gordon (who gave him the chain
mail of a Crusader he had found in the Sudan), Henry W. Longfellow, and
the poets Whittier and Emerson.

Expanding Lecturing and Teaching Opportunities

Midway through the year 1859, after a short series of lectures at the
London Institution, MacDonald was invited by the Philosophical Institution of Edinburgh and the Royal Institution of Manchester to lecture in
their cities, which he did—to larger and more approving audiences.
Around this time he was asked to contribute an article on the poet Shelley
for the Encyclopedia Brittanica. Trips to London from Hastings were frequent, as were visits with Lady Byron. She frequently sent her carriage for
them for a luncheon or "tea-dinner," and took the whole family entirely
into her heart. They stayed with her in London for two weeks while painting and wallpapering were being done at their home on the coast. And
though the amounts she gave them were never huge, her contributions
helped substantially to make life a good deal more comfortable for the
still growing family.

Upon the advice of Lady Byron and others, soon after the lecture tour
in the north, the MacDonalds moved into London, where the opportunities for work were increasing. It had become clear by this time that, so far
as his bronchial and asthmatic tendencies were concerned, London
suited him as well as anywhere else, if not better. About this time the Chair

of English Language and Literature at Bedford College came open, and MacDonald applied for it. The remuneration would be relatively small (30 to 40 pounds per year), but it would serve as a nucleus from which other work might grow, and MacDonald was pleased with the prospects after securing the Professorship.

Shedding light on his new post, Kathy Triggs explains: "The College, founded ten years earlier as a College run by women for women, was still in its infancy, lurching from one crisis to another. In many quarters it was frowned upon as lacking in propriety and orthodoxy. It was considered improper on the double score of being run by women, and of having male professors lecturing to the young ladies. The supposed unorthodoxy was largely because Francis Newman, the Cardinal's free-thinking brother, played an active part in its foundation. It was not always easy to attract professors, nor to pay them an adequate salary. As MacDonald was a new-comer to the lecturing scene, the post of Professor was attractive to him in spite of its low standing in the academic world. He was as grateful to Mrs. Reid for appointing him as she was for his willingness to be appointed."[3]

For the next several years, MacDonald's income was derived solely from teaching and lecturing and occasional magazine publications. There were no books for five years following *Phantastes*. Occasionally he preached, but never after this did he take any payment for it. And what-ever else he might be doing—teaching, helping the little family with their home lessons, upholding his wife in her domestic trials, or counseling the increasing number of people who gravitated to the MacDonald house-hold—henceforth he was *always* writing. Whether for immediate publica-tion or not, writing had by now become a true love, a passion, with him.

His stepmother, continuing to grieve over the loss of her husband, was still the recipient of an occasional letter of visionary faith. "May you know, when you are lying awake, that God is with you—our perfect good. My father is nearer Him now, and you will get nearer Him by losing my father. Even the bodily presence of Jesus in some degree prevented the disciples from finding God for themselves—the spiritual God, present to their hearts; and therefore it was expedient for them, as He said, that he should go away from them. . . . Louisa longs to have you with us. We should make you as happy as you can be now in this world, we think. And you would help us so much. . . . I am glad to hear Uncle and all of them are so kind. I should not wonder if they too learn more what my father was worth by his being taken away. . . ."[4]

For some time MacDonald had been working on a play, but all the publishers refused it. During this time, finances again dwindled to a very miserable state. In May of 1860 Lady Byron died, and just two weeks later another son, Ronald, was born, increasing the strain. One day not long afterward, Louisa went out to buy a few things and lost her purse in the omnibus, with the last sovereign they had. There was hardly food in the house for the children's dinner, and they simply did not know where to turn for help. It was as if God was calling them to practice on the physical plane the very words of comfort George had recently offered his mother on the emotional.

As the evening closed in, George and Louisa stood hand in hand, silently reflecting together on their plight, knowing they had been in like predicaments before, knowing that God would supply their need somehow, but wondering in what way—silently just waiting, as if for His answer. Outside a quiet and dreary rain fell. Just then they heard the postman walking up the steps. He dropped a letter in the box, and with a double knock on the door woke them from the solitary thoughts of their reverie.

The letter was from Lady Byron's executors, and a check (of which they had known nothing) was enclosed for 300 pounds.

By 1860, on the basis of his three books *Within and Without, Poems,* and *Phantastes,* George MacDonald's poetical gifts were fully recognized by most of the London critics. Nevertheless, for a few years nothing was published in spite of the direct encouragement by one publisher. MacDonald, however, continued to write—tirelessly, with painstaking and unflagging energy, though he was often bedridden with bronchitis, asthma, and painful headaches. More than one grave attack of haemoptysis (the coughing up of blood) came during the early sixties, and once he fell getting out of an omnibus, cutting his forehead terribly and arriving home nearly covered with blood and receiving a lasting scar from the incident.

"Mr. MacDonald, If You Would but Write Novels. . . !"

If *Phantastes* gave George MacDonald's literary career a boost, certainly another major turning point was the rejection of his drama, "If I Had a Father." His publisher, George Murray Smith, head of Smith, Elder, & Co.—a man of exceptional literary acumen, who had been the first to recognize the genius of *Jane Eyre* when he was but 23—told MacDonald that *Phantastes* held a unique place in literature. Smith did more than anyone to persuade the man who had long considered himself but a preacher and a poet that he had a gift for fiction, as well, and should use it. Upon the occasion of refusing his play, he said, "Mr. MacDonald, *if you would but write novels,* you would find all the publishers saving up to buy them of you! Nothing but fiction pays."

His words certainly proved to be prophetic, though it took a long time for MacDonald to realize it. Ironically, despite giving this great impetus to the author's future, Smith himself actually published only one of his novels, *The Portent.* Once MacDonald turned to fiction, Smith, Elder, & Co. refused the first two of his efforts, and by then, as he predicted, other publishers were eager to publish the works of this rising young literary star. Mr. Smith added, however, at the close of the conversation, "Yet I will publish any of your poetry."

The only thing to appear in print in the five years following *Phantastes* was *The Portent,* which appeared in serialized form in the *Cornhill Magazine* in 1860. The story is different, both from those books which preceded it and from those that came after, and it at once convinced friends and publishers that MacDonald did in fact possess skill in the art he had never tried before, the simple story narrative. Involving the ancient Highland belief in "second sight" (the capacity to "see" with the eyes of the spirit that which cannot be seen by physical sight, particularly the future and supernatural events)—of which gift George MacDonald would reluctantly admit that he himself had not a trace—*The Portent* is a spine-chilling tale of a young man who, in cataloging the neglected library of a great English house, falls in love with a mysterious stepdaughter who then haunts his mind until the book's end through many bizarre Hitchcock-like twists. The story is weird, dream-like, yet strangely compelling, not unlike *Phantastes* in some respects, yet wholly unlike it in others—far easier to read and without a touch of the spiritual or didactic—but whose "significance" (if indeed it *has* a significance) is perhaps equally difficult to grasp. Louisa once told an admirer that after reading *The Portent* she asked her husband for the story's meaning. His reply was, "You may make of it what you like. If you see anything in it, take it and I am glad you have it; but I wrote it for the tale."[5] The author received 40 pounds for its serialization and 30 for the copyright of the book four years later.

Meanwhile, MacDonald seemed willing to act upon Mr. Smith's advice and went to work converting his play into a lengthy novel entitled *Seekers and Finders*. But the budding novelist was still learning his craft, and the play ultimately was not adaptable. Notwithstanding Mr. Smith's prior encouragement, Smith, Elder, & Co. refused the book, and it was never published. In later years, both MacDonald's sons Ronald and Greville read the manuscript, and, in Greville's words, "endorse its author's decision that it had better remain unpublished"—which was his polite way of saying it was genuinely bad. Jointly they decided to destroy the manuscript.

In *Seekers and Finders* the character Robert Falconer first emerged, the man who would grow to be MacDonald's favorite personality of his own creation and the central figure of one of the most powerful of all his books. Significantly, the son which was born to him and Louisa in 1862 was named Robert Falconer MacDonald.

George MacDonald did not seek literary society as such. A phrase from the unpublished novel describing Robert Falconer no doubt illuminates the priorities of the author himself: "The merely professional literary party was an abhorrence to him. He said it made him feel sick—he could not help it. He took more pleasure in smoking a pipe now and then with an old cobbler somewhere about the Theobald's Road than in an evening with the most delightful literary society that London could furnish."[6]

Nevertheless, perhaps one of the great turning points of his writing career came at just such a party. At an informal evening supper, he and James Greenwood and others—possibly including George Smith, William Thackeray, G. H. Lewes, Leslie Stephen, Leigh Hunt, James Payn, and Henry S. King—were talking informally. Suddenly MacDonald's attention was arrested on hearing Manby Smith, the journalist, who had been talking to another, reciting a certain Scotch epitaph he had read somewhere.

"What's that! What's that!" MacDonald exclaimed, as though afraid of losing the precious thing that so instantly excited his imagination. "Say it again, Mr. Smith!"

So Smith repeated the words:

Here lie I, Martin Elginbrodde;
Hae mercy o' my soul, Lord God,
As I wad do, were I Lord God,
An' ye war Martin Elginbrodde!

The words seem so simple. Yet who can account for what triggers the imaginative senses in the brain? Something about the verse captivated his mind and took him over—the mystic in him ruminating over the intriguing theology of unknown Martin's audacious proposal, and the budding novelist in him already framing a story around this unpretentious beginning. He held it in his imaginative mind's eye and it grew, and eventually bore fruit manyfold.

MacDonald withdrew from the dinner party, his mind full of the possibilities, and within a short time a completed novel of over 400 pages lay before him. It was altogether distinctive from anything he had written before. Here was a light romance, a mystery, a popular novel for the masses rather than the cultured elite. There was no heavy symbolism like *Phantastes*; no eerie imagery as in *The Portent* (although it did contain its own spooky ghost-story portions as well); no narrative poetry like *Within and Without*. This new work more resembled Dickens and the other "popular" Victorian novelists who wrote for the public, not the literary journals.

But MacDonald's novel possessed an intrinsic difference. The spiritual teachings of its author came through just as vividly as if he had been standing in the pulpit. The man was still a preacher at heart. It was impossible for him to divorce the spiritual side of his life from the literary. Therefore, out of the mouths and relationships of the characters of his creation came spiritual truths—setting the style of writing found in this new novel apart from the works of MacDonald's contemporaries. The spiritually instructive novel was not a new form. But MacDonald at once transformed it to a completely new level of literary excellence. For here was no mere religious hack trying to patch together a potpourri of trite religious truisms under the dubious and flimsy covering of a "story." Here, instead, was a highly skilled and critically acclaimed poetic and mystical writer turning his imaginative instincts and his professional faculties to a new format.

A Unique Approach

The novel, entitled *David Elginbrod* in memory of the inspirational epitaph, was full of the color of MacDonald's homeland, the humble Scottish flavor reflected particularly through the vernacular dialect of his people. His early years in the north on the borders of the Highlands, and his more recent visits to Huntly, came through warmly, and his simple picture of life in a rural cottage is one that forever remains lodged in our minds. The figure of David Elginbrod was drawn from MacDonald's beloved father;

thus, in many respects, the book represents a return to its author's roots after having established himself with a certain degree of acclaim, but with limited breadth of success in the literary world. In fact, *David Elginbrod* and MacDonald's other Scottish novels were instrumental in leading to a whole movement of Scottish realistic stories, called "the kaleyard school" of fiction, in which the earthy values of humble individualism and rugged natural beauty of Scotland were exalted.

Perhaps what immediately set *David Elginbrod* apart from other similar novels of the time was MacDonald's way of intruding himself forcefully into the narrative, stopping the action momentarily and coming forward to speak directly to the reader. It was in this manner, as well as through the mouths of his characters, that MacDonald conveyed the spiritual truths he felt compelled to share. Telling a story was not enough; there was always a sense of spiritual mission behind everything he did. Not only did he "preach" in *David Elginbrod*, but the title character (as the first in what over the years emerged as a long line of similar MacDonald "saints") was unbelievably good, sensitive, compassionate, mature, knowledgeable, humble, warm, and Godlike. Such "spiritual" qualities were woven in and throughout a fairly intricate and certainly exciting and romantic story line. The new novel contained quite a mixture of varying ingredients.

The new form, however, did not appeal to the literary minded. Smith, Elder, & Co. found it hardly more attractive than *Seekers and Finders*. They rejected it, and so did every publisher in London. And ever since *David Elginbrod*, to the present day, MacDonald's novels are criticized, even by those who consider him a genius in other areas, because of the "uncohesive" way in which he wove plot and teaching together. Kathy Triggs says, "His novels *as novels* are flawed."[7] C. S. Lewis comments, "The texture of his writing . . . is undistinguished, at times fumbling."[8] And Robert Wolff adds, "*David Elginbrod* has many faults. Disjointed, long-winded, didactic. . . ."[9] Richard Reis perhaps summarizes this general critique many have made when he says, "There is no way to excuse his artistic faults—sentimentality, verbosity, preachiness, sheer lack of craft. Even his finest fantasies are too frequently disfigured by these same blights, especially of style. . . ."[10]

At times MacDonald's novels are, certainly, rather too long, verbose, with extended preaching or instructions that can become tedious. Reis is correct in pointing out a "lack of craft," which genuinely does exist at certain points: the plots sometimes get extremely thin, characters become stodgy and undeveloped, and there is very little artistic fictional fabric holding the story together. There are, perhaps, a half-dozen or so of MacDonald's more obscure novels which are genuinely bad. But they are in the minority. And it can hardly be helped that a writer with such a vast output as MacDonald would produce a few second-rate books. But these flaws, however, cannot be spread in blanket fashion over the whole of MacDonald's works.

A distinction must be drawn, then, between two ways of viewing MacDonald's fiction. The didactic *form* of MacDonald's novels is not necessarily intrinsically flawed. Critics who seek to compare MacDonald's realistic novels with other contemporary writing are judging them by standards that cannot apply to MacDonald. Quite simply, he was not writing the same kind of novel as his contemporaries, and therefore his books cannot be evaluated according to the same standards. He was offering a new slant on an already recognized literary style—and in so doing produced a whole new type of novel. His works must therefore be judged internally, on the basis of themselves, not their conformity or lack of conformity with other works of more traditional type.

In *David Elginbrod* and in many of the novels which followed it (with the exception of the problem books mentioned), George MacDonald was, in a sense, initiating a whole new literary genre. These are not "mere" novels. If the literary critics didn't appreciate them because they saw them as something *less* than what they were used to, it was because they did not have eyes to see that they were actually *more* than anything that had come before. Here was George MacDonald the preacher, the poet, the novelist, the image-maker, the Scot—all fused into one through this new medium which could give vent to *all* his gifts and ideas.

The following brief quote gives a hint of the flavor of the digressions which MacDonald wove through his story:

"The lessons went on as usual, and happy hours they were for all concerned. . . . Once a week, always on Saturday nights, Hugh stayed to supper with them; and on these occasions, Janet contrived to have something better than ordinary in honor of their guest. Still it was of the homeliest country fare, such as Hugh could partake of without the least fear that his presence occasioned any inconvenience to his entertainers. Nor was Hugh the only giver of spiritual food . . . to Hugh every day, many things were spoken by the simple wisdom of David, which would have enlightened Hugh far more than they did, had he been sufficiently advanced to receive them. But their very simplicity was often far beyond the grasp of his thoughts; for the higher we rise, the simpler we become; and David was one of those of whom is the kingdom of heaven. There is a childhood into which we have to grow, just as there is a childhood which we must leave behind; a childlikeness which is the highest gain of humanity, and childishness from which but few of those who are counted the wisest among men have freed themselves in their imagined progress towards the reality of things" (*David Elginbrod*, Ch. 6).

Of course, such a method of writing will hardly appeal to everyone. Not everyone appreciates the same forms of poetry. Neither can everyone be expected to appreciate the same types of fiction. One with no interest in spiritual content will undoubtedly have little use for George MacDonald's fiction. But for those eager for both a compelling story *and* spiritual instruction, his books stand unique in the literature of the day. To those looking for such a blend, this new approach of addressing the reader directly about spiritual things, begun with *David Elginbrod* and reaching its zenith in *Donal Grant* and *Paul Faber, Surgeon,* can be a distinctive find. Rather than seeming disjointed or uncohesive, these novels illustrate the powerful unity that is possible when all aspects of life—the higher spiritual dimension and the level of men's daily affairs—are brought together in harmony.

Capturing the essence of MacDonald's departure from the norm by the very title of his article, John Dyer wrote in the *Penn Monthly Magazine* in 1870 of George MacDonald as "The New Novelist." He tries to fit Mac-Donald into the age in which he wrote. "It is especially a theological age . . ." he says, hailing MacDonald for presenting "man as the son of a Father in heaven." God is real to him, stresses Dyer, and human life illuminated by His presence, and even the "preachy" passages are "thoughtful studies of human life," not "devout platitudes." He claims MacDonald to be the best portrayer of the Scots since Scott.[11]

More than one hundred years later, similar thoughts were echoed by Glenn Sadler, who said that MacDonald possessed an "oustanding talent for crossing literary types and age barriers"; and by Rolland Hein, who wrote: "In a day when so much Christian thought seems shallow and inadequate, bent as it is on reducing Christian prescriptions for human experience into simple formulas and four-step patterns, MacDonald reminds us how complex are our spiritual plights and how many-faceted is the truth."[12]

Thus *David Elginbrod* essentially inaugurated George MacDonald's true career, for as a novelist—a spiritual *and* an imaginative one—he was best known in his lifetime. Without realizing it, with this book he had turned a corner, making the transition from preacher to novelist. Through the change he would ultimately find his true congregation. And a vast audience it would become indeed!

Meanwhile, the book did not fare so well. The daughter of a Manchester friend happened to be visiting then at the MacDonald home, Tudor Lodge. Hearing of the manuscript's unhappy wanderings about the publishing houses of London, she asked if she might show it to her friend, Miss Mulock, author of *John Halifax, Gentleman.*

Realizing at once the book's merits, Miss Mulock took it to her own publishers, Hurst and Blackett, and told them they were fools to refuse it.

"Are we?" they asked. "Then of course we will print it without delay."

They gave MacDonald 90 pounds for the copyright. The book was published in August of 1863, and George MacDonald never again had difficulty in placing a book. It did not happen overnight; in fact, it took several more years for Mr. Smith's words to be fulfilled, but by the middle of the next decade George MacDonald had become one of the bestselling authors in Britain.

CHAPTER TWENTY-TWO

THE PUBLIC TAKES NOTICE
(1863–1867)

The publication of *David Elginbrod* vaulted its author immediately into a new literary realm. Until that time George MacDonald had been critically appreciated in a small and select (albeit growing) circle aware of his work. Suddenly his potential audience had increased a hundredfold. No longer was his congregation limited to a small church of fifty or a hundred, or the few thousands who were enthusiastic about poetry or fantasy; his audience was comprised of hundreds of thousands in the general reading public—a public whose Victorian tastes consumed stories such as MacDonald now produced as fast as they could be written.

A New Pulpit

There were undoubtedly moments of soul-searching during which MacDonald had to weigh God's call upon his life to be a preacher of His truths. There were those in the literary establishment who disdained the "popular novel" in favor of the intellectually sophisticated genres of poetry and symbolic fantasy. Yet imaginative and visionary George MacDonald had to face practical considerations at this stage of his life. First, all his efforts to "preach" God's gospel in a traditional sense from the pulpit had ended either in failure or illness. Second, he had a growing family to provide for—in 1863 there were eight children and another three would follow. Though he was a mystic, a preacher, and essentially a poet at heart—he once remarked, "I like preaching best, then writing poetry, then writing stories"—the expanding opportunities for writing, even in a popularized sense, might possibly be God's way of fulfilling his heart's desire to spread the message of God's love, and at the same time support his family.

History seems to indicate that George MacDonald came to that very conclusion. If Mr. Smith was right in saying, "Nothing but fiction pays," and if the public was hungry to buy adventure and romance, why could he not incorporate his spiritual themes into such a format? He had said he would not refuse to do anything he could honestly undertake. There were hungry mouths to feed. If fiction would feed them, his integrity as a father and husband demanded that he make every effort.

Concerning this pastoral aspect of his writing, his son Ronald once asked him "why he did not, for change and variety, write a story of mere human passion and artistic plot. He replied that he would like to write it. I asked him then further whether his highest literary quality was not in a measure injured by what must to many seem the monotony of his theme—referring to the novels alone. He admitted that this was possible; and went on to tell me that, having begun to do his work as a Congregational minister, and having been driven . . . into giving up that professional pulpit, he was no less impelled than compelled to use unceasingly the new platform, whence he had found that his voice could carry so far. Through stories of everyday Scottish and English life . . . he found himself touching the hearts and stimulating the consciences of a congregation never to be herded in the largest and most comfortable of [churches]."[1]

Whatever his thoughts may have been about the widening genres of his activity, it is clear from his output and remarkable diligence that George MacDonald threw himself into his work with great gusto the moment it became clear his books would sell. In the remaining seven years of the decade he produced another ten books—a remarkable achievement: seven novels, a volume of essays, another book of poems, and a collection of sermons.

Not only was he writing assiduously; now the public was buying. An explosion of popularity overwhelmed the works of George MacDonald. His books began to be pirated by unscrupulous publishers on both sides of the Atlantic (particularly in America), and copyrights were ignored. By the time he was 45 in 1870, George MacDonald's name was a household word in literary circles; his reputation in England rivaled that of his contemporary Charles Dickens, and his status as a spiritual muse and teacher was far-reaching. The calling of God he had felt upon himself ten years before (". . . I think God has chosen me for other work . . . to help the rest of his children") seemed at last to be reaching fruition.

Creative Depth Begins to Show

Certainly MacDonald found the form of the novel comfortable. Indeed, as good as the poems and fantasy had been, some felt that the realistic novel, especially when set in Scotland, in the dialect of his own people, with all the inherent cultural and historical nuances, was the most suitable vehicle of all for his imaginative expression. The moment he settled into the regular writing of fiction, everything seemed to "click." Following *David Elginbrod* in quick succession came *Adela Cathcart* (1864), a loosely plotted novel that was primarily a mode for the telling of a number of previously written short stories, and *The Portent* (1864), which had already appeared serially. His next novel was the Scottish *Alec Forbes of Howglen*

(1865), which many consider his best, that delightful story full of images from his own childhood in Huntly. One cannot read it without sensing how positively its author must have enjoyed every moment of its writing. Full of all the old places and sights, personalities and smells, pranks and escapades, it "touches" through the printed page that homeland of Scottish roots from which he had come. Next came *Annals of a Quiet Neighborhood* (1867), his characterization of Arundel, and—to satisfy the poet and lover of the land of faerie which ever remained an intrinsic part of his being—*Dealings With the Fairies* (1867) and *The Disciple and Other Poems* (1867). *Dealings With the Fairies* was MacDonald's first published collection of short stories, including "The Light Princess," "The Giant's Heart," "The Shadows," "Cross Purposes," and "The Golden Key."

Referring perhaps to these years between 1865–1867, which saw the appearance of four distinctive titles, Glenn Sadler comments: "He possessed a fully integrated genius, whereby the creations of faerie lore and the realities of his own childhood were one: and it is this feature that characterizes him best."

MacDonald's 1925 bibliographer J. M. Bulloch, whose bibliography in the February 1925 issue of the Aberdeen University Library Bulletin has become a standard, says of *Dealings With the Fairies*, "These stories have frequently been reprinted in various forms, and mark, perhaps, the greatest claim of MacDonald to a permanent place in English literature."[2] Others will no doubt dispute Bulloch's claim in favor of the poetry, the fantasy, the studies of literature, the sermons, or the fiction. But his words reveal the tendency all MacDonald readers seem to share of making great claims on behalf of their particular favorites.

Although MacDonald's second book, *Poems*, had been reissued in 1864 under the title *A Hidden Life and Other Poems*, the 1867 release of *The Disciple and Other Poems* marked a second collection of entirely new poetry.

Unspoken Sermons, Vol. 1 was published in 1867. MacDonald's doubting, non-Christian friend, English author and critic John Ruskin said, "They are the best sermons—beyond all compare—I have ever read, and if ever sermons did good, these will . . . very beautiful—unspeakably beautiful. If they were but true. . . . But I feel so strongly that it is only the image of your own mind that you see in the sky!"[3] Afterward came three more novels: first *Guild Court* (1868), subtitled "A London Story"; then *Robert Falconer* (1868), a towering masterpiece of characterization considered one of his finest novels, certainly one of the most spiritually compelling. About it his son Ronald says, "Whether I be right or wrong in discovering a greater homogeneity in *Alec Forbes* than in *Robert Falconer*, few of their readers, I imagine, will differ from me when I say that *Robert Falconer* is the high-water mark of George MacDonald's character drawing. The book contains at least four characters which have seldom been surpassed for truth, vigour, and loving humour: Dooble Sanny, Shargar, Falconer's grandmother, and the great Bob himself."[4] Finally appeared *The Seaboard Parish* (1868), about the life of a vicar and his family, a sequel to *Annals of a Quiet Neigh-*

borhood, a lazy story of life on the western seacoast of England.

It was a seven years worthy of an entire career for many men. But it had only begun. Fiction writing seemed to agree with MacDonald's lungs as well, for his health was much improved. Life within the MacDonald family continued in much the same manner, however. This success did not alter the financial stresses. There were no royalties, only a flat fee paid in advance, beyond which the author received nothing, whatever the sales. And of course he received nothing at all for the pirated unauthorized editions, which accounted for a large percentage of the total sales.

Louisa's father, Mr. Powell, now over eighty, had retired from business, had grown a beard (for which he had once silently condemned his son-in-law), and visited the family often. Another frequent visitor was Lewis Carroll, the shy, learned mathematician, who became intimate with the family and was known to the MacDonald children as Uncle Dodgson (his real name was Charles Dodgson). He asked George's opinion about a story he had been writing, which he called "Alice's Adventures Underground." George suggested that an experiment should be made upon his young family. Accordingly Louisa read the story to the children. When she came to the end all were heartbroken to see it end, one exclaiming that there ought to be sixty thousand volumes of it. From this enthusiastic reception, Uncle Dodgson was persuaded to present the world with one of its future classics, *Alice in Wonderland*.

Along with his friend Carroll, George MacDonald devoted a great deal of his attention in the 1860s to stories and fairy tales—usually first told for the little horde who would run for the platform of his knees and arms or the chair or floor beside him. Dramatically he read "The Giant's Heart," "The Light Princess," and probably many other of the stories that eventually found their way into print. And for these stories, supposedly "for children," he would be most remembered by succeeding generations at the time when his novels, sermons, and poems were being forgotten. At present, however, this forty-year-old bearded poet-turned-novelist was interested in making his own children laugh and cry, and above all *believe* in the magical world of fairies and thus, in their childlike way, in the kingdom of God.

The Demands of Public Life

Of this time, and of his father's response to the increasingly "public" nature of the life that was thrust upon him, with its demands and inevitable fame, Greville says, "The letters belonging to these . . . years . . . show us very plainly that the increasing freedom from care, notwithstanding the incessant work of lecturing and teaching;* the securer home and widening responsibilities; and, still more, the conviction that the world was so sorely in need of his message—these brought him, along with more

---

*He was still Professor at Bedford College and giving additional lectures and lessons as well.

happiness, freer utterance. . . . I have a strong suspicion, looking critically at his work, that, owing to his inherent modesty, he was slower than most great men in finding free play for his genius . . . yet he never questioned the light given him. . . . Now, however, with men and women of his own intellectual rank proud to be counted his friends, he grew more aware of his power . . . and . . . the conclusion cannot be avoided, when we compare *Seekers and Finders* with *David Elginbrod*, that his sense of art in fiction [had] changed extraordinarily. . . ."[5]

Even earlier, in 1860 when he was lecturing in Edinburgh, he found people were already beginning to "make much of him," giving him more honor than he cared for. He wrote to Louisa, "Just a few lines, dearest . . . I have not time for more, as I am busy preparing for my lecture tonight. The evening before last I was a little annoyed by the presence of Lord ___ . . . nothing but a Scotch lawyer and a bad one. His Stickship is one of the worst specimens of the worst phrase of low Scotch—why they asked him I can't think—but certainly they want to give me the *best* society in one sense! I would rather take tea with an old washerwoman. . . ."[6]

But even as the words are out of his mouth, we find ongoing evidence of his acute awareness of *self*.

"Just a little chat before I go to bed . . . all about my ugly self. Is it not strange that in the Christian law we can offer to God the most deformed and diseased thing we have got—ourselves? I have had a most strange, delightful feeling lately—when disgusted with my own selfishness—of just giving away the *self* to God—throwing it off me up to heaven—to be forgotten and grow clean, without my smearing it all over with trying to wash out the spot."[7]

Despite the loving manner in which George MacDonald depicts Scotland in his novels (surely the Scottish novels outshine the English novels with the possible exceptions of *Thomas Wingfold, Curate; Paul Faber, Surgeon; There and Back;* and *Annals of a Quiet Neighborhood*) and the radiant love he had for his homeland and its people, he nevertheless remained in and around London for most of the next two decades. In 1865 Ruskin wrote, "You know—I do think you would be happier in a country cottage—out of lecturing work and in peace. Only I *suspect* . . . that you can't do without London society."[8]

Greville responds to the comment with: "Indeed, one often wonders if Ruskin was not right in thinking a country life would have opened to my father a freer way for his greater powers. But . . . the thing that tied the author to town was the immediate and daily need to earn money by teaching."[9]

In the summer of 1865, George MacDonald took a long-desired and much-needed vacation in Switzerland. Unfortunately, Louisa was not in fit health to accompany him, so he traveled with his old friend William Matheson and another companion. Even though he was never well throughout the trip—asthma, lumbago, toothaches, and insomnia from intense headaches—he nevertheless gained a great deal. The trip to Switzerland, like every return to Huntly, provided invaluable input for his imaginative subconscious—much of the emotion of the trip revealing itself three years later in *Robert Falconer*, and the wondrous sights of the Swiss Alps bearing fruit in the descriptions of *Wilfrid Cumbermede*.

From Belgium he wrote Louisa: ". . . God be praised for that spire [Antwerp Cathedral]. . . . I [had to] go up though my head ached and I seemed worn out. 616 steps. . . ! I was on the point of crying several times with delight. . . . Oh how I should delight to build a cathedral—towers if nothing else. *God be praised!* was all I could say—as the Arabs say when they see a beautiful woman. It has filled and glorified me, and I could go home contented if I didn't see an Alp. . . . If I hadn't climbed that tower and had a breath of divine air, I should have been ill today. I went up ill and came down well. . . . Oh, for the mountains—God's church towers! . . ."

Then they traveled south through France: ". . . The town at which we stopped [Weissenburg] is a French-German one in Alsace. We had seen nothing so interesting before. . . . The lovely old town! with the water running through it, and the fine old church and the pretty women and the quaintest houses with rows of windows one above the other in every roof. I *must* take you there for a month some day. It is just the place to write a book in. . . . Will you come, sweet wife? Then we went on to Strasburg. And here again we found a glory of a city. I never saw anything to compare with it. . . . Then the cathedral—far beyond Cologne in every respect—built of red stone—no glass but stained in it throughout—dark and solemn. . . . I did what the others declared themselves unable for—I went up the tower and up the spire. . . . I went up as far as they would let me without an order from the Mayor, and all my weariness and fatigue was gone. And, darling, I am sure the only cure for you and me and all of us is getting up, up—into the divine air. I for my part choose the steeple-cure for my weariness. How will it be when I get amongst God's steeples? . . ."

Farther south into Switzerland: ". . . And the little town below is gay as a doll's house . . . for it is the time of an annual *Fest*. . . . The people come from all quarters of Switzerland. . . . We went to a meadow in the evening. . . . It was like a fair—with dancing places surrounded and half-hidden by boughs. We wanted to go into one of these, but were told that we must dance if we did, against which in my case there were two impediments, ignorance and lumbago [he suffered from rheumatism in the lower back]. . . ."

And at length they reached the region of the towering Jungfrau: "I am much better, dear, and have been out a good part of the afternoon. And if I had seen nothing else, I could now go home content. Yet I am not sure whether amidst the lovely chaos of shifting clouds I have seen the highest peak of the Jungfrau [the 13,640 foot mountain in the Alps south of Interlaken]. It is utterly useless to try to describe it . . . I hate the photographs, they convey no idea. The tints and the lines and the mass and the streams and the vapours, and the mingling, and the infinitude, and the loftiness, the glaciers and the slow crawling avalanches—they cannot be described.

"Once today, looking through the mist, I said with just a slight reservation of doubt in my heart, 'There, that is as high as I want to be,' and straightaway I saw a higher point grow out of the mist beyond. So I have found it with all the ways of God. And so will you too, dear love. . . . I said to them today that I should not [be able to] lie still in my grave if I had not brought you to see it. . . . I rather want to get home, for I have got all I wanted here—at least I have as much as I can take in now. . . . I *must* bring you here next summer if I can."[10]

His exultation culminated when he first beheld the Jungfrau peak, which he described in *Wilfrid Cumbermede*: ". . . The mist yet rolled thick below, but . . . far away and far up, yet as if close at hand, the clouds were broken into a mighty window, through which looked in upon us a huge mountain peak, swathed in snow. One great level band of darker cloud crossed its breast, above which rose the peak, triumphant in calmness, and stood unutterably solemn and grand, in clouds as white as its own whiteness. It had been there all the time! I sank on my knees . . . and gazed up. With a sudden sweep the clouds curtained the mighty window, and the Jungfrau withdrew into its Holy of Holies. I am painfully conscious of the helplessness of my speech. The vision vanishes from the words as it vanished from the bewildered eyes. But from the mind it glorified it has never vanished. I have *been* more ever since that sight. To have beheld a truth is an apotheosis. What the truth was I could not tell; but I had seen something which raised me above my former self and made me long to rise higher yet. It awoke worship. . . ." (*Wilfrid Cumbermede,* Ch. 15).

Life Grows More Complex

Maurice was born in 1864, Bernard Powell in 1865, and George (the eleventh and last) in 1867. Louisa was frequently tired, ill, emotionally distraught, and suffered recurring bouts of inferiority and unworthiness. In fifteen years she had eleven children: Lilia, Mary, Carolyn, Greville, Irene, Winifred, Ronald, Robert, Maurice, Bernard, George. She had been pregnant for eight years of months, in addition to nursing, recovery, and overseeing the care of nearly a dozen youngsters. In addition, she frequently had to nurse an invalid husband, fight abject poverty during the first of those years, and assume a large share of the responsibility of teaching her children at home. She taught music, dancing, and drama, etc.—both she and several of the children were accomplished musicians—while George taught mathematics and Latin. His imaginative bent, however, had its limitations. According to Greville, MacDonald's concentration on the higher and loftier elements came at the expense of the lower and more practical; he himself, he says, could hardly read at eleven. Moreover, Louisa had to move her household eight times in those same twelve years. No wonder George's laudatory words of praise for his wife were frequent, and no wonder too that he always made sure they had hired help for Louisa at home. She was a remarkable woman, and he was fully aware of the "pearl of great price" the Lord had provided for him. He instinctively knew that her devoted love and service, not only to the growing family, but to him personally, was as great a factor in whatever he was able to give the world as the words he spoke. Greville says, "My mother's constant vigilance over my father in his sickness and pleasure, his bodily and spiritual needs, is a very notable point in my parents' life. Always keen and instant, whatever her own ailing or weariness of heart . . . we realize [her] indefatigable zeal."[11]

Immediately upon his return from Switzerland, George MacDonald poured all his energies into his candidacy for the Edinburgh Chair of Rhetoric and Belles Lettres. Though George wanted the position, Louisa was relieved when the news came that another had been selected, for she had grave doubts whether her husband's bronchial tubes could weather the Edinburgh winters and biting winds. In spite of his continued attempts to gain university posts, he was providentially kept from receiving them. Through this repeated earthly failure, he was kept from the demands such a position would have created, and thus freed to write and give the world a legacy that might otherwise have been vastly limited. On his way north in application for the position, while visiting an old friend, he enjoyed a ride on horseback with the man's daughter. Her recollection of the visit in later years reflects on MacDonald's personality: "We all just loved him. One day he and I rode around Derwentwater together. I was a shy girl of about sixteen, but he talked so simply and interestingly, and just as if he liked all the things that I did, that I never forgot that ride. My father used to read to us all his books as they came out."[12]

During the time in the north he also visited Thomas Erskine, Thomas Carlyle, Dr. John Brown, Mrs. Batten, and Dr. Smeaton. At the time Louisa was in her eighth month of pregnancy with Bernard, and was suffering as she usually did at such times. Her letters reflect the changeableness of her emotions, yet the loving support she always managed to give her husband throughout it: "I do hope you will go and see Mr. Erskine, dear Husband; it will do you some good. They will give you some strength, if I have been giving you weakness. It will be some comfort to me . . . go, and stay more than a day. That Christian Erskine and that Prophet Carlyle will give you something—you who are always giving to others. I am doing very well. You can't think how strong I am. The last two nights I have slept all night, and am able to do a great deal in a quiet way in the day. . . ."

But she was clearly trying to put her best face forward, for after some news she continues: "I am simply ashamed of having talked with you with all my insane changes of mood. They have all been true [of] me. But why have I troubled you with them? Because I have for fifteen years and more felt as if what I felt was yours and interesting to you, especially when shut up with hideous thoughts [and] ugly truths. . . . One night God spoke to me. . . . Oh, the sweetness of that rest and sleep in him! That calm and trust in you! I can't tell you what it was like. . . . I will make no promises any more, but will try your way of making each present time do its duty. So shall you teach me yet if you will."

And her husband replies: "My darling, I shall love you more than ever.

I can hardly be sorry for your sufferings, if they made you hear one word from Him which I do think you would hear. Thank you with all my heart for trusting me in sending me what you had thought in the night. Do not be in the least anxious about me. I feel fairly well now. . . ."[13]

In 1866 A. J. Scott died and George MacDonald had to face a sorrow he had not known since his father's death eight years before. To Mrs. Scott he wrote: "He was—he is—my friend. He understood me, and gave me to understand him; and I think I did understand him to the measure of my inferior capacity. All my prosperity in literary life besides has come chiefly through him and you. . . . How glad and quiet he must be now the struggle is over! My heart clings to him. How I could have served and waited on him, had that been in my power or his need! Who knows but he may help us all now in ways that we cannot understand. But the best is, we are all going to him. The one God be with him and us. . . ."[14]

George MacDonald was now writing and producing his novels rapidly; they often appeared serially in magazines first, then as three-volume cloth-bound sets, then as single volumes. Most were quickly picked up by others than the original publisher. As a result, the majority of his books were found in a half dozen or more distinct editions within the first ten or fifteen years after their first printing. But Mr. Smith's words that the publishers would be saving up to pay his price was hardly fulfilled. His refusal to cater completely to "popular demand" undoubtedly kept him from making a great deal of money, for had he not had a higher calling his books would have been as immortal as those of Dickens.

Greville comments: ". . . perhaps we shall understand the reason why many of George MacDonald's novels failed to hold the place once given them. For it was just this: from his point of view, it was impossible to paint true pictures if he ignored the source of all light and colour and joy. . . . Never has his method been attempted before or since. . . . Even if his characters are sometimes too good or too wicked for credence, so were many authentic saints and kings. . . . But where George MacDonald overstepped the canons of modern art . . . lay in this alone, that he, the author, would sometimes, as if showman or chorus, take possession of his stage and stop the play's action to explain its characters' relation to Time and Eternity, or even to reproach his audience for their misplaced sympathies. Such interludes, however, used to be commoner than now. . . . George MacDonald, however, believing in Man and the joy and peace he might find in life if he would but accept it, is dismissed by the ordinary novel-reader because he is 'always preaching.' 'People,' he once remarked, 'find this great fault with me—that I turn my stories into sermons. They forget that I have a Master to serve first before I can wait upon the public.'. . . One thing was clear to him. Seeing that Life and Religion were as inseparable as the thought of a rose from its beauty; seeing also how men and women who denied this in their modes of living felt more comfortable so long as they stigmatized all open expression of it as cant, he at least must be outspoken whenever, wherever he had opportunity."[15]

In 1865 MacDonald became a lecturer in the evening classes at King's

College, London. Most of the students were Dissenters, but MacDonald had just begun to attend Anglican St. Peter's Church where F. D. Maurice was vicar. He got himself into difficulty for preaching in a small church that was deemed unacceptable by the college hierarchy, and one of his fellow professors was scandalized by seeing him actually taking Communion at the Church of England, St. Peters. The principal, however, understood MacDonald's position and honored his explanation, asking only that in the future when the lecturer on English Literature undertook public engagements to preach, he would refrain from mentioning his connection with King's College. About this same time, MacDonald avowed himself a member of the Church of England. To some this appeared a forsaking of his nonconformist, progressive ways. Yet though formal and steeped in history and tradition, the Church of England was considerably better suited theologically to a man of MacDonald's tolerant bent than the conservative Church of Scotland or any of the other dissenting Scottish or English denominations that had broken away from the established church or had been founded through the years. The differences among these were generally largely administrative in nature, and most dissenting groups remained heavily puritanical in their outlook. Possibly responding in measure to this decision of his own, some years later he wrote: "Do not mistake me; I believe as strongly as ever that the constitution of the Church of England is all wrong . . . but where I find my Lord preached as only one who understands Him can preach Him, and as I never could preach Him, and never heard him preached before, even faults great as those shall be to me as merest accidents. Gentlemen, every thing is pure loss—chapels and creeds and churches—all is loss that comes between us and Christ. . . . And of all unchristian things one of the most unchristian is to dispute and separate in the name of Him whose one object was, and whose one victory will be unity" (*Paul Faber, Surgeon*, Ch. 28).

He resigned his post at Bedford College in this year, and spent the summer of 1867 at Bude, far to the west on the Atlantic coast of Devonshire, the setting of *The Seaboard Parish,* which came out the following year. During those months the author wrote tirelessly. Of that time Greville wrote, "The breakwater was our joy, especially at high tides when the south-west wind brought furious, white-maned sea-horses scrambling over the sea-wall into the haven. My father, happy as his boys in dodging these drenching smotherers, would, with Maurice and Bernard, ages three and two, one under each arm, race across it to the Chapel-rock, and sometimes half up to his knees in the foamy water. The fascination of the sea's terror and loveliness must have been as strong as in his student days when he fought the winds by the bitter North Sea, though it could not now awaken the ecstatic melancholy of his boyhood."[16]

Reflecting, Greville continues: "*The Seaboard Parish* is not one of the strong novels, neither story nor characters being very convincing. [But] the incident of the drowned man was actually witnessed by us, and the incredible incident of a storm when two men leapt from the life-boat at the top of a wave to the main shrouds of a small schooner riding at anchor in the harbour, was told to my father by a coastguardsman with whom we hatched an invigorating intimacy. . . .

"Those days at Bude remain in my mind as the happiest of all my childhood's holidays; and chiefly because our father, in spite of his indefatigable writing, took more share in our romps and pleasures than I ever remember."[17]

Scottish coastline

CHAPTER TWENTY-THREE

THE NOVELIST
(1867–1873)

Upon returning from Bude, the search began for a larger house, for as on so many occasions in the past, the present house located at Earles Terrace in Kensington proved too small. A new home, named "The Retreat," proved a great success. The family occupied it, in conjunction with another in Hastings they rented about four years later, and with the exception of occasional winters and summers away, for 8 years. It was large, with nearly an acre of land, and perfect for raising the great brood, which George MacDonald used to say was "just on the wrong side of a dozen" (giving rise to the erroneous conclusion that he had thirteen children). The extra space also facilitated their entertaining and the lectures that he gave.

The Ministry of Entertainment

Entertainment on a larger scale than before was now possible. There was no ostentation, and refreshments, if abundant, were always kept simple. The house was located on the river, and on one occasion hundreds came to watch the boat races, including Alfred Lord Tennyson himself. Greville recalled the incident: "The serviceable children were worth double their number in servants; and once it was my glory to have rescued a cab from the human flood on the highroad half a mile away, and piloted it to the house for the Poet Laureate. What a great hand was his in its strong gentle grasp! What a deep, sad voice! I thought."[1] Later in the day Tennyson visited MacDonald's library. They discussed several books he had never seen, and he borrowed one that particularly fascinated him.

George's health during the first couple of years at the Retreat improved, but at the same time, even greater demands had come upon his and Louisa's energies. Not only was the family more hungry and active, and the need for housekeepers and nurses therefore increased, but the claims upon the house and the family for hospitality and ministry and generosity were enormous. "The more you give, the more is asked of you" is a common principle of life; similarly, "The more you give, the more that will be provided you, that you might give all the more." George and Louisa were both attractive; people were drawn to them. Their warmth and open-heartedness, their interest in others, the open-doored hospitality that was evident wherever they went, their charitable and benevolent spirits all combined to bring people their way. They drew people and problems and needs like magnets. Therefore, not only did they have an enormous family of their own, with more than their share of sicknesses to be attended to; but their household always seemed a great "bundle of life" for a wide variety of others—George's literary friends, Louisa's relatives, friends of the children, neighbors, puzzled young people searching out their faith, and those in physical want. The lectures, the holiday parties, the reading of fairy tales for groups of friends, and other forms of entertaining natural to their mode of existence made the Retreat a busy home with a great deal of activity.

All constituents of the social scale were involved: Ruskin came to Mac-Donald in his time of deepest need; social pioneer and reformer Octavia Hill (1838–1912) used the MacDonalds' home for her annual entertainments for the poor, reflected in *Weighed and Wanting*; Lord Mount-Temple (nephew of former Prime Minister Lord Melbourne and stepson of former Prime Minister Lord Palmerston) became very close with MacDonald, and waifs and strays collected in equal numbers.

Louisa was as large-hearted as her husband; there was always someone to be taken in. A certain Oxford graduate came begging in rags and remained several weeks. When at last George found employment for him on the staff of a London newspaper, he suddenly disappeared and never was seen again. A drunkard was brought in for reformation. Even an old broken-down horse was made the object of reclamation.

All did their share. The older children were now well into their teens, and genuine musical abilities were emerging. When people gathered, either a few or a hundred for the annual entertainment of the poor, some played the piano, some sang, one played the violin. Little family concerts were given—especially at Christmas time. Regularly small groups would gather to discuss world events, literature, social problems, or the faith. Everyone pitched in to help at such times, rolling up their sleeves—guests and family alike—to wash the dishes.

As their confidence was established among the poor, the whole Mac-Donald family went to the London slums, where George would retell the Gospel stories about Jesus and the rest would provide musical entertainment. During those days, the oldest daughter Lilia's gift for acting and Louisa's gift as a playwright and director were developing. The coach-house, though shared for a time with the family cow that supplied the children's needs for milk, was converted into a theater, where the multi-aged family (ages 3 to 18!) performed its plays until it ultimately had to be reconverted into a stable again. The highlight of those early dramatic per-

formances was Lilia Scott MacDonald's portrayal of Lady Macbeth opposite her father in the title role.

In a multitude of ways, therefore, this was a time of happy work for the
head of this energetic family. He had a house large enough for his children
to romp and to entertain guests and hold social functions. In addition, he
possessed a delightful study in which he could work freely, which an artist
friend had adorned and decorated for him in a sort of "barbaric splen-
dour" with reds and blacks and brass wall brackets and chandelier. So
huge was it—five windows in all!—that when the coachhouse was retaken
for equine purposes, the stage was set up at one end of this great study.

Significant too, the author had cause to feel good about the response
to his writings. His books had increased in market value, he was recognized in the first rank among living writers, and in 1868 his own university
in Aberdeen conferred upon him the degree of Doctor of Laws for his
"high literary eminence as a poet and an author." Worldly recognition had
never been his goal. But there was a satisfaction which came from knowing that at last his message was getting through.

Disastrous Travels

After a rigorous itinerary of lectures in Scotland in the early winter
months of 1869 (speaking 28 times in 5 weeks, in 28 different towns!) and
attacked as a result during the trip with hemoptysis (bleeding from the
lungs), followed by bronchitis and an asthma attack, plans were made for
the summer (four years after his first visit) to take Louisa to Switzerland as
he had longed to do. The cost was not a stumbling block now, but when
an invitation came for George to join a yachting trip to Norway, Louisa
insisted he do that instead. Though she would not be able to share it, she
knew it would be a more bracing and restful holiday for him, and quite
after his own heart, for he still loved the sea.

Recovery from the speaking tour was not complete, however, and
embarking on a new adventure so soon was ill-advised. Even the day of
the yacht's departure he wrote home complaining of feeling tired and
lame from a swollen knee. And though the seas were calm, the knee wors-
ened, as did his weakened condition, and thus he was unable to enjoy
what would have undoubtedly been one of the most marvelous experiences of his life. Instead he was confined to his cabin, steadily growing
worse as they traveled first to Lerwick and Unst in the Shetland Islands,
then on to Trondheim where he was hoisted up through the skylight of his
cabin and carried to a stateroom on board a steamer returning to England.
He had written Louisa at all hours—"Half-past three Monday morning, 21st
I think," reads one heading. But toward the end he was able to say, "Tomorrow the first end of my prayers will come at last. I shall be with you. Oh, I
have gone through some of the folds of the shadow of death since I saw
you, but the light has never ceased to shine. . . ."[2]

Writing to a friend, Louisa elaborates on the physical toll of the trip:
". . . He had never been well since his lecturing tour; and he had been

in bed for ten days with an attack of congestion of the lungs. Then this offer of five weeks of sea-life—the midnight sun, the fjords of Norway, etc., etc., no posts, no callers, no dinners—looked very health-giving, and we were both very hopeful about it. So he started.

"His first letter from Glasgow said that he had not been able to sleep from pain in his knee. . . . But then came another, after he had got on board, saying his knee was worse—and from Lerwick came worse news. . . . The doctors ordered leeches twice. . . . I heard no more after that, beyond that he had then been ten days in his cabin on his bed—no porthole even to look out at—sleepless nights, weary days—pain, pain, couldn't eat—could scarcely read, no woman near to attend him—not one face he had ever seen before about him—the most horrible noises going on about and around him. This was the last I heard for a week, when one morning I got a telegram to say . . . I was to meet him at King's Cross. . . .

"And oh! . . . I shall never forget what I saw on arriving at the platform. There was an invalid carriage and in it a man propped up with pillows looking as if he were in the last stage of consumption, with a horrid cough. I could scarcely believe it was George. His eyes were sunken, his cheeks hollow, and he was so weak that his voice, as hollow as his cheeks, could not speak three words together from weakness. I was not the only one who thought he was a dying man. Mr. A. Stevenson told me he looked *strong* to what he did when they carried him strapped to a stretcher in an open boat from the steamer to land. And so he had been carried from the yacht—from his own berth up *through* the skylight of his cabin on to the steamer when they were off the town of Trondhjem. . . .

"But he had suffered intensely, and who shall say those sufferings were not for other people—in what he may hereafter write. . . . He says himself that he had never had anything but the *luxury* of illness before, and it was well that he should know its real misery. . . . When we first laid him on his own bed he looked all round the room and cried with thankfulness. . . . He says though, it was nearly worth it all—the wonderful effect of the blue sky just above him as they laid him on the floor of his cabin when they took the skylight up. They lifted him up with cords. It was as if he looked out from his grave—the tall mast of the vessel rising from his cabin—that and the blue sky was all he saw—then he felt his Resurrection was come; but I should like you to hear him tell this. It was his one spot of joy. . . ."[3]

To the Pinnacle of Literary Success

This period of George MacDonald's life was one in which—from his searching beginnings, through a decade of apparent failure, followed by a decade of newfound success—his reputation climbed to the highest. The ten years between 1870 and 1880 were full of hard work and human acclaim, yet were accompanied by sickness and sorrow more than any other such period in his life. In the remarkable span between his 45th and 55th years, he turned out sixteen original works, in addition to a ten-volume set entitled *Works of Fancy and Imagination* (1871), chiefly reprints of already published works. *The Princess and the Goblin* (1872), the first of the two books involving Princess Irene and Curdie, was a book of time-less truths and symbols. It became one of his two or three most enduring classics and a perennial favorite with children of all ages. Another fantasy, *The Wise Woman*, was published in 1875. In addition, he brought forth his expanded collections of German translations of Novalis, to which had been added the Hymnbook of Luther and other poems from the German and Italian, which was entitled *Exotics* (1876); a history of English litera-ture and poetry, *England's Antiphon* (1874); and a collection of sermons, *The Miracles of Our Lord* (1870). About the latter, Charles H. Spurgeon said that it "contains many fresh, childlike, and . . . dreamy thoughts. It suggests side-walks of meditation."

Of sixteen books produced during this span, eleven were novels and several of them were among his very best. *At the Back of the North Wind* (1871) proved to be MacDonald's most enduring and bestselling book of all time. *Ranald Bannerman's Boyhood* (1871) gave simple insights into MacDonald's boyhood in Huntly. Next in quick succession came *Wilfred Cumbermede* (1872), for which the author received 1,200 pounds; *The Vicar's Daughter* (1872), the sequel to *The Seaboard Parish*, which thus completed the Marshmallows Trilogy and paid 1,000 pounds; and another Bannerman-like book, *Gutta Percha Willie* (1873).

After a two-year break came two of MacDonald's greatest achieve-ments, though in their own day they were not especially noteworthy: *Mal-colm* (1875) and *Thomas Wingfold, Curate* (1876). In certain respects, *Mal-colm* stands far above all other of MacDonald's works in plot and depth of characterization. Nowhere else is there such intrigue, such complexity, such twists, such multilayered mystery, such hints of romance, such a skill-ful weaving of clues and their resolutions, and such passages of unrelent-ing sheer dramatic action mingled with such poignant eternal struggles of the heart. But the plot is not the only way in which *Malcolm* is unique. A good deal of it is loosely based on MacDonald's own family ancestry from Glencoe through Culloden. It contains a host of memorable characters, each a personality that leaps off the page into the memory—the mad laird, Mrs. Stewart, Florimel, Barbara Catanach, Blue Peter, Sandy Graham, Miss Horn, Lord Lossie, Hector Crathie, Miss Horn's Jean, Lady Bellair, Meg Par-tan, not to mention Malcolm himself.

Of Duncan, Ronald MacDonald says: ". . . it may be doubted whether he ever equalled in clarity of characterization or profundity of loving humour his Duncan MacPhail, the blind piper of Portlossie. In his lofty, yet half savage sense of honour, his feminine tenderness, his berserk fits of rage, his jubilant piping, his love of personal finery undimmed by blind-ness, and in the poetic imagery of his speech; in his noble lament for Glencoe and his terrible cursing of Campbells; in his chivalrous worship of all women and his bitter hatred of one, Duncan, who must in the end confess himself a MacDonald, is at once the type of the Celt for his author, and the reconstruction (I suggest merely) of the influence upon his author of Highland tradition. Much that Duncan relates of Glencoe and Culloden, as well as certain passages in *Robert Falconer* concerning the 'blin' piper o' Portcloddie,' is family history."[4] *Malcolm* is a book absolutely *full* from beginning to end.

Following *Malcolm* came *Thomas Wingfold, Curate*, a book almost absent of plot and with only seven principal characters, a book so dramatically different in tone and pace and theme that it is hard to imagine they flowed from the same pen—a book unique in an altogether different way. For *Wingfold*, too, is "full," but with spiritual profundity rather than dramatic action. Through the story of the humble curate Wingfold, MacDonald unfolds one of his spiritual master strokes—outlining in a compelling fictional format the fundamental nature of salvation, the process of new birth, and the essence of God's forgiveness. If ever a book spoke out of the depth of its author's heart, *Thomas Wingfold, Curate* does.

Four more novels appeared during this period: the historical *St. George and St. Michael* (1876) set in 17th-century England; *The Marquis of Lossie* (1877), the gripping conclusion of Malcolm's story, the two making up a single unit; *Sir Gibbie* (1879); and the sequel to Wingfold's story, *Paul Faber, Surgeon* (1879)—which, as mentioned, furthers the portrayal of MacDonald's Arundel experience and whose plot may have inspired Thomas Hardy's *Tess of the d'Urbervilles*, written nine years later. Surely no period in MacDonald's life reflects such a strong output of classic novels as the years 1875 to 1880. *Sir Gibbie* is the story of the homeless and mute waif who grows in ministration and service to his fellows. In the end, he

Cullen House, site of fictional "Lossie House" in Malcolm *and* The Marquis of Lossie

inherits a title and a modest fortune, which he characteristically turns to the purpose of ministry. Like Robert Falconer, Thomas Wingfold, and Malcolm, it is the unique and magical character of "wee Sir Gibbie" that enchants the reader and lures him into Gibbie's world. If *Robert Falconer* is compelling in its weightiness, *Sir Gibbie* is compelling for its light, its brightness, the zest for life and the world as seen through Gibbie's eyes. Like so many of the characters of MacDonald's creation, Sir Gibbie is a boy who, once met, can never be erased from memory. And *Paul Faber, Surgeon* furthers and extends the parabolic insight into the nature of sin, forgiveness, and salvation, which was begun so forceably in *Wingfold*.

By the end of this decade, MacDonald was truly one of Britain's leading authors and was making a good deal of money. Whereas in the early 1860's he had been offered 30 and 50 pounds for a copyright, now he was being paid 700 to 1000 pounds for some of his novels. Wealth never came to the MacDonald household, however, and money flowed out as rapidly as it came in. The cost of supporting the household with all its attendants had mushroomed beyond all previous standards. Medical bills, enormous housekeeping and travel costs brought on by the physical necessity of wintering abroad in later years, and other expenses always seemed to keep financial demand one step ahead of supply.

The MacDonalds' friend and publisher Alexander Strahan began in 1869 a magazine, *Good Words for the Young*, intended to provide good literature for children. The following year Strahan offered MacDonald the editorship at a salary of 600 pounds a year, which temporarily bolstered the family finances wonderfully. But the magazine did not last long even though the contributions were first rate, from such as Charles Kingsley, William Gilbert, W. R .S. Ralston, as well as MacDonald himself. Its pages first revealed to the world *At the Back of the North Wind* with classic illustrations by Arthur Hughes, and *Ranald Bannerman's Boyhood*. But even as the magazine went downhill, MacDonald fulfilled three years of editing, the last two without remuneration. The strains were so great, however, that he afterward declared he would do no more editing at *any* salary. It lost him two close friends, one who charged that the editor refused his manuscript in order to make room for his own.

The Refinement of Ideas Continues

MacDonald's friend and mentor Frederick Denison Maurice, like A. J. Scott, was nearly twenty years older than George MacDonald. Like Scott, Maurice had repudiated many sacrosanct doctrines, which had resulted in his expulsion from King's College, London, and the strength of Maurice's personality attracted MacDonald to become a lay member of the Church of England. There was discussion between the two for collaboration on a book of sermons, prayers, and hymns, but Maurice's health failed shortly thereafter and nothing became of it.

Upon Maurice's death in 1872, MacDonald, as was often his custom, having also written in memory of A. J. Scott and Lady Byron, wrote a poem entitled "Thanksgiving for F. D. Maurice," which was included in his published *Poetical Works* in 1893. One stanza of the poem was omitted from the published version; it would no doubt have stirred up as much controversy in his day as it is likely to in our own.

> He taught that hell itself is yet within
>   The confines of thy kingdom; and its fires
> The endless conflict of thy love with sin,
>   That even by horror works its pure desires.[5]

The words certainly shed light on the continued progress of George MacDonald's thoughts. He continued all his life to make seemingly contradictory statements, refusing to conform to any one dogmatic label on this most controversial of issues, which followed him throughout his career: "He [Wingfold] was a servant of the church universal, of all that believed or ever would believe in the Lord Christ, therefore of all men, of the whole universe. . . ." (*There and Back*, Ch. 31). Further MacDonald says, "thousands of half-thinkers imagine that, since . . . hell is not everlasting, there is then no hell at all. To such folly I for one have never given enticement. . . . I see no hope for many, no way for the divine love to reach them, save through a very ghastly hell. Men have got to repent; there is no other escape for them, and no escape from that."[6]

Commenting on the dual sides with which MacDonald seems always to approach any discussion of hell, C. S. Lewis said, "The Divine Sonship is the key-conception which unites all the different elements of his thought. I dare not say that he is never in error; but to speak plainly I know hardly any other writer who seems to be closer, or more continually close, to the Spirit of Christ Himself. Hence his Christ-like union of tenderness and severity. Nowhere else outside the New Testament have I found terror and comfort so intertwined. . . .

"In many respects MacDonald's thought has, in a high degree, just those excellences which his period and his personal history would lead us to expect least. . . . Reaction against early teachings might on this point have very easily driven him into a shallow liberalism. But it does not. He hopes, indeed, that all men will be saved; but that is because he hopes that all will repent. He knows (none better) that even omnipotence cannot save the unconverted. He never trifles with eternal impossibilities."[7]

A Popular Lecturer

The health of the MacDonald family was always mediocre, one or more generally ailing. Along with the enterprise and vigorous output of the father, the decade of the '70s produced many changes, death touching the close-knit family upon repeated occasions. Louisa's father, Mr. Powell, died in 1870 at 91.

By this time the letters received by George MacDonald from people all over the country were innumerable—thankful, abusive, argumentative on this or that point of doctrine, questioning, seeking advice, both criticizing and praising his work. Louisa answered the worshiping and adoring young ladies who suffered from being "misunderstood." The author himself was always as tender as he could be with young poets seeking his counsel, and replied with whatever help he could give.

In the days before radio and television, when the intellectual climate was perhaps more "sophisticated" than today, a chief form of both learning and entertainment came from lectures given by men of renown. In his younger days, attending lectures provided a fashionable social occasion for student George MacDonald, and he himself became popular as a lecturer in later years. When he was lecturing in Scotland in the late 1860s, one lady wrote, "All Aberdeen seemed to be crowded that night into the Mechanic's Institute to hear him speak."

Lecturing could be extremely lucrative for one who drew large crowds, for the agent as well as the speaker himself. Lecturing bureaus, therefore, were competitive and always on the lookout for a "hot prospect" on the basis of whose name they might make a few thousand pounds. Dickens and Thackeray had already been to the United States on a lecturing tour, and by late 1871 a similar venture was pressed upon George MacDonald.

It is doubtful that under ordinary conditions he would have complied, for the work was desperately taxing, and the traveling schedule exhausting. And though at present there was no evidence of tuberculosis or lung hemorrhaging, he yet suffered from bronchitis and terrible attacks of asthma. But the offer of a U.S. tour was tempting, for at the particular time the proceeds from his books were not quite keeping up with the demand on his bank account. So the invitation was accepted for the latter part of the year 1872, a tour planned to last between six and eight months, and arranged through the leading lecture agency of Redpath and Fall, with the condition that he should not have to lecture more than five nights a week and that his fee should be 30 pounds per lecture. He and Louisa projected the trip would bring in between three and four thousand pounds, which would greatly reduce several pressing bills.

The author's fitness for such an undertaking was questionable. A lecturing tour in the north in the spring of that same year left him nearly at the point of exhaustion. Writing to Louisa on the eve of reaching home, he said, "I shall be very glad to get home. *Oh the work undone that snarls at my heels—not to say the work unbegun.* But I think it is to teach me to trust and learn more and not be anxious."[8] He was clearly a man energetically driven toward his goals!

In May MacDonald visited Huntly, taking eight-year-old Maurice with him. Though he was working on the proofs of *The Vicar's Daughter* on the train, his particular reason for going was to visit Cullen, the site of boyhood holidays on the coast north of Huntly, for the purpose of its being the center of a new novel that had germinated in his mind, a book to be called *Malcolm*. He stayed at 26 Grant Street while working on the book, one of whose distinctive features is its sweeping and uncompromising *trueness* to the place; it is a book whose setting *lives*.

After returning south, in September George and Louisa and sixteen-year-old Greville sailed for Boston, leaving 20-year-old Lilia in charge of the rest of the young family, which now ranged in ages down to five.

The American Tour of 1872

In *George MacDonald and His Wife*, Greville devotes 43 pages of his biography to the American tour, disproportionate for only eight months in his father's life but clearly a highlight in his own life. The material for it is "wonderfully rich," as he says, because of Louisa's daily and lengthy letters home to her children, and the reactions to American places and people, and the little trials and joys of travel make for fascinating reading.

The tour began in Boston, and from that point there were speaking engagements in Providence, New York, Philadelphia, Scotch Plains, N.J., Washington, Baltimore, Jersey City, Williamsport, Pittsburg, Cincinnati, Dayton, Altoona, Pa., Chicago, St. Louis, Buffalo, Detroit, Ann Arbor—in addition to Canada—to name but a few. In many of the cities there were return visits—in all a total of between a hundred and a hundred and thirty lectures; there is no record of an exact count.

Louisa said of her husband, "He was the bear who must dance when his keeper, Mr. Redpath, shook the chain." And though it became obvious early into the tour that the scheduled work was too heavy, no changes were made. There was scarcely any consideration for the long and tiring daily journeys that had to be made *before* every speaking engagement.

View of Cullen from the Scaurnose—site of Malcolm *and* The Marquis of Lossie

And in addition, the lecturer (never one to conserve his energy even when prudence indicated such might be in order) accepted many invitations to preach without fee whenever he might squeeze it in. It remained for Louisa on many occasions to keep him away from social functions that had been planned in his honor, or to cancel—on account of illness—long-advertised lectures.

Despite the arduous schedule, the MacDonalds loved America—until winter, bad accomodations, freezing snows, and illness began to dampen their enthusiasm by degrees. Acquaintance was made and a number of lasting friendships were formed with many eminent Americans, including the poet Whittier, James Fields, Oliver Wendell Holmes, Rev. H. Bellows, and Rev. Phillips Brooks. MacDonald lunched with Ralph Waldo Emerson, visited Henry Wadsworth Longfellow, and struck up a close and lasting friendship of mutual high regard and respect with Mark Twain.

The reception of the poet-novelist-preacher on the other side of the Atlantic in "the colonies" was tremendous. In most places the halls were filled, everywhere people clamoring for Robert Burns. Greville recalls the opening talk, "This was his first lecture in America and his first anywhere on *Robert Burns*. But the second on the same subject was at the much larger Lyceum in Boston itself; and it was then that the public discovered . . . his power of inspired, uplifting criticism, in no way spoiled by his just facing of facts. Through his wise and weighty, poetic and passionate words, without notes or help other than a little volume of Burns's works, he set the man before them, the lover, the romantic ploughman, the poet, in true portraiture, while his sins and shortcomings were fully accredited to him. I must have heard him lecture on Burns over forty times, I think, in the States, and used to declare that on every occasion it was a different lecture. It was new to an American audience to hear such eloquence unbuttressed by academic elocution. . . . Here is my mother's description of the *Burns* lecture [in a letter home] . . .

"'. . . The people are so kind and glad to see Papa. I can't tell you how very happy it seems to make some people to look at him. . . . It was very pleasant to hear different people tell of the way Papa's books had come to them, and the good and comfort they have been to them. . . . Papa's lecture at Boston on Wednesday was the great event of the week to us. . . . There were two thousand eight hundred and fifty ticket holders, besides a few that got in as friends. Such a hall! . . . '"9

But then later, as the tour was about to end, having by now nearly had her fill of Burns, she wrote: "DEAREST MY DEAR LILY," she says, ". . . Sometimes I break down a little, and then your and the others' dear letters build me up again. I had a feast yesterday in yours . . . you toiling away like a mother bee to send your sisters to their enjoyments and profit, you darling love. You are all darling loves—as I think you all round, I feel so rejoicing and happy. I don't know how to keep my cup from running over.

"No, I don't keep it—it's always running over and filling up faster than ever—like those tremendous outpourings of those big lakes down into the

Niagara rapids and basins which we saw last Sunday.... Papa lectured during a tremendous thunderstorm.... I hope to-morrow will be finer for *R. Burns*.... To-morrow's will be the fortieth lecture I have heard on that poor but talented genius! The long and short of which is that 'he did as well as he could, but he might have done better'...."[10]

Personal Response to *The Man*

One phenomenon was clearly at work, according to Louisa, in his own day, which both Greville and Ronald allude to in their writings about their father, and which continues to this present day—the extremely personal reactions people have to George MacDonald. During the American tour it wasn't enough for people to come and listen to a famous man speak: they wanted to meet him, touch him, shake his hand, get close to him, and tell what a particular book of his had meant to them. People had highly personal and emotional responses to him. Something about the man drew them through his words. And though it has been more than a hundred years since most of his books were written, that same warm and human response continues today. I don't know how many times, because of my own interest in George MacDonald, I have received a letter or a shake of the hand from someone who just wants to express "what George Mac-Donald has meant to me." It's a unique reaction, totally unlike what one usually feels upon reading a particular book by a particular man, a desire to communicate, to express common ground, to relate to a similar mental journey, and to share common hope and vision.

Such intimate response to a man known only through hundred-year-old books comes because he himself was a highly *personal* author. His books do not exist in a vacuum. The personality and values and beliefs and perspectives of George MacDonald the man come through the printed page. Therefore upon completing one of his works the reader has an inward sense of *knowing* the man. And knowing him fosters a desire to relate to him on a personal level. He is no longer a mere "author"; George MacDonald becomes a friend.

This marvel certainly was in evidence during MacDonald's American tour of 1872-73. All over the country, people responded *personally* to George, and even to Louisa. They were no stage-actors, no unapproachable celebrities, but rather the couple next door to whom anyone might come day or night.

Loved Wherever He Went

George MacDonald's speaking repertoire included *Hamlet, Tom Hood,* the lyrics of Tennyson, *King Lear, Macbeth,* and Milton. But the favorite subject with American audiences was always Scot Robert Burns. Greville comments, "I remember how my father, after speaking for over a hundred minutes, dropped into a chair in the reception-room somewhat exhausted with the effort and the wonderful audience; how James T. Fields shook him by the hand, his eyes full of tears, and declared there had been nothing like it since Dickens; and how Redpath came rushing at him with this almost angry anticlimax, 'See here Mr. MacDonald, why didn't you *say* you could do this sort of thing? We'd have got 300 dollars a lecture for you!'"[11] The author had sent the agents no advance press-cuttings or testimonials whereby they might gauge his ability, which was customary. His modesty, as can be seen, cost him dearly; he could probably have received twice as much per lecture as he actually was paid.

In Philadelphia he faced a packed house of 3,500, a larger audience than he had ever spoken to in his life. In Boston the family was roused out of bed in the middle of the night; a terrible fire was raging in the heart of the city and spreading rapidly. The fire was contained, however, and they were in no danger. In December George was struck down with a severe attack of bronchitis, and quite a number of lectures had to be canceled. Louisa wrote home, ". . . I never saw him more prostrate except, of course, at the time of the Manchester illness. It is very serious this attack for him— we do not know yet whether he will be able to lecture again at all, and if he does he can scarcely make up all he has lost before the close of the lecture season. But if he can but get what will cover the debts that trouble him I do not think we ought to mind about more. . . ."[12]

But with surprising resiliency he recovered quickly and was able to resume the tour in January. Greville's words, in which he quotes a letter home from Louisa, tell how they came close to losing him. "On Christmas Eve we travelled from Elmira to Jersey City. It was a terrible journey. We were constantly stopped by great snowdrifts in the cuttings. The stoves in the cars, being dependent upon swift motion for their draught, refused to burn. We were three hours late, half-frozen and famished. My father's asthma was bad and became alarming as we stepped out into the deep snow. No one met us, for we had crossed by the wrong ferry to a wrong depot, others being misled with us. Fortunately our hotel was not many yards away; but I thought we should never get him alive through the snow:

"'. . . He stood gasping in the street holding onto Greville's arm, tears rolling down his cheeks as if he would die then and there—and could not move for whole minutes, though it was only across the road he had to go to get to our inn. But the thermometer was five degrees below zero, and he said afterwards the air felt like strong acid cutting up his lungs. It was agony for him, and it was agony to see him. . . .'"[13]

But Greville's reminiscences also reveal the humor of the sixteen-year-old, and we can imagine what fun the trio had in their lighter moments.

"We three would play whist—either with dummy or a three-handed game invented by my father. Even merry we often were, and would write verses in competition on more ludicrous events, to send home to our dear ones. . . . Often we had to stay at very bad hotels, the food being deplorable. Steaks were universal—veritable *pieces de resistance*. Their sole value was to the proprietor; for their defiance even of the knife made it possible to present the same slabs of leather at breakfast, dinner and supper again and again, until, possibly because of their damage to the cutlery, they were discarded to pave the side-walks. My mother liked the tomatoes, cranberries, and green corn on which she often dined; but my father could digest none of such things, and, but for the fact that good milk and eggs were always to be had, would have often done ill. If I ate the steaks, it was to spite the manager.

"In the middle of February we visited Cincinnati, where my father had second cousins. My mother's account of these is good reading. The lectures, however, were not well received. But what could we expect when the population was chiefly pigs, and even driving a buggy through the snorting throngs that filled roadway and side-walks everywhere, scarcely roused them? Cincinnati was then known as Porkopolis. . . .

"One amusing incident deserves recording. Very soon after the lecturing tour had been determined upon—as early, I think, as February 1871—my father had had an invitation from the Burns Society in New York to be their guest at the annual dinner on the poet's birthday. He accepted, and asked whether these Scots in New York followed the custom set by the Caledonian Society in London—of appearing at the annual dinner in full dress kilt. The reply was that it was *de rigueur* for those who were Highlanders to wear their native costume. So my father of course took his kilt with him—even sword, dirk, and skean dhu. And to Delmonico's on January 24th he went in his MacDonald tartans—and was the only guest not in black swallow-tails and white tie! He was greeted with rapturous delight, and being the guest of the evening, had opportunity, in responding to the toast 'Scottish Literature,' for explanation and apology, and for vowing vengeance upon his most particular friend who had so misled him!"[14]

A touching letter from Louisa to Maurice on the occasion of his ninth birthday must be recorded. This letter is full of pathos, for the little boy would live but six years more and had less than a year earlier lost his godfather, F. D. Maurice. Little did his mother dream how soon he would follow.

From Altoona, Pennsylvania, on February 16, 1873, she wrote: "MY DEAREST MAURICE, I was very sorry I couldn't write to you on the 7th of February, my darling, precious little son—you are not forgotten by your Father and Mother. . . . People that love each other can't be very far off each other, though a great big sea comes in between the bodies of them. Love joins us, doesn't it, dear boy? When you are thinking about me you have got me, and when I think about you I know you are mine. I know God gave you to me and so you are mine; and I can think of your dear face and the loving little kiss and the loving little way you have of doing things for me: that brings you quite close to my mind, and then my heart holds you very tight when I get hold of you so! . . . But all your life God will be nearer to you than I can ever be, and He can help you more than Papa or I ever can. You are more His even than mine. We may often mistake you, or be so far away from you that we cannot look at you and speak to you just the minute you want something; but God the Great Father will never misunderstand you and He is always near you and helps every time you call to Him. Even when you only wish you could speak to Him, He will help you to speak—making you want it. So, dear darling Boy, you must take care not to send Him away, but ask Him to come into you more and more. . . .

"The people that come to speak to Papa all say the same thing almost, in all the different cities hundreds of miles away from each other. They all say 'that he seems like an old friend to them,' or that they have known him so long and have spent so many pleasant hours with him; or often they say they have learnt so much from him that they want to 'clasp him by the hand.' . . . On Friday we went to Indiana, a small city, but it has a very large and handsome Court House, where the judges sit. When we passed this handsome building in the morning there was a large blue banner hanging out, and on it in silver letters I saw, *'George MacDonald, England. Eminent Scotch Orator.* Subject, *Robert Burns.'* Yet at such a rich place no one asked us to tea or dinner and we had to go to the sort of Inn that you couldn't help fancying all night that robbers might be in the next room; and the master of the Inn looked as if he might be the greatest villain of all. I thought Ronald would have made up lots of robber and murder stories out of that horrid, dirty house and dark passages. . . . We got up and had our breakfast and walked down to the station. The only light we had was the moon which shone very brightly on the new fallen snow—and how it sparkled! . . . We got to a junction at 8:30, where there was only a shed, and they told us we must wait there till 11:30—such a wretched place! and snow still thick on the ground. But we sent Greville (our courier you know) to go and look if there was anything of a town: he came back in about five minutes and said there was a little hotel near. Oh, Maurice, I *was* so glad! for Papa had begun to be asthmatic, and though there was a stove in the shed all the poor men and rough farmers' boys were round it and spitting out their tobacco juice all round it. Gladly we followed Greville, and in three minutes we went into the daintiest toylike hotel—Glen Hotel, it was called—I ever saw. A man took us into a pretty, little parlour with Brussels carpet and a couch and a stove fire and a Bible and a hymn-book and *Pilgrim's Progress* and a volume of sermons. He soon made it nice and bright, and said we should have some breakfast. So though we had had a nasty breakfast at 5:30 at Indiana, we were quite ready for the nicest breakfast we had had for many days at 8:30. The man's wife cooked it and his little son—Ronald's age, I should think—waited on us. Papa really enjoyed the meal of eggs and tea and hot cakes and nice rolls and cheese and butter and milk. The country about was so lovely with hills and rivers and trees that I daresay people go there in the summer. . . . We had nearly three hours very comfortable there. Papa and I slept, Greville read us to sleep. . . . When we came away the landlord shook hands with us. He had been so kind and charged so little. . . . Your own, Mother."[15]

And another from Ann Arbor to Lilia is of equal interest.

"DEAREST LILY," she wrote. "We came here on Thursday. Your dear letter came in like an unexpected jewel among our beach stones. . . .

"*After service, Sunday night.* Father has been preaching so divinely, so simply, so powerfully. All the other places in the town, except the Episcopalians, shut their churches that their ministers and their congregations

might have the opportunity of hearing him. If ever, dear, he was truly elo-
quent, it was to-night; if ever he was speaking the truth as if by the power
of the Spirit within him, it was to-night. I hung on every word as an utterance from the voice of the Father speaking through him. . . . The effect was
tremendous, the listening was silence itself. He was so overcome afterwards that I was afraid for him—and he has to lecture to-morrow. . . . There
seemed such a Presence there. . . . He's in bed now—the dear saint, the
preacher, the Man of God. . . . I begin to think he ought to manage to
preach always—but how? God knows best. I'm sure we don't—he or I.
How people do love him, Lily! It's wonderful and yet it's not either—when
they tell you what his writing has done for them. . . ."[16]

The MacDonalds were invited to tea—Louisa refers to it as a "severe
tea"—where they visited with Longfellow and the great Episcopalian
preacher Phillips Brooks. Of MacDonald's preaching Brooks was later to
comment: "Among the many sermons I have heard, I always remember
this one by Mr. George MacDonald, the English author . . . over and
through it all it had this quality: it was a message from God to these people
by him. . . . As I listened, I seemed to see how weak in contrast was the
way in which other preachers had . . . challenged my admiration for the
working of their minds. Here was a gospel! Here were real tidings. And
you listened and forgot the preacher."[17]

The duration of the tour was extended to make up for the engagements
missed because of illness, but some of the local lecture bureaus occasionally refused to pay the full fee because of the lecturer having broken his
schedule. A great farewell dinner was held in Boston with many dignitaries
present to bid adieu to the Scotsman, who had now been in the United
States almost eight months. Before they left, Mrs. Whitney, author of *Gay-
worthys*, initiated a "Copyright Testimonial" for which they raised over
$1,500 in recognition of the thousands of MacDonald books sold in Amer-
ica that had brought the author no remuneration.*

End of the Tour

A few days before the MacDonalds were scheduled to depart, a depu-
tation of deacons from one of New York's fashionable and wealthy
churches came to call. Their assignment, however, was of a slightly different nature than the call of exactly twenty years earlier by a group of deacons from Arundel's Congregational chapel. Indeed, the tables had been

---

*The matter of copyright prompted a discussion that led to a long-lasting correspon-
dence with Mark Twain, and the two writers became quite good friends. They
exchanged books with each other and discussed at some length the idea of cooper-
ating on a novel so as to secure copyright on both sides of the Atlantic, Twain having
early in his career had the same trouble in England that MacDonald was now having
in the U.S. However, the project never materialized. As a result of his time in America,
MacDonald made contact with U.S. publishers, and thereafter most of his books were
published simultaneously in both countries, thus falling under both European and
American copyright laws.

turned! The Fifth Avenue committee, he was informed, had come to offer him the pastorate of their church at a yearly stipend of twenty thousand dollars. Though the offer was staggering, representing more money per year by double or triple than he had yet made in a cumulative fifteen years of writing—the equivalent salary to an English bishop—without hesitation he refused it on the spot.

In May of 1873, some fifty of MacDonald's more prominent literary friends invited him, in token of public gratitude, to give a farewell lecture on Hamlet, for which he would receive the gross proceeds. May 19th was fixed as the day and the huge Association Hall was packed, though "The Tribune" said: "If everyone in New York who had been made better and gentler by his teachings had gone to this lecture, no house ever built would have held them." On the podium with him, to deliver to the lecturer the farewell greetings of his American friends, was an impressive roster: William Cullen Bryant, Dr. J. G. Holland, R. W. Gilder, Mark Twain, Charles Dudley Warner, Bret Harte, Whitelaw Reid, George W. Curtis, Dr. Abram Coles, Thomas Moran, and Dr. Henry Bellows, who himself gave the farewell greetings on behalf of himself and the others.

In response, MacDonald's concluding words were:

"For the kindness I have received in America I am very grateful. We came loving you, and knowing that we should love you yet more; and instead of being disappointed, our hearts are larger and fuller for the love of so many more friends than we had before. If word of mine could be of any value, the love between the countries will surely be at least a little strengthened by your goodness, which, if only in honesty, but yet more in happiness, we are compelled to carry back with us. Your big hearts, huge in hospitality and welcome, have been very tender with me and mine— so patient with my failures and shortcomings. And as you and I, whatever befall, will never find misunderstandings possible, so may it be with our fellow countrymen, yours and mine. Never let us misunderstand each other whatever we do. Let there be no lies between us. Let us know that, whatever vain rumours of dislike and annoyance and ill-natured criticism come to us, they arise only among the triflers on both sides; let us know that the thinking and honest men of boths sides are just like each other, that they care for each other and believe in each other. . . . I trust and hope that we in England and you in America who have the same blood, and the same language, and the same literature, the same Shakespeare, not to speak of the same Bible, will only be the better friends for everything that compels us to explain what we mean to each other."[18]

A brief letter to Lilia about her mother, from one of her parents' dear new American friends, seemed to summarize at least one perspective of the trip:

"*. . . You don't know how she carried all hearts by storm here! We expected that of the father—but the mother took America by surprise.*"[19]

CHAPTER TWENTY-FOUR

"THE MIRACLE OF IMAGINATION"

If George MacDonald's novels brought him a degree of commercial success, and if the literary world's giants in Britain and America lauded his praises, it was because his novels made good reading, his poetry sang, and his fantasy stories made the imagination soar. Yet notwithstanding his recognition on these levels, George MacDonald's greatest contribution to the world lies in the spiritual realm. There lies his true uniqueness—both in his own time, and for generations to come.

When George MacDonald emerged "out of the black Sabbath of a Calvinist town," it was by what Chesterton called "a miracle of imagination." His choice of phrase is illuminating: a *miracle* of *imagination*. A spiritual "miracle" in the full, God-infused, supernatural, scriptural, extra-worldly sense had been wrought at the hand of the God-inspired, God-created "imagination" that at once unites heart, mind, and soul into a thorough oneness both with God and the nature He made. For MacDonald none of the false dichotomy existed between the two. For MacDonald the world of "faerie" *was* the kingdom of heaven.

The Fusing of Religion and Creativity

Neither miracle nor imagination was new. Clerics and ecclesiastical expositors, evangelists, and prophets had been proclaiming the miracle for centuries. Likewise, imagination had experienced a rich history, especially in Britain. Imagination abounded—from Shakespeare to Dickens, Burns to Scott.

But suddenly in the middle of the 19th century came a man who at once fused the two into a simple and yet compelling majestic harmony.

The imaginative poet from whose mouth could break out rhymes worthy of the best of Burns:

> And now, where'er my feet may roam,
> At sight of stranger hill
> A new sense of the old delight
> Springs in my bosom still,
> And longings for the high unknown
> Their ancient channels fill.

would unexpectedly turn his verse all at once toward the miracle of God's life blossoming within him:

> For I am always climbing hills,
> From the known to the unknown—
> Surely, at last, on some high peak,
> To find my Father's throne.

This was something no Burns, no Shakespeare, no Scott could do. As great as their imaginations were, they were locked in the earthly realm. As much as they might stir up "longings" for something more with their imaginative insights, stories, and verses, they had no "miracle" to give.

Equally it was something no evangelist, no gospel expositor, no devotional writer, even no "inspirational novelist," and certainly no Calvinist preacher had ever done. Concerned only with the so-called religious side of life (i.e., the *miracle*), their imaginations had been left behind, leaving only formula, ritual, dogma, and the lifeless phrases and proof texts of the Shorter Catechism in the drab Calvinist towns of their theology.

MacDonald was able to achieve this harmony in all things because he saw the Spirit of God in everything. "Not a maggot can die any more than a Shakespeare be born without him. He is either all in all, or he is not at all." His imaginative eyes perceived the miracle in all things.

"All about us, in earth and air, wherever the eye or ear can reach, there is a power ever-breathing itself forth in signs, now in daisy, now in wind-waft, a cloud, a sunset; a power that holds constant and sweetest relation with the dark and silent world within us. The same God who is in us, and upon whose tree we are the buds, if not yet the flowers, also is all about us—inside, the Spirit; outside, the Word. And the two are ever trying to meet in us; and when they meet, then the sign without, and the longing within, become one light, and the man no more walketh in darkness, but knoweth whither he goeth" (*Thomas Wingfold, Curate*, Ch. 82).

To neither of man's limited notions of miracle nor imagination did George MacDonald give his soul. Because his soul was God's, *both* were able to unite and emerge from within him in a way that was new and powerful, yet difficult to apprehend at first. In his early years, neither side could grasp this unique fusion between miracle and imagination. As a result neither side "wanted" him. He was cast adrift, alone to make his attempt to find the unity he knew was there. His imaginative notions did not fit the mold of Arundel's interpreters of the divine truth. Assuming he had forsaken the divine for the so-called secular, they washed their hands of him. But equally in the struggling formative years of his writing career, when he began to infuse his fiction with the "miracle," the critics found it unacceptable. "We don't want your preaching," they said in effect. "If you're going to write novels, stick to the imagination."

Thus between the two poles George MacDonald continued to stand . . . and grow . . . and write. But he would not alter his divine commission.

As time passed, and both the souls *and* the imaginations of men, women, and children the world over began to respond in their innermost beings to the writings and thoughts of the man, the time ultimately came when both the miracle and the imagination claimed him for their own. By no accident, within a few days at the conclusion of his American tour, the highest representatives of both organized Christianity and the literary world pledged him unlimited allegiance—with the offer of one of America's most prestigious pulpits and the laud of America's greatest collection of assembled literary personalities.

But he had said, "To no system will I subscribe." Therefore he would not accept their pulpit. Neither would he alter the spiritual content of his writing, though his publishers at times assured him great money could be made by catering a bit more to the public appetite, as did others of his contemporaries. His guiding principle remained, "I have a Master to serve first."

Therefore, his writings came to occupy a unique position in 19th-century literature. Conveying spiritual truths, he did not rely on spiritual words alone. Instead he used the imagination to bypass didacticism and inject truth into the heart and inner mind in ways at once simpler and yet more profound than mere instruction could ever accomplish. What words of sermon or exposition could convey with such disarming simplicity the truths in certain of his fairy stories? In *The Princess and the Goblin*, Irene's ancient grandmother explains why the moonlight in her beautiful room must never go out, though "it does not happen above five times in a hundred years that anyone does see it. . . . Besides—I will tell you a secret—if that light were to go out, you would fancy yourself lying in a bare garret on a heap of old straw, and would not see one of the pleasant things round about you all the time" (*The Princess and the Goblin,* Ch. 11).

Later when the princess brings the miner-boy Curdie to see her grandmother, instead of the great room and the beautiful woman, he sees only the bare attic and the heap of musty straw and a ray of sunlight through a hole in the roof. The incident is told with such simplicity that no argument against its truth comes to mind. Inevitably and without question we accept the profound truth that only the pure in heart have imagination enough to see God.

His stories, characters, and profound nuggets of imaginative truth strike home on deeper levels than is possible through the words of others whose focus is limited to one dimension or the other. Rose Goodwin, author of *Verse For Little Children*, recalls her memory of meeting this particular book and its author. "Nothing could happen that could make my first introduction to him pass from my memory. Such a poignant ecstatic experience, at such an age (I was only six years old) was too profound, too thrilling for time to do other than deepen the impression. . . . Those starry, vanishing walls! That fire of roses! The mysterious lamp that could shine through impenetrable stone! I had been reading steadily since I was four. I knew Grimm, Anderson, Lewis Carroll, etc. but never, never had I read *anything* approaching this!"[1]

C. S. Lewis says that George MacDonald's writing "goes beyond the expression of things we have already felt. It arouses in us sensations we have never had before, never anticipated having, as though we had broken out of our normal mode of consciousness and 'possessed joys not promised to our birth.' It gets under our skin, hits us at a level deeper than our thoughts or even our passions, troubles oldest certainties till all questions are reopened, and in general shocks us more fully awake than we are for most of our lives."[2]

The Foundational Role of Nature

For George MacDonald the imagination was God's. It had come from Him and it reflected His creativity and character. "It is God who gives thee thy mirror of imagination," he wrote in *Paul Faber, Surgeon*, "and if thou keep it clean, it will give thee back no shadow but of the truth. Never a cry of love went forth from human heart but it found some heavenly cord to fold it in" (*Paul Faber, Surgeon*, Ch. 7). This conviction that God was everywhere stimulated MacDonald's grand and moving descriptions of nature, rooted in imagination. "God, like . . . light," he wrote, "is all about us, and prefers to shine in upon us sideways" (*Weighed and Wanting*,

Elk grazing in Highlands near Balmoral Castle

Ch. 13). Examples of such imaginative views of nature are numerous: his books are literally full of them. In *Donal Grant*, he wrote of the smells brought by the wind: "The scents the wind brought with it on its way over field and garden and moor, came to him sweeter than ever they had seemed in his life before; they seemed seeking to comfort him. . . . The wind hovered about him in a friendly way, as if it would fain have something to do in the matter; the river rippled and shone, as if it knew something worth knowing which had yet to be revealed. For the delight of creation is verily in secrets, but in secrets only as revelations upon the way . . ." (*Donal Grant*, Ch. 1).

In *Thomas Wingfold, Curate* he compares nature with Scripture: "Then what has nature in common with the Bible. . . ? She has a thousand things. The very wind on my face seems to rouse me to fresh effort after a pure and healthy life! Then there is the sunrise! There is the snowdrop in the snow! There is the butterfly! There is the rain of summer, and the clearing of the sky after a storm! There is the hen gathering her chickens under her wing! I begin to doubt whether there be the commonplace anywhere except in our own mistrusting nature, that will cast no care upon the Unseen" (*Thomas Wingfold*, Ch. 41). In *What's Mine's Mine* he talks of the "mystery" of nature: "She began to feel a mystery in the world, and in all the looks of it—a mystery because a meaning. She saw a jubilance in every sunrise, a sober sadness in every sunset; heard a whispering of strange secrets in the wind of the twilight; perceived a consciousness of unknown bliss in the song of the lark;—and was aware of a something beyond it all, now and then filling her with wonder, and compelling her to ask 'What does it, what can it mean?'" (*What's Mine's Mine*, Ch. 35). And in *There and Back* he sees the Lord in the rising of the moon: "The moon kept rising and brightening, slowly victorious over the pallid light of the dead sun; till at last she lifted herself out of the vaporous horizon-sea, ascended over the tree-tops, and went walking through the unobstructed sky, mistress of the air, queen of the heavens, lady of the eyes of men. Yet she was lady only because she beheld her lord. She saw the light of her light, and told what she saw of him" (*There and Back*, Ch. 66).

For George MacDonald, the miracle and imagination were *one*. "God's imagination . . . ," he wrote, "is the birth and truth of things" (*Salted With Fire*, Ch. 4). Therefore he could, as a poet and an imaginative novelist, make the reader believe what the ecclesiast in the pulpit never could—because the poet touched the imaginations. His truths struck root on a deeper and more foundational level of awareness than words, circumventing the limitations of the conscious mind with its analysis and logical arguments.

This illuminating quality of his writing has been called a "magic torch"—the imagination is magic, and the truths MacDonald conveyed (the "miracle") were light indeed. Often the so-called "inspirational" or "religious" writers of his day took the gaiety and warmth out of their stories by turning them into mere Gospel tracts. MacDonald's light, on the other hand, did not weaken the imaginative vessel, but rather strengthened it. He wrote no tracts; the light that was within him giving rise to his imaginative genius spilled out onto the printed page in spite of himself. Didactic words were hardly necessary, although they are found in his books. The torch was indeed a magic one. The unpretentious innocence of his imagination revealed the miracle without having to discuss it. And even in his didactic moments of straightforward preaching in his novels, the words of argument themselves are not the primary vehicle that in the end communicates truth. Rather the characters themselves, and the interplay of their relationships when pitted against the problems inherent in the plot are vehicles of the truth.

Greville says, "His appeals to the imagination are . . . inspiration indeed. . . . In some prophetic epigram or 'celestial wit,' he will reveal the truth suddenly, convincingly, like the drawing of a nebulous veil from the sky-piercing Jungfrau . . . we light upon this—and then never forget it; *'Freedom is the unclosing of the idea which lies at our root and is the vital power of our existence. The rose is the freedom of the rose-tree'"* (*Donal Grant*, Ch. 30). Or consider the brevity and simplicity of his description of conversion, about which others have written volumes without communicating so much: "The spiritual fluid in which his being floated had become all at once more potent, and he was in consequence uncomfortable. A certain intermittent stinging, as if from the flashes of some moral electricity, had begun to pass in various directions through the crude and chaotic mass he called himself, and he felt strangely restless. It never occurred to him—as how should it?—that he might have commenced undergoing the most marvellous of all changes—one so marvellous, indeed, that for a man to foreknow its result or understand what he was passing through, would be more strange than that a caterpillar should recognize in the rainbow-winged butterfly hovering over the flower at whose leaf he was gnawing the perfected idea of his own potential self—I mean the change of being born again" (*Thomas Wingfold, Curate*, Ch. 11).

North Wind

Many have pointed to *At the Back of the North Wind* as possibly the greatest, because it is the simplest, of all MacDonald's prophetic attempts to unite miracle with imagination. So smoothly do we pass from one world to the other in its pages that before we are through, the two have been fused into one; Diamond's imagination has become *real*. Greville says, "All the strength of its teaching is allusive—an appeal to the imaginative seeing of a truth rather than a claim for its passive acceptance. . . . Who, for instance, can logically accept the doctrine that, God having made the whole world, he being moreover all powerful and all good, everything in the world *must* be good, however much . . . appearances deny the claim?[3] Yet North Wind's statement, as one of God's messengers, about the ship she has to sink strikes something deeper in our hearts than the force of logical, preconceived arguments: "I will tell you how I am able to bear it, Diamond: I am always hearing, through every noise, through all the noise

I am making myself even, the noise of a far-off song. I do not exactly know where it is, or what it means; and I don't hear much of it, only the odour of its music, as it were, flitting across the great billows of the ocean outside this air in which I make such a storm; but what I do hear, is quite enough to make me able to bear the cry from the drowning ship. So it would you if you could hear it" (*At the Back of the North Wind*, Ch. 7).

Wolff comments: "Of all MacDonald's works, *At the Back of the North Wind* has remained the best-known, delighting and disturbing generation after generation of children. It takes place in two worlds, the real world of everyday Victorian London, and the dream-world of the imagination of Diamond, the coachman's son. . . . With equal matter-of-factness, and no change of pace, MacDonald narrates the events that take place in both worlds; so that the dream world seems a natural extension of the real world. . . . We are not here dealing with an explicit transfer from the world of reality to the world of dreams, as in *Phantastes* or the *Alice* books, which are purely dream narratives. For adults, *At the Back of the North Wind* is like Hoffmann's *Golden Pot*: as if falling asleep, almost without warning, we pass from one world to the other, and at times the two worlds are fused. No doubt this is one of the reasons why the book gives children the shivers."[4]

Even the book's imagined narrator furthers the truth that to MacDonald imagination was real with one of the simplest, yet most moving, conclusions MacDonald ever wrote: "I walked up to the winding stair, and entered his room. A lovely figure, as white and almost as clear as alabaster, was lying on the bed. I saw at once how it was. They thought he was dead. I knew that he had gone to the back of the north wind" (*At the Back of the North Wind*, Ch. 38).

Greville adds further: "True feeding of the child is more subtle a thing than psychologist can fathom. George MacDonald did fathom it—and in a way that was absolutely matchless. Magic and mystery, nonsense and fun—in no egregious fashions of the day, but in enduring forms of beauty. . . . *North Wind* is full of light, always renewing itself to this day."[5]

And Ronald writes: "*At The Back of the North Wind* . . . seems to stand, in its mystery and simplicity . . . far above its fellows. Here, for child and man alike, George MacDonald gives us the two worlds coexistent; not *here* and *there*, but both here and now. And its three great persons, North Wind, Diamond the boy, and Diamond the cab-horse, speak more wisdom than will ever be spoken about them."[6]

All George MacDonald's writings were consistent, communicating the same essential truth—that in everything God was to be seen. Thus, as his son says, his "poetical mysticism . . . will hold sway over human hopes and spiritual strife long after the logical ecclesiasticism of [others] is forgotten,"[7] because he touched his readers on all levels—especially the subconscious and emotional level of the imagination.

A poet? Yes. A mystic? Yes. But neither a poet nor a mystic (like so many) for whom poetry or mysticism were ends in themselves—rather, a spiritual mystic whose imagination was always pointing to the One who was his life.

MacDonald's Reply to the Charge of Being Unorthodox

In the climate of his day, this "spiritual" God-directed foundation of George MacDonald's writings was difficult, even impossible, for many traditional minds to fathom. Like Curdie, they walked into the palatial room only to see the bare attic and dirty straw, though MacDonald was standing beside them all the while describing the grandmother most vividly. His writings were truly only for those with "eyes to see and ears to hear." Like his Master who cast the nuggets of His truth into the form of parables so that only the pure in heart would be able to discern their meaning, MacDonald cast the truths of his being into an imaginative mold.

It is true that critics of George MacDonald abound. To this very day there are those who read one or more of his books and wonder why such-and-such a character didn't get saved. Some readers question MacDonald's doctrinal purity because of a doubt voiced by a certain character. Sometimes MacDonald was presenting his own beliefs; other times he was expressing his own spiritual debates.

Throughout his own life there were multitudes to whom his books ministered, yet others (especially in the organized circles of religion) who honestly considered him a heretic against the doctrines that comprised their faith. But such criticism did not alter his convictions. From the pulpit or platform he could hold multitudes enthralled with his tender and compassionate words, but at other times fierce could be his denunciations of pharisaism and false priorities in the church. He feared no one, and boldly proclaimed what he felt compelled to speak. His vehicle for communicating the *miracle* was the *imagination*, and he never tried to make his approach more orthodox to satisfy the tradition-minded. He was forging new ground as a spiritual communicator—using new forms for ancient ideas.

Some accused him of turning his back on the church, whereas in reality the greatness of his imagination led him into higher realms of faith, realms they were unable to comprehend. He received a letter from a lady in the mid-1860s asking him why he had lost the "old faith." His reply is unusually candid and thorough, setting down with great clarity just how deep his faith was, despite what many would regard as "unorthodox" views. His reply straightforwardly sets forth the clear priorities of his commitment to his God. Through his own words we see clearly to Whom he sought to lead others through imaginative writings.

"Have you really been reading my books, and at this time ask me what have I lost of the old faith? Much have I rejected of the new, but I have never rejected anything I could keep. . . . With the faith itself to be found in the old Scottish manse I trust I have a true sympathy. With many of the forms gathered around that faith, I have none. At a very early age I had begun to cast them from me; but all the time my faith in Jesus as the Son of the Father of men and the Savior of us all, has been growing. If it were not for the fear of its sounding unkind, I would say that if you had been a disciple of his instead of mine, you would not have mistaken me so much. Do not suppose that I believe in Jesus because it is said so-and-so in a book. I believe in him because he is himself. The vision of him in that book, and, I trust, his own living power in me, have enabled me to understand him, to look him in the face, as it were, and accept him as my Master and Savior, in following whom I shall come to the rest of the Father's peace. The Bible is to me the most precious thing in the world, because it tells me his story; and what good men thought about him who know him and accepted him.

"But," MacDonald continues, those who hold to "the common theory of the inspiration of the words, instead of the breathing of God's truth into the hearts and souls of those who wrote it . . . are in danger of worshipping the letter instead of living in the Spirit, of being idolators of the Bible instead of disciples of Jesus. . . . It is *Jesus* who is the Revelation of God. . . . Jesus alone is The Word of God.

"With all sorts of doubt I am familiar, and the result of them is, has been, and will be, a widening of my heart and soul and mind to greater glories of the truth—the truth that is in Jesus—and not in Calvin or Luther or St. Paul or St. John, save as they got it from Him, from whom every simple heart may have it, and can alone get it. You cannot have such proof of the existence of God or the truth of the Gospel story as you can have of a . . . chemical experiment. But the man who will order his way by the word of the Master shall partake of his peace, and shall have in himself a growing conviction that in him are hid all the treasures of wisdom and knowledge. . . .

"One thing more I must say: though the Bible contains many an utterance of the will of God, we do not need to go there to find how to begin to do his will. In every heart there is a consciousness of some duty or other required of it: that is the will of God. He who would be saved must get up and do that will—if it be but to sweep a room or make an apology, or pay a debt. It was he who had kept the commandments whom Jesus invited to be his follower in poverty and labour . . .

"From your letter it seems that to be assured of my faith would be a help to you. I cannot say I never doubt, nor until I hold the very heart of good as my very own in Him, can I wish not to doubt. For doubt is the hammer that breaks the windows clouded with human fancies, and lets in the pure light. But I do say that all my hope, all my joy, all my strength are in the Lord Christ and his Father; that all my theories of life and growth are rooted in him; that his truth is gradually clearing up the mysteries of this world. . . . To Him I belong heart and soul and body, and he may do with me as he will—nay, nay—I pray him to do with me as he wills: for that is my only well-being and freedom."[8]

CHAPTER TWENTY-FIVE

ITALY
(1873–1887)

The years 1873 and 1874 were good, happy years spent at the Retreat. Of the American tour Greville says, "I do not think my father brought home with him much over a thousand Pounds," but this seems doubtful unless he overlooked the fact that he had already sent money home previously. Despite the fact that they had to pay a good portion of their own expenses during the eight months, when the number of lectures is realized, and is added to the Copyright Testimonial of $1,500 and the Farewell Lecture, the figure must have been higher. And Greville notes later that the tour did give his father "temporary alleviation of his debts."

In the autumn of 1873 George and Louisa, with two of the girls, again visited Huntly and Cullen, for last-minute preparations on *Malcolm*, in its final stages. Visits from new American friends began almost immediately, including one from Mark Twain. (Twain wrote about a book exchange with MacDonald: "I'll send you the book . . . as soon as it issues from the press. . . . I will take *At the Back of the North Wind* in return, for our children's sake's; they have read and re-read their own copy so many times that it looks as if it had been through the wars."[1] Seventeen years later, in 1899, Twain wrote to another friend about the death of his daughter three years earlier: "How desperately I have been moved tonight by the thought of a little old copy in the nursery of *At the Back of the North Wind*. Oh, what happy days they were when that book was read, and how Suzy loved it!"[2])

Tubercular Troubles of a New Generation

In 1874 daughter Mary first caught scarlet fever, from which she recovered. But not long thereafter tuberculosis began to affect her. Thinking the riverfront location of the Retreat was possibly to blame, the MacDonalds began to spend more and more time down on the coast at Hastings, where for a couple of years they had also maintained a home. They began to search for an alternative in the London area as well. After a couple of short-term rental tenancies, in the fall of 1875 they leased a pretty and newly built house at Boscombe and named it "Corage," the first word in George MacDonald's anagram and personal family motto: "Corage! God mend al!" Aware of their shortcomings in the education of Greville, George and Louisa brought in a tutor to teach the four younger boys Latin, mathematics, and other related subjects.

George's health continued up and down, especially during winters. Now that Greville was attending medical school in London and was being largely supported in *his* education by his father, as the father himself had been by his own years earlier, bills and finances were still a factor of concern. Partially to relieve the financial burdens, and partially to fulfill herself creatively, Louisa took steps about this time to produce some of the family theatrical successes for the public. They were so successful, both artistically and financially, that she was encouraged to continue. She rented a hall and the first genuinely "public" performance of *The Pilgrim's Progress* was given at Christchurch in Hampshire in 1877, on March 8th— their 26th wedding anniversary.

Throughout these years George MacDonald's work became more and more urgent to him. His letters seem always trying to balance the work he wanted to do with the sicknesses that kept preventing him:

". . . This illness compels me to change my plan and finish one volume before I write the whole. If it pleases God that I do that, it must be the best way, though I can't quite see that it is. . . . I am very stupid. My windows are darkened—*all but the skylights*. But I think I shall soon be all right again. . . ."[3]

Edward Hughes, nephew of the renowned artist Arthur Hughes, who was a friend of the MacDonalds and the illustrator of several MacDonald volumes, had proposed to Mary. However, her condition was now rapidly deteriorating. By the autumn of 1877 she had become so diseased in the lungs that it was decided she must spend the winter in Italy. Louisa wrote to a wealthy old relative of hers, appealing for a loan of 300 pounds to help them make the trip for this young cousin of his. In a very affectionate letter full of conventionally religious jargon, he regretted that he had to "decline her request." But the trip had to be made, money or no money. So Louisa, along with four of the children, made the journey to Nervi, where they rented a home called the Palazzo Cattaneo for the winter. Remaining behind to finalize the dismemberment of the Retreat, which they had now left for the last time, and to conclude negotiations for *Paul Faber, Surgeon*, which his publisher had at first refused, George and the others followed, joining them on the Mediterranean about a month later. When all was settled, only 400 pounds were received for the book, less than half of what he had then been receiving. The fine man of business to whom Louisa had written died the next year, childless, with an estate valued at over 100,000 pounds.

Though the dry heat of Italy was physically rejuvenating for George, the next two years proved perhaps the heaviest burdened of all the nearly thirty of their marriage. Mary died at Nervi in April of 1878, two months before her 25th birthday. They had faced the rapid consumptions of Alec and John, the poet's brothers, and had suffered through little Bella's latter days, but now perhaps for the first time the full tragedy of death assailed them. In Mary the desire for life and the strong sense of its worth remained forceful until the very last, even as her emaciated, cough-racked body clung to the love of her parents and the beauty of the earth. She knew what was coming and her soul was at peace. Yet she wanted desperately to live, and they never gave up hoping. Thus the blow, when it came, was overwhelming.

Though two months prior to Mary's death George wrote, "Surely the father is with us, and the shadow that seems to deepen is but the shadow cast from his hands by the light of his countenance,"[4] Louisa, as Greville says, was "shaken to the very foundations of her soul." "The loss," he goes on, "was not less terrible that ten other darling worlds remained hungry for her care, nor that their father was still needing her support and comforting."[5] For March and April—during Mary's final days—George had had a six-week bout with invalidism himself, still troubled in his lungs, though under the warm Italian sun the attack was far less severe. It took six months for the tears finally to dry over Mary's death. "Love Me, Beloved," written so many years ago, had anticipated death. And nothing in all George MacDonald's writings, published and unpublished, can compare with the beauty and tenderness of his personal letters of consolation written to friends upon the loss of a loved one. Touching the eternal, the dominant theme of all such letters was the emphatic truth that death is but the beginning of true life. Yet now he found that such words could not ease his own wife's pain.

The healing hand of time ultimately closed the wound in Louisa's soul, but could never hide the scar. Mary's illness, however, possibly proved to be one of the instruments that prolonged the life of her father, for the climate in Italy turned out so restorative to George that they decided to remain for another year. When the lease on Palazzo Cattaneo was up, they rented the Villa Barratta at Porto Fino for an additional twelve months, about halfway between Genoa and Spezzia, so secluded a spot that they could only reach it by rowboat. Writing to a friend, MacDonald was apparently contemplating another lecture tour: "We do not return to England this year. We live cheaper here, and another winter of Italy will do much for me and perhaps make me able to encounter another in America. . . ."[6] And Lilia wrote to a friend, "Here we have such a domestic, secluded, delicious life and see three times as much of Papa as we used to at home. He is hard at work as ever. The country all about us is lovely even in winter."[7]

The previous year, before leaving England, no doubt as a result of his close friendship with the Mount-Temples, George MacDonald had been presented to the Queen's daughter, Princess Alice, at Buckingham Palace. Because of her influence, and possibly that of other of his influential friends, Queen Victoria granted him a Civil List Pension of 100 pounds per year. He received notification of it in a letter from Lord Beaconsfield's secretary just before leaving for Italy. In addition to the financial blessing, he was named in a friend's will as the beneficiary of a substantial sum, a sad monetary windfall. Reflecting on death and growing older, he wrote to a friend: ". . . Yes, I have never known such a time. Friend after friend going. . . . But our hope is in heaven. God comes nearer and nearer. If only we went as fast as he was drawing us. . . . If we would but understand that we are pilgrims and strangers! It is no use trying to nestle down.

"Things look much better for me now, I thank God, in money ways. He will keep me short, I daresay, as will probably always be best for me, but he will enable me to die without debt, I do think. Mr. Russell Gurney has left me 500 Pounds, which will go far to clear me off, I hope—would almost, if I were not straitened for present cash. But I do not want this talked about. . . . *Paul Faber* will be out in . . . October, and a new story . . . is more than half done. . . ."[8]

Though the heat was a tonic to George, through the summer following Mary's death Louisa was extremely frail and could hardly move about. In their own little boat George and the boys would row out into the little bay. Much of every day was spent swimming in the sea. The "new story" was none other than the masterpiece *Sir Gibbie*. Its completion at Porto Fino demonstrated that along with renewed physical strength came mental and emotional vigor as well. Though written entirely in Italy, the clarity of MacDonald's memory of his homeland is vivid. *Sir Gibbie* is one of the most picturesque and moving of his Scottish novels, the scenes from the Deeside no less *real*, considering the author was a thousand miles away when he penned them. Even though he lived for decades in both England and Italy, to Scotland he always returned for his strongest work.

Death Comes Close

So the year 1879 dawned with renewed hopes. However, before three months had passed, new grief had overtaken them. Maurice, not the healthiest of the children and troubled by an abscess in the knee earlier and with tuberculosis already at work, caught pneumonia and after a brief eighteen-day illness suddenly died. He was but fifteen. Letters first from George, then from Louisa, both to the same friend, speak of a more victorious outlook. *Weighed and Wanting*, written just after Maurice's death, contains a lovely characature of the peaceful boy in Mark of the story, as well as an autobiographical glimpse into the effect of his death on the family.

". . . It is a sore affliction, but though cast down we are not destroyed. Jesus rose again glorious, and to that I cleave fast. My boy is of course dearer to me than before, and we shall find him again, with his love as fresh as the life that cannot die. Not a murmur escaped him. His contentment was lovely and his soul strong to the end—his obedience perfect—and his rest in God marvellous."[9]

"Alas, that we should be such complaining, difficult children to bear the gifts and the discipline of the father! He has, as it were, given stronger and better life back into the hands of my husband, and yet he has taken to himself that strong young life that seemed to be preparing so vigorously, so manfully for the soldiership to which he was called. . . . Ah! dear friend, it is so wrenching: and yet why strive with the Giver because He cares *more* for his lovely gift than we did or can? We love to think the sweet daughter and son are together. . . . Surely some day, even here, I shall be able to thank the Father for taking him to himself: at present I cannot get further than asking, as I heard Maurice himself in a whisper doing, for 'all to be taken away that now makes it hard to say *Thy will be done*.'. . .

"I wonder whether you will be surprised to hear that we are intending to act our Bunyan's *Pilgrim's Progress* wherever we can. We have already made four engagements, the results of which will pay—and more—our journey home. But then we must have some more in order to pay our journey back. It is so wonderful to have Mr. MacDonald writing away without cough or asthma—day after day. . . ."[10]

Surely this time of growth was at the root of the words MacDonald would later write to a friend at the tragic loss of his son:

"Dear Old Friend,
What can I say to you, for the hand of the Lord is heavy upon you.

The River Dee and the surrounding countryside known as Deeside—site of fictional River Daur and opening scenes of Sir Gibbie.

But it is his hand, and the very heaviness of it is good. . . . There is but one thought that can comfort, and that is that God is immeasurably more the father of our children than we are. It is all because he is our father that we are fathers. . . . It is all well—even in the face of such pain as yours—or the world goes to pieces for me.

It is well to say 'The Lord gave and the Lord hath taken away,' but it is not enough. We must add, And the Lord will give again: 'The gifts of God are without repentance.' He takes that he may give more closely— make *more ours*. . . . The bond is henceforth closer between you and your son. . . .

> To give a thing and take again
> Is counted meanness among men;
> Still less to take what once is given
> Can be the royal way of heaven!
>
> But human hearts are crumbly stuff,
> And never, never love enough;
> And so God takes and, with a smile,
> Puts our best things away awhile.
>
> Some therefore weep, some rave, some scorn;
> Some wish they never had been born;
> Some humble grow at last and still,
> And then God gives them what they will."[11]

For Louisa, in spite of this double tragedy, these years in Italy brought renewed hope that possibly God had given it to them as a land of promise where, as her son rather glowingly phrased it, "her prophet was to find rest for his tired brain, health for his constantly ailing body, air for his spiritual wings."[12] His returning vigor was clearly evident to those closest to him, and was reflected in the books of this period, which are some of his strongest.

Faith usually requires an ordeal to test and validate its worth. Surely the years 1878–1879 provided that ordeal in George and Louisa Mac-Donald's walk of faith. On many previous occasions he had written about the intrinsic role of doubt in the fortification and vitalization of one's trust in God. And yet now, putting the words to work in his own life did not come automatically. During this time he wrote: ". . . Never had I so many worldly mosquitoes about me, but they don't get within my curtains much. I grow surer and surer . . . and I don't think I shall be long ill. I have seldom been quieter in mind than this day—but I am sometimes hard put to it with the Apollyon of unbelief. . . ."[13]

Such words seem almost shocking in light of the rock of faith demonstrated in other letters. But for George MacDonald, faith was never static. It was always growing, moving, always being tested, always doubting . . . then reaching still higher for the next plateau of stronger and deeper conviction of God's truth and goodness. A man or woman is *more* to be respected, not less, for being able to admit to what so many of us try to hide—doubt, despair, stumbling failures. Ready to confess weakness,

MacDonald was an intensely human man; not one to put on the pedestal of greatness with a halo about his head, but a man whose earthly example shows us the direction from which the light is coming. Even as all those around him, especially his own family, relied on this man as a mainstay of spiritual courage and tenacity, he himself seemed unaware of the strength that had slowly blossomed through the years of doubt and trial—always expressing the need for more growth, greater trust, always aware of the great lack of the deep dependence on God he longed to see reflected in his life. Doubt—even unbelief—can be a tool in God's hand wielded, in the lives of those who allow it, for the *strengthening*, not the destruction of faith. The faith of Hebrews 11:1, which "is the substance of things hoped for, the evidence of things not seen" is rooted in divine knowledge, worked out—"proved"—in the battle lines of painful human suffering.

In two of his books, written in this period of heartache, he clarifies the faith that cannot be sustained only on an intellectual level, speaking to himself as well:

"To make things real to us, is the end and battle-cause of life. We often think we believe what we are only presenting to our imaginations. The least thing can overthrow that kind of faith. The imagination is an endless help toward faith, but it is no more faith than a dream of food will make us strong for the next day's work. To know God as the beginning and end, the root and cause, the giver, the enabler, the love and joy and perfect good, the present one existence in all things and degrees and conditions, is life. And faith, in its simplest, truest, mightiest form, is—to do his will in the one thing revealing itself at the moment as duty. The faith that works miracles is an inferior faith to this—and not what the old theologians call a saving faith" (*Donal Grant,* Ch. 1).

He then goes on to affirm there is a deeper way of knowing than by the intellect. "A man may look another in the face for a hundred years and not know him. Men *have* looked Jesus Christ in the face, and not known either him or his father. . . . Do you ask why no intellectual proof is to be had? I tell you that such would but delay, perhaps altogether impair for you, that better, that best, that only vision, into which at last your world must blossom—such a contact, namely, with the heart of God himself . . . as, by its own radiance, will sweep doubt away forever. Being then in the light and knowing it, the lack of intellectual proof concerning that which is too high for it will trouble you no more than would your inability to silence a metaphysician who declared that you had no real existence. It is for the sake of such a vision as God would give you that you are denied such a vision as you would have. The Father of our spirits is not content that we should know him as we now know each other. There is a better, closer, nearer than any human way of knowing, and to that he is guiding us across all the swamps of our unteachableness, the seas of our faithlessness, the deserts of our ignorance. . . . The mists and the storms and the cold will pass—the sun and the sky are forevermore" (*Paul Faber, Surgeon,* Ch. 32).

One more book belongs to these days, inspired by the sufferings brought on by the loss of his two children, a book whose full title perhaps reveals more about it than anything that could be said: *A Book of Strife in the Form of the Diary of an Old Soul*. It was an intensely private book, whose brief daily poems offer tiny windows into the sometimes tired, sometimes hurting heart of their author. It was not a book George Mac-Donald wrote for the public in the same way as his others. It was printed privately, and few efforts were made to distribute it widely. In fact, mentioning the book in a lecture, John Ruskin raised many questions among his listeners. A reviewer of the lecture wrote, "Mr. Ruskin instanced Mr. George MacDonald's *Diary of an Old Soul* as a proof that Faith and Poetry were still united. . . . Everybody is asking to-day what that *Diary* is. Nobody seems to have heard of it until Mr. Ruskin mentioned it. I believe it has not been advertised, indeed is sold almost privately. . . ."[14] But George Mac-Donald had written it for himself, to express the pains of his heart, with their correspondent quiet joys.

Between England and Italy

Between 1879 and 1887 the large household spent each winter in Italy, a tremendous undertaking that would not have been possible without the income generated by *The Pilgrim's Progress* and a few other plays. These were given in the summer all over England and even in Scotland. A house had been planned and built in the late 1870s, named Casa Coraggio (House of Courage), located in Bordighera, Italy, only about three or four miles from the French border on the Italian coast. Contributions for the house were made by many of the MacDonalds' wealthy friends, the Queen's daughter Alice, and others of the nobility. It was a huge home, giving them ample space to entertain and give lectures, and had an immense study for the writer. Every fall the MacDonalds retired to Bordighera, where their new home quickly became the center of life for a rapidly growing colony of intellectual Scots and English in the area.

At first George had been less than enthusiastic about the drama presentations. But he supported them, knowing that his wife felt a sense of mission about it, in much the same way as he felt about his writing. If God had led her into it, he would back her all the way. For Louisa, the acting troupe, whose company was large and by this time involved many more than their immediate family, had become a spiritual enterprise equal to her husband's expositions via the printed page. Her directional gifts and interpretation of *The Pilgrim's Progress* had a profound impact on most who saw it, being a true spiritual art form. There were many, however, especially relatives, who were against it for a variety of reasons. Louisa persevered, however; lives were touched, and the hard work was always rewarded by the Italian winters beneath gorgeous blue skies, olive woods, palms and roses, and the serenity of Casa Coraggio. Louisa was both director and mother to her company. In 1881 Louisa adopted two little girls and subsequently their ailing mother, who appeared at death's very door. For the next seven years they lived as part of the family at Casa Corraggio, the two children educated by Louisa's own daughters.

The settings and props for the plays were made by Louisa and her girls. Musical accompaniment for the singing of the actors was provided by nothing more than a piano and sometimes a violin. George worked on his proofs backstage while waiting for his call as Mr. Greatheart, the name by which he gradually became known among his close friends in after years. In 1881 the daughter of the Bishop of Carlisle had been bitterly disappointed at having been sick and therefore prevented from seeing the play. When a friend told George about her, he quietly picked up a bit of paper, wrote on it, folded it, and gave it to her, saying, "Give that to her with my love." Presumably the disappointment of the young girl was healed by the message:

> Pain and sorrow,
> Plough and harrow,
> For the seed its place to find;
> > For the growing
> > Still the blowing
> Of the Spirit's thinking wind;
> > For the corn that it will bear,
> > Love eternal everywhere.[15]

Tuberculosis continued to stalk the MacDonald clan; Grace's lungs gave way in 1884 and she followed Mary and Maurice.

A Hospitable Home

The big home at Bordighera was always open. On Wednesday afternoons throughout the winter, George would read or expound upon his favorite literature. During some winters, he offered courses on Dante or Shakespeare. On Sundays sometimes a hundred or more would gather. Louisa would play a fine pipe organ that had been donated for the house, and direct a choir—also organized and trained by her. At eight o'clock George would take his seat by the fire and read or expound upon Scripture. One visitor said it was worth a journey from London to hear him read the forty-third chapter of Isaiah. Another recalled a simple word of wisdom he first heard from that chair: "If anyone tells me it is an easy thing to speak the truth, I should tell him that he had never tried it."[16]

Greville recalls the scene, "I have many vivid pictures of my father hung in the long gallery of my life. They glow in colour, and . . . this [one] had a niche and illumination all its own: the old man with his white head and beard, his searching blue eyes with crimson velvet cap, seated in low armchair by the fire, two candles on a little gate-legged table before him, the red glow of the olive logs occasionally breaking into flame and lighting up the green and red tiles, just as his words of fire leapt into flaming life and drove out the dark shadows from our souls. I recall no other light in the great room, and its contrast with the listeners so still and rapt. At last my father would, perhaps quite unexpectedly, rise and kneel, so that all, needy or critical, whatever their creed or hope, must feel their hearts opening out to God. . . . And then came a blessing, wonderful in its quiet, deeply penetrating, almost tremulous words . . . of . . . benediction; then a deep silence, and perhaps the organ softly rolling forth Handel's Largo from the far Jerusalem. Still and quiet even now, the guests would at last rise and go down the wide stone stair and out beneath the flashing stars of the huge Italian sky."[17]

Christmas was always a happy time, with carol singing, a large Christmas tree, Italian children, and great hospitality—the house was always full of guests and relatives. Even if the beauty and extent of the geniality was greater, the simplicity was reminiscent of the first Christmas at the Tackleway with its penny toys and books and oranges and storytelling by the young father. Lord Mount-Temple in his *Memorials* talks about one memorable Christmas he spent in Italy:

". . . On Christmas Eve, we were dining in our little room looking on the olive wood, and we heard the sound of many voices, and looking out, lamps glimmered among the trees, and figures carrying lanterns and sheets of music. Who should they be but the dear MacDonald family visiting the houses of all the invalids of the place, to sing them carols and bring them the glad tidings of Christmas."[18]

Another instance of Louisa's imagination and resourcefulness in entertainment, as well as her sense of humor, appeared in an invitation to their friends for a New Year's Eve celebration, verses supplied by her husband, with *his* sense of humor, of course:

> Please come on Monday
> The day after Sunday,
> And mind that you start with
> Something to part with;
> A fire shall be ready
> Glowing and steady
> To receive it and burn it
> And never return it.
> Books that are silly,
> Clothes outworn and chilly,
> Hats, umbrellas or bonnets,
> Dull letters, bad sonnets,
> Whate'er to the furnace
> By nature calls "Burn us!"
> An ancient, bad temper
> Will be noted no damper—
> The fire will not scorn it
> But glory to burn it!
> Here every bad picture
> Finds refuge from stricture;
> Or any old grudge
> That refuses to budge,
> We'll make it the tomb
> For all sorts of gloom,

The out-of-door path
For every man's wrath.
All lying and hinting,
All jealous squinting,
All unkind talking
And each other balking,
Let the fire's holy actions
Turn to ghostly abstractions.
All antimacassars,
All moth-egg amassers,
Old gloves and old feathers,
Old shoes and old leathers,
Greasy or tar-ry,
Bring all you can carry!
We would not deceive you:
The fire shall relieve you,
The world will feel better,
And so be your debtor.
Be welcome then—very—
And come and be merry!

GEORGE AND LOUISA MACDONALD
Bonfire at 7 P.M.
Dancing at 8.

CASA CORAGGIO
Dec. 31st, 1885[19]

Even in fun, George MacDonald's deep beliefs could not but spill over in a parable of the purifying of God's fires! The former message of sermons now found outlet in handwritten party invitations.

In Italy George also took up bookbinding (a lifelong fascination) as a more serious hobby. Hours on end he spent with paste and paper and parchment and scraps of leather, enjoying more than anything the restoration of old and damaged books. His love for books from this new angle found its way into *There and Back*, the third novel involving the character Thomas Wingfold, which was written in Italy as MacDonald was teaching himself the art.

In February of 1887, a dreadful earthquake struck the coast of Italy, devastating the villages of the poor. Even Casa Coraggio, with its solid stone walls, lost a tower and suffered a good deal of cracking. The household was thrown into a havoc for weeks and was opened to some of the nearby families whose houses had fallen in.

George wrote to a friend: "... We have had the most extraordinary time—terrible indeed in its awfulness. That one shock was worth having lived to know what power may be. You knew it must be none other than God. No lesser power could hold the earth like that, as if it were 'A very little thing,' and shake you as if your big house were a doll's fly.... Don't be anxious about us. We are all right...."[20]

As usual, the earthquake found its way into a book with great realism, as had the floods of Scotland that MacDonald had witnessed as a boy. *A Rough Shaking*, the only of MacDonald's novels partially set in Italy, was written about a year later.

Of this autumn period in his parents' lives, Greville comments: "Greater happiness was theirs, I think, during this period, even if the multifold sadness of migrating hopes kept their eyes increasingly upon the horizon. . . . Material comfort was added in more than one beautiful home of their own, and much quiet joy came from my father's increasing influence in the thoughts and faiths of men. . . ."[21]

CHAPTER TWENTY-SIX

THE VALLEY OF THE SHADOW
(1887–1905)

George and Louisa lived the rest of their lives, with intermittent temporary changes, at Bordighera. The drama productions ended in 1888, but George's writing did not diminish in the least. He had begun to use a typewriter in the early '80s, no longer writing out every manuscript in longhand. And during the ten years of that decade (1880–1890), fifteen new titles were released, in addition to several reprints: seven novels; two volumes of poetry—*Diary of an Old Soul* (1880) and *A Threefold Cord* (1883)*; two volumes of sermons—*Unspoken Sermons, Vol. 2* (1885) and *Unspoken Sermons, Vol. 3* (1889); two collections of essays on literature—*Orts* (1882) and *The Tragedie of Hamlet* (1885)†; and a collection of short stories entitled *The Gifts of the Child Christ and Other Tales* (1882).

The novels were: *Mary Marston* (1881); *Castle Warlock* (1882), for which the author received 400 pounds, a novel set in the Highlands south of Huntly in the little valley of "the Cabrach," where the MacDonalds occasionally had vacationed when George was a boy and which so characterizes MacDonald's vision of the father-son relationship; *Weighed and Wanting* (1882); *Donal Grant* (1883), the gripping and suspenseful sequel to *Sir Gibbie,* which boasts one of MacDonald's saddest endings; *What's Mine's Mine* (1886), a Highland tale set in the remote region north of Inverness, full of clan history and Highland flavor, a true "historical" adventure, an accurate picture of the disintegration of the clan structure that took place in the Highlands of Scotland in the late 18th and early 19th centuries; *Home Again* (1887); and *The Elect Lady* (1888).

Most of MacDonald's novels appeared initially in three-volume sets.

---

*The subtitle for this volume was "Poems by Three Friends, edited by George Mac-Donald"; it contained the poetry of Greville Matheson, George MacDonald, and George's brother John Hill MacDonald.

†Ronald calls this "George MacDonald's greatest achievement of literary interpretation . . . a work of deep insight and high scholarship."[1]

Customarily, he would first write a sketch or outline for the entire book. If this was satisfactory to the publisher, he would then begin and the publisher would release each of the segments as he completed them. A one-volume edition would usually follow shortly after the completion of the whole. The writing schedule was particularly taxing in that he had to fit it around numerous speaking engagements and the drama performances during the 1880s.

The Passing of Lilia

With the passage of years, death seemed to be closing in on all sides. Almost every year brought new grief, and with it fresh challenges. His letters of consolation continued to be, not only meaningful to their recipients, but illustrative of the vision that sustained their writer as the sun gradually set upon his life. He wrote from Casa Coraggio in Bordighera:

BELOVED FRIEND

Do not start at the warmth of my address, for brief as was our opportunity of knowing each other, it was more than long enough to make me love you. I write because I hear you are very ill. I know not a little about illness, and my heart is with you in yours. Be of good courage; there is a live heart at the centre of the lovely order of the Universe—a heart to which all the rest is but a clothing form—a heart that bears every truthful thought, every help-needing cry of each of its children, and must deliver them.

All my life, I might nearly say, I have been trying to find that one Being, and to know him consciously present; hope grows and grows with the years that lead me nearer to the end of my earthly life; and in my best moods it seems ever that the only thing worth desiring is that his will be done; that there lies before me a fulness of life, sufficient to content the giving of a perfect Father, and that the part of the child is to yield all and see that he does not himself stand in the way of the mighty design.

But why do I write thus to you who may know all this, tenfold better than I? Just because I want to come near to you in your illness. . . . Christ speaks of the world's goods as not ours—as things that cannot be ours, but are in their nature foreign to power of possession. Our own things are the riches towards God. What I may have in this kind I offer you, in love and sympathy with you and yours.

May the great life whose creating power of Love be with you and make you strong and comfort you. . . .

May he make you triumph over pain and doubt and dread, and restore you to perfect, divine health. . . .[2]

The friend was restored to "perfect, divine health" even sooner than MacDonald had anticipated; he died before the letter reached him.

And to a very close friend after the death of her husband, he wrote:

"Yes, dear, it is a hard time for you, but he is drawing you nearer to himself. You will have, I think, to consent to be miserable so far as loneliness makes you miserable, and look to him and him only for comfort. But the words that the Lord speaks are spirit and life. We are in a house with windows on all sides. On the one side the sweet garden is trampled and torn, the beeches blown down, the fountain broken; you sit and look out, and it is all very miserable. Shut the window. I do not mean forget the garden as it was, but do not brood on it as it is. Open the window on the other side, where the great mountains shoot heavenward, and the stars rising and setting, crown their peaks. Down those stairs look for the descending feet of the Son of Man coming to comfort you. This world, if it were alone, would not be worth much—I should be miserable already; but it is the porch to the Father's home, and he does not expect us to be quite happy, and knows we must sometimes be very unhappy till we get there."[3]

By now Greville was a practicing physician who would eventually write not only his biography of his parents (1924) and his own autobiography, *Reminiscences of a Specialist* (1932), in which he recalls growing up in the MacDonald household, but also a number of novels of his own. Ronald too, after his contribution to *From a Northern Window* (1910), would go on to become a novelist in his own right. Ronald married in 1888, and went to the United States for the sake of his wife's health, but she died in 1890. His eldest sister, Lilia, joined him there for several months to keep house and offer what consolation was possible.

But the "family attendant," as MacDonald occasionally called it, was hounding this fair young woman of 38 years herself. Lilia had been a great joy to her parents. Her portrayal of Christiana in *Pilgrim's Progress* had earned her a wide reputation, and she had been urged by many to join the theater in London, where it was felt she would become highly successful. Her parents urged against it because of the questionable moral quality of theater life in the city. She respected their wishes, remaining with them her entire life. She had grown into mature womanhood, helped to raise all the younger children, and had now come to share life with George and Louisa on the equal plane of adulthood. She had truly become a sister to them as well as a daughter. The following letter from her father while she was with Ronald in America seems to anticipate what is coming, though at the time neither of them knew it. The occasion is her thirty-ninth birthday in January of 1891.

DEAREST CHILD,
    I could say so much to you, and yet I am constantly surrounded by a sort of cactus-hedge that seems to make adequate utterance impossible. It is so much easier to write romances where you cannot easily lie, than to say the commonest things where you may go wrong any moment. . . . I can only tell you I love you with true heart fervently, and love you far more because you are God's child than because you are mine.—I don't thank you for coming to us, for you could not help it, but the whole universe is "tented" with love, and you hold one of the corners of the great love-canopy for your mother and me. I don't think I am very ambitious, except the strong desire "to go where I am" be

ambition; and I know I take small satisfaction in looking on my past; but I do live expecting great things in the life that is ripening for me and all mine—when we shall all have the universe for our own, and be good merry helpful children in the great house of our Father. I think then we shall be able to pass into and through each other's very souls as we please, knowing each other's thought and being, along with our own, and so being like God. When we are all just as loving and unselfish as Jesus; when like him, our one thought of delight is that God is, and is what he is; when the fact that a being is just another person from ourselves is enough to make that being precious—then, darling, you and I and all will have the grand liberty wherewith Christ makes free—opening his hand to send us out like white doves to range the Universe.

Have I now shown that the attempt to speak what I mean is the same kind of failure that walking is—a mere, constantly recurring recovery from falling? . . .

I have still one *great* poem in my mind, but it will never be written, I think, except we have a fortune left us, so that I need not write any more stories—of which I am beginning to be tired. . . .

My dear love to Ronald. I could not bear you to leave him any more than you could yourself. Tell him from me that Novalis says: "This world is not a dream, but it may, and perhaps ought to become one." Anyhow it will pass—to make way for the world God has hidden in our hearts.

Darling, I wish you life eternal. I daresay the birthdays will still be sparks in its glory. May I one day see that mould in God out of which you came.

> Your loving
> FATHER[4]

When Ronald's spirits revived, Lilia returned to Casa Coraggio to nurse a friend who spent the winters at Bordighera and who was now suffering from tuberculosis. Though by this time everyone was aware that the disease was contagious, she waited upon her friend day and night. The dying woman would often refuse food and medicine except from Lilia's hand, so that she fed the starved fire with her own life. George, then sixty-seven, seeming wonderfully fit for his work, was away on his final lengthy lecturing tour of England, Scotland, and Wales when news of his daughter's friend's death came, her final days being terrible ones. Lilia's devotion was so total that her own infection seemed inevitable, and the signs of it were immediate.

While away George again visited Huntly where his cousin James, with whom he had grown up, was now in possession of the Farm. He wrote, ". . . I have just returned with James from the churchyard where the bodies of all my people are laid—a grassy place, and very quiet, in the middle of undulatory fields and with bare hills all about. But I see the country more beautiful than I used to see it. The air is delicious, and full of sweet odours, mostly white clover, and there is over it much sky. I get little bits of dreamy pleasure sometimes, but none without the future to set things right. 'What is it all for?' I should constantly be saying with Tolstoi, but for the hope of the glory of God. . . ."[5]

The losses of this period were not all from death. In September came news that the bank where they had over 2,000 pounds in savings had gone under and everything was lost. As all his life George MacDonald had refused to insure either his life or his possessions, this account had been the only bequest he had for his wife and family in the event that he could no longer create earnings with his pen; it was the first time in their long marriage they had actually been in possession of a "surplus." Yet the grief they felt seemed minimal, almost humorous, and there was never a word of reproach to the trustee responsible for the unwise investment.

There was never even a slight hope for so much as a temporary improvement for Lilia. Writing to his wife while in London with Greville at the end of his lecture tour, MacDonald says: ". . . My memory gets so troublesome—I suppose by my brain being tired. I have things to tell you, and then by the time I sit down to write, I cannot remember them. . . . For Lily, it seems just the old story of ups and downs. But we must remember that we are only in a sort of passing vision here, and that the real life lies beyond us. If Lily goes now, how much the sooner you and I may find her again! Life is waiting us. We have to awake—or die—which you will—to reach it. Only let us believe the great way, and trust altogether. When I come, I shall be able to help you. . . . We have had a nice talk, Greville and I, at and after lunch. . . .

"'Has he been overworking himself,' he asked a patient concerning her husband who had gone out of his mind. 'Oh, dear, no! We belong to the landed gentry,' was her reply! . . ."[6]

A heart-rending letter from Louisa to George then tells of Louisa's journey by train with Lilia and the two other girls and of Lilia's self-control—sitting straight upright, showing no fatigue, and without so much as a cough, yet the life dying within her. Then she adds the poignant words: ". . . But oh! she did suffer!—and indeed all her life she has been an intensely suffering soul. Knowing all I do now of what unintentional agonies we have made our children suffer all the while having a heart full of love and intended good-will to them, I could not *dare*, of my choice, have over again such a lovely family as was given to us to rear and teach and guide. Well, thank God, with all our mistakes and come-shortednesses, the children are and have been all trying to do their duty, and in their measure serving their God. . . ."[7]

To his wife in the first week of November (1891), one week before he was due home, George wrote, ". . . This is your birthday, dearest. I hope you are full of hope in it. Though the outer decay, the inner, the thing that trusts in the perfect creative life, grows stronger—does it not. God will be better to us than we think, however expectant we be. . . .

"Dearest, my love to you on this your birthday—a good day for me. I thank God for you."[8]

And the very next day he wrote again, saying, ". . . I may as well use this paper which wrapt my last lecture-fee to write my next to last letter to you. . . . My work is done and I am better now than when I began it—48 lectures in 58 days. . . . I hope I shall be able to help you in the nursing. . . .

"G. says I have 15 or 20 years' work in me yet. The doctors say a man's age is the age of his arteries, and there is no decay, no age in mine. He says there is not an unsound spot in me. . . ."[9]

George reached Bordighera on November 8, and Lilia died in his arms exactly two weeks later at 39.

Bunyan's Mr. Greatheart had come to bid Christiana farewell at the river's edge as she preceded him to the other side. How prophetic the words became that they had so often played to one another on the stage!

Quoting from the book, Greville poignantly paints the picture of the father and daughter:

"'So the Post from the Celestial City presented her with a letter. When he had read this letter to her, he gave her therewith a sure token that he was a true messenger, and was come to bid her make haste to be gone. The token was, an arrow with a point sharpened with love, let easily into her heart, which by degrees wrought so effectually with her, that at the time appointed she must be gone. . . . She called for Mr. Greatheart, her guide, and told him how matters were. So he told her he was heartily glad of the news, and could have been glad had the post come for him, saying, 'thus and thus it must be; and we that survive will accompany you to the river side.'

"While the coffin was carried into the church the congregation joined in the singing, 'My God, my Father, while I stray.' The tremulous, subdued voices showed how deeply everyone was mourning the loss of a cherished friend, that woman who, from her very childhood, had been a mother to old and young. Her father could hardly leave the grave: he came back twice after all others had left, and it was with difficulty he was at last led away. The day was terribly wet: all nature was lamenting.

"'But Christiana answered, "Come wet, come dry, I long to be gone: for however the weather is in my journey, I shall have time enough when I come there to sit down and rest, and dry me." . . . The last words she was heard to say were, "I come, Lord, to be with thee, and bless thee!" So her children and friends returned to their place, for those that waited for Christiana had carried her out of their sight. At her departure her children wept.'

"Only one picture of Mr. Greatheart hangs in my [mental] gallery. I see him clad from shoulders to feet in chain-mail and camail, with the white, red-crossed surcoat and his great two-handed sword. He has seen Christiana disappear in the Dark River, and then comes down to the listeners who wait upon his every word, saying, 'Thanks be to God who has given us the victory!'"[10]

MacDonald's own words of several years earlier to the wife of a departed friend surely echoed the sentiments with which he would seek to find comfort for him and his wife at this loss of their firstborn:

MY DEAR MRS. MCLEOD

I almost dread drawing near you with a letter. It seems as if all one could do, was to be silent and walk softly. Yet I would not have you think me heedless of you and your sorrow. And yet again, what is there to say? Comfort, all save what we can draw for ourselves from that eternal heart, is a phantom—a mere mockery. Either one must say and the other must believe that there is ground for everlasting exultation, or comfort is but the wiping of tears that for ever flow.

The sun shines, the wind blows soft, the summer is in the land; but your summer sun and your winter fire is gone, and the world is waste to you. So let it be. Your life is hid with Christ in God, at the heart of all summers—so 'comfort thyself' that this world will look by and by a tearful dream fading away in the light of the morning. I do not know how I may bear it when similar sorrow come to myself, but it seems to me now as if the time was so short there was no need to bemoan ourselves, only to get our work done and be ready.

And, dear Mrs. McLeod, if you will not think me presuming, may I not say—Do you not find your spirit drawing yet closer to the great heart that has *seemed* to leave you for a while? I ask this, because I think the law of the spirit or really the law of the universe; that as, when the Lord vanished from the sight of his friends, they found him in their hearts, far nearer then than before, so when any one like him departs, it is but, like him, to come nearer in the one spirit of truth and love. . . .[11]

Final Works

As incredible as it seems, the MacDonalds were still harassed for lack of money. To a friend he wrote: ". . . I don't know that ever I *seemed* worse off. I say *seemed* because I do not acknowledge the *look* of things. I am spending borrowed money now, and see no way but to borrow more. If I had a good offer for my house I would sell it. . . . You see, I have only one son off my hands yet—that makes it so heavy with two of them away from home. [This was written in 1885 when Ronald (studying medicine) and Bernard were both away at school, and of the sons only eighteen-year-old George MacKay remained at home.] However, they cause me no other burden whatever—thank God. . . . What do you think? It is very odd how those who have plenty seem to stick to their money when others are most in want of it. But business is a strange country to me. . . ."[12]

Another letter, written to his son Greville at the end of 1886, seems to anticipate the steady advancement of his years: "When a man comes to feel quiet confidence and hope, even when the life he *feels* is indeed not worth living, then he is getting ready fast. When one in a dream can welcome the thought of the sun and the active day, he is worth waking. But many of us will not consent to leave our coffins till we have made them tidy. I don't think Jesus folded his death garments: the angels did that after he had gone out of his three days' chamber. This is not quite coherent, but it may make *thinks* in you. May you have a divinely good Christmas."[13]

The years following 1890 saw a steady though diminishing output of original books including *Lilith*, which many of the more symbolically inclined critics point to as his crowning achievement. In addition there was a rising swell of reprints and new editions of previously published works. There were seven novels; the first complete edition of his poetry, the two-volume *The Poetical Works of George MacDonald* (1893); an edited edition of Sir Philip Sidney's poems, entitled *A Cabinet of Gems* (1891); and one final volume of sermons, *The Hope of the Gospel* (1892). The seven novels were: *A Rough Shaking* (1890); *There and Back* (1891)—the third of the books involving the character Thomas Wingfold, but not in a strict sense a "sequel" to either of the other two; *Flight of the Shadow* (1891)—a somewhat eerie and nonspiritual tale of a similar tone to *The Portent* written so many years earlier; *Heather and Snow* (1893)—a homely and simple Scottish tale; *Lilith* (1895); *Salted With Fire* (1897)—his last Scottish story, revolving once again around a repentant minister; and *Far Above Rubies* (1898), a short book which might more accurately be described as a novelette.

Louisa never quite recovered from Lilia's death, and gradually began to weaken. By the mid-1890s they were both into their seventies. George continued to write. *Lilith* was begun in 1890, yet because Louisa and others did not care for it, it was laid aside for a time and not finally released until 1895. As soon as MacDonald began it, he said he was possessed by a feeling that it was a mandate from God, for which he himself was to find the form and clothing and words. Therefore, its writing was to him more like a "transcription" than a piece of original work. The manuscript was unlike anything else he ever wrote, running from page to page with few breaks into new paragraphs, scarcely sufficient punctuation, and hardly a word altered until later revisions.

When *Lilith* was released it attracted little notice, being so dramatically different from what the public had come to expect from the Scotsman. And though it is not for everyone, its resemblance in figurative mystery to his first prose book affords it a place of stature as representative of his final years. Echoing a note of sad melancholy through its symbolism, it reads as a fitting climax to his long career, portending death, harkening back in the style of the allegory to his first fantasy, *Phantastes*, the two works seeming to enclose like bookends a career that produced fifty-three books. Before embarking on a discussion of his father's poetry, Ronald said, "I find myself impelled . . . to pass through the hall of entrance where stand *Lilith* and *Phantastes*, one on either hand, like two strange sphinxes, with each its constant form, and each with its ever changing beauty of countenance—sphinxes asking questions which none will regret his endeavour to answer. . . ."[14]

Many are enchanted by *Lilith:* H. G. Wells is said to have commended it, while others can make little sense of it—a statement which is true of *Phantastes* as well. This has no bearing upon a person's literary capacity, but only upon the simple fact that MacDonald's different genres speak to different people on distinctive levels. Greville comments: "*Lilith* indeed, needs reading and re-reading before the heart of its magic is reached; and even then much may be missed by those who are not already intimate with its writer's spirit and style. My mother, though I do not think her mind had lost any of its elasticity, was troubled by the book's strange imagery; her distress gave my father real heartache, so that he began to question his ability to utter his last urgent message."[15] Greville concludes, "I lay all this stress upon the importance of *Lilith* because I am writing my father's life; for it was not only the majestic thought of his old age, but portion also of the suffering that, mercifully near the end, led him up to his long and last vigil. And here I append the closing words of his [next to] final book: 'God is deeper in us than our own life; yes, God's life ... which we call *ours;* therefore is the Life in us stronger than the Death, in as much as the creating Good is stronger than the created Evil.'"[16]

The Advance of Years

George's pace began to slow, though not quite so soon as his wife's. His letters to many friends reveal that the passage of time and growing old are on his mind.

1892

... I have no impulse toward public work this year. I do not think I should feel at all sorry if I were told I should never preach or lecture again. Somehow I have very little feeling of doing good that way. But let everything always be as our Father wills. . . .[17]

1893

I gather from your last letter that you are now fifty years of age. I am nearly twenty years your senior ... but if I do not in all things, I do in all essential things feel younger than when I was a child. Certainly I am happier and more hopeful, though I think I always had a large gift of hope. It has been the one constitutional power of life in me—none of my making surely! . . .

I am rather driven with work, I think sometimes; but if my faith were stronger, as I hope it is on the way to being, I should never feel that. . . .[18]

1893

I can't do it, even to oblige you. . . . I never have and never will consent to be interviewed. I will do *nothing* to bring my personality before the public in any way farther than my work in itself necessitates. Pardon my brevity. I have begun again to work, but writing takes all the strength I have to spend. . . . My memory plays me sad tricks now. It comes of the frosty invasion of old age—preparing me to go home, thank God. Till then I must work, and that is good. . . .[19]

1894

... I am a little better, I think, and begin to imagine it possible I should one day begin another book. But I continue very weak mentally. I am only able to read and understand books worth reading, mixed with a good story now and then. . . .[20]

1894

Next month I shall be 70, and I am humbler a good deal than when

I was 29. To be rid of self is to have the heart bare to God and to the neighbour—to *have* all life ours, and possess all things. I see in my mind's eye, the little children clambering up to sit on the throne with Jesus. My God, art thou not as good as we are capable of imagining thee? Shall we dream a better goodness than thou hast ever thought of? Be thyself, and all is well.[21]

1896
... My wife and I are somewhat tired *by* life, but not tired *of* it.[22]

1897
... He it is who checks and admonishes and turns us into the right way. I have felt both his bit in my mouth and his spur in my flank and desire that he may take and have his own strange and *therefore* perfect way with me, whatever may be my foolish way of judging it. Would that my being were consciously filled with the gladness of his obedience! Nothing less can content me. . . .[23]

1898
... I have been indeed unable to think, and still more to know what I was thinking. Indeed I feel sometimes as if I were about to lose all power of thought. . . . I am drawing nearer to the time I shall have to go. I do not think it will be just yet, and it is a good thing we should not know when the call will come, but may He give me what readiness he pleases. . . .[24]

Confiding to his son Greville, as he reflected on his life, he made what to us must sound like an incredible statement:

"I have had no great troubles or afflictions, no hardships to face, no terrible griefs. I don't know why. It could not be that I did not need them; perhaps I shall be given them yet in the new life."[25]

The remembrance of another, in the year 1888, illuminates the portrait of George MacDonald as he reached the end of his long life, even more than his own letters, which necessarily, coming from within him, cannot show what he looked like to others. A friend recollects his first meeting with George MacDonald:

"I went with no little nervousness, but his reception put me at ease at once. I was struck by his appearance, of course—that beautiful kindly shrewd face. . . . It seemed to me (if I may reverently say so) as if I were talking to S. John the Apostle. I never think of Dr. MacDonald without instinctively thinking of S. John. There was in him that gentleness and humanity and strength—a depth of fire below the surface in spite of all his sweetness—that I fancy were characteristics of the disciple Jesus loved.

"Well, we sat in the library—where boxes were being packed and books lying about the room, prior to departure for Bordighera. And then I opened my heart to him as I had hardly ever opened it to any stranger before. Doubts and fears—sore burdens just then—were bluntly put before him, and he sat and listened with the utmost patience. It was strange—and yet it was not strange—to find myself talking to him so freely. I saw, I felt, his holiness and nearness to God, and yet I should not have been afraid to confess to him most secret sins. There was a humanity about him, and a searching honesty, which, along with his sympathy, made me feel that he would understand me. He would not cast me out.

"I suppose men and women felt like this when they talked with our Lord. His holiness attracted them, and His love and pity encouraged them to come and open up their hearts, sure that He would not drive them away. . . .

"I forget much of his reply, but I remember this: 'I should not be surprised,' he said, 'if God has not some special work for you to do.' I cannot describe the comfort those simple words gave me. Then this tension of mind was a discipline, and meant good. I could bear it, and perhaps one day thank God for it.

"Then just before I left he said—and I can hear him now—'But after all, whatever help or comfort any one may try to give you, it is but to follow the advice of Jesus. "Enter into thy closet, and shut thy door, and pray to thy Father in secret"—pour out your heart to God—get down on your knees—He will help you as no one else can, and will give you an answer of peace.'

"I left him with 'uplifted head,' and thankful heart—but only years unfolded to me the depth of his words."[26]

For most of his adult life George MacDonald had suffered from eczema. Diet and many types of treatment for the itching and inflamed skin disease had been tried—sulfur baths, homeopathy, hydropathic systems, and many remedies and regimens of different specialists—but nothing helped. Until the worsening of his itching, he had always been a great sleeper, and could lie down and fall asleep at almost any moment. The winters in Italy had steadily diminished his tendency to bronchitis and asthma, but toward the middle of the 1890s the eczema grew gradually worse until his sleep was seriously affected.

He exercised little, his books providing his chief solace from work and "recreation." He was still reading, now binding old books as well. At Bordighera he taught himself both Spanish and Dutch. His mind remained vigorous until well into his 73rd year; his mental powers never suddenly dropped away. The following passage from *Paul Faber, Surgeon* reveals more of its author than the characters about whom he wrote it: "It is foolish to say that after a certain age a man cannot alter. That some men can not—or will not, (God only can draw the line between these two *nots*) I allow; but the cause is not age, and it is not universal. The man who does not care and ceases to grow, becomes torpid, stiffens, is in a sense dead; but he who has been growing all the time need never stop; and where growth is, there is always capability of change: growth itself is a succession of slow, melodious, ascending changes" (*Paul Faber, Surgeon*, Ch. 28). But the eczema became so torturous and kept him from sleeping that even waking hours became an exhausting agony. He realized that his brain sometimes would not respond to his imagination, though he disciplined himself to read regularly, as if to force his fatigue into "some renewal of life." Even this eventually became impossible.

Louisa remained devoted to serving him, always hoping for his recovery, always encouraged by the instances of wit and humor that would suddenly break through. Once his breakfast egg was unusually large, and he quietly remarked, "It must have taken two hens to lay that one." But the fatigue was clearly taxing both body and brain. His hand grew shaky and the need increased for more constant nursing than Louisa and Irene (38), the only one of the eleven still at home, could give. Louisa was 75 and not strong herself. A trained man and woman were hired to help, and George's gratitude, for even the slightest things, was touching.

His suffering was terrible, as though Satan was being allowed one final try of his hand to see if this saint could survive a testing of his faith. His dejection was not unlike Job's, and he began to feel that the Lord had indeed forsaken him.

To this time belong these verses, though the original contained many erasures and changes and were left in a totally unpolished state.

> Come through the gloom of clouded skies,
>> The slow dim rain and fog athwart,
> Through East winds keen and wrong and lies,
>> Come and make strong my hopeless heart.
>
> Come through the sickness and the pain,
>> The sore unrest that tosses still,
> The aching dark that hides the gain—
>> Come and arouse my fainting will.
>
> Through all the fears—that spirits bow—
>> Of what hath been or may befall,
> Come down and talk with me, for thou
>> Canst tell me all about them all.
>
> Come, Lord of Life—here is thy seat,
>> Heart of all joy below, above—
> One minute let me kiss thy feet
>> And name the names of those I love.[27]

The Passing of an Era

In 1899 at 74, as Greville describes it, "something seemed to break." George MacDonald suffered a stroke, which left him without power of speech. A great peace seemed to come over him, his skin cleared completely, and his old power of sleep returned. All at once he seemed to have been removed to another world—still *in* this, but not *of* it.

For the next five years he spoke scarcely one word. He accepted all that was done for him with gentle gratitude, obeyed whatever he was told to do. Like an innocent baby, he was now a complete invalid, always with a look deep in his eyes of "a constant waiting for something at hand," reminiscent of his words in *Lilith*, "All the night long the morning is at hand." That far-off look of wistful inquiry never left him. His deep blue eyes lost none of their sparkle, and with his voice now gone, these eyes became the fullest expression of his personality, reminding those around him of the words he had written of little Diamond in *At the Back of the North Wind*—"those blue eyes that seemed rather made for other people to look into than for himself to look out of."

In 1900 Greville bought some land at Haslemere in Surrey, south of London, and built a home for them there, probably designed by Irene's husband-to-be, an architect. It was named "St. George's Wood," and there George and Louisa settled. There were lovely gardens and three acres of woodland about it. In the summer he was well known by sight as he was taken out for his daily ride in either his wheelchair or a carriage. Young neighbor children rode up and down the road on their bicycles that they might see "the grand old saint" in his red cloak and white suit and grey felt hat. Here George and Louisa celebrated their golden wedding anniversary in 1901, with children, grandchildren, nephews, nieces, and many friends gathered about them. Louisa was bright and young-eyed, and whoever observed her husband closely would see that whenever she left the room his gaze would follow her and remain on the door until she returned; then he would sigh contentedly.

But eventually Louisa, worn out with age and disappointed hopes for her husband's recovery, realized that he would never regain his power of speech, and that other more skillful nurses could do more for him than she could in her waning strength. A great despondency came over her, and the devoted care of her daughter Irene was the only source of consolation. Greville adds, "Yet to the last she sent me tender notes and encouragements about my father."

Louisa died in January 1902 at 79. For some days Irene and Winifred, both of whom were with her at the last, dared not tell their father, almost afraid he would be unable to grasp the truth. When they finally did he wept bitterly.

For the next two and half years, until her marriage in 1904, Irene scarcely left her father. He spent much of his time in bed. But even then, whether lying down or sitting dressed in a chair, the countenance of his white-topped head was a beautiful one. And still the look of anticipation remained in his deep blue eyes. Whenever the door opened, his head would quickly turn in a moment of expectancy, and then, seeing it was not Louisa, he would sigh deeply and turn back to begin his waiting again, still keeping the long vigil till she and their Lord came for him.

After Irene's marriage, her father was moved to Winifred's home. And there, at Ashtead in Surrey, George MacDonald died on September 18, 1905, at 80 years of age, after several months of loving care from his youngest daughter, Winifred Louisa Troup. Despite his wish to be buried at Huntly, his body was cremated and the ashes buried at Bordighera beside the body of his wife.

> Autumn clouds are flying, flying
> O'er the waste of blue;
> Summer flowers are dying, dying,

Late so lovely new.
Labouring wains are slowly rolling
    Home with winter grain;
Holy bells are slowly tolling
    Over buried men.

Goldener light sets noon a sleeping
    Like an afternoon;
Colder airs come stealing, creeping
    From the misty moon;
And the leaves, of old age dying,
    Earthly hues put on;
Out on every lone wind sighing
    That their day is gone.

Autumn's sun is sinking, sinking
    Down to winter low;
And our hearts are thinking, thinking
    Of the sleet and snow;
For our sun is slowly sliding
    Down the hill of might;
And no moon is softly gliding
    Up the slope of night.

See the bare fields' pillaged prizes
    Heaped in golden glooms!
See, the earth's outworn sunrises
    Dream in cloudy tombs!
Darkling flowers but wait the blowing
    Of a quickening wind;
And the man, through Death's door going,
    Leaves old Death behind.

        (*Poetical Works*, vol. 1, "Autumn Song")

EPILOGUE

CHAPTER TWENTY-SEVEN

GEORGE MACDONALD IN THE TWENTIETH CENTURY

George MacDonald probably spoke as often on death as he did any other subject. Over and over throughout his writings, the theme is clearly evident that death is the real beginning of life. In *David Elginbrod* he wrote: "I think of death as the first pulse of the new strength shaking itself free from the old mouldy remnants of earth-garments, that it may begin in freedom the new life that grows out of the old. The caterpillar dies into the butterfly. . . ." (*David Elginbrod*, Ch. 54).

His words to Mrs. A. J. Scott after the death of her husband surely reflect the feelings of those closest to MacDonald at the time of his own death in 1905. Indeed, it is almost eerie how wonderfully—though he would never have written them about himself—these comments, written some forty years earlier, apply to their own author's passing: ". . . He who has left us was the best and greatest of our time. Those who know him best will say so most heartily. But we have no more lost him than the disciples lost their Lord when he went away that he might come closer to them than ever. Life is not very long in this place. . . . All we have to mind is to do our work, while the chariot of God's hours is bearing us to the higher life beyond."[1]

To George MacDonald, death never severed a relationship. When his own brothers, father, sisters, children, and friends had gone, his single perspective was always the greater life into which they had entered. His own passing was not the end of his life, but the continuation of his life in new form.

> Now I grow old, and the soft-gathered years
> Have calmed, yea dulled the heart's swift fluttering beat;
> But a quiet hope that keeps its household seat

Is better than recurrent glories fleet.
To know thee, Lord, is worth a many tears;
And when this mildew, age, has dried away,
My heart will beat again as young and strong and gay.

(Diary of an Old Soul, Oct. 16)

Thus George MacDonald's death in 1905 does not end his biography. Not only does his spiritual being remain alive, but by the very nature of his work as a writer, his life lives on through his stories, teachings, characters, sermons, and poems. The complete picture of MacDonald reaches far beyond 1905, into the 20th century, and to the present day.

The Coming of a New Age

In one sense, George MacDonald epitomized the ideal Victorian author. His Christian morals and principles exemplified in literature what Queen Victoria would have seen practiced in the government and indeed throughout all aspects of British life. So fond was she of MacDonald's ideas that she gave a copy of *Robert Falconer* to each of her grandchildren.

The Victorian era ended with the Queen's death in 1901, however, and the impact upon Britain and the world was more far-reaching than a mere transferral of the monarchy in London. A comprehensive metamorphosis, the seeds of which had been planted during Victoria's lifetime, was in the process of turning society inside out. The entire political framework of the world was being revamped. The birth and growth of the Labour Party completely altered Parliament's decision-making process in Great Britain. The old feudal and manorial systems—dying slow deaths for centuries—finally gasped their last. Socially, economically, and politically, old norms were being thrown out. Technological breakthroughs, given impetus by World War I, found their way into the daily lives of countless millions on both sides of the Atlantic—automobiles, electricity, airplanes, automation, radios, music, fashions, telephones, urban growth, industry.

These were profound changes. The world in the first two decades of the 20th century was a world in upheaval. The 19th century, which ended with Victoria's death, was in reality hundreds of years different in outlook than the modern age, which was in full swing twenty years later. Between 1900 and 1920 yawned a gulf, not of two decades, but of two centuries.

The world of Victorian Britain was a world in large measure content with itself. The middle and wealthy classes enjoyed their status and their pleasures without compunction. The volcano of unrest was brewing beneath them, but it had not yet boiled over. For the upper classes the late 19th century was a tranquil world of horses and carriages, country manors, afternoon teas, leisurely walks, lazy summer days, garden parties, and visits with one's neighbor. This was the literate public that enjoyed MacDonald's books—the very types of persons around whom many of his novels were built. They were educated, had time to read, and generally shared MacDonald's Victorian value system and the easy-going pace of his novels.

A book's length mattered little. There were no pressing engagements. A book could be 400, 500, or 600 pages. Happy endings and sound morals made them all the better. Poetry was popular. In the upper reaches of society literacy was high. There was a familiarity with the classics, the great poets, and Shakespeare; most had at least a passing acquaintance with Latin and often another language or two.

This all changed dramatically with the coming of the fast-paced 20th century. Life intensified. Literacy (in the sense of familiarity with "literature") gradually lessened. Interest in poetry waned. Happy endings and moralistic sermonizing were no longer desirable. And the accelerated momentum of life became too rapid to accomodate a 600-page slow-moving story. The so-called "Victorian novel" fell out of favor for more "realistic" books without the naivete of the happy ending. More "serious" themes, social problems, and personal psychoanalysis came to the fore. No longer did the modern "sophisticated" reader want his heroes to be saints; now the public called for "flawed" heroes and unsolved problems and bitter relationships that did not immediately heal themselves at the book's end. Thus Thackeray, Dickens, Scott, and Stevenson gave way to Shaw, Fitzgerald, Steinbeck, and Maugham.

Even more profound than these social changes—though intrinsically linked to them—was the spiritual outlook of the new century. As in most other ways, the ideals and attitudes of the Victorian era came to be viewed as behind the times and unenlightened—moralistic but untrue. Even though on a personal level the virtues of Christianity may have been lost much earlier, yet there remained throughout the 19th century—in both the U.S. and Britain—a mental allegiance to the old value structure that had its roots in the Bible. To what extent they may have been practicing its principles in their daily lives may be open to question, but most men and women vaguely considered themselves Christians, believed in God, and were therefore in agreement with the majority of the foundational principles that undergirded the teachings of men like MacDonald.

But the 20th century altered all this. God and the principles of Scripture ceased to be of interest to most individuals. In the 20th century this gradual change, with roots extending back centuries, came to be felt through all levels of society. As a result, everything was recast with a decidedly altered value structure—organized religion, politics, relationships, music, and especially literature. Homiletic and moralistic novels, and religious poetry and essays no longer held the interest of the general public, but were relegated to a small minority.

All these factors taken together had a tremendous negative impact on George MacDonald's popularity as a writer. For the modern mentality everything about his books was wrong. They were too long, too slow-paced, the heroes too good, the endings unrealistic, the saints too unbelievable, the themes too simplistic, and the sermonizing too evident and disruptive to the flow of the story. His poetry, like most other poetry, was gradually ignored. Public tastes had changed, and George MacDonald fell out of vogue.

Most of his books continued to enjoy some popularity after his death; new editions continued to be printed through 1910 and 1915. Several "centenary" editions were published in 1924 to commemorate the hundredth year after his birth—*Tragedie of Hamlet*, *Lilith*, and *Fairy Tales of George MacDonald*. That same year his son Greville's biography, *George MacDonald and His Wife*, was published. The following year J. M. Bulloch's extensive bibliography of George MacDonald's works was released in the Aberdeen University Library Bulletin.

But as the 20th century progressed, Victorian, Christian George MacDonald gradually fell further and further out of step with the new era's different drummer. The novels, though many had been bestsellers in their own day, one by one went out of print, along with the sermons, essays, and poems. By the 1950s George MacDonald—of whom it was written: "In their day his writings enjoyed immense popularity, excited bitter controversy, elicited long articles in the serious critical journals, and brought him fame—and . . . love. . . ."[2]—had been reduced to a mere literary historical footnote. Within a few years, not a single one of his full-length novels remained in print in either the U.S. or Great Britain, though often they could be found in secondhand bookshops. The man who had drawn standing-room-only crowds in Chicago, Boston, Manchester, Edinburgh, and London, whose books rivaled those of Dickens in sales and popularity, had been forgotten.

Faerie Lives On

The demise of MacDonald's popularity was not total, however. Curiously, the 20th century—though turning its back on poetry and the moralistic—*did* develop a thirst for the land of faerie. Most critics had always admitted that his children's stories, his fairy tales, and particularly his adult fantasies (which some reviewers hailed as forming an entirely new literary genre) were, even in the 20th century, among the best ever written. On the basis of this particular phase of his writing G. K. Chesterton said of him: "If we test the matter by originality of attitude, George MacDonald was one of the three or four greatest men of the nineteenth century."[3] C. S. Lewis commented, "What he does best is fantasy. . . . And this, in my opinion, he does better than any man. . . . MacDonald is the greatest genius of this kind whom I know."[4] And W. H. Auden asserted: "In his power . . . to project his inner life into images . . . which are valid for all, he is one of the most remarkable writers of the nineteenth century."[5]

Therefore, MacDonald's books in which the fairy element was strong remained in print and continued to attract moderate interest—*Phantastes, Lilith, The Princess and the Goblin, The Princess and Curdie, The Wise Woman, The Golden Key, The Light Princess*, some collections of short stories, as well as MacDonald's bestseller through the years, *At the Back of the North Wind*.

Despite this overall waning of the popularity of MacDonald's books with the public, with *individuals* MacDonald never lost his influence.

Wherever his books—no matter how old and worn—found their way into receptive hearts, the impact of George MacDonald's life lived on. Story after story is told of the discovery of some "old, forgotten volume" of George MacDonald's—by children, by teenagers, by adults—which changed the reader's whole outlook, which opened new worlds in the mind or imagination or spirit. The few such stories that have been made public by those who have recorded them hint at the abundance of similiar experiences untold.

G. K. Chesterton, that eminent early 20th-century Catholic theologian, poet, journalist, mystic, biographer, and bestselling mystery writer (1874–1936), commented: "I . . . can really testify to a book that has made a difference to my whole existence, which has helped me to see . . . a vision of things . . . so real. . . . Of all the stories I have read . . . it remains the most real, the most realistic, in the exact sense of the phrase the most like life. It is called *The Princess and the Goblin*, and it is by George Mac-Donald. . . ."[6]

Writing in his little book, *The Victorian Age in Literature*, Chesterton says further, "George MacDonald, a Scot of genius . . . could write fairy tales that made all experience a fairy tale."[7] J. R. R. Tolkien (1892-1973) called his fairy tales "stories of power and beauty."[8] W. H. Auden (1907-1973), writing an introduction to the 1954 reprint edition of *Phantastes* and *Lilith*, said, "*The Princess and the Goblin* is, in my opinion, the only English children's book in the same class as the Alice books, and *Lilith* is equal if not superior to the best of Poe."[9]

Probably the best-known modern association with George MacDonald comes from C. S. Lewis (1898-1963), that foremost author of forty books with sales in the multiple millions, indeed one of this century's most "well-known" Christians. His almost reluctant purchase of a MacDonald book ultimately triggered his own process of conversion. "It must be more than thirty years ago that I bought—almost unwillingly . . .—the Everyman edition of *Phantastes*. A few hours later I knew that I had crossed a great frontier."[10] So great, in fact, was Lewis's indebtedness to MacDonald—upon repeated occasions in his own writing he credits MacDonald with beginning his own progressive journey toward Christianity out of atheism—that he later had a fictionalized MacDonald act as heavenly guide in his own *The Great Divorce* (1946), and compiled an anthology of quotations from MacDonald's sermons (*George MacDonald: An Anthology*, 1946) in the introduction to which he says, "I have never concealed the fact that I regarded him as my master; indeed I fancy I have never written a book in which I did not quote from him."[11]

So the impact of George MacDonald has continued, albeit quietly, through the years. One almost imagines that his son Ronald's words could have been written in 1950, 1960, or 1970 rather than in 1910; they seem so apt in any age, pinpointing this love for the man that has continued for so long after his death: ". . . there is abundant evidence not only that the more vigorous of the Scottish novels and all the fairy tales have a perennial public, but also that there is a personal George MacDonald tradition healthily active. I cannot tell how strangely, I cannot remember how often . . . I have encountered some flash of a smile, some reminiscent anecdote, some kindness, or some quaint proof of a newer generation's almost personal affection for the man known only from *Robert Falconer* filtered through a parent, of *At the Back of the North Wind*, read or listened to many years ago."[12]

Once Again in the Public Eye

Elizabeth Yates (1905–2001), still another 20th-century writer who owed a personal debt to MacDonald, in 1936 compiled a collection of MacDonald's poetry.* Nearly thirty years later (1963), observing with sadness the dearth of MacDonald fiction available and recognizing the shifts in public taste which were responsible, she undertook the task of "editing" *Sir Gibbie* to make it shorter and more readable for the drastically changed modern literary palate.

A turning point had come in MacDonald's own career when he moved from the previous formats he had originally preferred to the popular novel. He recognized that he could convey his message to a vastly larger audience by adapting himself to a mode that would be more readily available and read by more people. In a similar way, in light of the reading tastes of contemporary men and women, Yates's effort to edit, shorten, and translate the now difficult Scots dialect was an attempt to accomplish for the novels, whose form had become outdated, exactly what MacDonald had himself done: to make the message appropriate for the contemporary public. To do so in MacDonald's day meant moving from fantasy and poetry to the novel; to accomplish the same in this day meant modifying the novels so they could be received with something of the same enthusiasm they were in his own day. On a very pragmatic level, how much better that the public be reacquainted with MacDonald, even in edited format, than for his books to remain obscure, out of print, and impossible to find!

In her introduction to her new edition of *Sir Gibbie*, Yates offers another of these "stories of discovery":

"Some years ago a friend asked, 'Have you ever read *Sir Gibbie*?'

"'No,' I answered, wondering what I had missed.

"'Oh, but you must.'

"And I meant to read *Sir Gibbie*, but the book had long been out of print and there seemed no copy easily available in either bookstore or library.

"Then, one day, my friend quietly took down *Sir Gibbie* from her shelf and put it into my hands. It was an old copy, small of print, and worn. She did not say, even then, why I should read it or what it was about. . . .

"'You'll like it,' she said patiently, 'and don't be put off by the Scotch dialect. It's more readable than it looks.'

"But I was put off by it and found myself during the first fifty pages

---

Gathered Grace (Cambridge: W. Heffer and Sons), 1936.

setting the book down many times. Then, suddenly it seemed, I reached the point where Gibbie . . . became real and imperative. He took me by the hand, as I read, and led me through the streets of the old gray Scottish city and up the slopes of Glashgar where he ran through the heather with the sheep. . . .

"The book defied hasty reading but . . . from the moment it caught me up I was conscious of a breadth and depth and height of feeling such as I had not known for a long time. It moved me the way books did when, as a child, the great gates of literature began to open and first encounters with noble thoughts and utterances were unspeakably thrilling. But this was different, too. It was as if a wind blew over me, coming from heights even higher than that of Glashgar. I wanted not to put the book down until it was finished, and yet I could not bear to come to its end. Once at its last page, I felt I would have to do what I had often done as a child—turn back to the first page and begin reading all over again. I longed to tell everyone I knew to read it. . . . It would not do to tell them anything about it. This was not only a book, it was an experience."[13]

Through the years occasional critical attention had been paid to Mac-Donald. Articles, though unpredictable, were regular, and chapters on MacDonald appeared regularly in publications more specifically concerned with C. S. Lewis, J. R. R. Tolkien, and other of the British "mythopoeic" types, which were somehow mysteriously linked together. At the Wheaton College library in Illinois, the Marion E. Wade Collection was established to house works by and promote interest in the collected works of these writers—C. S. Lewis, G. K. Chesterton, J. R. R. Tolkien, Dorothy Sayers, Owen Barfield, Charles Williams, and George MacDonald. But even then the interest in the 19th-century Scotsman was sporadic, MacDonald always remaining the shadowy figure in the background. Behind the scenes, he was completely eclipsed by the fame of Lewis and Tolkien, though according to Lewis he could be seen as foundational to them all.

Greville MacDonald wrote in 1924: "These books will assuredly be read yet again when the world has grown wise enough to appreciate their writer's singleness of vision and the open road between him and God."[14]

Perhaps in fulfillment of these words, in the 1970s a resurgence of interest in George MacDonald began to be noticed in wider spheres, focusing initially on increased circulation of the fantasy writings. Little pockets of George MacDonald books began to be found in bookstores throughout the United States, the renewed interest linked primarily at first to C. S. Lewis as more people became aware of the affiliation between the two British authors. The burgeoning sales of Lewis's *The Chronicles of Narnia* generated spin-off interest in MacDonald's *Princess* and *Curdie* stories and his other fantasies as well. In the late 1970s, Wheaton professor Rolland Hein issued four volumes of edited sermons and quotations, attempting—as had Yates earlier—to simplify MacDonald's writings so they could again enjoy more widespread impact in the 20th century. In 1980, the George MacDonald Society was formed in London to generate further interest in MacDonald.

Clearly the memory of George MacDonald was not dead. Though kept alive by a slender thread during the forty or so years of the mid-20th century, the essential "life" of it was unchanged. Like the old and disused garden where Polwarth dug in *Paul Faber, Surgeon*, the seeds of life were just waiting for the opportunity to blossom once again: "'Perhaps you are not aware, ma'am,' he began . . . 'that many of the seeds which fall to the ground, and do not grow, yet, strange to tell, retain the power of growth. . . . It is well enough known that if you dig deep in any old garden, such as this one, ancient—perhaps forgotten—flowers will appear. The fashion has changed, they have been neglected or uprooted, but all the time their life is hid below'" (*Paul Faber, Surgeon*, Ch. 41).

Richard Reis recently wrote, "There are many signs that MacDonald's eclipse will not last. . . . It seems at least probable that MacDonald will be given more attention in future literary histories. He is a more important writer . . . than a number of his better-known Victorian contemporaries. . . . MacDonald's minor fame survives, however, because he speaks to a later time than his own."[15]

So throughout the years, men and women such as C. S. Lewis and Elizabeth Yates and Rolland Hein continued to spade the ground and upturn the soil where the long-buried seeds of George MacDonald's imaginative work had been concealed, waiting for the ancient, forgotten flowers to reappear. During this time, however, in the genus of the primary emphasis of MacDonald's life work—the novel—there was still no apparent widespread revival of interest. Even Yates's groundbreaking effort with *Sir Gibbie* was only moderately successful, and was temporarily withdrawn from publication.

Resurrection

By 1980 it had been a hundred years since the pinnacle of Mac-Donald's popularity. A hundred years earlier MacDonald had completed the most industrious decade of his life, including his highly successful lecture tour of the U.S. Exactly a hundred years later, the "second wave" of great impact began, witnessing the bursting into full flower of the forgotten seeds so long buried. For in the 1980s, the growing swell of interest at last seemed to come into fruition, foreshadowed by the likes of Lewis, Yates, Chesterton, Hein, and MacDonald's sons—with the new publication by Bethany House Publishers in Minneapolis of MacDonald's novels in edited form.

This re-releasing of MacDonald's fiction in redacted format proved to have a parallel impact on the reading public as had MacDonald's own turning to a fictional format in the 1860s. Several became bestsellers—something that had not been said of a MacDonald title in nearly a century (notably Bethany's edited edition of *Malcolm, The Fisherman's Lady*, Michael Phillips, ed., which ultimately sold over 200,000 copies and thus sparked the MacDonald renaissance into full flame)—and this led to new editions of other of his works, new critical studies, increasing articles, and a number of foreign translations. Suddenly the garden of old forgotten seeds and flowers seemed fairly bursting with new growth.

CHAPTER TWENTY-EIGHT

THE LEGACY

Complex Simplicity

Since his first publication in 1851, people have been trying to interpret the person, views, thought, and character of George MacDonald on the basis of what he wrote. As a partial result of his translations of Novalis in that year, the leaders of his congregation "interpreted" him to be unorthodox and later asked for his resignation. And from that point on, MacDonald has been the subject of much analysis—readers and critics, clergy and laymen, literary experts and self-appointed guardians of the faith have tried to pigeonhole him into one camp, viewpoint, doctrinal position, or psychoanalytic slant or another. At the same time, biographers have tried to get inside his psyche, reading into his writings everything from an Oedipus complex to a death wish.

Perhaps George MacDonald has attracted a long and persistent line of critics and analysts precisely because he was at once an extraordinarily complex and yet an extremely simple man. His imagination, his thought processes, his reasoning powers, his gift of communication, the incisiveness of his logic, the breadth of his knowledge, the force of his wisdom, his insight into man, the probing depth of his ever-expanding awareness of God's nature were all far-reaching indeed. Yet simultaneously, he held an exceedingly uncomplicated faith. He believed that God *is,* that God is love, that in obedience to God's principles truth can be found, that God loves all men completely, and will never stop redeeming and purifying them until the job is accomplished, and that all of life is therefore to be viewed through the perspective of God's immediate presence as He carries out that work in mankind.

Fatherhood and obedience. Rarely in life do these two qualities go hand in hand. The complexities of the thinker, the poet, the philosopher, and the theologian do not ordinarily inspire childlikeness of faith. Theologians foster theological networks. Philosophers contrive philosophical theories. Poets devise odd rhymes and complicated images to communicate the yearnings of their hearts. George MacDonald simply did not conform to any preconceived mold. Seeming to fit a certain standard at one point, he was soundly criticized for not adhering to some other aspect of the standard. The man who seems liberal at one moment and conservative the next makes his fellows uncomfortable. Neither side will have him because he doesn't nicely conform to the lines they have drawn.

Such a man was George MacDonald. One moment he preached the most basic of salvation sermons—"Come, then, sore heart, and see whether his heart cannot heal thine. He knows what sighs and tears are. . . . Brothers, sisters, we *must* get rid of this misery of ours. It is slaying us. It is turning the fair earth into a hell, and our hearts into its fuel. There stands the man who says he knows: take him at his word. Go to him who says in the might of his eternal tenderness and his human pity, *Come unto me, all ye that labor and are heavy-laden, and I will give you rest. Take my yoke upon you, and learn of me; for I am meek and lowly in heart: and ye shall find rest unto your souls. For my yoke is easy, and my burden is light*" (*Thomas Wingfold, Curate*, Ch. 46). The next, he lectured to thousands on the skeptic Robert Burns, and then he published a volume that offers a new interpretation to Shakespeare's *Hamlet*.

He fit no mold. The Calvinists in his own day weren't comfortable with him because he was always delving into things "outside" the faith. His views were out of step and unsettling. He refused to be denominationalized. He maintained unconventional points of view about what one's priorities as a Christian should be. He was accepting toward unbelievers and chastised the clergy and religious systems.

Thus all his life his writings and views elicited argument. He went against the grain, upset the norms, refused to adhere quietly to the status quo. He was too controversial, his teachings too new, his interpretations of Scripture too outlandish.

A Different Drummer

So George MacDonald marched on to a different drummer, and those with ears to hear *heard* his message, while others pointed to specifics in his writing that did not fit the mold of their view. But recognizing and accepting MacDonald as God's man is the only way to apprehend the legacy he left the Christian world. For whatever the significance of the many literary contributions he made, that legacy is primarily a spiritual one. It is in the spiritual realm that he sought to impact men's hearts, thoughts, attitudes, and priorities; and it is only in the spiritual realm that he can be fully appreciated and set in the context of history.

MacDonald *was* a complex man. But because his faith was so simple, so centered immovably in the character of God, MacDonald's imaginative creativity was free to roam wherever it chose. The universe was the Lord's and he was therefore free to explore all of it. There was no question he could think of, no conjecture his mind could frame, no thought that could come into his brain, no place he could go that didn't fall under the sovereignty of

God. Therefore, as a writer and thinker, MacDonald posed bold—sometimes frightening—questions. He did not fear allowing his author's pen to probe into any of life's dark corners, for he knew God was there. He explored the spiritual battleground between God and Satan. His writings reveal a familiarity with the demon world and a knowledge of its ways. He rolled up his sleeves and jumped into the middle of the fray between conflicting churches and opposing beliefs. He was especially pointed in his attacks against professional religiosity. In nearly every one of his books he explores the dream world with an insight decades ahead of its time. His psychoanalytic understanding (seen through his treatment of dreams, relationships, and the key role he consistently gives to childhood in all of his work) predates both Freud and Jung. His break from Calvinistic legalism, which bound so much of Protestantism in the 19th century along with others of similar bent, helped blaze the trail for the whole spectrum of 20th-century Christianity, from liberal to evangelical. MacDonald's influence upon the writings of influential 20th-century personalities, even if indirectly, can be seen in the likes of G. K. Chesterton, C. S. Lewis, Francis Schaeffer, J. R. R. Tolkien, Dorothy Sayers, Charles Williams, Madeleine L'Engle, and many others.

The "complexity" that gave birth to his varied interests allowed George MacDonald a freedom most writers by nature cannot enjoy. His writings were as diversified as his many enthusiasms. He was in love with life. It all held fascination for him, from the flower to the ancient poet to the stories of the Old Testament to his Gaelic clan heritage. Poems and stories came forth naturally. In everything he perceived the imaginative and the eternal. He *enjoyed* spinning tales; the reader of *Alec Forbes of Howglen* or *Sir Gibbie* or *Malcolm* can feel his delight. At other times he spins totally different sorts of yarns with equal relish. *The Portent* could easily qualify as an episode of "The Twilight Zone," or as a ghost story told by a particularly imaginative teenage boy to his companions around a campfire. His God-centered outlook was so total that he was not bound to "spiritualize" every word he wrote. His imagination was free, and it soared.

The Legacy

It is all too easy to allow an interpretation of MacDonald's life to degenerate into a doctrinal statement. People naturally "line up" or "take sides" on this or that question, discussing specific doctrines rather than looking beyond them to the foundational, and far greater, issues which MacDonald's life as a whole generates. To discuss George MacDonald's life solely in the context of this or that theological issue, however, is to miss the larger impact of the man's faith.

Perhaps certain ideas George MacDonald believed will turn out to have been wrong. Such can be said about each one of us. But this biography was intended neither as a "case" in support of MacDonald's positions, nor as a supportive argument for points of MacDonald's theology. His life was one of significance, one therefore which should be told—not because of his specific positions on specific issues, but because of the One toward whom he always pointed. Where MacDonald was wrong, undoubtedly he has been given more light by now, as we all will one day receive more light at those points where our vision is presently obscured. If we are distracted by the doctrinal tangents, however, we miss the lasting importance of George MacDonald, a man whose writings reflected his own burning desire to live in total oneness with and obedience to the commands and priorities and principles of his heavenly father, a God of creativity, imagination, goodness, and love.

George MacDonald pointed single-mindedly toward a personal God of love whom we have the opportunity to joyfully obey. His life is a call to a lifestyle of simplicity and obedience, a call to singleness of mind and purpose in that obedience. It is a challenge to the Christians of the world to practice daily, in the next five minutes, their faith in God. It is an exhortation to holiness. It is a call to live like Jesus. That is primarily the legacy he has left us.

The True Biography

As MacDonald himself emphasized, his life lives in his books. And that is where the *real* biography is to be found. This limited biographical effort can merely point you in that direction—to the true essence of the man as revealed in what he wrote. In his writings we come to *feel* him. George MacDonald was a thoughtful boy who began early to ponder the questions of life. But until we live through that process with young Robert Falconer, we haven't really "felt" the essence of George MacDonald's childhood. The clan loyalties of the MacDonald family extend back to Culloden and Glencoe and form the very fiber of George MacDonald's heritage. But until we "live" that past through the turbulent emotions of *Malcolm's* Duncan MacPhail, we cannot "feel" the depth of clan loyalty that is the foundation of historic Scotland. MacDonald loved the innocence of childhood, nature, and the Scottish mountains and streams and fields. But until we experience those loves through the eyes of wee Sir Gibbie as he finds his way up Daurside to Glashgar, we have not *felt* Scotland, childhood, and nature. George MacDonald had an unusual approach to dreams and a gentle wisdom concerning death. But until we *experience* Diamond's living dream in *At the Back of the North Wind* these will be mere words alone.

Therefore, the true biography is to be found elsewhere—in the more than fifty volumes that flowed from George MacDonald's pen. That is where we discover the essence of the man—not in any single one, but in the totality of his life's work. (Information on availability of MacDonald titles, both original and redacted, and on *Leben*, the magazine dedicated to MacDonald's legacy, can be obtained at the address and Web site found on the last page of this book.)

Why is his writing his true biography? His own son says, "I have heard of men whose lives were coloured by religion. But George MacDonald's life *was* religion; and . . . his iridescent imagination gave its colour to the religion that was his. . . .

"Because his religion was his life, he could no more divide the religious from the secular than a fish separate swimming from water . . . this is not a man with a 'religious side' to his nature; nor was he . . . a 'one sided' man. But the many sides of him shone in one only light; the two lungs breathed one air. . . .

"I have no space . . . to pile up here story upon story of this man's good deeds, his kindly acts, and of his sudden sympathetic apprehension, swift as the flash from the blue of the eyes, which never, I believe, launched a bolt not generous, and seldom one not kindly.

"Thrice, in a halting attempt to put him upon paper, have I been reminded . . . of his eyes as they were wont to look at me. . . . His personal influence was founded, I think, largely upon the keen interest he showed in any man's tale of himself, and upon his characteristic habit of expecting and believing the best of every man until he knew the contrary; and when I consider the scope of his friendship and acquaintance, it seems not a little wonderful how seldom he was imposed upon.

"If he did not love all men, it is a grievous charge against some . . . Great as I think this man's work, I set his conduct of life relatively even higher. . . . If he could read this he would say, smiling, that he was planted early where the ground was richest. . . .

"The ideals of his didactic novels were the motive of his own life . . . a life of literal, and, which is more, imaginative consistency with his doctrine. . . . There has probably never been a writer whose work was a better expression of his personal character. This I am not engaged to prove; but I very positively assert . . . that in his novels, his fantastic tales and allegories, and most vividly, perhaps, in his verse, one encounters . . . the same rich imagination, the same generous lover of God and man, the same consistent practiser of his own preaching, the same tender charity to the sinner with the same uncompromising hostility to the sin, which were known in daily use and by his own people counted upon more surely than sunshine."[1]

In short, George MacDonald must be "experienced." His works are too intricate to be reduced to analysis. For this reason, all who are interested in him must write their own biographies. For every man or woman, a different book or poem or sermon will be the *one* that speaks the loudest. *Phantastes* did it for C. S. Lewis; the fairy tales accomplished it for G. K. Chesterton; *Sir Gibbie* for Elizabeth Yates. MacDonald's son Greville appreciated *Phantastes* and *Lilith* most highly. His son Ronald likened the poetry to "the inner sanctum." For some it has been the Scottish novels, for others the sermons. One man's eyes fairly glow when he talks of the genius of insight he has discovered in *The Portent*. In MacDonald's home town of Huntly, to this day he is referred to by some as "our poet." One reader said, "People like Donal and Robert and Malcolm and Gibbie . . . are people we want to know more about and to learn from as they go through real everyday life." And about her reading of *Robert Falconer*, one young woman said, "I feel the Spirit of God speaking to me all the way through it, and even months later, it still kindles in me a greater desire to be a servant like Robert Falconer, and ultimately, like Jesus Christ."

MacDonald's legacy, indeed, lives on. The seeds of those ancient and forgotten flowers of George MacDonald's garden lie waiting for us to dig and unearth and bring back to light.

APPENDIX

THE WORKS OF GEORGE MACDONALD

Categorizing and chronologizing George MacDonald's writings is extremely difficult for several reasons. Nearly all his books were released in many different editions by a variety of publishers. *David Elginbrod, Alec Forbes of Howglen,* and *Robert Falconer,* for instance, were issued in at least twelve editions between 1865 and 1900, *Annals of a Quiet Neighborhood* in fifteen. And even his more obscure novels were released in four or five varieties. In America, where he was very popular and widely pirated, texts and titles were sometimes altered, and the lack of copyrights and scanty records on the part of the publishers make any kind of tracing of the books virtually impossible.

Secondly, MacDonald had a passion for polishing and re-editing. He constantly was reworking his poems, with the result that every new edition of poetry contained newly worded poems by the same title, but with slight variations from ones that had been released earlier. An example is the book *Adela Cathcart,* which contained whole different collections of stories from one edition to another.

He not only reworked his material, title changes were frequent. Thus *Orts* became *A Dish of Orts* and was released in the U.S. as *The Imagination and Other Essays. The Gifts of the Child Christ* became *Stephen Archer and Other Tales.* And the magazine parable released as *A Double Story* became *The Wise Woman* when first published in book form, only to later be released by two other publishers as *Princess Rosamond* and *The Lost Princess*—four titles in all.

All the short stories and poems were released in many distinctive formats with different contents. *The Twelve Spiritual Songs of Novalis* were expanded to fifteen (nine new and six from the 1851 edition) and added to other German and Italian translations to make up *Exotics.* Later *Rampolli* was released, which combined *Exotics* and *Diary of an Old Soul.* With every successive publication of poetry, changes were made until the 1893 release of *The Poetical Works of George MacDonald* (2 Vol.), which contained his longer poems *Within and Without, The Disciple,* and *A Hidden Life,* with a complete collection of 435 remaining poems of varying length.

When all is listed and analyzed, George MacDonald produced 53 books (37 fiction and fantasy, 2 distinctive collections of short stories, 3 literary books, 5 volumes of sermons, and 6 distinctive volumes of poetry), though in his lifetime the number of separate editions of this material no doubt exceeded four hundred.

CHRONOLOGICAL LISTING OF GEORGE MACDONALD'S BOOKS

1851 *Twelve of the Spiritual Songs of Novalis*—privately printed
1855 *Within and Without: A Dramatic Poem*—Longman, Brown, Green
1857 *Poems*—Longman, Brown, Green
1858 *Phantastes: A Faerie Romance for Men and Women*—Smith, Elder
1863 *David Elginbrod*—Hurst & Blackett
1864 *The Portent: A Story of the Inner Vision of the Highlanders Commonly Called the Second Sight*—Smith, Elder
     Adela Cathcart—Hurst & Blackett
1865 *Alec Forbes of Howglen*—Hurst & Blackett
1867 *Dealing With the Fairies*—Alexander Strahan
     The Disciple and Other Poems—Alexander Strahan
     Annals of a Quiet Neighborhood—Hurst & Blackett
     Unspoken Sermons, 1st Series—Alexander Strahan
1868 *Robert Falconer*—Hurst & Blackett
     Guild Court: A London Story—Hurst & Blackett
     The Seaboard Parish—Tinsley Brothers
1870 *The Miracles of Our Lord*—Strahan & Co.
1871 *At the Back of the North Wind*—Strahan & Co.
     Ranald Bannerman's Boyhood—Strahan & Co.
1872 *The Princess and the Goblin*—Strahan & Co.
     Wilfrid Cumbermede: An Autobiographical Story—Hurst & Blackett/ Scribner
     The Vicar's Daughter—Tinsley Brothers
1873 *Gutta Percha Willie: The Working Genius*—Henry S. King
1874 *England's Antiphon*—Macmillan
1875 *Malcolm*—Henry S. King/Lippincott
     The Wise Woman: A Parable—Strahan & Co.
1876 *Exotics: A Translation of the Spiritual Songs of Novalis, the Hymn Book of Luther and Other Poems From the German and Italian*—Strahan & Co.
     St. George and St. Michael—Henry S. King
     Thomas Wingfold, Curate—Hurst & Blackett
1877 *The Marquis of Lossie*—Hurst & Blackett/Lippincott
1879 *Sir Gibbie*—Hurst & Blackett/Lippincott
     Paul Faber, Surgeon—Hurst & Blackett/Lippincott

1880 *A Book of Strife, in the Form of the Diary of an Old Soul*—privately printed
1881 *Mary Marston*—Sampson Low/Lippincott
1882 *Warlock O' Glenwarlock*—Sampson Low/Harper
Weighed and Wanting—Sampson Low/Harper
The Gifts of the Child Christ, and Other Tales—Sampson Low
Orts—Sampson Low
The Princess and Curdie—Lippincott/Chatto & Windus
1883 *Donal Grant*—Kegan Paul/Harper
A Threefold Cord: Poems by Three Friends—privately printed
1885 *The Tragedie of Hamlet*—Longmans, Green
Unspoken Sermons, 2nd Series—Longmans, Green
1886 *What's Mine's Mine*—Kegan Paul/Harper
1887 *Home Again: A Tale*—Kegan Paul/Appleton
1888 *The Elect Lady*—Kegan Paul/Munro
1889 *Unspoken Sermons*, 3rd Series—Longmans, Green
1890 *A Rough Shaking*—Blackie & Sons/Routledge
1891 *There and Back*—Kegan Paul
The Flight of the Shadow—Kegan Paul, Appleton
A Cabinet of Gems: Cut and Polished by Sir Philip Sidney, Now for Their More Radiance Presented Without Their Setting by George MacDonald—Elliot Stock
1892 *The Hope of the Gospel*—Ward, Lock, Bowden
1893 *Heather and Snow*—Chatto & Windus/Harper
1895 *Lilith*—Chatto & Windus/Dodd, Mead
1897 *Salted With Fire*—Hurst & Blackett/Dodd, Mead
1898 *Far Above Rubies*—Dodd, Mead

SOME OF THE MORE PROMINENT NINETEENTH-CENTURY REPRINTS AND COLLECTIONS

1864 *A Hidden Life and Other Poems* (formerly *Poems*)—Longman, Green
1871 *Works of Fancy and Imagination* (10 Volumes)—Chatto & Windus
1880 *Cheerful Words by George MacDonald* (Topical selections edited by E. E. Brown with an introduction by James T. Fields)—Lothrop & Co., Boston.
1883 *Stephen Archer and Other Tales* (formerly *The Gifts of the Child Christ, and Other Tales*)—Sampson Low
1876 *Dramatic and Miscellaneous Poems*—Scribner
1893 *A Dish of Orts* (formerly *Orts*)—Sampson Low
1883 *Imagination and Other Essays* (American edition of *Orts*)—Lothrop
1886 *Cross Purposes and the Shadows* (reprinted from *Dealings With the Fairies*)—Blackie & Sons
1887 *Poems by George MacDonald* (a small one-volume collection)—E. P. Dutton, New York

1890 *The Light Princess and Other Fairy Stories* (reprinted from *Dealings With the Fairies*)—Blackie & Sons

1890s *Cure for Thought-Taking* (selection)—Warren and Wyman, New York

1893 *Poetical Works of George MacDonald,* 2 Volumes (some new, mostly reprints)—Chatto & Windus

1893 *Scotch Songs and Ballads* (reprinted from *The Disciple and Other Poems*)—John Rae Smith

1894 *Beautiful Thoughts From George MacDonald* (Selected daily readings)—James Pott & Co.

1897 *Rampolli: Growths From a Long-Planted Root*, being translations chiefly from the German, along with *A Year's Diary of an Old Soul* (*Exotics* with a few additions plus *The Diary of an Old Soul*)—Longmans, Green

1907 *The Pocket George MacDonald* (selections compiled by Alfred H. Hyatt)—Chatto & Windus

A CATEGORIZATION OF GEORGE MacDONALD'S WORKS

FULL-LENGTH FICTION

Realistic Scottish Novels

David Elginbrod (1863)
Alec Forbes of Howglen (1865)
Robert Falconer (1868)
Malcolm (1875)
The Marquis of Lossie (1877)
Sir Gibbie (1879)
Warlock o' Glenwarlock (1882)

Donal Grant (1883)
What's Mine's Mine (1886)
The Elect Lady (1888)
Flight of the Shadow (1891)
Heather and Snow (1893)
Salted With Fire (1897)

Realistic English Novels

Annals of a Quiet Neighborhood (1867)
Guild Court (1868)
The Seaboard Parish (1868)
The Vicar's Daughter (1872)
Wilfrid Cumbermede (1872)
St. George and St. Michael (1876)
Thomas Wingfold, Curate (1876)

Paul Faber, Surgeon (1879)
Mary Marston (1881)
Weighed and Wanting (1882)
Home Again (1887)
A Rough Shaking (1890)
There and Back (1891)
Far Above Rubies (1898)

Realistic Junior Fiction

Ranald Bannerman's Boyhood (1871)

Gutta Percha Willie (1873)

Imaginative and Symbolic Adult Fiction

Phantastes (1858)

Adela Cathcart (1864)

The Portent (1864)

Lilith (1895)

Imaginative Junior Fiction

At the Back of the North Wind (1871)

The Princess and the Goblin (1872)

The Wise Woman/The Lost Princess/A Double Story (1875)

The Princess and Curdie (1883)

SHORT STORIES
(Published in many different editions and groupings)

A Journey Rejourneyed

Angels' Song

Birth, Dreaming, Death

Broken Swords

Butcher's Bills

Carasoyn

The Castle

Cross Purposes

The Cruel Painter

Giant's Heart

Gifts of the Child Christ

Golden Key

Gray Wolf

If I Had a Father

The Light Princess

Little Daylight

My Uncle Peter

Papa's Story

Photogen and Nycteris/Day Boy and Night Girl

Port in a Storm

The Shadows

Snow Fight

Stephen Archer

Uncle Cornelius: His Story

Wow o' Rivven

A Child's Holiday

Adela Cathcart (1864)—different editions of this book contain different collections: *The Light Princess/The Shadows/The Giant's Heart/Wow o' Rivven/Broken Swords/The Cruel Painter/The Castle/Snow Fight/My Uncle Peter/A Child's Holiday/Birth, Dreaming, Death*

Dealings With the Fairies (1867): *The Light Princess/The Giant's Heart/The Shadows/Cross Purposes/The Golden Key*

Works of Fancy and Imagination Vols. 5–10 (1872): *Phantastes/The Portent/The Light Princess/The Giant's Heart/The Shadows/Cross Purposes/The Golden Key/Carasoyn/Little Daylight/The Cruel Painter/The Castle/Wow o' Rivven/Broken Swords/The Gray Wolf/Uncle Cornelius*

The Gifts of the Child Christ, and Other Tales (1882): *Gifts of the Child Christ/History of Photogen and Nycteris/Butcher's Bills/Stephen Archer/Port in a Storm/If I Had a Father*

POETRY

Within and Without (1855)

Poems (1857)—72 in all: *A Hidden Life/Gospel Women* (16 poems)/*Miscellaneous Poems* (55 poems)

The Disciple and Other Poems (1867)—73 in all: *The Disciple/Scotch*

Songs and Ballads (10 poems)/*Miscellaneous Poems* (62 poems)
  Works of Fancy and Imagination Vols. 1–4 (1872): *Within and Without/ A Hidden Life/Poems* (4 poems)/*The Disciple/Gospel Women* (16 poems)/ *A Book of Sonnets* (7 poems)/*Organ Songs* (29 poems)/*Violin Songs* (15 poems)/*Songs of the Days and Nights* (8 poems)/*A Book of Dreams/Roadside Poems* (10 poems)/*Poems for Children* (13 poems)/*Parables* (22 poems)/*Ballads* (6 poems)/*Scotch Songs and Ballads* (14 poems)
  Exotics (1876): German Translations (From Novalis, Schiller, Goethe, Uhland, Heine, Von Salis-seewis, Claudius)/From the Dutch of Genestet/ From Unknown German Author/From Petrarch/Milton's Italian Poems/ Luther's Song Book
  Diary of an Old Soul (1880)
  A Threefold Cord (1883)
  A Cabinet of Gems (1891)
  Rampolli (1897): *Exotics/Diary of an Old Soul*
  Poetical Works of George MacDonald Vol. 1 (1893): *Within and Without/ A Hidden Life/A Story of the Seashore/The Disciple/Gospel Women* (16 poems)/*A Book of Sonnets* (14 poems)/*Organ Songs* (46 poems)/*Violin Songs* (30 poems)/*Songs of the Days and Nights* (8 poems)/*A Book of Dreams/Roadside Poems* (17 poems)/*To and of Friends* (11 poems)
  Poetical Works of George MacDonald Vol. 2 (1893): *Parables* (32 poems)/*Ballads* (6 poems)/*Minor Ditties* (13 poems)/*Motes in the Sun* (21 poems)/*Poems for Children* (22 poems)/*A Threefold Cord* (159 poems)/ *Scots Songs and Ballads* (38 poems)

SERMONS

Unspoken Sermons, 1st Series (1867): The Child in the Midst/The Consuming Fire/The Higher Faith/It Shall Not Be Forgiven/The New Name/The Heart With the Treasure/The Temptation in the Wilderness/The Eloi/The Hands of the Father/Love Thy Neighbor/Love Thine Enemy/The God of the Living
  Unspoken Sermons, 2nd Series (1885): The Way/The Hardness of the Way/The Cause of Spiritual Stupidity/The Word of Jesus on Prayer/Man's Difficulty Concerning Prayer/The Last Farthing/Abba, Father!/Life/The Fear of God/The Voice of Job/Self-Denial/The Truth in Jesus
  Unspoken Sermons, 3rd Series (1889): The Creation in Christ/The Knowing of the Son/The Mirrors of the Lord/The Truth/Freedom/Kingship/ Justice/Light/The Discipleship of Jesus/Righteousness/The Final Unmasking/The Inheritance
  The Miracles of Our Lord (1870): The Beginning of Miracles/The Cure of Simon's Wife's Mother/Miracles of Healing Unsolicited/Miracles of Healing Solicited by the Sufferers/Miracles Granted to the Prayer of Friends/ The Casting Out of Devils/The Raising of the Dead/The Government of Nature/Miracles of Destruction/The Resurrection/The Transfiguration
  The Hope of the Gospel (1892): Salvation From Sin/The Remission of Sins/Jesus in the World/Jesus and His Fellow Townsmen/The Heirs of Heaven and Earth/Sorrow the Pledge of Joy/God's Family/The Reward of

Obedience/The Yoke of Jesus/The Salt and the Light of the World/The Right Hand and the Left/The Hope of the Universe

LITERARY BOOKS AND ESSAYS

England's Antiphon (1874)—a history of the religious poetry of England

Orts (1882): *The Imagination: Its Functions and Its Culture/A Sketch of Individual Development/St. George's Day, 1564/The Art of Shakespeare, As Revealed by Himself/The Elder Hamlet/On Polish/Browning's "Christmas Eve"/"Essays on Some of the Forms of Literature"/"The History and Heroes of Medicine"/Wordsworth's Poetry/Shelley/A Sermon/True Christian Ministering/The Fantastic Imagination*

The Tragedie of Hamlet (1885)

GEORGE MACDONALD'S FAMILY TREE

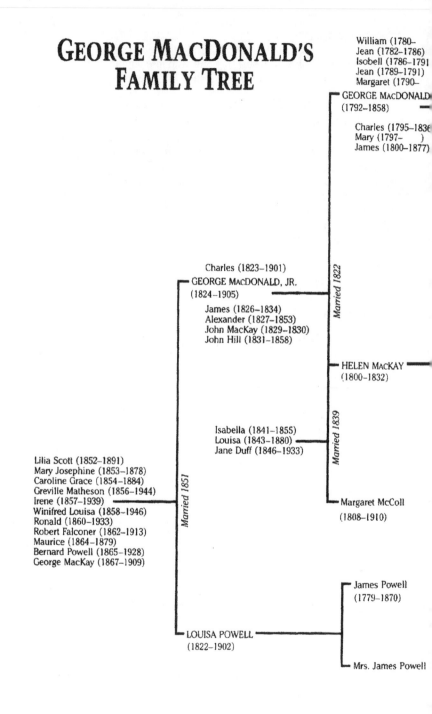

William (1780–
Jean (1782–1786)
Isobell (1786–1791
Jean (1789–1791)
Margaret (1790–
GEORGE MACDONALD
(1792–1858)
Charles (1795–1836
Mary (1797–   )
James (1800–1877)

Charles (1823–1901)
GEORGE MACDONALD, JR.
(1824–1905)
James (1826–1834)
Alexander (1827–1853)
John MacKay (1829–1830)
John Hill (1831–1858)

Married 1822

HELEN MACKAY
(1800–1832)

Isabella (1841–1855)
Louisa (1843–1880)
Jane Duff (1846–1933)

Married 1839

Lilia Scott (1852–1891)
Mary Josephine (1853–1878)
Caroline Grace (1854–1884)
Greville Matheson (1856–1944)
Irene (1857–1939)
Winifred Louisa (1858–1946)
Ronald (1860–1933)
Robert Falconer (1862–1913)
Maurice (1864–1879)
Bernard Powell (1865–1928)
George MacKay (1867–1909)

Married 1851

Margaret McColl
(1808–1910)

James Powell
(1779–1870)

LOUISA POWELL
(1822–1902)

Mrs. James Powell

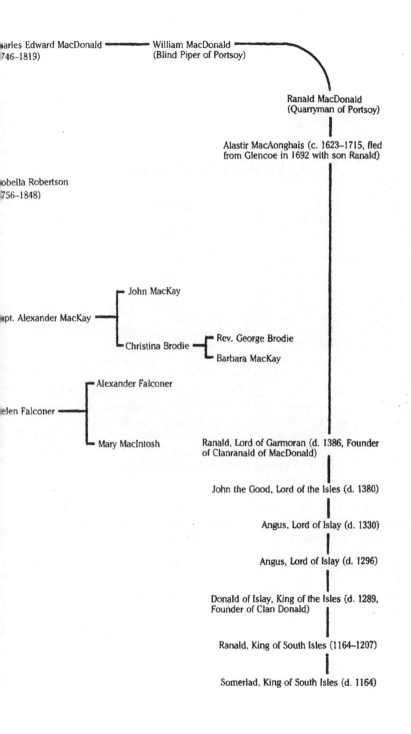

arles Edward MacDonald
746–1819)

William MacDonald
(Blind Piper of Portsoy)

Ranald MacDonald
(Quarryman of Portsoy)

Alastir MacAonghais (c. 1623–1715, fled
from Glencoe in 1692 with son Ranald)

obella Robertson
756–1848)

John MacKay

pt. Alexander MacKay

Christina Brodie

Rev. George Brodie

Barbara MacKay

Alexander Falconer

elen Falconer

Mary MacIntosh

Ranald, Lord of Garmoran (d. 1386, Founder
of Clanranald of MacDonald)

John the Good, Lord of the Isles (d. 1380)

Angus, Lord of Islay (d. 1330)

Angus, Lord of Islay (d. 1296)

Donald of Islay, King of the Isles (d. 1289,
Founder of Clan Donald)

Ranald, King of South Isles (1164–1207)

Somerlad, King of South Isles (d. 1164)

AUTHOR'S NOTE

For nearly thirty years it has been my vision and "life's work," in a sense, to reacquaint the public with this remarkable man whose story you have just read. My reasons have not been to glorify George MacDonald or place him on a pedestal in my own or anyone else's mind, but because I am convinced that his perspective on God and His ways is one that God's people sorely need, and thus that his life and message and outlook must not be lost sight of.

Toward that end, my personal objectives have been sixfold: (1) To produce *edited* versions of MacDonald's dialect-heavy Scottish novels. The purpose of redacting these masterpieces in the beginning was a practical one—hopefully to interest a contemporary publisher (skeptical about dense 500-page Victorian tomes) to publish and promote them, and also to make MacDonald's stories and spiritual wisdom available and compelling to a new and less literarily patient reading audience. (2) To produce high-quality editions of MacDonald's *original* works that would stand the test of time and insure that MacDonald's legacy endured into future generations. (3) To produce additional books, studies, and materials *about* MacDonald, which included this new biography of MacDonald. (4) To author my own original books emphasizing similar priorities and perspectives as did MacDonald, and, to the extent the marketplace allowed, to adapt myself to MacDonald's style in order to turn readers comfortably from my own work to his. (5) To produce a periodical offering bold and challenging ideas and keeping alive the legacy of George MacDonald. (6) Ultimately to work toward the establishment of a George MacDonald Center in Scotland to insure the continuation of MacDonald's legacy in his own homeland.

Though it has taken thirty years and has been a slow process (though a labor of love), most of these components of this vision are in place. Just last year (2004), the magazine *Leben* got underway, encouraging readers toward bold-thinking Christianity and dedicated to the legacy of George MacDonald and my own spiritual vision. And continuing, in a sense, where the edited novels left off, in a new partnership with Bethany House, we are now inaugurating a series of modestly edited nonfiction topical writings by George MacDonald, the LIFE WITH GOD series.

To subscribe or order...

   Leben (issued quarterly)
   Wisdom to Live By (leatherbound hardback collection of over 1,300 quotes from all the published books of George MacDonald)

And for information and availability regarding...

   The Sunrise Centenary Editions of the Works of George MacDonald (leatherbound cloth facsimile reprints of the original 19th-century works)
   The LIFE WITH GOD series of nonfiction writings by George MacDonald
   Availability of THE NEW CLASSICS (the edited novels of George MacDonald)

Write to:
   Michael Phillips
   % Sunrise Books
   P.O. Box 7003
   Eureka, CA 95502

Or see: *www.macdonaldphillips.com*

ENDNOTES

Introduction
1. Greville MacDonald, *George MacDonald and His Wife* (London: George Allen and Unwin Ltd., 1924), p. 546.
2. Ronald MacDonald, "George MacDonald: A Personal Memoir," *From A Northern Window* (London: James Nisbet, 1911), pp. 56, 58.
3. Louise Collier Willcox, "A Neglected Novelist," *North American Review*, 183 (Sept. 1906), p. 403.

Chapter 1
1. C. Edward Troup, "Notes on George MacDonald's Boyhood in Huntly," *The Deeside Field* (Aberdeen, date unknown), p. 63.

Chapter 2
1. Greville MacDonald, op. cit., p. 54.
2. Ronald MacDonald, op. cit., p. 80.
3. Greville MacDonald, op. cit., p. 112.
4. Greville MacDonald, op. cit., p. 55.
5. Greville MacDonald, op. cit., p. 56.
6. Greville MacDonald, op. cit., p. 56.

Chapter 3
1. C. Edward Troup, op. cit., *The Deeside Field*, p. 63.

Chapter 4
1. Greville MacDonald, op. cit., p. 59.
2. Greville MacDonald, op. cit., p. 59, April 23, 1850.
3. Greville MacDonald, op. cit., p. 62, August 15, 1833.
4. Greville MacDonald, op. cit., p. 66, approx. 1837.

Chapter 5
1. Glenn Edward Sadler, in the "Afterword" to *Lady of the Mansion*, reprint edition of *The Portent* (San Francisco, Calif.: Harper and Row Publishers, 1979), p. 163.

Chapter 7

1. Glenn Edward Sadler, unpublished informational poster on George MacDonald in the Brander Library in Huntly.
2. Greville MacDonald, op. cit., p. 69, October 28, 1841.
3. Greville MacDonald, op. cit., p. 68, January 5, 1841.
4. Greville MacDonald, op. cit., p. 69, October 28, 1841.
5. Greville MacDonald, op. cit., p. 75.
6. Greville MacDonald, op. cit., p. 78.
7. Greville MacDonald, op. cit., p. 78.
8. George MacDonald, unpublished. Quoted by Robert Lee Wolff, *The Golden Key* (New Haven, Conn.: Yale University Press, 1961), p. 3.

Chapter 8

1. Greville MacDonald, op. cit., p. 72.
2. Greville MacDonald, op. cit., p. 73.
3. On the German romanticists, Rolland Hein sheds light by saying: "The German Romantics were marked by a tendency to contemplate and idealize man, his emotions, and his position in the cosmos. They were convinced that all things are related and that the universe is characterized by a pervading unity, a unity discoverable to man's reason governed by his intuition. They were much concerned that man's reason be viewed in light of his total being rather than allowed to become his controlling faculty, discrediting the imagination and destroying man's spirit. In addition, they had an appreciation for individuality and a conviction that one's life can have an inner harmony commensurate with that which they saw in the outer universe. To them, the most important aspect of man's inner being is his yearning after the eternal and the infinite—a type of spiritual love which draws man toward the divine. This love finds its counterpart in the love of man for woman, so that passionate love mirrors spiritual love. Lastly, they were convinced that poetry is absolute reality, ultimate truth, knowledge itself." Rolland Hein, *The Harmony Within* (Grand Rapids, Michigan: Wm. B. Eerdmans, 1982), pp. 7–8.
4. Greville MacDonald, op. cit., p. 74.

Chapter 9

1. Greville MacDonald, op. cit., p. 80.
2. Greville MacDonald, op. cit., p. 80.
3. Greville MacDonald, op. cit., p. 85.

Chapter 10

1. Greville MacDonald, op. cit., p. 92, November, 1845.
2. Greville MacDonald, op. cit., p. 108, 1846.
3. Greville MacDonald, op. cit., p. 109, May 22, 1847.

Chapter 11

1. Greville MacDonald, op. cit., p. 83, 1868.
2. Greville MacDonald, op. cit., p. 98.

3. Greville MacDonald, op. cit., p. 105.
4. Greville MacDonald, op. cit., p. 102.
5. Greville MacDonald, op. cit., p. 102.
6. Greville MacDonald, op. cit., p. 105–106.
7. Greville MacDonald, op. cit., p. 94, June 15, 1846.

Chapter 12
1. Greville MacDonald, op. cit., pp. 110–111, Summer, 1848.
2. Greville MacDonald, op. cit., p. 113.
3. Greville MacDonald, op. cit., p. 113, Summer, 1848.
4. Greville MacDonald, op. cit., p. 115.
5. Greville MacDonald, op. cit., p. 117, October 23, 1848.

Chapter 13
1. Greville MacDonald, op. cit., p. 118.
2. Greville MacDonald, op. cit., p. 119.
3. Greville MacDonald, op. cit., p. 121–122, May 12, 1849.
4. Greville MacDonald, op. cit., p. 122, May 15, 1849.
5. Greville MacDonald, op. cit., p. 123–124.
6. Greville MacDonald, op. cit., p. 128.
7. Greville MacDonald, op. cit., p. 124–125.
8. Greville MacDonald, op. cit., p. 120–121, August 6, 1849.
9. Greville MacDonald, op. cit., p. 121.
10. Greville MacDonald, op. cit., p. 129–130, February 23, 1850.
11. Greville MacDonald, op. cit., p. 130.
12. Greville MacDonald, op. cit., p. 131–132, May 24, 1850.
13. Greville MacDonald, op. cit., p. 132, May 31, 1850.

Chapter 14
1. Robert Lee Wolff, *Gains and Losses: Novels of Faith and Doubt in Victorian England* (New York: Garland Publishing, Inc., 1977), pp. 1–2.
2. Louise Willcox, op. cit., *North American Review*, p. 403.
3. Greville MacDonald, op. cit., pp. 12–14.
4. Ronald MacDonald, op. cit., *From a Northern Window*, pp. 87–88.
5. Robert Lee Wolff, op. cit., *Gains and Losses*, pp. 345–346.

Chapter 15
1. Greville MacDonald, op. cit., p. 136, August 28, 1850.
2. Greville MacDonald, op. cit., p. 227, July 2, 1855.
3. Greville MacDonald, op. cit., p. 137, January, 1853.
4. Greville MacDonald, op. cit., p. 137, August 30, 1850.
5. Greville MacDonald, op. cit., p. 131, April 29, 1850.
6. Greville MacDonald, op. cit., p. 138, October 4, 1850.
7. Greville MacDonald, op. cit., p. 138–139, October 16, 1850.
8. Greville MacDonald, op. cit., p. 140, October 24, 1850.
9. Greville MacDonald, op. cit., p. 142, October 29, 1850.
10. Greville MacDonald, op. cit., p. 145, November 7, 1850.

11. Greville MacDonald, op. cit., p. 145–146, November 15, 1850.
12. Greville MacDonald, op. cit., p. 147, December 17, 1850.
13. Greville MacDonald, op. cit., p. 148–149, December 27, 1850.
14. Greville MacDonald, op. cit., p. 149–150, January 9, 1851.
15. Greville MacDonald, op. cit., p. 150, January, 1851.
16. Greville MacDonald, op. cit., p. 152–153.

Chapter 16
1. Greville MacDonald, op. cit., p. 154–155.
2. Greville MacDonald, op. cit., p. 154–156.
3. Greville MacDonald, op. cit., p. 155, July, 1853.
4. Greville MacDonald, op. cit., p. 155, April 15, 1851.
5. Greville MacDonald, op. cit., p. 158.
6. Greville MacDonald, op. cit., p. 158.
7. Greville MacDonald, op. cit., p. 158, February 6, 1852.

Chapter 17
1. Robert Lee Wolff, op. cit., *Gains and Losses*, p. 340.
2. Greville MacDonald, op. cit., p. 156.
3. Greville MacDonald, op. cit., p. 178.
4. Greville MacDonald, op. cit., p. 179.
5. Greville MacDonald, op. cit., p. 180.
6. Greville MacDonald, op. cit., p. 180, July 27, 1852.
7. Greville MacDonald, op. cit., p. 185, May 20, 1853.
8. Greville MacDonald, op. cit., p. 182, Summer or Autumn, 1852.
9. Greville MacDonald, op. cit., p. 183.
10. Greville MacDonald, op. cit., p. 183–184, July, 1853.
11. Greville MacDonald, op. cit., p. 184, April 29, 1853.
12. Greville MacDonald, op. cit., p. 184–185, May 20, 1853.
13. Greville MacDonald, op. cit., p. 185–186 June 3, 1853.
14. Greville MacDonald, op. cit., p. 187, July, 1853.

Chapter 18
1. Greville MacDonald, op. cit., p. 160–161.
2. Greville MacDonald, op. cit., p. 161.
3. Greville MacDonald, op. cit., p. 168.
4. Greville MacDonald, op. cit., p. 172–173, April 5, 1853.
5. Greville MacDonald, op. cit., p. 194.
6. Greville MacDonald, op. cit., p. 206, December 30, 1853.
7. Muriel Hutton, "The George MacDonald Collection," *Yale University Library Gazette*, #51 (New Haven, Conn., 1976), p. 78.
8. Greville MacDonald, op. cit., p. 204, December 21, 1853.
9. Greville MacDonald, op. cit., p. 199, September 7, 1853.
10. Greville MacDonald, op. cit., p. 199. September 7, 1853.
11. Greville MacDonald, op. cit., p. 201, September 26, 1853.
12. Greville MacDonald, op. cit., p. 195.

13. Greville MacDonald, op. cit., p. 207.
14. Greville MacDonald, op. cit., p. 197–198, 1853–1854.

Chapter 19
1. Greville MacDonald, op. cit., p. 212–213, June, 1854.
2. Greville MacDonald, op. cit., p. 213, June 26, 1854.
3. Greville MacDonald, op. cit., p. 213–214, July 19, 1854.
4. Kathy Triggs, *The Seeking Heart* (Basingstoke, England: Pickering & Inglis, 1984), p. 73.
5. Greville MacDonald, op. cit., p. 216–217.
6. Greville MacDonald, op. cit., p. 218.
7. Greville MacDonald, op. cit., p. 224.
8. Greville MacDonald, op. cit., p. 226, June 3, 1855.
9. Greville MacDonald, op. cit., p. 228–230, July 2–4, 1855.
10. Greville MacDonald, op. cit., p. 237–238.
11. Greville MacDonald, op. cit., p. 233–234.
12. Greville MacDonald, op. cit., p. 237, July, 1855.
13. Greville MacDonald, op. cit., p. 232, July 5, 1855.
14. Greville MacDonald, op. cit., p. 234, July 8, 1855.
15. Greville MacDonald, op. cit., p. 234, July 9, 1855.
16. Greville MacDonald, op. cit., p. 235, July 10, 1855.
17. Greville MacDonald, op. cit., p. 235–236, July 11, 1855.
18. Greville MacDonald, op. cit., p. 239–240, July 14, 1855.
19. Greville MacDonald, op. cit., p. 243, July 20, 1855.
20. Greville MacDonald, op. cit., p. 241, July 14, 1855.
21. Greville MacDonald, op. cit., p. 244, July 25, 1855.
22. Greville MacDonald, op. cit., p. 244, July 28, 1855.
23. Greville MacDonald, op. cit., p. 243, July 17, 1855.
24. Greville MacDonald, op. cit., p. 246, August 1, 1855.
25. Greville MacDonald, op. cit., p. 244–245, approx. July 29, 1855.
26. Greville MacDonald, op. cit., p. 246–247, August 3, 1855.
27. Greville MacDonald, op. cit., p. 247, August 6, 1855.
28. Greville MacDonald, op. cit., p. 247–248, August, 1855.
29. Greville MacDonald, op. cit., p. 248.
30. Greville MacDonald, op. cit., p. 248, August, 1855.
31. Greville MacDonald, op. cit., p. 249–250, August, 1855.
32. Greville MacDonald, op. cit., p. 250–251, August, 1855.
33. Greville MacDonald, op. cit., p. 251, August 26, 1855.
34. John Calvin, *Institutes of the Christian Religion* (III, ix, 5), 1536.
35. Greville MacDonald, op. cit., p. 252, September 27, 1855.

Chapter 20
1. Greville MacDonald, op. cit., p. 262, March, 1856.
2. Greville MacDonald, op. cit., p. 264–265.
3. Greville MacDonald, op. cit., p. 272–273, 1857.
4. Greville MacDonald, op. cit., p. 273.
5. Greville MacDonald, op. cit., p. 280–281.

6. Greville MacDonald, op. cit., p. 283, December 2, 1857.
7. Greville MacDonald, op. cit., p. 286–287, December 25–27, 1857.
8. Greville MacDonald, op. cit., p. 288, January 2, 1858.
9. Greville MacDonald, op. cit., p. 289, 1858 or 1859.
10. Greville MacDonald, op. cit., p. 290, Spring, 1858.
11. Greville MacDonald, op. cit., p. 290–291, April 18, 1858.
12. Greville MacDonald, op. cit., p. 292, June, 1858.
13. Greville MacDonald, op. cit., p. 292–293.
14. Greville MacDonald, op. cit., p. 37, August 27, 1858.
15. Greville MacDonald, op. cit., p. 294.
16. Greville MacDonald, op. cit., p. 295, August 26, 1858.
17. Greville MacDonald, op. cit., p. 295–296, October 15, 1858.

Chapter 21
1. C. S. Lewis, *George MacDonald: An Anthology* (London: The Macmillan Pub. Co., 1947), p. xxxiv.
2. Robert Lee Wolff, op. cit., *The Golden Key*, pp. 4–5.
3. Kathy Triggs, op. cit., *The Seeking Heart*, p. 57.
4. Greville MacDonald, op. cit., p. 303, January 19, 1859.
5. Greville MacDonald, op. cit., p. 318.
6. Greville MacDonald, op. cit., p. 321.
7. Kathy Triggs, op. cit., p. 72.
8. C. S. Lewis, op. cit., p. xxvi.
9. Robert Lee Wolff, op. cit., *The Golden Key*, p. 182.
10. Richard Reis, *George MacDonald* (New York: Twayne Publishers, 1972), p. 143.
11. John Dyer, "The New Novelist," *The Penn Monthly Magazine*, 1, 6 (June 1870), 217, 219, 220.
12. Rolland Hein, op. cit., *The Harmony Within*, p. xii.

Chapter 22
1. Ronald MacDonald, op. cit., *From a Northern Window*, p. 67.
2. John Malcolm Bulloch, "A Bibliography of George MacDonald," *Aberdeen University Library Bulletin* (Vol. V, No. 30, February 1925), p. 693.
3. Greville MacDonald, op. cit., p. 337, December 18, 1868.
4. Ronald MacDonald, op. cit., p. 96.
5. Greville MacDonald, op. cit., p. 324.
6. Greville MacDonald, op. cit., p. 325, January 6, 1860.
7. Greville MacDonald, op. cit., p. 326–327, March 7, 1861.
8. Greville MacDonald, op. cit., p. 332, February 8, 1865.
9. Greville MacDonald, op. cit., p. 332.
10. Greville MacDonald, op. cit., p. 347–351, Summer, 1865.
11. Greville MacDonald, op. cit., p. 226.
12. Greville MacDonald, op. cit., p. 354, early Fall, 1865.
13. Greville MacDonald, op. cit., p. 357–358, August 17, 1865.
14. Greville MacDonald, op. cit., p. 359, February 9, 1866.
15. Greville MacDonald, op. cit., p. 374–375.

16. Greville MacDonald, op. cit., p. 369.
17. Greville MacDonald, op. cit., p. 370.

Chapter 23
1. Greville MacDonald, op. cit., p. 379–380.
2. Greville MacDonald, op. cit., p. 394, June 28, 1869.
3. Greville MacDonald, op. cit., p. 395–396, July 22, 1869.
4. Ronald MacDonald, op. cit., p. 76–77.
5. Greville MacDonald, op. cit., p. 398.
6. George MacDonald in Introduction to *Letters From Hell* by Valdemar Thisted (London: Bentley & Son, 1886), p. viii.
7. C. S. Lewis, op. cit., *George MacDonald: An Anthology*, p. xxx–xxxii.
8. Greville MacDonald, op. cit., p. 414, Spring, 1872.
9. Greville MacDonald, op. cit., p. 424–425, October, 1872.
10. Greville MacDonald, op. cit., p. 454, April 6, 1873.
11. Greville MacDonald, op. cit., p. 425.
12. Greville MacDonald, op. cit., p. 430, December 3, 1872.
13. Greville MacDonald, op. cit., p. 434, late December, 1872.
14. Greville MacDonald, op. cit., pp. 444–445, 442–443.
15. Greville MacDonald, op. cit., p. 447–449, February 16, 1873.
16. Greville MacDonald, op. cit., p. 456, April 19, 1873.
17. Brooks, Phillips, *Lectures On Preaching* (1904), p. 16.
18. Greville MacDonald, op. cit., pp. 459–460, May 19, 1873.
19. Greville MacDonald, op. cit., p. 461, June 6, 1873.

Chapter 24
1. Greville MacDonald, op. cit., p. 377.
2. C. S. Lewis, op. cit., p. xxviii.
3. Greville MacDonald, op. cit., p. 362.
4. Robert Lee Wolff, op. cit., *The Golden Key*, p. 148.
5. Greville MacDonald, op. cit., p. 363.
6. Ronald MacDonald, op. cit., *From a Northern Window*, p. 103.
7. Greville MacDonald, op. cit., p. 401.
8. Greville MacDonald, op. cit., p. 373–374, approx. 1867.

Chapter 25
1. Greville MacDonald, op. cit., p. 458, September 19, 1882.
2. Greville MacDonald, op. cit., p. 458, 1899.
3. Greville MacDonald, op. cit., p. 471–472, undated.
4. From an unpublished letter, dated April 7, 1878, in the National Library of Scotland.
5. Greville MacDonald, op. cit., p. 484.
6. Greville MacDonald, op. cit., p. 484, May 12, 1878.
7. Greville MacDonald, op. cit., p. 486, 1878.
8. Greville MacDonald, op. cit., p. 487, June 19, 1878.
9. Greville MacDonald, op. cit., p. 489–490, March 19, 1879.
10. Greville MacDonald, op. cit., p. 490, April 10, 1879.

11. Greville MacDonald, op. cit., p. 536—the poem quoted is entitled "The Giver" and is found in *The Poetical Works of George MacDonald*, Vol. 2.
12. Greville MacDonald, op. cit., p. 494.
13. Greville MacDonald, op. cit., p. 475, Autumn, 1877.
14. Greville MacDonald, op. cit., p. 497.
15. Greville MacDonald, op. cit., p. 504–505.
16. Greville MacDonald, op. cit., p. 509.
17. Greville MacDonald, op. cit., p. 508.
18. Greville MacDonald, op. cit., p. 511.
19. Greville MacDonald, op. cit., p. 512.
20. Greville MacDonald, op. cit., p. 514, March 8, 1887.
21. Greville MacDonald, op. cit., p. 501.

Chapter 26
 1. Ronald MacDonald, op. cit., p. 91.
 2. Greville MacDonald, op. cit., p. 528–529, June 16, 1881.
 3. From an unpublished letter, dated April 7, 1878, in the National Library of Scotland.
 4. Greville MacDonald, op. cit., p. 517–518, January 4, 1891.
 5. Greville MacDonald, op. cit., p. 520, July 13, 1891.
 6. Greville MacDonald, op. cit., p. 524, October 13, 1891.
 7. Greville MacDonald, op. cit., p. 525, October 30, 1891.
 8. Greville MacDonald, op. cit., p. 525, November 5, 1891.
 9. Greville MacDonald, op. cit., p. 525, November 6, 1891.
10. Greville MacDonald, op. cit., p. 526–527.
11. Greville MacDonald, op. cit., p. 416, July 7, 1872.
12. Greville MacDonald, op. cit., p. 531, January 10, 1885.
13. Greville MacDonald, op. cit., p. 535, Christmas, 1886.
14. Ronald MacDonald, op. cit., p. 100–101.
15. Greville MacDonald, op. cit., p. 548.
16. Greville MacDonald, op. cit., p. 555–556.
17. Greville MacDonald, op. cit., p. 539, June 15, 1892.
18. Greville MacDonald, op. cit., p. 542, January 22, 1893.
19. Greville MacDonald, op. cit., p. 542, June 11, 1893.
20. Greville MacDonald, op. cit., p. 542, June 18, 1894.
21. Glenn Edward Sadler, in the "Afterword" to *Flight of the Shadow* (San Francisco: Harper & Row Publishers, 1983), p. 249.
22. Greville MacDonald, op. cit., p. 539.
23. Greville MacDonald, op. cit., p. 544–545, October 7, 1897.
24. Greville MacDonald, op. cit., p. 545, Good Friday, 1898.
25. Greville MacDonald, op. cit., p. 544.
26. Greville MacDonald, op. cit., p. 537–538.
27. Greville MacDonald, op. cit., p. 559–560.

Chapter 27
 1. Greville MacDonald, op. cit., p. 359, February 9, 1866.
 2. Robert Lee Wolff, op. cit., *The Golden Key*, p. 4.

3. G. K. Chesterton's obituary article in the London *Daily News*, Sept. 23, 1905, p. 6.
4. C. S. Lewis, op. cit., p. xxvi, xxviii.
5. W. H. Auden, in Introduction to *The Visionary Novels of George Mac-Donald*, ed. Anne Fremantle (New York: The Noonday Press, 1954), p. v–vi.
6. Greville MacDonald, op. cit., p. 9.
7. G. K. Chesterton, *The Victorian Age in Literature* (New York & London: Williams and Norgate, 1913), p. 152.
8. J. R. R. Tolkien on flyleaf of *The Golden Key* by George MacDonald (New York: Farrar, Straus, & Giroux, 1967).
9. W. H. Auden, op. cit.
10. C. S. Lewis, op. cit., p. 20.
11. C. S. Lewis, ibid.
12. Ronald MacDonald, op. cit., p. 72.
13. Elizabeth Yates in Introduction to *Sir Gibbie* by George MacDonald (New York: E. P. Dutton, 1963), pp. v–vi.
14. Greville MacDonald, op. cit., p. 378.
15. Richard Reis, op. cit., p. 143.

Chapter 28
1. Ronald MacDonald, op. cit., pp. 112, 84–86, 58–59.

INDEX